World In Motion

Simon Hart

World In Motion

Simon Hart

Photography from
The Peter Robinson Football Archive

First published as a hardback by deCoubertin Books Ltd in 2018.

First Edition.

deCoubertin Books, Studio I, Baltic Creative Campus, Liverpool, L1 OAH
www.decoubertin.co.uk

ISBN: 978-1909245655
Republic of Ireland edition: 978-1-909245-78-5

A CIP catalogue record for this book is available from the British Library.
Cover design by Thomas Regan/Milkyone.
Images by Peter Robinson Football Archive.
Typeset by Leslie Priestley.
Printed and bound by Standart.

FOR MUM

CONTENTS

INTRODUCTION

THE KREMLIN, MOSCOW. IT IS THE EVE OF THE 2018 WORLD CUP finals draw and it is hard to imagine a more alluring location as I leave behind St. Basil's Cathedral and approach the red-brick, fifteenth-century Spasskaya Tower. For the world's press, this tower, built into the huge wall that marks the western edge of Red Square, is the route into the Kremlin, the traditional heart of Russian power. I pass the guard at the foot of the giant gate and step through into the snow-laden interior.

English-language signs for 'Media Centre' lead past a line of gold-domed churches and cathedrals and on to the Kremlin's Palace of Congresses: a place built for Communist Party gatherings but tomorrow the setting for Gary Lineker, the main draw presenter, and his support cast of fellow World Cup greats to pick the balls and chart the way ahead for the 32 teams at Russia 2018.

Another global showpiece awaits, with all its joys and controversies, but this is not the reason I am here. Instead, as I stand in the media zone waiting for Fabio Cannavaro, Italy's 2006 World Cup-winning captain and one of Lineker's draw assistants, my thoughts are on a tournament receding into an ever distant past.

Italia '90 is further away today than the 1966 World Cup, England's moment of glory, was in 1990. For any English football fan over the age of 35, though, the mere mention of Paul Gascoigne's tears and Luciano Pavarotti's 'Nessun Dorma' and the national team's thrill-ride to the semi-finals can still make the soul smile.

As a journalist, I have covered World Cups on four different continents, from Japan to Brazil via Germany and South Africa, but none prompts the same stirrings of nostalgia as that 1990 tournament – seen, in my case, through seventeen-year-old eyes in the lounge of the family home in Liverpool.

When Fabio Cannavaro stops to speak to me, it becomes clear that Italia '90 cast its spell on him too. He was certainly closer to the action as a sixteen-year-old ball boy inside the Stadio San Paolo in Naples on the night Argentina broke the hopes and hearts of the hosts in a semi-final just as dramatic as the one between England and West Germany.

'Of course I cried,' he remembers, flashing his Colgate smile. 'I was a child with a lot of passion.'

The purpose of this book is to examine the impact of Italia '90 across the globe and Cannavaro is one name on a long list of more than a hundred people I spoke to who witnessed at first hand the power and emotion of that World Cup 28 years ago.

It was a tournament which took place at a pivotal moment in the sport's evolution; the advent of the Premier League and Champions League was around the corner, the influence of television was growing, and the world of football was about to become a much smaller place. In a sense, it acted as both a last hurrah and a searchlight on the future. It had a direct impact on the way the game would be packaged and played in the decades to follow.

To gauge fully this impact, I travelled to eleven countries over a period of ten months, an itinerary which included Cameroon, whose footballers emerged as the darlings of the tournament.

'The victory of a whole continent' is how the *Cameroon Tribune* described their victory over Argentina in the opening match – the first for any sub-Saharan African nation at a World Cup and the cue for a groundbreaking run to the quarter-finals. FIFA responded by guaranteeing greater representation thenceforth for the countries of CAF, the African confederation. 'Their demand is justified,' declared Franz Beckenbauer, West Germany's coach. 'The Africans have caught up.'

To emphasise the excitement that must have shaken Cameroon, this was the first time its twelve million people – the population in 1990 – had been able to follow their team's World Cup matches live on television.

They were not alone in taking a big step forward. Tournament newcomers Costa Rica and the Republic of Ireland both progressed to the knockout rounds. It was a World Cup of consequence too for the United States, restored to the world's elite after a forty-year absence, and the United Arab Emirates, who gained a deeper understanding of the sport's soft power.

As for Europe's Eastern Bloc nations, competing in Italy as seismic changes unfolded with the Iron Curtain's collapse, it was a moment for a generation of footballers when old realities crumbled and new doors opened – and some of the personal testimonies gathered, on journeys to Russia, Czech Republic, Slovakia and the Balkans, evoke a lingering bittersweetness.

It was a World Cup with more novelties than most: Fair Play flags, statistics on our TV screens (RAI, the host broadcaster, offered a table at the end of each half listing shots on goal, saves, corners, fouls and offsides), and England's first-ever penalty shootout. It also heralded significant changes to the Laws of the Game – a point underlined to me in an illuminating interview in Zurich with Sepp Blatter, the former FIFA president.

One of my most memorable encounters was with Totò Schillaci, Italy's bolt-from-the-blue centre-forward who won the Golden Boot for his six goals at his home World Cup – yet scored only one other international goal in his entire career. Schillaci, a Sicilian then more at ease speaking in his regional dialect than Italian, explained one autumn afternoon in Palermo his struggles to cope with the attention his feats attracted, and it is difficult to imagine a World Cup footballer today, with their cottage-industry entourages, suffering in this way. (Oliver Bierhoff, the Germany team manager, today uses the term 'independent entrepreneur' for his players.)

Similarly, Roger Milla's story has a thick slice of romance that would be virtually impossible to find reproduced in 2018. It is a story he recounted to me at his home in Yaoundé, the Cameroonian capital, remembering how he stepped out of semi-retirement on the Indian Ocean island of Réunion to lead defences a merry dance with the Indomitable Lions.

Another highlight was lunch at a restaurant in Argentina named Italia '90, and owned by Sergio Goycochea, the man who began the World Cup as the

Albiceleste reserve goalkeeper and ended it as hero of two penalty shootouts.

It is these human stories, combined with the transformative background events, which make Italia '90 so compelling. It is a tournament whose participants, I learned, inspired a Costa Rican film and a Czech play. Irish writer Roddy Doyle set his novel *The Van* against the backdrop of World Cup mania in Dublin, where half a million people turned out to welcome back Jack Charlton's team. (Such was the hold of the tournament on Ireland that the *Limerick Leader*, seeking the advice of a local pharmacist, ran a front-page article afterwards headlined 'World Cup fever could lead to withdrawal symptoms'.)

In England, there was *An Evening with Gary Lineker*, the play by Arthur Smith and Chris England centred on a group of friends sat around watching England's semi-final match. Smith tells me, 'It was a more insulated world then. There wasn't football on the telly all the time, so any individual game that was on had a greater impact and you'd all gather and watch it together.'

A World Cup then came with a Christmas-morning tingle. Four whole years had passed since Mexico '86 and the last month of wall-to-wall football on television.

In the words of journalist Adrian Tempany, writing in *And the Sun Shines Now*, his outstanding book on the Hillsborough disaster and football's development thereafter, '... its magic belonged to another age, one of scarcity and rarity.'

In my research, I heard a resonant line from ITV commentator John Helm, who, early in the Cameroon-Romania group-stage match in Bari, told his viewers: 'Cameroon today [are] playing in green shirts, red shorts and yellow stockings. It's not often we see anything like that in England.'

He was right. The World Cup was an explosion of colour into our living rooms. In the 1989/90 season, not a single European club competition match was broadcast live on the BBC or ITV – not even the European Cup final. To the football watcher born after 1990, after the arrival of football's satellite age, the rarity factor cannot be overstated.

During the English season leading up to Italia '90, there were twelve domestic top-flight matches broadcast live, compared with 168 in 2017/18. Moreover, the armchair viewer had to wait until 29 October 1989 and the meeting of Liverpool and Tottenham Hotspur, fully ten weeks into the season, for the first live match.

Arsenal and Liverpool had produced the most gripping finish to any league season the previous May with the north London side's last-gasp, title-grabbing 2-0 victory at Anfield. It was a match broadcast live by ITV on a Friday night but it had evidently not altered the thinking of the rights holder, who considered that people were more likely to stay at home and watch football once the clocks had gone back and the longer nights had set in.

For its part, the BBC screened eight FA Cup ties live that season – including, for the first time, both semi-finals on the same day. With the Liverpool-Crystal Palace and Manchester United-Oldham Athletic matches yielding thirteen goals between them, this was the first Super Sunday before the phrase had even tripped off the tongue of a Sky Sports executive. (And like that 1989 Liverpool-Arsenal classic, it provides a loud call for nuance from those drawn to a simplistic, Year Zero reading of the subsequently remodelled game).

For European football enthusiasts, meanwhile, the only continental action came from Wednesday night highlights on BBC's *Sportsnight* or ITV's *Midweek Sports Special*.

If there was little international club football on our television sets, so there were few players from abroad in the old First Division. On the last weekend of 1989/90, just fifteen players involved came from beyond the British Isles. Only two would go to the World Cup: Sweden's Glenn Hysén and Roland Nilsson, then with Liverpool and Sheffield Wednesday respectively. The World Cup in 1990 seemed like a voyage of discovery.

The first World Cup tournament I had embraced, the first such voyage of discovery, had been España '82. I once sat in the manager's office at Wycombe Wanderers' training ground and heard Gareth Ainsworth, who, like me, had turned nine in the weeks leading up that World Cup, reminisce about running out of his house to replay the action in the back garden of his family home in Blackburn.

I still recall my own fascination with the *Radio Times*' 1982 World Cup preview magazine. There was the exciting discovery, made while poring over it on a bench on the promenade at Grange-over-Sands, that there was a team in Chile called Everton. The El Salvador team profile, meanwhile, contained a grim account of the death of one of their players: shot by guerrillas, with his body found dumped in a dustbin. I was hooked.

There were also hours spent playing the England World Cup record, 'This Time (We'll Get It Right)', and Scotland's admittedly superior 'We Have A Dream'. Eight years on, I went down to Woolworths and bought an even better record, New Order's 'World In Motion'.

The fact the 1990 finals were taking place in Italy had enhanced the anticipation. This was a place where everything felt bigger and better: the United States of Football. As the introductory voiceover in FIFA's official film of the tournament put it: 'Italy had become the spiritual home of the modern game.'

Italy had the teams – AC Milan, Juventus and Sampdoria completed a clean sweep of 1990's European prizes – and it had the stadiums too, five of them with capacities upwards of fifty thousand. Champions Milan recorded an average attendance of 57,890 in that 1989/90 season when Old Trafford's 39,077 was as good as it got for the English game.

As for the continental competitions, the old First Division's finest were still in the chill of exile following the ban put in place after the 1985 Heysel Stadium disaster.

So much was different then, and stepping back into the Palazzetto dello Sport for the World Cup finals draw on 9 December 1989 demonstrates the point.

Luciano Pavarotti – the big, beaming tenor with the big, booming voice – performs 'O Sole Mio' and 'Nessun Dorma', while Sophia Loren brings some bouffant-haired Hollywood glamour. On ball-picking duties is a cast of World Cup winners: Pelé, Bobby Moore, Daniel Passarella, and – in outrageous, *Dynasty*-style shoulder pads – Bruno Conti.

Giorgio Moroder, the Italian record producer and songwriter, is present too. His freshly composed official tournament song, 'To Be Number One', gets an airing – as does 'Notti Magiche', the Italian version. More than one thousand journalists look on.

To the modern viewer, there is something endearingly unpolished about proceedings. The top tier of the auditorium is filled with schoolchildren who respond boisterously to the cues of presenter Pippo Baudo. They chant 'Sophia' at *Signora* Loren and, in a foretaste of his cartoon-villain role at Italia '90,

6

throw in a few whistles when Diego Maradona's name is mentioned.

These whistles come during Loren's brief Q&A with Baudo, an exchange noteworthy for its candour. After naming Maradona as her favourite player, she is asked to provide a tip for visitors to Italy and, with her reply, touches instead on the fear of hooliganism – a fear which had ensured, before a ball was picked, England's presence out of harm's reach on Sardinia. 'I hope they come here with the mindset of tourists and not warriors,' says Loren.

She even displays an ambivalence towards football which would have the sport's PR machines combusting were it to happen now, when she is asked how much her children are looking forward to the World Cup: 'My sons don't really follow football.'

The feel of an old-fashioned Saturday night variety show is heightened by the appearance of the tournament's stickman mascot – represented by eight lycra-suited dancers in tooth-paste stripes of green, white and red with half-footballs on their heads. His name, Ciao, was chosen following an eleven-week polling process involving over 30 million votes cast – and featuring the regrettable demise of rival contenders Bimbo and Dribbly.

One of the most intriguing sights is found directly behind Sepp Blatter, the twinkle-eyed, 53-year-old FIFA general secretary, as he conducts the draw ceremony itself. The backdrop shows the flags of the 24 competing countries. Above his left shoulder is the USSR; on the row below are Czechoslovakia, Romania and Yugoslavia: all countries in a state of upheaval following the fall of the Berlin Wall.

Seven months later, two days before the World Cup final, Nato declared a formal end to the Cold War. Never again would the names Czechoslovakia, USSR and West Germany appear on the World Cup map.

England's own place on the football map would shift considerably too in the near three decades between Blatter apologising – in Italian and French – for conducting the 1990 draw in English and Gary Lineker's turn as master of ceremonies in the Kremlin.

The national side's enthralling run to the semi-finals of Italia '90 and the drama of a shootout defeat by West Germany gave a sense of rebirth to the English game, with their clubs' five-year exclusion from Europe brought officially to an end six days after that epic night in Turin.

England had begun the tournament deliberately detached from the mainland but if there were outbreaks of trouble in Cagliari, Rimini and Turin from their feared supporters, by the latter stages a different narrative had taken over as a cheeky-faced poster boy called Paul Gascoigne – a player of rare, game-changing spontaneity – led his team, and their hitherto vilified manager Bobby Robson, on a journey out from the shadows.

Italia '90 fever at home grew with the progress of Robson's side. In the wake of the quarter-final victory over Cameroon, off-licences and takeaway shops reported sales up by forty per cent.

Chris Waddle's decisive penalty miss in the semi-final against West Germany was the cue for a record electricity surge of 2,800MW, the equivalent of 1,120,000 kettles being switched on at the same time – which is probably precisely what happened given the record estimated TV audience of 26.2 million. One tabloid newspaper reported that in Enfield, north London, a man had celebrated Gary Lineker's semi-final goal by running through a glass patio door.

By the time it all finished, Fabio Cannavaro was not the only one watching who was ready to cry. My hope is that this book will explain just why Italia '90 meant the world to so many people all around it – and why its legacy endures.

FIRST ROUND

The big bang

THE 1990 WORLD CUP BEGAN WITH A BANG. AND NOBODY FELT IT more than Claudio Caniggia. If Argentina 0 Cameroon 1 was the most seismic opening result of any World Cup, there is arguably no more famous a foul in finals history than the one Benjamin Massing, the west African nation's huge central defender, effected on Caniggia, the long-haired Argentina forward, with two minutes remaining of the tournament's curtain-raiser at the San Siro on 8 June 1990. It is certainly hard to think of a more laughably blatant one.

Not for Massing the sly rake of studs down calf or other such acts of cunningly disguised destructiveness. No, this was full-frontal stuff, cartoonish in its crudeness. It was like a mischievous Quentin Tarantino remake of that classic scene from the 1970s BBC comedy series *Some Mothers Do 'Ave 'Em* where the accident-prone Frank Spencer is flying down the street, out of control on a pair of roller skates. In that sequence, Spencer hurtles across a junction, zigzagging between a Mini and a Ford Capri, and then squeezes beneath the trailer of a passing truck. Here, the flying Caniggia evades two green shirts but then, splat – the haulage truck, aka Massing, flies into the frame and simply wipes him out.

'It's a nice thing for me,' grins Massing. 'Wherever I go, it's, "Ah, he's the one who did the tackle on Caniggia." Everywhere. Everyone says it to me, even when I went to Equatorial Guinea a few years ago for the Cup of Nations. It's what people recognise me for. So I have to say, it's affection I get more than anything else, and if it was a source of money, I'd be a rich man.'

He begins his retelling of the incident with teammate Emmanuel Kundé, the first man in Caniggia's path, and, as he puts it in French, '*un partisan de la non-aggression*'. It is not meant as a compliment. 'He'd come off with his shirt spotless, just as he'd come on,' he says with a frown. 'Then I saw Victor [Ndip], who was my direct partner. We knew each other's game well. He couldn't get to him. When Caniggia hurdles him, I said, "Shit, this is dangerous."'

The cheetah-quick Caniggia had originally picked the ball up five yards outside his own box. He had passed Kundé as he crossed the halfway line, then hurdled – just – the raised boot of Ndip.

Ndip's nibble had left him striving to regain full balance and his head was down and arms flailing as Massing steamed in.

'I was marking Diego [Maradona], but I left him,' he adds. 'I thought, "If he's got time to get his balance and pass the ball, we're stuffed." That's why I came in on him like a truck. I got to Caniggia and flew in on him. I wasn't thinking that clearly. I was a bit wound up that he'd got past my two colleagues. Knowing that he was breaking clear, and about to get his head up, that was going to be dangerous.

'And that's why I really went for it.'

He really did. 'No leavy go' is what Massing's defensive partner Ndip, from the Anglophone south-west of Cameroon, would shout at the French-speaking Massing in pidgin English during matches – don't let him go. There was no leavy go for poor Caniggia.

Massing claims he once ran 100m in 10.1 seconds. In he flew, landing on the Argentinian's left foot and sending him skidding across the turf.

Five Argentina players rushed over to protest to referee Michel Vautrot, as Massing bent down to pull back on the boot which had left his foot with the force of his challenge.

None of the World Cup's thirteen previous opening matches had witnessed a red card. This one had now seen two, with Massing following teammate André Kana-Biyik into the dressing room. Kana-Biyik thought that the match must be over at the sight of his teammate. 'He starts raising his arms and he's expecting me to do the same,' Massing recalls. 'He says, "What's going on?" so I tell him, "No. They've sent me off too."'

To underline the size of the shock witnessed by the crowd of 73,780 inside the San Siro that evening, it is worth noting that no team from south of the Sahara had ever won a World Cup finals match before.

Three Maghreb nations had – Tunisia in 1978, Algeria in 1982, and Morocco in 1986 – but this was a first for black Africa. And they had not beaten just any team. Rather, in front of 150 countries watching around the world, Cameroon had upset Diego Maradona's Argentina; the holders felled by the 500-1 outsiders.

The impact of Senegal's scalping of reigning champions France in the opening game of Korea/Japan 2002 does not compare. Then, Senegal had a starting XI made up entirely of players based in France (compared with just one Ligue 1 player for *Les Bleus*). Cameroon's 1990 team, by contrast, included five home-based players – officially termed as amateurs.

Only five of their 22-man squad played top-level football abroad. François Omam-Biyik, their match-winner, had – like Massing – spent the preceding season in France's second tier.

For Cameroon, it was the springboard for their history-making run to the quarter-finals. Moreover, it was an evening which set the tone perfectly for what was to follow at Italia '90.

There was controversy, drama, brutality. There were pantomime heroes and villains. And, at the end of it, huge headlines.

To review the action through the softer prism of 21st-century sensibilities invites the occasional shudder – and sympathy for Maradona, who rises wearily off the turf more than once, with something approaching stoicism. The final foul count read Cameroon 28 Argentina 9. Each of substitute Caniggia's first four runs earned a clattering, with Massing's crushing contribution still to come.

Not that the crowd, who had whistled loudly through Argentina's anthem, cared. The two red-carded Cameroonians left the pitch to cheers.

To the Milanese, Maradona, who had just taken the Serie A title down to Naples in the south of the peninsula, was the bogeyman.

When Napoli collapsed spectacularly – and, some suggested, suspiciously – in the 1988 title race, Maradona said, 'Today, the racist Italy has won'. During Argentina's preparatory camp in Austria, he had returned to the same theme, speaking of Napoli's title triumph as 'the revenge of the south against the racist north'.

The Argentina skipper mined the same seam with his sardonic response following this opening upset: 'The only pleasure I got this afternoon was to discover that thanks to me, the people of Milan have stopped being racist. Today, for the first time, they supported the Africans.'

EDÉA LIES ON CAMEROON'S ROUTE NATIONALE 3 CONNECTING THE administrative capital, Yaoundé, set among the hills of the Central region, with Douala, the country's main port in the south. It is a single-lane highway cut through a lush forest landscape. Or, as Martin Etongé, the local journalist sharing the back seat, sighs, 'This is a death trap.'

The toll stops along the route feature cash collectors stood roadside in orange work coats. This is a country of bright colours – even the security guards wear yellow.

On the outskirts of Edéa, we reach the Hostellerie de la Sanaga, a hotel named after the river that flows behind it, a river running out into the Gulf of Guinea.

Tall, thin coconut trees frame the view.

The date is 28 April 2017. We are here to meet Benjamin Massing. He arrives in a Toyota Corolla which looks to have taken almost as many bumps as Diego Maradona did on that unforgotten evening in Milan.

He is now a chief of the Bakoko, the people native to Edéa. His business card explains he is a third-class chief and includes the honorific *Sa Majesté* – His Majesty – and he certainly looks the part.

Over his pale checked shirt he wears a black waistcoast complemented by a long, matching skirt. A large necklace hangs around his neck, displaying three lion teeth. He has a broad, handsome face and – belying the memory of *that* tackle – a surprisingly gentle manner.

Inside the hotel, a meeting of chiefs is about to begin, with the environmental impact of a local mining project on the agenda.

It is a role he combines with his vice-presidency of the national footballers' union. 'You have to settle disputes between members of your community,' he explains. 'At the end of a tribunal, you've got to make a ruling that's fair for everybody.'

It was here in Edéa that three of Cameroon's principal actors in the drama of 8 June 1990 shared their formative football moments. Massing and Kana-Biyik, the two defenders dismissed to the San Siro dressing room, became friends after the latter left his home village of Pouma, thirty miles away, to attend school in the town.

Kana-Biyik then introduced Massing to his younger brother, François. The man who would head the goal that stunned Argentina was already the owner of a prodigious leap, as Massing explains.

'Omam-Biyik played his first match here because his older brother, Kana-Biyik, came to school here, and when there were days off, he'd come and stay with us for a couple of days. He'd stay a couple of nights – Friday, Saturday – and then go back to school on the Sunday. That was when we started to play. We started playing for a local club while still at the *lycée*. During the holidays, he said to us, "I've got a little brother, and he's really good."

'At the time, François didn't play as a forward; he was a libero. When we went to the inter-district competition, François came. We realised then that at every corner, he was the one jumping the highest to win the ball.'

It was in the 67th minute of Italia '90's opening match that the rest of the world discovered what Massing had seen as a teenager.

'He had this timing,' adds Massing. 'He knew how to do it. I don't think he'd ever jumped as high as that, though.' There were only two Cameroon players against five defenders in the Argentina penalty box to attack a free-kick from the left flank. As the ball landed, Cyrille Makanaky, the dreadlocked midfielder, got a foot to it ahead of Néstor Lorenzo, sending it looping over to the far post.

There, Omam-Biyik, aided by the negligence of Roberto Sensini beside him, had a near-clear leap at the ball. Up he rose, hanging in the air. His header was tame, yet Nery Pumpido, Argentina's goalkeeper, fell lazily onto the ball and it escaped beneath him. 'Disaster for Pumpido,' said Barry Davies, describing it to the BBC viewers.

The goal came six minutes after his brother's red card for clipping the heels of Caniggia. Kana-Biyik blew three kisses to the crowd as he stepped off the pitch. The ten men became nine two minutes from the end.

By today's standards it would be absurd to defend Cameroon's tackling.

Maradona did not manage a shot on goal that day, but he did suffer twelve fouls. It was in this climate of casual brutishness that FIFA decided, in the wake of Italia '90, that enough was enough.

Massing does not hide the intent to intimidate. 'We knew full well that Maradona wasn't a player you could play against normally. He was somebody you had to brutalise a bit, so he'd lose a bit of heart. We knew that with Maradona, you had to hit him. It wasn't all about finesse with him. He liked a battle. He didn't say anything to you. He had the same logic.'

It is an extraordinarily frank insight into a defender's mindset at the time. In truth, self-preservation might have been driving Maradona's logic, as he reflected later in his autobiography, 'Cameroon had really given us a kicking.'

And yet, in Cameroonian minds, there were question marks against the red cards. 'For the first, for Kana-Biyik, the referee really got it wrong,' Massing says of the straight red issued for a challenge that occurred forty yards from goal with another defender in close attendance.

'In our era, we African footballers had a lot of problems with European referees. Maybe we played too hard. Maybe there were problems with racism. With Vautrot, it wasn't the first time we had a match together, and there were times he blew for fouls which weren't.

'Put simply, it's a contact sport, and the contact in football isn't like in boxing where you get weighed, see you're both the same weight, and then face each other. In football, you can weigh eighty kilos and be up against someone who's sixty-two kilos. And if you go into a challenge and he goes down, it doesn't mean you've committed a foul; it means he's lighter than you.'

A similar attitude is found in the World Cup reports in the *Cameroon Tribune* newspaper. The country's main paper said of the opening match, 'Under the pretext of protecting football from violence, in accordance with FIFA's wishes, Vautrot went too far, showing clearly a reverential fear for Maradona and company.'

The paper speculates that Vautrot 'even came to mix up the Cameroon players' in his decision to dismiss Kana-Biyik.

The sense of injustice finds expression too in a cartoon showing goalkeeper Thomas Nkono comforting a sniffling, kneeling Maradona with the words,

'It's Monsieur Vautour, er ... Vautrot who's had you. A lion is twice as dangerous when he is wounded.' *Vautour*, in French, is vulture.

✱

CAMEROON HAD PARTICIPATED IN THE WORLD CUP FINALS ONCE before, in 1982 in Spain, where they departed the tournament unbeaten after draws with Peru, Poland, and Italy. It was after that tournament that Thomas Nkono, the subject of offers from clubs in Spain and Brazil for his outstanding displays, joined Spanish club Espanyol, the start of an enduring association with the Barcelona club, where he is now the long-serving goalkeeper coach.

Nkono meets me one bright, spring lunchtime at Espanyol's training ground, the Ciudad Deportiva Dani Jarque. Outside stands a statue of Jarque, the defender who died suddenly in 2009 and whose name Andrés Iniesta wore on a t-shirt after his winning goal in the 2010 World Cup final.

Nkono may now, at sixty, be spectacled and bald-headed, but the trademark black tracksuit bottoms are still on – just as they were on those hot, humid evenings of Italia '90. It was a habit born out of practicality.

'We trained on a dirt pitch in Yaoundé,' he says, flashing an easy smile. That pitch, incidentally, is still there today, still being used by his old team, Canon Yaoundé.

Looking back, Nkono explains that Cameroon's 1982 side had 'more individual talents' than their 1990 successors – notably a then thirty-year-old Roger Milla and Nkono himself, whose nickname 'Mr Fifty Percent' told of the difference he made to his team.

The Lions ended level on three points in their group with Italy, the eventual winners, and with an identical goal difference of zero. However, the *Azzurri* had scored one goal more and thus progressed.

Eight years on, Cameroon's preparations for Italia '90 were mixed. They performed poorly at the Africa Cup of Nations in Algeria that March, falling at the group stage after defeats by Zambia and Senegal.

Meanwhile, the recall of the now 38-year-old Milla, following a decree by national president Paul Biya, had drawn raised eyebrows – and frowns – from some of the junior members of a squad unconvinced by the merits of reintroducing a man in semi-retirement on the Indian Ocean island of Réunion.

'At the start, some people didn't understand it,' says Nkono of the internal debate that went on. 'The players who knew him better did. I have a great friendship with Roger.

'When he was at Montpellier, I'd visit him there, as it's only three hours away. We'd won a lot together and done a lot in African football, and were the leaders – myself, Roger, [Emmanuel] Kundé, [Stephen] Tataw. We were quite strong, and the youngsters accepted it. We said to Roger he'd have to wait and be our joker, but he'd succeed that way, and so it proved.'

At their camp in Yugoslavia, the team won two and lost two of their five fixtures against local club sides. There was uncertainty over the merits of the playing system which, Nkono says, led to a switch from 4-4-2 to a 4-4-1-1 spearheaded by Omam-Biyik. Nkono, who had played all three matches at Spain '82 as Cameroon captain, had his own particular anxiety over the decision of Valeri Nepomniachi, the squad's Russian coach, to favour Bordeaux goalkeeper Joseph-Antoine Bell as his No1 for the World Cup.

Nkono and Bell had had a career-long rivalry – a blessing for their country with one spurring on the other – but Nkono was reluctant to stand in the shadows.

He duly confronted Nempomniachi, a reticent figure who communicated with his players through an interpreter. 'I came from Espanyol after the best season of my life, got to Yugoslavia, and before starting the preparations, I had to sit down with the coach, his interpreter, and his assistants.

'He said, "You're not going to start."

'I said, "Why not?"

'He said he was going to change the system in defence and use a high line. He said his decision was taken. I was ready to go back. Espanyol were in the second division and playing to win promotion. In the end, my wife convinced me to stay.'

As it was, Nkono would feature in the opening match against Argentina, though the player himself only discovered this on the morning itself.

The reason was that Bell – ever outspoken – had given an interview to *L'Équipe*, the French sports daily, criticising Nepomniachi's preparations and predicting a defeat against the South Americans. Nkono had not anticipated the late twist.

'I was going to be in the stand with my wife. It wasn't like today, when everyone has a phone. I called her the day before and said I had the tickets, and tomorrow we'd meet up and go in together.

'I was in the same room as Omam-Biyik. I said, "François, sleep well, because tomorrow, you're going to score a goal."

'The next day, we had breakfast, and at midday, we had a team meeting, but the coach's interpreter came to me and said the coach wanted to speak to me. I was with [third goalkeeper] Jacques Songo'o in his room and said to him, "I bet he says I've got to play". It was around eleven o'clock.

'The coach said, "How are you to play?"

'I said, "You said I couldn't play. I have to think about it, I'm going to call my wife." But I couldn't get hold of her, as she'd gone out. I kept calling the reception.

'The meeting was at 12.30, and at 12.15 the federation called me. They said, "They've told us you don't want to play."

'I said, "Yes, because the coach said I wasn't going to play, and I'm not ready."

'They said, "We're going to decide, because Bell isn't going to play." There'd been some declarations from Bell in the French press, they were quite strong, and he was out. In the end, I said, "You can tell the head of state I'll play for him."

'When my wife called me at lunchtime, I said, "We can't meet up now, love."

'"What's wrong?"

'"Because I have to play now."

'She couldn't eat after that.'

The goalkeeper saga was not the only source of last-minute panic. There was some confusion over the official squad list too, with a wrong date of birth for Jean-Claude Pagal one of several discrepancies.

Three different versions were submitted to FIFA in the end. À *la camerounaise*, as Benjamin Massing puts it.

FOR DEFENDING CHAMPIONS ARGENTINA, THE FOCUS, AS EVER, WAS on Diego Maradona, their inspirational leader and the dominant figure of the 1986 World Cup.

On the eve of the opening match, Carlos Menem, his country's president, announced the thirty-year-old's new status as an ambassador for Argentinian sport and presented him with a diplomatic passport at the San Siro.

As a reflection of this status, the beige-suited Menem waited in front of a couple of hundred journalists at the stadium's media centre until Maradona, in Argentina shirt and tracksuit bottoms, had completed his pitch walkabout and was able to join him on the dais.

Waiting for Maradona was nothing new, of course. The previous summer, Napoli had done just that after the player responded to his club's refusal to permit him a transfer to French side Olympique Marseille by prolonging his summer break in Argentina.

He cancelled his return flight to Naples 34 times. When he returned, he had a beard and was seven kilos overweight.

In his autobiography, *El Diego*, Maradona details the efforts undertaken to ensure his readiness for his third World Cup. He had entered spring 1990 suffering from excruciating pain in his lower back, unable to train and overweight once more. Yet, after returning to the Napoli team on 11 March against Lecce, he began a series of weekly visits to the Italian Olympic Committee's Institute of Sports Science in Rome and embarked on a rigorous fitness programme and diet.

Physician Dr Henri Chenot likened his charge to 'a Rolls Royce abandoned in a garage', yet by cutting his sugar and salt intake and eating only fruit, vegetables, cereals, and white meat, Maradona lost four kilos inside three weeks.

On the Argentina squad's arrival at the World Cup base in Trigoria, he had his own exercise machine installed in the gym at a cost of sixty thousand dollars.

If Maradona was losing weight, the squad selection of Carlos Bilardo, still at the helm four years after the team's triumph in Mexico, had left him with a heavy heart. Although he had pushed successfully for the inclusion of Claudio Caniggia, he felt keenly the exclusion of Jorge Valdano, a scorer in the Mexico '86 final and somebody he has described as 'the only man capable of lifting my spirits with a single word'.

Valdano had formed part of Argentina's inner circle in Mexico along with José Luis Brown, a late withdrawal because of injury, and Ricardo Giusti who was struggling for fitness along with Jorge Burruchaga, Julio Olarticoechea and Oscar Ruggeri. In Maradona's eyes, the World Cup-winning spine of 1986 was broken.

And yet, they had Maradona.

The mere sight of him in the corridors of the San Siro was too much for a couple of Cameroon players. As defender Victor Ndip recalls, 'Alphonse Yombi and Roger Feutmba started crying before the match when they saw Maradona.'

Out on the pitch, the opening reels of Italia '90 had begun to whir. Gianna Nannini – sister of the Formula 1 racer Alessandro Nannini – and Edoardo Bennato performed the official tournament song. A choir from La Scala sang parts of 'Aida'.

One hundred and sixty models oozed glamour in the creations of four Italian designers, one for each of the continents involved.

A giant ball, adorned with hundreds of decorative daisies, rose from the centre of the pitch and floated up and out of the stadium. The cynical-minded might suggest it was an unwitting augury for the anti-football that would follow.

Meanwhile, there were colourful happenings offstage too. The testimony of an unnamed employee from the local organising committee tells of the 'many condoms' left littering the VIP toilets that evening, suggesting that Italia '90's low-scoring trend did not apply to Milan's beautiful people.

The most striking thing of all, of course, was the San Siro itself; a great space station of a stadium, whose newly added third tier had raised the capacity to 80,000. From down on the pitch, the dramatic, red roof girders framed a rectangle of sky.

To English eyes, this was supersized football, a Cecil B. DeMille makeover. At the time the old First Division's biggest arena was the 50,726-capacity Old Trafford. John Williams, an associate professor in sociology at Leicester University and author of fifteen books on football, was attending the match on a research trip for the Football Trust and he articulates the wow factor: 'There was no stadium like it in England – no stadium of that size and of that completely enclosed aspect. That was all going to come in the post-Taylor years. It was absolutely alien to the English experience.'

Yet, as Victor Ndip points out, African football could do big scale too. 'I'd been in the national team four or five years, and it was just like in Surulere in Lagos, when I was in the junior national team and there were 120,000 spectators. When I saw the crowd at the San Siro, to me, it was very simple.'

✱

THE INTERACTION BETWEEN THE ARGENTINA AND CAMEROON teams, limbering up inside, in the same warm-up space, held its own fascination. It was there that Cameroon gained a psychological foothold.

Eugène Ekéké, later a scorer against England in the quarter-finals, remembers: 'The Argentinians started warming up, and our players were a bit intimidated. One player started watching Maradona juggle the ball and says, "We're dead here." We couldn't carry on like that, so we decided to start making some noise.'

It would not be the only time that Cameroon's battle songs would leave an impression on their Italia '90 opponents. 'The Argentinians came in and started singing, so we started singing even louder,' recounts Nkono.

Roger Milla adds, 'We couldn't understand them, but we thought they were making fun of us. When we started singing loudly, they left.'

For Maradona, his teammates' subdued mood prompted a call to arms back in the Argentina dressing room as he shouted out, 'Fucking c'mon! This is a World Cup, and we're the world champions.' Over in Cameroon's dressing room, Ekéké, a Christian whom the other players knew as *le Pasteur* – the Pastor – led a prayer. Ekéké has not forgotten his words: 'I said, "Lord, we're in this contest like David against Goliath. Nobody thinks we can win, but as with David, show your glory because you like to take small things and make something great with them."

'We were less afraid now, and we started singing. We got into the tunnel, and you had us on the right and Argentina on the left. We were singing, *"Frères camerounais, nous allons gagner, nous allons gagner, nous allons gagner au nom du Cameroun".* The message, delivered in his entrancing light baritone, is clear – Cameroonian brothers, we're going to win.

'I think it was the Argentinians who were wary now,' he adds. 'Our stopper, Benjamin Massing, stopped in front of Maradona and looked at him. We have a technique here, when you look deeply into their eyes. And he did that.'

Mind, the big defender got a surprise at what he saw. 'He combed his hair,' Massing grins. 'It was like somebody going to a night club, sprucing himself up.'

Maradona continued to catch the eye in the on-field preamble. After shaking the hand of his Cameroon counterpart, Stephen Tataw, he flicked the ball up and let it bounce four times up into the air off his shoulder; a sudden flashback to his days as an Argentinos Juniors ballboy entertaining half-time crowds with his tricks.

It is a sight that has remained with Roger Milla, sitting on the bench ahead of his first late cameo of the competition. 'Perhaps he did that for us – to discourage us, to say, "We're the world champions, we're here, and we're going to crush you." We thought, "OK. You play the game on the pitch, not on your shoulders."'

And, in the case of Thomas Nkono, who had not even expected to be on that pitch, you play the game as slowly as possible. 'Maradona actually said to me, "Weren't you not meant to be playing?"' begins the goalkeeper thrust unexpectedly into the firing line.

'In my career, those first fifteen minutes were the hardest I had, in terms of getting my concentration fixed on the game. The plan was very simple. Knowing the morphology of the Cameroonians, to get into the game was difficult for us. We had to break the rhythm of the game. So, every action began with me. I broke up the rhythm, I gave it to my defence, they gave it back to me.'

It was a case of building up confidence and growing into the contest. By playing lots of back passes – thirteen, to be precise, by half-time.

When it is put to him that the subsequent change to the back-pass rule was a consequence of the actions of teams like Cameroon, Nkono, who would be booked for time-wasting at 0-0 in the next match against Romania, lets out a laugh 'It was because of me. I'm the one who made life more difficult for goalkeepers!'

Victor Ndip does not disagree: 'Thomas Nkono would push the ball forward and say, "OK, you climb up", and then, he'd kick it one step, pick the ball back up and just look at that time wasted.'

If that was part one of Cameroon's plan, part two involved stopping Maradona. It is something of a paradox, given the naivety they attribute to themselves elsewhere in this book – perhaps recklessness is a more apposite word – but Cameroon's game was built on strong defence and spontaneous attack.

'Any Cameroonian who played football would know our system of play was built on defence,' says Benjamin Massing. 'We had forwards who could score at any moment. That wasn't a problem. We didn't calculate how to score a goal.

'We calculated how to defend our goal. And we had the good fortune in that period that Cameroon always had great goalkeepers and – for at least fifteen years – strong defenders of a certain profile. Two years before, we'd won the Nations Cup in Morocco scoring only four goals.'

For Maradona, they devised a relay system. 'It wasn't easy to man-mark him,' he adds, explaining how Maradona played like 'a piston', dropping back in search of the ball, then driving back upfield with the sphere at his feet. 'We said, "We'll mark out our half in squares. As soon as he gets in such a zone, you take him. As soon as he leaves your zone, leave him and I'll take him."

'But he was very mobile. We'd been watching him for months – Argentina cassettes, Napoli cassettes, we saw exactly how he played. He had the same way always of starting his attacks, so it wasn't complicated. You just needed the physical capacity to be able to follow him all the time and to be physically right when you went into a challenge with him, because he was tough.'

For Argentina coach Carlos Bilardo, it was no surprise when the rough stuff began. He had travelled out to watch Cameroon at the Africa Cup of Nations and was forewarned. 'They'd told me in the Argentinian embassy, "Be careful with Maradona, because they're going to kick him," so I already knew.'

And had he passed the warning on? 'No. I didn't see it as important.'

The Times' headline the following morning, 'Argentina cut down to size', was a fair summary of the Cameroonian approach. Massing's first caution came after nine minutes when he clattered into the back of Maradona. His partner Victor Ndip followed him into referee Vautrot's book for a savage challenge on the same player after 23 minutes. Leading a counter-attack, Maradona had wriggled away from Massing and lifted the ball past Ndip, who caught him with a boot at chest height.

I meet Ndip in a bar in Buea at the heart of Cameroon's English-speaking south-west region. It is a lively university town sited on the eastern slopes of Mount Cameroon, the country's highest peak, and reached on a scenic road through banana and rubber plantations.

There is a cooling mist rolling down from the summit as Ndip turns his thoughts to Maradona, and his own red mist.

'It was something that happened instantly,' he says. 'There's no way I'd have planned to do such a foul on somebody, it just happened like that. You saw it happen in 2010 in South Africa – it was the same situation with [Nigel] De Jong.'

He is referring to the Dutchman's chest-high challenge on Spain's Xabi Alonso in the World Cup final. Needless to say, in 1990, the award of just a yellow card for such an offence caused no such uproar.

As one of the Cameroon squad's home-based players (earning, he estimates, 'about £75 a month' playing for Canon Yaoundé), he insists he was thrilled to be sharing a pitch with Argentina's skipper.

'I was so inspired to see Maradona, the best player in the world, but something came to me that the football is round and the field is flat, so we have to go onto the field and see what's there.'

MARADONA'S OWN BEST WORK THAT EVENING WAS UNDONE BY the failings of those around him. His vision and precision would have put both Abel Balbo and Jorge Burruchaga through on goal but for their poor touches.

Oscar Ruggeri failed with a free header when picked out by Maradona's dead ball. To the Argentina skipper's dismay, Balbo had begun the match ahead of Claudio Caniggia, and the Udinese-based forward would waste a pair of second-half openings too.

Clarín, the country's best-selling newspaper, shared this frustration: 'It's inexplicable because Caniggia standing is worth more than others running.'

For their part, Cameroon did not just seek to destroy. They sprang forward with speed and the cheers of the crowd in their ears, with skilful ball players Louis-Paul Mfédé and Makanaky prominent.

In the 21st minute, Makanaky nearly brought about the opening goal. Omam-Biyik played a brilliantly-weighted, angled ball across the penalty box to meet his run, and though José Basualdo got a foot to the ball ahead of Makanaky, he diverted it over his own goalkeeper, Nery Pumpido, and towards the goal. Néstor Lorenzo, racing back, pushed it past the post before it could cross the line.

'We had individuals who knew how to use the ball,' says Benjamin Massing. 'In midfield, Louis Mfédé was practically the most talented player of his generation. Roger Milla and François Omam-Biyik were great technicians.

Cyrille Makanaky was another with a great mastery of the ball.'

Their golden reward came with Omam-Biyik's strike with 23 minutes remaining. It was a goal which shook the football world. A photo of it hangs on a wall in the national museum in Yaoundé, yet this was a moment with no need for hindsight to appreciate its significance.

'When the referee blew the final whistle,' attests Victor Ndip, 'I looked directly into the crowd and I saw my president Paul Biya and all those other presidents greeting him and I felt tears running down my ears.' The headline on the front page of the *Cameroon Tribune* read simply, '*Historique!*'

As Cameroon celebrated, Maradona refused initially to leave the dressing room and attend the post-match press conference, but was persuaded by an Italian official that his absence would only start another fire. 'It was my worst moment in football,' is how Bilardo, his coach, described it to me.

Clarín had little sympathy: 'Even 100 victories in a row could not wipe away the memory of such a humiliation.'

Amid the Argentinian complaints about Cameroon's approach, midfielder Burruchaga said the referee 'should have been tougher' though Michel Vautrot's own view is that as referee of the opening match, he had a remit to 'set the tone'.

FIFA had instructed its referees to take a hard line on professional fouls, and threatened that those who failed to comply would be sent home.

But could he have been stricter still in enforcing the directives? 'How?' he retorts. 'By sending off even more Cameroon players? And to have it said I'd fixed the match in the event of an Argentinian victory?

'Each big competition produces some precise instructions which FIFA uses to deliver a message to the whole world – the accent is often put on whichever football cancer is damaging the spectacle at that time. In 1982 in Spain, for example, it was respecting the distance at free-kicks.

'Perhaps it was the time to stop the escalation [of fouls] which could have ruined the end of the match,' he says of the first of the two red cards. 'It's normal that the country which has two players sent off at this level of competition considers it severe. It wasn't easy for me because I spoke the same language as the Cameroonians and they were trying to unsettle me, saying things like, "We know you've had instructions to favour the Argentinians as defending champions."

'But at the end of the match, Roger Milla came to shake my hand, and I remember telling him, "You can thank me because you've gone into legend now for beating the world champions with nine men."'

In this, at least, he could not have been more correct. The Cameroon bandwagon had begun to roll.

Island games
Part 1 – England

A BLOOD-STAINED ENGLAND SHIRT. IT IS THE DEFINING IMAGE OF Terry Butcher's ten-year international career. It was the defining image, too, of England's qualifying campaign for Italia '90. At the Råsunda Stadium, during the 0-0 World Cup qualifying draw with Sweden, the England centre-back had played on after receiving five stitches to a still-leaking head wound. By the end his white shirt was scarlet.

'It should've been seven stitches, but he only put five in,' says Butcher, flicking through the mental album of that night in September 1989. 'I had to go out again, and there was still an inch of open wound. I'd gone to head the ball, and it might have been [Johnny] Ekström who got a touch at the last minute, and I've just smashed his head. I knew it was a bad one because you put your hand to your head straight away – it was on the forehead, and there was hardly any flesh there.

'I was captain, and that made it even more important to get on with it. Bobby Robson was never in any doubt about taking me off at half-time. The pictures are quite famous – everybody on the pitch, including the referee, had some of my blood on their jerseys and shorts. What it led to was that because of the worry about AIDS and infection, players would have to go off and be stitched up. I wouldn't have been allowed back out nowadays, because it was quite a lengthy stitching process.

'We got battered but ended up getting a nil-nil draw which was a crucial point, and then a nil-nil the following month in Poland got us on the plane to Italy. People were so transfixed by my image, as I virtually had a red shirt on. I always say to people, "If you're going to cut your head, cut it when you're wearing an all-white kit, as it looks far more dramatic." I've had people who've gone to fancy-dress parties as me.'

Butcher is speaking to me at the Holiday Inn in Ipswich. He takes off his plastic-framed glasses as he sits down, orders a cup of tea, and begins to reminisce with the same fluency found in his BBC radio commentaries. It is not just the spoken word he values. 'I still use a fountain pen and write letters,' says the 59-year-old. 'My father used to get me to spell words. I had to spell them correctly before I got down from the dinner table. I could be a proofreader. I spot mistakes left, right and centre.'

If that does not sound like the head-banging centre-back of lore, the man who played Iron Maiden cassettes on the England team bus, it would not be the first time Butcher surprised us. In the 26th minute of England's World Cup semi-final against West Germany, ten months after his Stockholm blood fest, Butcher presented a wholly contrasting image as he skipped on to a loose ball, strode up to the centre-circle, and duly back-heeled the ball to Paul Gascoigne.

As a symbol of the transformative powers of Italia '90, a tournament now considered the turning of a page for English football, it was not bad at all: the English-oak defender serving up a palm-tree trick. 'I back-heeled the ball to an England player which was like, "Wow,"' he grins. 'I was quite pleased with that.'

Dunking a ginger biscuit into his tea, Butcher continues: 'Defending was strong, uncompromising. It was in your face – go for the ball and the ball's there somewhere but you take everything. I couldn't play as I did then in today's football, but you'd have to adapt, and it'd be a totally different preparation and mindset, anyway.

'I'd have loved to play today. I wasn't a bad passer – I used to like getting on the ball and bringing it out. I like to think I'm an old version of John Stones, but I could defend a bit better than John, stick my head in a bit more. John's too pretty for a centre-half.'

The Butcher back-heel was a doubly-fitting motif, given his relationship with Bobby Robson, the England manager who had given him his league debut at Ipswich Town in 1978, and with whom he helped the provincial club win the UEFA Cup – and finish top-flight runners-up – in 1981. He and Robson would bump into each other most mornings while walking their dogs.

By 1990, both men were preparing for their last World Cups. It would be Butcher's third and, at 31, there were concerns about his starting place. 'Mark Wright had come on really well, Des Walker was there, and I'm thinking, "I'm going to struggle to get into the team,"' he says. 'I'd peaked, and I knew this was my last tournament.'

The same applied to Robson, whose eight-year reign as manager was entering its last act. History tells us that at Italia '90, he would oversee England's best World Cup performance outside of their 1966 conquest on home soil. Within two days of the semi-final loss in Turin, Jeff Powell was lauding him in the *Daily Mail* for 'rekindling the English love affair with the great game invented on our island more than a century ago'.

A knighthood and national-treasure status would follow before his death in 2009, yet Robson spent much of the two years leading up to Italia '90 in the cross hairs of the press.

Although he had guided England to the last eight at Mexico '86, the team's dire showing at the 1988 European Championship, where they lost all three matches, had nearly brought about his departure, with the Football Association declining his offer to resign. After a 1-1 draw in Saudi Arabia later that year, the *Daily Mirror* declared, 'In the name of Allah, go', while the *Sun* screamed, 'England Mustafa new boss'.

England were the only team in the world to qualify for Italy without conceding a goal, but the negativity intensified with newspaper allegations about Robson's private life and, as Italia '90 approached, the Football Association declined to offer the 57-year-old a new contract. Bert Millichip, the FA chairman, is believed to have said he either had to win the World Cup or go, and yet Robson's subsequent decision to find employment with PSV Eindhoven sparked a tsunami of outrage and indignation.

'PSV Off Bungler Bobby' was the *Sun*'s headline. An even more striking example of the newspapers' savagery came from the *Today* newspaper in an article headlined, 'A Liar, A Cheat ... And Not Fit To Lead England'. It proceeded to describe Robson as a 'shambles of a man [who] stands accused of being a liar, a cheat and a traitor. He has been all these to his wife for many years ... Tomorrow he takes that team to Italy for the World Cup. He is not fit to lead it.'

Robson's widow, Lady Elsie, remembers: 'He'd been told by the FA that the World Cup would be the end of his England career, and PSV had said they'd like him to go there. At that time between the tabloid papers, there was a big war going on, between the *Mirror* and the *Sun*, and he was caught up in that.'

She is sitting in the front room of the terraced house in Fulham that was Robson's pied-à-terre in the capital. With us are Mark and Paul, two of Sir Bobby's three sons. The former recollects a time of 'complete anarchy within the press, who could say and do what they wanted. For us as a family, that was upsetting, but there was nothing you could do about it. It was part and parcel of the whole package – selling newspapers and writing rubbish stories. Obviously, Dad didn't appreciate that, because he wasn't a man who tolerated poor behaviour, fools, lies, or made-up stories. I didn't spend much time with Dad because he was a football manager, but I distinctly remember he was deeply hurt, really.'

For all the damaging discourse, Lady Elsie remembers her husband as a man who did not carry grudges. 'He rose above all that, which not many people can do. He knew the ups and he knew the downs, and he knew how to lose gracefully. And that was the art that that generation of football coaches grew up with, but it's not so any longer.'

The inner strength instilled by Robson's north-east upbringing provided an important bulwark. At seventeen, as an electrician, he had gone down the same pit at Langley Park colliery in which his own father worked for more than half a century.

'He was down the mine at Langley Park for fifty-two years. He missed one shift and was actually at the coalface,' says Mark Robson of his grandfather. 'That's where the toughness came from, without doubt. It helped Dad in his career that when it all got really nasty, he could probably step back a bit and have a think about what Granddad went through. With all the criticism during his England career, he must have thought, "Do I jack this in?" but I don't think he thought about it very long. It was, "This is where I want to be, I'm proud and I'm from the north-east and you have to be tough".

All the same, Mark continues, 'the nastiness' – and he cites a photo that appeared in the press of his father relaxing on his hotel balcony in Italy – tested that toughness and even 'possibly spoiled' his Italian experience. 'They stayed in Sorrento up on the hillside there, and someone pictured him through the bushes,' he recalls.

Happily, a more welcome photograph of Robson would appear in the English newspapers on 6 July, two days after his side's semi-final defeat. He has a cigar in his left hand and a smile of satisfaction on his face.

Paul Robson says, 'I remember the advert he did for Hamlet cigars. There'd been all this doubt and criticism, and they obviously got to the semi-final, and there was a big spread in the newspaper of dad smoking a cigar – it was the satisfaction of proving his critics wrong, if you like. He got paid quite a lot of money as well – ten thousand pounds.'

'Did he?' is Lady Elsie's rejoinder. 'He didn't tell me!'

TURIN, AND VINDICATION, LAY A LONG WAY DOWN THE TRACK during the early stretch of England's first-round campaign in Sardinia. Terry Butcher did not help his manager by butting an opponent during the final warm-up match in Tunisia, where Steve Bull's goal earned an underwhelming 1-1 draw. 'Nutter' was the headline in the *Daily Mirror* on 4 June, and Butcher does not deny the charge. 'I head-butted him,' he says. 'The guy put his arms around me like a cage and didn't allow me to get out. I just went, "No, you can't do this, I'll elbow you." He laughed at me, so I nodded to Gazza; Gazza played a free-kick in, and I just stuck my head down. I got his cheekbone.

'When we flew to our base camp in Sardinia, we had a debrief, and Bobby Robson showed us the whole video, and when my incident came on, the players all got up and applauded, because it was the most blatant head-butt you'll ever see in your life. Bobby Robson went bananas, because he'd defended me from the press and said I didn't mean to do it, when there was nothing more obvious.'

As the opening Group F game against the Republic of Ireland came nearer, another headache for the manager was the fitness of captain Bryan Robson, who was struggling with a heel problem. The Manchester United midfielder had departed the 1986 finals in Mexico with a dislocated shoulder suffered in the second group match against Morocco. Robson would start the Ireland game despite compounding his fitness problems with a noteworthy late-night mishap.

Butcher explains, 'What happened was we'd organised a breakout, and about eight of us went to a local bar. Chris Woods was arm-wrestling. It was hilarious – singing and dancing and the locals joining in. Then, we came back to the hotel and had a few drinks, and then Bryan Robson went into Gazza's room.' It was there that Robson, captain of England, tried to tip Gascoigne off his bed. He was wearing flip-flops. Down came the bed and off went Robson's right toenail. 'It just caught me on the big toe,' confirms Robson.

Butcher describes the team meeting the following morning: 'At eight-thirty, there was a knock on the door from Don Howe: "Team meeting!" We never normally had a team meeting, and we're thinking, "Oh my God, we've been rumbled". We went down, and Bobby Robson went right through the whole squad. He was probably the most animated I've ever seen him. He said, "Look, the captain of our country is in danger of not playing in the World Cup." I thought, "Well, we were dancing on tables the night before, and he looked pretty good to me."'

It was not just alcohol which helped bond that group of England players. A dispute with the English press prompted a period of radio silence from the players and, moreover, forged a siege mentality which, argues Butcher, 'worked to our advantage more than anything else'.

The cause was a *Daily Mirror* front-page story on 14 June about a female hostess – 'stunning Isabella Ciaravolo' – who had allegedly been expelled from the England base 'amid rumours of hi-jinks with players'. When Bobby Robson said the actions of the press could 'torpedo the players and torpedo the spirit', the *Mirror* responded with a comment piece declaring that 'Bobby Robson is a poor England manager who is now blaming anybody and everybody for his own mistakes, past, present or future.'

Patrick Barclay, now chair of the English Football Writers' Association, was in

Sardinia covering the World Cup for the *Independent*. He remembers, 'Robson was grumpy, he was in the mood to lash us. I'll never forget – we had a press conference with him and no players in a hut near a little training ground in Sardinia. It'd been bucketing down immediately after the training session had finished, and all the press ran out of what had previously been sunshine and through this rain to cram into this hut, where he was giving his press conference.

'One of them was Mike Langley of the *Sunday People*, a wonderful journalist but quite sharp of tongue in his columns. He said, "Before the conference starts, Bobby, my wife is visiting me at the moment and given the inclement weather would it be alright if she stood at the back of the room, out of the rain?" Robson snapped back: "Buy her an umbrella, Mike. Next question."'

The strain was manifest – and a departure, Barclay stresses, from Robson's usually amenable manner. 'The excellence of his management was he was collegiate, he would listen. Although he was a very able man he did have that insecurity, that open-mindedness. At press conferences he could see dangerous areas but he could also see the journalists' point. I'd guess "daft as a brush" [Robson's description of Gascoigne] came from one of these sessions. He'd go in and you'd say to him, "Bobby some unfortunate publicity about Gascoigne we have to ask you about." "Oh no, I'm not getting into that." "But do you not think this kind of publicity is a distraction for the squad?" "No, it's not something I want to get into." What you did then was you waited. You had to just wait. He couldn't bear the silence and he'd break the silence himself. "It's not something I want to get into at all ... I can understand why you're asking." And then you'd have it. You just had to wait because he was an instinctive communicator and incorrigibly honest. We knew that if we waited, he was like a fish that couldn't resist the bait. I say that as somebody who loved him. We all loved him – maybe not as much then as we did after, because the England manager and the English press is always a tough relationship.

'He rounded on the press, but I am absolutely certain it was the players who banned us. I can remember them laughing at us as we drove away from a training session. I remember [Gary] Lineker winking. As for the other players, I don't know if they were giving V-signs but that was definitely the message.'

Indeed, when defender Paul Parker, standing on the steps of the team bus after one training session, started a conversation with a reporter he knew, Michael Hart of the *Evening Standard*, Paul Gascoigne's response was to throw a cup of water at his teammate (though Parker told me this was just 'Gazza being Gazza').

England's opening game with the Republic of Ireland did little to change the mood. They had lost 1-0 to the Irish in their first match of the 1988 European Championship. This time, it finished 1-1.

Lineker, the six-goal Golden Boot winner at Mexico '86, added to his collection with the opening goal after nine minutes when, freed by Chris Waddle's angled ball over Ireland's back line, he chested it past the outrushing goalkeeper, Packie Bonner, then won a race to bundle it over the line. Kevin Sheedy's 73rd-minute equaliser, however, brought a draw.

Thanks to YouTube, it is a fixture perhaps best remembered by many England fans today for Lineker's mid-match loss of bowel control. Thankfully for Lineker, now the face of the BBC's football coverage, there were only eleven cameras inside the stadium (not the 37 you get at a World Cup today) and ultra-high definition had not yet been invented. Butcher recalls, 'We saw him rub his backside on the halfway line and thought, "What's he doing?"'

The Italian media wondered something similar about the entire England team. 'No football please, we're British' was the *Gazzetta dello Sport*'s headline. 'Derby in English means boredom' wrote the *Corriere della Sera*. 'Is this all there is to England?' asked *La Repubblica*.

Back at home, the response was even more scathing. The *Sun*, in a fuming front-page diatribe titled 'Bring 'em home' raged, 'Maggie Thatcher has hinted darkly that if our fans got out of hand she would call the whole team home. Don't wait, Mrs T. We can't face another night like that.'

IF THE ITALIANS CONSIDERED ENGLAND CULPABLE OF STONE-AGE football, a bigger preoccupation for the hosts in the approach to Italia '90 had been the country's supposed cavemen supporters. Butcher's shirt was not the only blood-stained one: Bobby Robson's press conference after the team's final qualifier in Poland was interrupted by a travelling supporter from Manchester who burst into the room with blood pouring from a wound in his forehead sustained when rival fans began hurling bottles and stones at each other.

It was anything but an isolated incident and the story of England at Italia '90 cannot be told without considering happenings off the field.

Only five years had passed since the Heysel Stadium disaster, when a surge by rioting Liverpool fans contributed to the deaths of 39 Juventus supporters, killed as a wall collapsed in the antiquated venue before the European Cup final.

Five years before that, fighting between England followers and Italian spectators pockmarked the national side's 1980 European Championship match against Belgium in Turin; the tear gas used by police spread to the pitch and led to a pause in play.

English teams had endured a ban from Europe's club competitions in the five years since Heysel and now, on the eve of the World Cup, UEFA said it was ready to re-open the door but deferred a final decision until after the tournament.

After all, it was only two years since English fans had run amok in Düsseldorf during the 1988 European Championship, bringing 381 arrests and the withdrawal of an earlier FA application for the readmission of English clubs to Europe. In September 1989, 100 England fans were arrested and deported from Sweden after the World Cup qualifying match in Stockholm. Prime Minister Margaret Thatcher had urged the FA to 'consider very carefully' withdrawing England from the finals.

Luca Cordero di Montezemolo, general manager of the 1990 World Cup organising committee, remembers 'three or four meetings' with Colin Moynihan, the British government's minister for sport. 'He was very worried,' he tells me. 'My rule was to first of all give assurances that we were able to control the situation very well and also to present to him a very clear project.' Namely, to put England on an island closer to Corsica than to the Italian mainland. 'There was a very good reason: for safety [security]. Because you can't arrive on Sardinia unless you're the best swimmer in history, or by plane or by boat, so it was very easy to control everybody from the airport and from the port.'

Once the England fans reached Sardinia, its population newly boosted by seven thousand law enforcement officers, the daily hooligan-watch dispatches began. On 6 June, the *Gazzetta dello Sport* led its Group F coverage with news of the expulsion of Paul Scarrott, a notorious football thug – or 'the king of the hooligans', as the paper labelled him. The reports of arrests and anti-social behaviour kept coming: fourteen detained after a confrontation with police in downtown Cagliari three nights before England's opening fixture; another three arrested for stealing bed sheets and trashing a room in their boarding house.

Fortunately, this drip, drip of unhappy headlines was only part of the story surrounding England's supporters, for Italy proved the setting for a groundbreaking initiative by the Football Supporters' Association (as the Football Supporters' Federation was then called) to improve the lot of travelling fans.

Thanks to the efforts of FSA volunteers, Italia '90 became the first World Cup with a fans' embassy.

Today, when tens of thousands of football lovers descend on major tournaments – an estimated 500,000 supporters from across the UK attended Euro 2016 – information points for travelling fans are ubiquitous.

In June 1990, the landscape was very different. Huge numbers had yet to start following England. This was only the national team's second World Cup on European soil since the 1950s, and the on-field failings and off-field fighting at the 1988 European Championship did little to entice fresh followers.

It was also five years before the advent of budget airlines (2.69 million passengers passed through Luton International Airport, as it was then, in 1990 compared with 15.8 million in 2017).

Hence, it was possible to roll into Cagliari and pick up a ticket for England v Netherlands, the highest-profile Group F fixture, from a tout for half the face value.

Steve Beauchampé, one of the two main embassy organisers, recalls, 'One of the things we offered people was advice on how to get tickets. England's following was not massive. It was about six thousand for the Ireland and Dutch games, and less for Egypt. It got a little bit bigger on the mainland, but even for the semi-final, it was probably only about nine or ten thousand.

'There were sociologists out there – John Williams, Rogan Taylor, Adrian Goldberg who was working for the Sir Norman Chester centre. You had the journalists, too. I remember thinking, "How many people are actually here to cause trouble, and how many are here to monitor it?" The whole way the tournament was framed in the build-up to it in England and Italy was around hooliganism. Some journalists didn't understand the distinction between a hooligan and an ordinary fan.'

Beauchampé had been active in the early days of fanzines – he helped establish *On The Ball*, a Birmingham-based publication – and became involved in the nascent supporter movement that gathered strength with the founding of the FSA in 1985. Its voice became increasingly audible in the wake of the Hillsborough disaster, as Beauchampé notes: 'Hillsborough made a massive difference to the way the football authorities regarded the FSA. A number of people, most of all Rogan Taylor, handled that impeccably, and we, as an organisation, albeit for the worst of reasons, received a major lift.'

As Italia '90 approached, John Tummin, an FSA colleague, proposed a satellite office in Sardinia and came up with the phrase 'football embassy'. The task of realising the plan fell to Beauchampé and Craig Brewin, leader of the London branch. It was Brewin, then working as a finance officer for a London borough, who put up the money.

'We got a grant from the Football Trust but didn't know that was coming through until about the week the tournament started,' he explains. 'So, I said to Steve, "I'll underwrite it and pay all the bills for the first few weeks." It was about five thousand pounds.'

They hired a suite of rooms on the first floor of the offices of Ansa, the Italian news agency, in Cagliari. Beauchampé adds, 'The office was a base, but we spent time outside, handing out guides wherever we found people. Obviously, this was pre-mobile phone and internet, and then word of mouth gets around that there's this place for England fans. We'd be out till midnight and later, just handing stuff out and seeing the nightly toing and froing between fans and police and Italians.'

For the England fan on Sardinia, there were bumpy experiences. Supporters entering the stadium for the opening game against Ireland, for instance, had all their coins confiscated. Later that night, a group of England fans found themselves in a confrontation with a gang of Italians outside the railway station after they were unable to return to their out-of-town camp sites, owing to a scarcity of buses. 'It was a couple of miles' walk back into town from the stadium, and a lot of people would have to find somewhere to bed down around the station, the bus station or the port, or stay up all night,' Beauchampé says.

One night Craig Brewin had one of his car windows smashed while driving a pair of English fans away from a trouble spot. Yet, he plays down the severity of the skirmishes that would be reported enthusiastically by the press. 'There were a few stand-offs in the town late at night, but there'd be fifty or sixty people at most, and there were probably five thousand England fans there.'

Brewin believes the mood music from the British government – negative messages from Moynihan, Margaret Thatcher's sports minister, who had made a successful appeal for an alcohol ban on match days – did not help matters at a time when positive action was being taken, such as the FA's founding earlier in 1990 of the official England supporters' club. 'We were thinking most people were going there for a holiday, but he seemed to be talking as if everyone was going there to cause trouble, and you cannot possibly know that, particularly if the people with tickets had all been vetted by the FA as well,' he says.

Another member of the FSA team in Cagliari was Kate Quill, who was helping out as a volunteer interpreter, and she takes a similarly sympathetic view. 'For many it was their first trip abroad,' she says. 'Many fans had simply bought a flight and made no preparation at all. They were unbelievably naive.

'In Sardinia, the younger fans were clearly overwhelmed during the first few days – the heat, the foreign language, the different currency, the stunningly beautiful, and very sophisticated and self-composed, local girls. Just the general beauty and elegance of Italy was unsettling to them, I think. They stuck out like sore thumbs, but as we bumped into them again in different cities as the tournament progressed, it was clear some of them were enjoying Italy.

'I often felt that one of the biggest barriers to mutual understanding came down to very simple things. Italian culture is essentially a visual one, and they place a huge amount of importance on outer respectability. They take enormous pride in their appearance, and public displays of drunkenness or undignified behaviour are deeply frowned upon, across all classes and all income groups. So here they were, confronted by men stripped to the waist, sometimes quite overweight, bearing tattoos – which weren't fashionable as now – sunburned chests, and smelling pretty bad because they were sleeping in campsites, or in the railway station, or on someone's floor for the night. Add in a few beers before midday, and it's really not a good look in Italy.'

Before the first match in Group F, leading Sardinian newspaper *L'unione Sarda* wrote an editorial in response to an attack on three England fans by locals, in which it said, 'Maybe it was inevitable after people have talked about nothing else but violence for months, but the island has been taken over by hooligan psychosis with a result that every male English citizen between fifteen and sixty becomes indelibly stamped as the hooligan.'

It was the second fixture, England's meeting with the Netherlands on 16 June, which many had foreseen as potentially explosive. The previous autumn, an Ajax-Austria Vienna UEFA Cup tie was marred by visiting goalkeeper Franz Wolfhart being struck by an iron bar – an incident leading to a one-year UEFA ban for the Amsterdam club – while the next month, two Feyenoord hooligans threw nail bombs into an Ajax section during a league game.

Violence did erupt on 16 June, but there was no involvement from the travelling Dutch fans, already then kitted out in those now trademark bright-orange costumes.

The trouble originated, rather, with an England supporters' march to the stadium. The FSA had warned people not to take part. One of the leaders of the march, Beauchampé remembers, was 'this guy who was involved in the London branch of the FSA and was a bit dodgy. The police came to see us and said no to this march. When we told him it'd get out of hand, he used this phrase which is engrained in my mind: "If the police put up barriers, the lads will smash right through them."'

The most dramatic account of what came next is found in Bill Buford's book *Among The Thugs*. He writes, 'With the world's media bearing down on them, the supporters wanted to take on an island militia that had been preparing for this event for months. The lads wanted to fight the police.'

Buford's book relays a sequence of events which begins with a policeman firing a handgun into the air and ends with fans charging down a hill towards an Esso station, where a plate glass window is shattered. It was here that the Italian police responded and John Tummin, an embassy volunteer monitoring the march, was assaulted by Antonio Patea, the assistant police deputy.

'Patea was a nasty piece of work,' Beauchampé asserts. 'The very first time we met him, all he could see was England fans as hooligans. John went up and spoke to him about the way the police were batoning fans, and he hit John across the face.'

John Williams, an author and associate professor from Leicester University, was present in Cagliari and offers his own interpretation: 'The problem was you had lots of young men who'd been told for months this was going to be an extraordinary event, so there was a lot of wish-fulfilment. They've had too much to drink and get a bit excited, and the police are itching to demonstrate what they're here for, as a lot of them had been flown in from the mainland – and as you saw in the miners' strike here, if you don't have local police officers they feel somehow detached from their responsibility to the local community.

'The British police kept saying, "We'd have done this completely differently," but if you go to a country where they have a riot force, you're pretty much guaranteed to get what happened there if your fans are like England fans who are overtly challenging, drink too much, are very loud and look collectively threatening.'

Williams goes on to relate an exchange with one England fan in a bar afterwards. 'He had his arm in a sling and had clearly been knocked around a bit. He told us he was a plumber from London. When we asked what had happened, he said he'd flown in in the morning for the game and had immediately been caught up in some of the running around. He was chased and had been hit by a riot police officer with a truncheon and was carted off to hospital. He hadn't even seen the game. We were commiserating with him and he said, "Oh no, it's been great; I've had a fantastic adventure."'

If powerless that evening, the FSA embassy did deliver many positives according to Brewin. One example was a raffle of England equipment to raise funds for research into sickle cell anaemia, a disease unusually common on Sardinia.

Brewin explains, 'We organised football matches with the locals which the England travel club still do regularly now. We'd try to arrange a meeting with local fans wherever we went. I remember driving around Naples and trying to find the leader of the Napoli ultras, just to talk to him and share experiences.'

Brewin's only previous England away game had come when the magazine

When Saturday Comes had organised a coach trip to Albania for a World Cup qualifier in March 1989 to allow right-minded England fans the chance to watch the national team – only to end up engaged in a confrontation with a separate coachload who were making Nazi salutes.

He expounds, 'I wanted to do it because I wanted to put on a show for the people back home – to show how England fans can behave and how they should behave and to try to send out a message to other people who'd want to follow England: that, actually, a lot of people who go and watch England raise money for charity and are mixing with the local community.

'I wanted to present to the world a different view of the England football fan, whereas Steve [Beauchampé] wanted to do something for football fans that needed doing because no one else was going to do it.

'We both had a different view of why we were doing it, and I think we probably achieved both. Steve and I did another one in Sweden in '92. In '94, we didn't go and in '96, it was in England, so there was a long period where they weren't doing them. It started again in '98 when I wasn't involved. Everyone does them now. Maybe we were ahead of our time.'

FOR ENGLAND'S FOOTBALLERS, THE NIGHT OF THE SECOND GROUP F match against the Netherlands was the night they began to show they were not a team out of touch with their time.

It was the night of a tactical tweak which many interpreted as a great leap forward: the adoption of a sweeper system.

It was an unprecedented ploy during Robson's eight-year reign, and a widespread rumour was that Robson's gamble was the result of player power. However, Graham Turner – then a journalist for *El País* and a friend of Robson since the late 1950s when he coached him in the Oxford University football team – visited the England manager at the squad's base in Sardinia and suspected the hand of Don Howe, the assistant manager, at work.

'He [Robson] was talking about it and asking, "Do you think this could work?"' he says. 'He'd think deeply about things. He was the same in his dealings with the media. He'd think things over and try to see the other side. I think it was Don.

Don was much more of a tactician. They talked it through a lot.

'He felt it helped to motivate the players as well to do something different to break the mould, if you like, and get them thinking about the football mechanisms as opposed to everything that was going on on the periphery.'

Terry Butcher adds, 'There was all this talk about player power and delegations, but that was never the case. Don [Howe] and the gaffer, Bobby, already had it in their heads what they wanted to do. We just gained momentum from that. We had so many experienced players and good players that you could change systems and it wouldn't matter.

'Mark Wright was the best sweeper because he was able to read the game very well and he was really comfortable bringing the ball out. We were all comfortable on the ball, apart from Paul Parker.'

In the new system, Parker came in as a right wing-back in place of full-back Gary Stevens, with Stuart Pearce on the other side. The centre-backs were Butcher and Des Walker with Wright sweeping. Wright, *The Times* reported, had actually played as a sweeper only three times for his club, Derby County. Parker, a centre-back with Queens Park Rangers, had not played at full-back since leaving Fulham three years earlier. Even before the team's friendly against Tunisia, Robson had Parker working on the training ground in the right-back position, though the player himself – despite his speed and intelligence – had reservations.

'I was an out-and-out defender, to be perfectly honest – I was inexperienced and playing out of position,' he told me when I interviewed him in 2010. 'Chris Waddle helped me through it – as a player and as a mentor, he talked me through it.'

Robson had wanted three central defenders to avoid a repeat of the nightmare endured by his two centre-backs, Tony Adams and Wright, facing Ruud Gullit and Marco van Basten during the 3-1 defeat by the Netherlands at the 1988 European Championship.

His starting XI, trying out the sweeper system, had actually lost 1-0 to the second string in a practice match yet come the evening of Saturday 16 June, the monochrome of the previous Monday's game against Ireland now gave way to a big splash of colour.

In truth, this was down as much to the first signs of Paul Gascoigne's blossoming on the global stage as to the sweeper system. It was a night when the Tottenham Hotspur midfielder showed an absolute absence of inhibition, tugging playfully on Gullit's dreadlocks and giving defender Ronald Koeman a taste of his own *Oranje* medicine with a Cruyff turn. This nearly brought a famous goal too, only for Steve Bull and Gary Lineker to miss by inches the inviting cross that followed.

Pete Davies, the writer given rare access to England's players for *All Played Out,* a fabulous on-the-ground account of their 1990 campaign, was watching that night in the Stadio Sant' Elia. He highlights the significance of Gascoigne's display, 'The Cruyff turn in the corner gets picked out, when he leaves two defenders for dead behind him – but for me it is the way he was in Gullit's ear, utterly fearless. He was stood next to Gullit, taking the piss. You could sense this radiation from him: "Give me the ball. I'm not frightened of anybody."'

Afterwards, as Bobby Robson enthused over Gascoigne's performance – 'He ranked with anybody as the best player on the pitch' – it was possible to see a parallel emerging with England's Mexico '86 campaign. Four years earlier, Robson had discovered his best team after the loss of Bryan Robson and Ray Wilkins, to injury and suspension respectively. After 64 minutes of the Netherlands game, Robson limped out of the World Cup once more with a torn Achilles – a problem which would prove beyond even Olga Stringfellow, the faith healer flown over to Sardinia – yet England finished the match with renewed conviction.

They so nearly won it, too. Lineker had a first-half goal disallowed. He and Bull each spurned openings with only goalkeeper Hans van Breukelen to beat. Then, in injury time, after Gascoigne had burst upfield from his own half to win a free-kick, Stuart Pearce's strike found the far corner of the net. Unfortunately, the referee had signalled for an indirect free-kick.

'That gave us massive belief,' says Terry Butcher, who spent the evening as the right centre-back in the new system. 'I hardly got a kick. I played against Hans Gillhaus, who played for Aberdeen. He played left wing [rather than as a striker], and I was the biggest right wing-back in the world, and we just stood out there. Bobby Robson was expecting [Wim] Kieft, the big striker, to play, and I was to mark him. Van Basten was to be marked by Des Walker, who did a brilliant job on him, and Mark Wright swept.'

It is worth recapping what it meant for England to match the European champions as they did that evening, while experimenting with a new formation. 'England herald new dawn' was the headline accompanying *The Times'* match report the following Monday as its football correspondent, Stuart Jones, hailed Robson for 'daring to play the Netherlands at their own sweeping game'.

This was an England side whose players were not playing in UEFA's club competitions, save for Chris Waddle at Olympique Marseille and the quartet based north of the border at Glasgow Rangers: Terry Butcher, Trevor Steven, Gary Stevens and Chris Woods. Indeed, the lure of European football, and the bigger money on offer at Ibrox, meant that for the only time in history, there was a Scottish club contributing the most players to an English World Cup effort.

Incidentally, England's last World Cup campaign before the dawn of the Premier League also featured a player who never played top-flight football: Wolverhampton Wanderers' Steve Bull, a goalscorer who had helped Wolves climb from the fourth division to the second. When the England starting XI was read out before the last group game against Egypt, announcing that he was starting the match, Bull's name actually got the loudest cheer.

As it was, England's fans had already found their pied piper in Paul Gascoigne. And they already had a tune too. Two weekends previously, New Order had leapfrogged Adamski and Seal's 'Killer' to reach the top of the UK chart with 'World In Motion'. It was the England World Cup song and it provided another piece in that summer's jigsaw. Peter Hook, the band's then bassist, declares, 'I do think "World In Motion" is the best song that's ever been done for a World Cup without a doubt.

'It was right at the peak of acid house and the Haçienda [the Manchester music venue] so we were flying as high as a kite and that was the icing on the cake to get the World Cup song – and then to get our only ever number one was a bit bizarre because you look at all the other great songs we've done, none of them got to number one but the England World Cup song did.'

Football songs were nothing new, of course. Twenty years earlier, England's Mexico-bound squad had reached the chart summit with 'Back Home'.

However, good football songs were as rare as Saharan snow – something they knew only too well in West Germany where, in 1990, Jürgen Klinsmann was playing air saxophone and Karl-Heinz Riedle shaking a maraca on the video of their World Cup ditty, 'We're already on the Brenner Pass'. (Germany's USA '94 effort, recorded with the Village People, was no improvement either.)

Here was a happy exception and it was Tony Wilson, the late Mancunian impresario, who masterminded the project. Hook relates, 'He was at a do somewhere and the head of PR for the Football Association [David Bloomfield] was at the same do and he was talking to Tony because he was a big Joy Division and New Order fan and he said to Tony, "The thing I hate is that whenever we have a football song it's done by people who are awful and I wish we could get somebody to do it who was good." Tony simply said to him, "Well, why don't you ask New Order?."'

According to Hook, 'the song was in two halves, which is quite ironic isn't it.' The first half came from band members Stephen Morris and Gillian Gilbert, who used an electro-pop tune they had been working on as part of the soundtrack to a BBC series, *Reportage*. 'Half of "World In Motion" was left over from this, it was an idea that they had,' says Hook. 'Barney [Sumner, the lead singer] then came up with an idea of his own which was where the music changes halfway through and we just then stuck them together.'

Sumner's Italo-house section culminates in John Barnes's rap. 'The rap was Keith Allen's idea,' Hook adds of the actor who had been introduced to the band by Wilson. 'He decided that we needed some help and suggested Keith Allen because he was a mad football fan. That appealed to us because it was a bit mad and when we met Keith we realised he was fucking mad. And we all got swept along from there.'

Hook's retelling of the day of the recording, at Led Zeppelin guitarist Jimmy Page's Sol Studio in Berkshire, close to England's then training base at Burnham Beeches, is almost as entertaining as the song itself, which opens with an extract from Kenneth Wolstenholme's famous 1966 World Cup final commentary ('Well, some of the crowd are on the pitch') and concludes with the brilliant daftness of the closing refrain of '*Arrivederci*, it's one on one'.

According to Hook's autobiography, *Substance*, Wilson arrived at the studio with a 'bag of coke' for the band and 'a brown envelope' for each of the players involved – John Barnes, Paul Gascoigne, Chris Waddle, Peter Beardsley, Steve McMahon and Des Walker. 'There wasn't a great deal of interest from anybody in the Football Association or the team and Tony found it difficult to get everybody involved,' he explains to me. 'Really it was only because there was the culture of pound notes that he got them down because he paid them all in cash for helping.'

There were plenty of refreshments too. 'We got a few beers in and vodka and champagne, more for us than anything else. We were off our nuts but we were shocked by how they descended on it. They raided it like a team of locusts. Gascoigne was the wildest.'

Also in the studio that day was former Liverpool midfielder Craig Johnston, who had co-written the 1988 'Anfield Rap' for the Merseyside club, and had come along with Barnes. It was Johnston who contributed the line 'We ain't no hooligans/This ain't a football song'.

Hook adds, 'When the England team came to sing on it, it was doubled in length. Craig Johnston really got stuck into the lyrics. Gascoigne then had a go at rapping and he was terrible. Beardsley had a go, he was shocking. And John Barnes did it and it was just like magic.

'By the time we got to do the rest of the backing vocals, "*Arrivederci* it's one on one" and all that, the team were getting a bit bored, they were also a bit drunk and didn't last long, to be honest.

'All of a sudden they stood up and left. We said, "Where are you going?" and they went, "Oh we're off now, we've got to open a Topman store."

'It was wild and to watch Gascoigne drink three bottles of champagne from the neck of the bottle and then drive a Mercedes following the team... As we were waving them off, we were thinking, "Jesus, there's an accident waiting to happen".

'Tony was devastated because he'd paid them all a few grand in cash when they came in and all they'd done was walk in, get pissed and then fuck off to open a Topman. I think we were more aware, shall we say, of its possible significance than they were.'

This being the time of the Madchester scene – 'Like Woodstock for Manchester' as Hook describes it – the band wanted to call the song 'E for England' as a nod to the drug ecstasy. 'We had a massive argument,' he explains.

'Tony and Keith Allen were desperate to call it that and it was the FA that said no. They said they'd drop it because they knew what we were doing.

'We also had some good arguments because I was saying, *"Arrivederci,* it's one on one", that's "Goodbye, it's one on one", it doesn't make sense. *"Buongiorno,* it's one on one" has just not got the same ring, has it, but for some reason it really bothered me that it was *"Arrivederci".* That doesn't make fucking sense. But, of course, a great tune is a great tune. No one cares as long as you can sing it in the bath. And "World In Motion" was one of those songs that you could sing in the bath.'

Speaking to me on the twentieth anniversary of Italia '90, Barnes, the first black player to represent England at the World Cup finals, played down the meaning of the song and his role: 'The change in football in the Nineties was because of the Premier League. The fact I was rapping on it didn't have any bearing on anything.'

That said, this was only twelve years since Viv Anderson had become England's first black international footballer. Moreover, it was the same summer in which Geoff Hurst, England's 1966 World Cup final hero, sat in a BBC TV studio and described Bobby Robson's side as 'the nigger in the woodpile' during a discussion on the potential World Cup winners before the semi-final against West Germany. Garth Crooks, the first black chairman of the Professional Footballers' Association, was sitting right beside him.

Others, therefore, would beg to differ about the significance of the song. Sociologist John Williams says: 'That fusing of popular culture with football, the music and the New Order song felt — to me, at least — like a multi-cultural England team had been accepted for the first time. I'd been travelling with England for research during the Eighties, and it was horrible the way some England fans treated some black players who played for England. Now you had Des Walker and Paul Parker in the team too, and we felt like we were modernising.'

BACK IN THE HOLIDAY INN IN IPSWICH, IT IS EVIDENT THAT NOT every aspect of modern football is to the liking of Terry Butcher. Each generation looks quizzically, at times, at the next, and Butcher is no different as he compares the dynamics of his 1990 England squad with their successors today.

'There were no cliques, no black or white tables, nothing like that whatsoever – we just had a laugh, you could sit with anyone,' he says. 'We enjoyed it. There was silliness and pranks. We'd go out to inspect the pitch, and Gazza would kneel down behind someone, and Chrissie Waddle would push the guy and over he goes. It happened all the time.

'You didn't have the headphones and the phones where you go out there and you're speaking to people on the phone. We didn't have the internet. You spoke with each other: card schools, race nights; we had Monopoly, we had to make it fun, and the players had to work at it, and it wasn't all given to us.

'We really had a good time, but when we played, we meant it – we really did mean it, it meant everything to us. The Champions League matters a hell of a lot now. It's definitely taken away a lot of the presence that international football had and a lot of the glory.'

Considering the reasons behind England's brush with glory in Italy, he cites leadership – 'There were a lot of captains in the team, a lot of big, experienced players' – and he also cites laughter, before giving a flavour of the pranks and mischief that brought that group together.

Butcher begins by detailing the sting that took place during one of the squad's race nights. Videos would be sent over of race meets, for the players to bet on. On this particular occasion, the players got a sneak preview. For the first three races, they deliberately backed losing horses. The fourth race was a different matter. 'Fred Street [the squad's physio] got into the fourth race and showed it to everyone. We all knew. It was hilarious. We all had money on the one who won it, who was an outsider. The boys are laying odds, laying odds, laying odds, and you could see Shilts [Peter Shilton], and you could see Gary Lineker [the two bookmakers], because they roomed together – and you could see them going white because they thought if this horse comes in they are going to be thousands of pounds out, and it came in! The boys were up on the tables ...' Grainy footage of the scene featured in the BBC's 2000 documentary about the England team, *Three Lions*, and it shows Shilton with a nonplussed look on his face as Gascoigne cries out in the background, 'Look at my wad! Look at my wad!'

Evening meals were another opportunity for mirth, particularly for the

Rangers contingent who staged a back-to-front night. 'We came in with our clothes back to front, hat back to front, glasses on the back of the head,' says Butcher. 'We walked in backwards, and we ordered the ice cream first, then the main meal, then the soup. The players loved it.'

There was more of the same the night before England earned their place in the last sixteen – courtesy of Mark Wright's header, from a Paul Gascoigne free-kick, which secured a narrow victory over Egypt. Butcher did not appear in that game, owing to Bobby Robson's decision to revert to a back four, but he did his bit to keep spirits high in the lead-up. He explains, 'The last night before the Egypt match, me, Chris Woods, and Gary Stevens decided to wear our England blazers along with our England tie and our England shirt, and then to wear jockstraps – no trousers – and black socks and shoes.

'We gelled our hair and had sunglasses. We arranged with the waiters to set the table with long tablecloths, so they couldn't see we had our jockstraps on. We had the bottles of wine on the tables, but they were empty bottles filled up with fizzy water.

'We got in really early, and as the players came in, we were like, "Come on, boys," and were toasting their health and drinking. Then Don Howe came in with Bobby Robson, and Bobby was going apoplectic. All meal, you could see he was really agitated. Our plan was to have the starter and main course, then get up and wish the lads all the very best and then go back to the room, get the shellsuit on and then come back in for dessert and coffee.

'That was the plan, but who walks in but the whole international committee – Bert Millichip, Jack Wiseman, in all their glory. We're sitting down thinking, "We've just got jockstraps on, what are they going to think of us?" After the main course, we just said, "Let's just do it." We got up to walk out, and the players gave us a standing ovation. And as we got to the top of the stairs to go out, we just bared our backsides to the whole of the England squad and the international committee. It broke the ice for the evening.'

Island games
Part 2 –
Republic of Ireland

THE RAIN CAME DOWN IN CAGLIARI. OCCASIONALLY, SO TOO DID the ball. It was England v Republic of Ireland, the 1990 World Cup match with the least football played. Just 49 minutes, according to FIFA's official timers.

And yet whenever he goes back to Ireland, the night of 11 June 1990 is a night that Kevin Sheedy never stops hearing about. It was, after all, the night he scored a nation's first World Cup finals goal.

'I was at the races in Punchestown, and there was a couple there who came up to me,' he says, citing a trip made in 2015. 'They lived in the same town but never went to the same places. On the night of England-Ireland, they were at the same venue watching the game, and when I scored, they hugged and kissed each other. After that, they started going out and when I met them, they were celebrating their wedding anniversary. You don't really realise the impact off the pitch. I've had cats and dogs named after me, but nobody actually getting married thanks to me, so that was good.'

The goal in question had a value greater than any that his famed left foot delivered for his acclaimed Everton side of the mid-1980s. 'I had great moments with Everton, but just to score in a World Cup and be Ireland's first-ever goalscorer is a piece of history no one will ever take away from me,' adds Sheedy. It cancelled out Gary Lineker's scrambled early effort and earned the Republic of Ireland their first World Cup point.

My meeting with Sheedy takes place in a study room at Everton's Finch Farm training ground, shortly before his departure from his role as the club's Under-18s coach for a new challenge in Saudi Arabia. Sitting in his blue training kit, he proceeds to describe in detail his 73rd-minute strike.

'It was a long kick from Packie Bonner, which he did a lot up to [Tony] Cascarino, and I was always good at getting second balls and reading where the ball's going to drop. I managed to pick up the second ball, and I tried to make a pass through, and it got intercepted by Steve McMahon who'd just come on as a sub. He wasn't up to speed with the game and tried to play a square ball to Gary Stevens, and I intercepted it with a good first touch and just hit it.

'As soon as I hit it, I knew it was in because of all the years of doing finishing practice and scoring goals. It was a clean strike, and it was always arrowing for Peter Shilton's bottom-left hand corner. It was a great moment.'

It was a flash of class in a mongrel match described as 'a shameful insult to the game of football' by the great Scottish sports writer Hugh McIlvanney. Yet for the noisy contingent in green, banging their bodhráns – the traditional goatskin-covered drums that remain the Irish fans' instrument of choice – waving their flags and out-singing the English, it was the first in a series of cherished moments.

Thanks to Sheedy's surgical precision, the Irish World Cup story was up and running; a story, it has to be said, of some contradictions. This was a team that did not, technically, win a single game in Italy, yet received a heroes' welcome on a scale never seen before or since. A team managed by an Englishman, Jack Charlton, and manned by a good number of players born outside of Ireland that gave the country its greatest sporting party. A team that played a defiantly uncomplicated game – primitive, their critics said – yet breathed confidence into a changing nation.

When Ireland played Italy in the quarter-final in Rome, an estimated ninety per cent of the 3.5m population were watching. There had been only 5,100 people in attendance at Lansdowne Road for a summer friendly against Mexico six years earlier. At the time of Charlton's appointment, in February 1986, Gay Byrne, presenter of the country's most popular chat show, state broadcaster RTÉ's *The Late Late Show*, remarked, 'I have just been handed a piece of paper here which says that Jack Charlton has been appointed manager of Ireland ... whatever that means.' If indifference reigned then, by 1990, the so-called Boys in Green were making a record with U2's Larry Mullen, 'Put 'em under pressure', echoing Charlton's tactical mantra.

The U2 connection was fitting. Culturally, an anything-is-possible era had dawned – from Bono and Co gracing the cover of *Time* magazine in 1987 (and subsequently grabbing a Grammy for *The Joshua Tree*) to the 1990 Oscar success of *My Left Foot,* the film about the Irish writer and painter Christy Brown, which earned five nominations and awards for Daniel Day-Lewis as best actor and the Dublin-born Brenda Fricker as best supporting actress.

Looking back, Kevin Moran, another Dubliner, remembers 'an upsurge of a great Irish feeling'. The established narrative has subsequently entwined soccer success with the tale of the Celtic Tiger, Ireland's economic growth which began gradually after the 1973 accession to the European Community, then accelerated in the late 1980s and through the boom years of the 1990s. 'It hasn't got to do with the Irish soccer team or anything like that,' argues Moran, 'but it was very much a part of the feel-good factor, without a shadow of a doubt, and there was a great feel-good factor all round, with how the country was going economically. The growth rate was just phenomenal. If you look at GDPs at the time, it was eight or nine per cent per year or more even, and at the same time there was this upsurge in the Irish soccer fortunes as well which everybody loved.'

Moran, a Gaelic footballer who became a Manchester United footballer and later a successful player agent, observes that Italia '90 was special as Ireland's first big sporting celebration on the global stage.

'Gaelic football is our national game, but it's not international, it's parochial. You come to an All-Ireland final, and you'll never see an atmosphere like it, but it's just those two counties enjoying it. From an international point of view, we never got on to the big stage until Euro '88. When it came, I've always maintained it wasn't just soccer people, it takes over the whole country as such.'

Tony Cascarino, the striker who had made his debut in 1985 and remained in the team until 1999, suggests, 'We were like a rock band which suddenly became big. Ireland isn't like England. There aren't many other stars in other industries. Because we came across from England and played our football in England, when we came to Ireland, we were treated like gods. Everywhere we went was free, every drink we had was free. I loved the excitement of being around the team, because we went from also-rans to household names. People would stop us on the streets, they'd want to chat with us, want to meet Jack. For a six-year period from '88 up until America '94, it was utter madness.'

FOR IRELAND, THE MAN BEHIND THE MADNESS WAS JACK CHARLTON, a.k.a. Big Jack, big brother of Bobby and one of England's 1966 World Cup heroes. He did not even receive a reply from the Football Association when he applied for the job of England manager a decade earlier. Mind you, he was not the Football Association of Ireland's first choice, either. When seeking a replacement for Eoin Hand, the FAI had turned initially to Billy McNeill, then Manchester City manager, but failed to negotiate a deal with City chairman Peter Swales for his part-time services. Then, after Charlton's inclusion on a short list of four – alongside Bob Paisley, Johnny Giles and Liam Tuohy – he received only three votes from the FAI's eighteen-man executive in the initial secret ballot to decide on their choice of manager.

In a process detailed by Paul Rowan in his fine book on the Charlton era, *The Team That Jack Built*, Paisley, Liverpool's most successful manager and a last-minute addition to the list, received nine votes in that first round – one short of the required total. Yet, the manner in which FAI president Des Casey, who had close ties with Liverpool, had unexpectedly presented Paisley as an eleventh-hour option prompted a backlash from committee members. Charlton, after four ballots, was the beneficiary. He had never seen Ireland play a live game of football.

By then, Irish soccer had a long history of muddling through. Until Johnny Giles's reign as player-manager – which began in the same 1973/74 season that he won the league title with Leeds United – a selection panel would name the squad. According to Mick Meagan, who, from 1969-71, served as the first Ireland team manager, the directors of Irish club sides on the panel would push for their own players' inclusion 'to put them in the shop window for a transfer to England'.

Spool forward to the mid-1980s and Eoin Hand, Charlton's predecessor, took his wife along to Moscow to cook for the squad before a match against the Soviet Union, owing to concerns about the food in their hotel. Hand had previously had to sleep in an apartment rented by Irish journalists at the 1982 World Cup after the FAI, unable to grasp why their manager would wish to attend the tournament, declined to arrange his accommodation and accreditation. Another story from the Hand era concerns a race between Mick McCarthy and journalist John O'Shea: when the latter said he could outrun the defender, Hand accepted the bet and urged his reluctant player to take part, telling him, 'Well, I've bet him fifty quid, and if you don't race him, I'll lose it.' Tony Cascarino, an amused spectator that day, chuckles: 'Mick won by an ant's cock. It was unreal. Imagine a journalist having a race with an England player.'

In fairness to Hand, his team had lost out on a place at the 1982 World Cup in controversial fashion. In a qualifying group with Belgium, France and the Netherlands, as well as Cyprus, they finished in third place – ahead of the Dutch, but behind France on goal difference and a point short of Belgium. In their final home qualifier, they earned a pulsating 3-2 victory over the France side who would reach the Spain '82 semi-finals. It was their last away qualifier, seven months earlier, which did the damage, though – they lost to an 88th-minute Jan Ceulemans goal, having earlier seen a Frank Stapleton strike ruled out unjustly.

Whatever the size of that injustice, by the last days of Hand's reign, Ireland were sliding. Kevin Sheedy remembers, 'He had top players like Liam Brady, Frank Stapleton, Mark Lawrenson, and he couldn't really handle them; they just ruled the roost. When Jack came in, it was a real breath of fresh air. It was Jack's way or the highway.'

Charlton's approach was, put simply, route-one. Albeit, Sheedy insists, with a caveat. 'In those days, Watford and Wimbledon were playing long balls but didn't have the quality. If you've got the likes of Denis Irwin, Steve Staunton, Chris Hughton playing longer balls, they weren't just fifty-fifty balls; they were balls the striker had a chance of winning, and we played in the opposition half, which was unique in international football in those days.

'We got the ball in their half, and we closed. We had Andy Townsend, Paul McGrath, Ray Houghton, myself, Cascarino, [John] Aldridge who all bought into the style of football and were winning the ball in the opposition half. With the quality we had, we were causing them problems. Everybody said it was long ball, but it was long ball with quality, which a lot of people underestimate.'

And it worked. Ireland qualified for the 1988 European Championship – their first major tournament finals – as winners of a group including Belgium, Scotland, and Bulgaria. Then, in their opening match of the finals in Stuttgart, they beat England 1-0 through a Ray Houghton header. After a 1-1 draw against the USSR, they missed out on the semi-finals only because of Dutchman Wim Kieft's fortuitously headed goal eight minutes from the end of their third group fixture.

'That was a defining moment for the next ten years,' remembers goalkeeper Packie Bonner. 'We beat England, which, for Ireland in particular, was a big country to beat. It was our first competitive game in any major competition; it got momentum going; it got the crowd, the media, everybody on our side. You couldn't do anything wrong after that.'

Tony Cascarino says, 'We were a really hard side to beat in '88. Jack had a really good squad, and look at our team – all playing for top clubs. We got eliminated by Wim Kieft's freak goal, but we matched that fantastic Dutch team all the way. Jack always said he missed one thing – he wanted a blistering-quick striker, and he felt we could have gone even further if we'd had that.

'It's really hard describing Jack without laughing, because he was a real maverick. I remember him doing a team talk, and he says to Liam Brady "Ian". Ian Brady's the mass murderer, and we're all pissing ourselves laughing.'

If names escaped him, an intuitive understanding of his sport did not. 'He understood world football in how African teams might play, Scandinavians, Eastern Bloc,' Cascarino continues. 'He'd always be very thorough in how he saw them play and was determined we didn't change. I liked it because my instruction was simple. It was basically, "You pull on the full-backs when we've got it at an angle, and if the centre-half comes out and tries to pick you up, fight him because there's a space now that my midfield runner can run into in the eighteen-yard box and get on the end of crosses."

'When I first played for him, I once said, "Jack, on corners, who am I picking up?" and he looked at me and said, "You pick up a big one. In my team, big ones pick up big ones, and little ones pick up little ones." I started laughing, but we never conceded a goal from a corner.

'Jack was very ABC – simplify everything. You knew in uncertain terms your job and if you didn't do it, you got pulled off. John Sheridan made his debut in Spain, and he said to me, "What do I do? Jack hasn't spoken to me." I said,

"John, just chip it into the gullies and don't do a one-two with the centre-forward – if you do a one-two, he'll bring you off." He said, "Well that's my game, I'm a short, neat, and tidy footballer." I said, "John, don't do it." All John did all night was chip it in the gullies to no one. Wasted balls. Jack never said a word to him. He was delighted with him.'

Remembering another game against Spain, the 1-0 home victory in World Cup qualifying secured by a Míchel own goal, Cascarino adds, 'Jack said, "Don't play through midfield" because Míchel was such a good footballer. He said, "He'll run the show so bypass him" so all we did was keep bypassing their midfield — Míchel couldn't get the ball, and he kept shouting, "Rugby!" We just threw the kitchen sink at them, and they hated it. Jack refused for us to play any other way. He said, "You won't beat them, you have to play ugly."'

Cascarino's 88 appearances for Ireland were, for a period, a national record. Speaking to me one lunchtime in a pub by London's Waterloo station, fresh from one of his regular radio appearances on talkSPORT, he recalls enthusiastically the experience off the pitch under Charlton.

A stalwart of Don Revie's storied Leeds United side – and later manager at Middlesbrough, Sheffield Wednesday, and Newcastle United – Charlton instilled a strong togetherness, just as he had seen Revie do at Elland Road.

Previously, Ireland players would arrive at the team hotel for internationals and then see the Irish-born members of the group disperse to visit their families, in cars laid on by the FAI. No longer.

Cascarino grins as he recounts the routine: 'We'd be absolutely lambasted today. We'd arrive in Dublin in the [Sunday] afternoon as a team, we'd go for a drink in Malahide, and that'd go into the early hours of the morning. We'd train in the morning, but training was always put back till Monday afternoon because the lads were in such a bad state.

'We'd get up, have our bowl of soup, have the worst training session in the world, but Jack didn't really care; we just got a sweat on us. Then he'd say, "Right, pictures today," and we'd go to the pictures in Dublin. Half the players would disappear to the billiard hall or went to the pub to have a drink. This was Monday night, two days before the international. We'd then get up Tuesday, have a really light training session and play the game. That was our build-up. Kevin Sheedy would have turned up on a Zimmer frame for it.

'I used to laugh as Kevin would turn up and go, "I've done my hamstring". "Why haven't you pulled out?" I'd ask. He'd reply, "I'm not missing the trip." I know the England players were very envious of us, because they were imprisoned. You'd talk to them at club level, and they'd say, "You lot do what you like". England were always perceived as better than us, but they couldn't beat us. I played at Chelsea; Dennis Wise was there, and Dennis had got a few caps, and he'd say to me, "One England cap is worth fifty Irish caps" as if playing for England is far bigger and better, and I'd say, "Yeah, but you can't beat us, Den." I also remember David Platt running out with his England kit on at Villa and having it on in training, the actual top. Me and big Paul McGrath were like, "Really?" England were put on a pedestal.

'Of course, when we crossed the white line, we were very serious too, but there was an enormous amount of fun. I remember Jack saying to me, when having dinner the night before a game, "If you want a pint before dinner, have one – don't have a fizzy drink. What are you drinking that Coke crap for?" Very old school and very off the wall.

'In Italy, we played Trivial Pursuit, which was hilarious. Jack would have "Jack's team", which consisted of the staff, against the team [players]. The chaplain would be the judge and Jack would be going mental with him, effing and blinding and calling him a cheat because he'd refuse answers Jack didn't quite get spot-on. We'd all be cracking up. Jack was so determined to win and he was really the only one who knew answers to stuff. Some of his staff weren't the smartest. He'd be so determined to win, his face would go red with thunder, and he'd call the chaplain a "daft cunt."'

Kevin Sheedy recalls this hatred of losing erupting while playing the card game Hearts with Charlton on the bus to Ireland's opening European Championship finals game against England in 1988. Sheedy had put down a card which jeopardised his manager's chances of winning. 'He was renowned for his tightness, and I hit him with the Queen of Spades, and he said, "If you don't pick that up, you won't be sub," and he was deadly serious. When I got to the ground, I didn't know till the team sheet was up that I was sub.'

Beneath the gruff demeanour, though, Cascarino saw some sensitivity in

Charlton and remembers his difficulty in telling midfielder Gary Waddock he had missed the cut for the World Cup. 'Over the years, I saw there were times you could tell he'd get upset, and his best way of dealing with it was to be as hard as nails. That's how Jack worked. We were in Malta before Italia '90 and he literally told Gary Waddock by the carousel, waiting for our bags, that he was going to send him back. He felt terrible about it.

'I also remember walking through the foyer in our hotel in Sicily, and he came across and went to me, "You're out, you're not playing Sunday against the Dutch." I went, "Why?" He said, "You were shit against the Egyptians, you're out." That was it – and I'd been our top scorer in qualifying. But Jack was incredibly sensitive, and no one saw that unless you were around him on a regular basis. We were playing cards in a room once, and a guy had a big sweep-over on the telly — we were laughing, and he just lost it. He went, "You're fucking taking the piss, you lot. Bobby lost his hair at twenty, and fucking idiots like you lot were taking the piss out of him." He went into an absolute meltdown. I always remember that.'

WITH HIS ITALIAN SURNAME AND CHIRPY LONDON-NESS, TONY Cascarino was considered the ne plus ultra of a defining feature of the Charlton years: a recruitment system which exploited to the maximum the one-grandparent rule. In the case of the Kent-born Cascarino, he had actually travelled to Madrid to watch England play Spain at the 1982 World Cup. The next World Cup match he attended, he was playing against them. 'If you'd said to me, "Eight years later, you'll be playing for Ireland against Italy in the quarter-finals of a World Cup," I just couldn't have imagined it.'

Cascarino rippled the waters in 2000 when, in his autobiography, *Full Time,* he declared himself 'a fake Irishman'. He explained how he had genuinely believed his Irish maternal grandfather, Michael O'Malley, qualified him to play for Ireland; only later, after the rejection of a passport application, did he learn that O'Malley was not a blood relative. Eventually, after 64 caps, he did receive a passport.

He insists he would qualify today 'because of the adoption law. My mum was adopted. I would do. I had a very Irish upbringing because my granddad lived with us, and he was from Mayo.'

Charlton was not the first Ireland manager to look across the Irish Sea for talent. There is an oft-told tale of Londoner Terry Mancini, on his international debut in 1973, turning to a teammate at the end of the Irish anthem and sighing, 'I hope ours isn't as long.' In the 1980s, meanwhile, the Brighton & Hove Albion and Liverpool striker Michael Robinson – a player who had once told *Shoot!* magazine that his professional ambition was to 'play for England' – arranged for his mother to get an Irish passport so he would be eligible.

However, Charlton went further than before. His starting XI against England in Cagliari included accents from London, Cornwall, Liverpool, Glasgow, mid-Wales and south Yorkshire. It became, in a sense, a triumph for the Irish diaspora. This is a theme explored by Dermot Bolger – the Irish novelist, poet, and playwright – in his one-act monologue, *In High Germany*, which offers a study of identity, longing, and dislocation against the backdrop of Euro '88.

At one point, protagonist Eoin, an Irish emigrant in Germany, says, 'I thought of my uncles and my aunts scattered across England and the USA. Of every generation shipped off like beef by the hoof. And at that moment it seemed to me that they had found a voice at last.' And this through a game which the Gaelic Athletic Association – the governing body of the country's traditional sports, notably Gaelic football and hurling – had actually banned its members from participating in, along with other 'foreign' sports like cricket, hockey and rugby. To them, soccer was the 'garrison game', the game played by the occupying British troops, and the ban remained in place from 1905 until 1971.

Two decades on from 1971, the cultural impact of the Ireland football team's efforts cannot be overstated, according to Colm Tóibín, the esteemed Irish novelist, who was at Italia '90 reporting for the *Sunday Independent*. 'It was a lifting of the spirit in the place, which happened to coincide with a number of things,' he begins. 'What Dermot [Bolger] has written about was the whole idea of identity, of this foreign game, soccer – but also these guys with English accents playing for the Irish because they were the peoples from emigration. So, there's a whole sense that this is Ireland going out beyond itself, and it culminated in that year with the election of Mary Robinson [as Ireland's first female president], which really was very unexpected.

'Very quickly [you had] that whole idea of the economy growing and the Celtic Tiger beginning, but that summer, there were a number of things being talked about – the way the fans had behaved, and the fact that a good number of the players were not actually local lads but the result of the complexity of Irish identity, which is that so many people had gone to England, and also that this was being managed by Jack Charlton who became a national hero, and that made it an easier relationship [with Britain].

'All of those things gathered. Some of them were coming anyway but when something like that happens, with the extraordinary economic miracle of Ireland, which I suppose began around that time, you're always looking for moments where you're saying, "There's a moment where I almost saw this could happen."

'I know someone laughed at me for saying this, but I must have been down at the front at one of those games, and I looked behind and had a sense of what it might have been like for people signing up in 1914 to join the First World War from Ireland and going out … all men, all young, all enthusiastic, all somehow crossing a line of a certain sort. I just got a glimpse of that and thought it worth recording. There were a lot of ordinary Irish people gathered together – all men, all young, all innocent, all full of hope about something.'

And most definitely not English. Tóibín remembers the thousands of Irish who arrived by ferry from Sicily, their own team's island base, for that opening match against England in Sardinia on 11 June. 'The narrative of the time was the English were thuggish and the Irish were gentle and sweet … I don't know if you've come across this,' he says wryly. 'The only people who didn't know about this were the Italian police. The Irish fans simply had no interest in being hooligans – they were absolutely determined that there wouldn't be one article printed or one thing happened that would suggest they were hooligans as well. This was noticeable as even the smallest group would say, "Oh my God, we want to make clear we're not the English." I thought this was something journalists were making up, but actually it turned out to be true. There was a constant wave of Irish fans going up to Italian cops, smiling and waving at them, and the Italian cops got to realise the Irish were entirely different. That was part of the thing that happened on the two islands.'

*

THE QUESTION OF IDENTITY IS ON THE AGENDA TOO IN MICK McCarthy's manager's office at Ipswich Town's training ground. 'Quite clearly, I'm sat speaking to you in a broad Yorkshire accent, so I'm not from Ireland, am I? But my father was Irish, and I was very much aware of my – for want of a better word – Irishness from a very early age,' says the captain of Ireland's 1990 team, clad this lunchtime in his training-pitch attire of black club sweatshirt and Adidas bottoms.

'I went to school, a junior school in Worsbrough Bridge, with all the Irish Catholics who went to church – the McHughs, the McQuails, the Keatings, the Morgans – all the Irish kids. My father is Irish, and I remember asking him, "Am I English or Irish?" "Half and half" was the answer, which is fair enough – the diplomatic answer, with an English mother. We were very much an Irish-Catholic family growing up in England, so when I got the shirt and pulled it on, it was a bit like, "Well, I'm suddenly not fifty-fifty any more now; I'm Irish." It may sound twee, but that's just how I felt.'

Roy Keane evidently felt otherwise when, during his rabid rant at McCarthy, then Ireland's manager, at the team's pre-finals camp on the Pacific island of Saipan – which led to the Irish captain quitting the national squad on the eve of the 2002 World Cup – he told the Yorkshireman, 'You shouldn't be managing my country.'

McCarthy is not here to discuss that episode. There is the briefest recollection of the fall-out ('It was the general election and it was seventeen pages in before it got a mention in the Irish papers; it was all about Saipan and the World Cup'), but he will reflect on another identity, the footballing one, which was a big talking point too in the Charlton years.

'I loved him as a bloke. I thought he was refreshingly honest, brutally honest, but I like that. He didn't suffer fools gladly. He took that team over and made it into a very good team. And not [the way] everybody liked, but I love that fact. We were doing to teams what they didn't like. We were beating teams who didn't like being beaten by us because of the perceived way that we played. I loved the fact Jack stuck to his guns, and despite everything, he was a success.'

McCarthy, it seems fair to say, is a man cut from the same cloth as his uncompromising former manager. Take the Barnsleyite's dry response when asked about the modern game – 'Next year will be modern, won't it? It'll be more modern than this' – yet the man who committed most fouls at Italia '90 has his shades of grey too.

'For all that I'm the archetypal centre-half, apparently, my favourite ones have been [Franz] Beckenbauer, Mark Lawrenson and [Franco] Baresi – so none of them in my mould,' he reveals. 'Beckenbauer, I loved. I had to get a manager once to tell me to stop hitting it with the outside of my foot. "If I see you pass it with the outside of your foot again, I'll fucking kill you."'

McCarthy's unfussy approach served him well with Charlton, given the character that the Englishman wished to stamp on his Republic of Ireland team. Certain easier-on-the-eye players fared less well. Lawrenson, the stylish Liverpool defender, faded from sight owing to the Achilles injury which eventually ended his career.

Liam Brady missed the 1988 European Championship through injury and would play no part in Italia '90 after Charlton removed him ten minutes before half-time, and two minutes after the loss of an equalising goal, during a 1-1 friendly draw with West Germany in Dublin in September 1989. Charlton would later tell journalist Paul Rowan, 'With Ireland, you see, they don't give up their fuckin' heroes easily, so you've really got to show 'em.'

Brady, who felt humiliated, played only once more for his country – his testimonial game against Finland in the month before the finals. McCarthy says, 'I remember him taking Liam off in a game against Germany, and that put the marker down. He put Andy Townsend on and I thought at that time, "That's a big pair of gonads, that."'

The treatment of Brady would be just one of the arrows fired Charlton's way by his strongest critic, Eamon Dunphy, in response to the paucity of Ireland's play in their opening two games in Italy.

A one-time Manchester United apprentice whose club career had peaked with Millwall (a period later recounted to excellent effect in his account of his last season at The Den, *Only A Game?*), Dunphy was an analyst with RTÉ and a *Sunday Independent* columnist, and he saw Charlton's football as a rejection of Irish soccer principles. For his part, Charlton considered Dunphy's fierce criticisms as a betrayal, given that they came from an ex-professional.

Dunphy had already alienated McCarthy, who remembers his own reaction during the 1988 European Championship when Charlton brought Dunphy to dinner at the team's hotel. 'Eamon Dunphy had been giving me stick ever since I went there – I was too slow, I couldn't turn, I couldn't play, I wasn't good enough. Jack invited him in for a bite to eat. I saw him walk in and I said, "What the fuck's he doing in here?" He [Charlton] said, "I've invited him" and I said, "If he's staying here, I ain't." I went, and Frank Stapleton too. Going home on the plane, we were reading the paper: it was Dunphy giving out even more stick to me, and that's when Jack turned on him as well.'

Hostilities intensified at Italia '90. Even the Ireland players admit the opening draw with England was a match to forget, Sheedy's goal aside. 'We were preparing for this warm weather, and we got this pissy old night in Barnsley,' says McCarthy.

'I hated that game,' adds goalkeeper Packie Bonner. He recalls how Ireland had struggled with diagonal balls aimed over McCarthy's shoulder for Gary Lineker when the teams met in Stuttgart in 1988. The England forward's opening goal was more of the same. 'It was that type of diagonal ball played between myself and Mick. I couldn't come, and he couldn't deal with it.'

For Kevin Moran, it would have been worse but for a lucky escape. 'I do remember an incident with [Chris] Waddle where he threw me a dummy in the box and went by me. I stuck my foot out and I caught him. I immediately jumped back and put my hands up in the air and said, "Never touched him, ref."'

Dunphy's response was a *Sunday Independent* column six days later, headlined 'British football died of stupidity', in which he lamented the 'narrow minds' of a line of coaches – starting, he argued, with Alf Ramsey and Don Revie, and leading to Charlton – who favoured functionalism over aesthetics.

'Yes, these islands have become football's Third World,' he wrote, 'an insular, unenlightened province of the international game which has elsewhere found it possible to reconcile individualism with team play.'

Dunphy was just warming up. He really got going when seated in the RTÉ studio during the ensuing goalless draw with an unambitious Egypt side. 'Egypt was a horrible game,' McCarthy admits. 'We weren't a team that would pick holes in anybody with silky, free-flowing football. We'd put it in their half and play in there, [but] Egypt sat back, and we tried everything – corners, free-kicks, long throws – and they repelled everything we could offer.'

Ireland ended that second Group F fixture ahead by 17-3 on crosses, 8-1 on corners and 6-1 on attempts on goal. Bonner had so little to do in goal that the *Gazzetta dello Sport* declined to award him an individual rating.

Dunphy's response in the studio at full time – which had smoke rising from the RTÉ switchboard – was as follows: 'I feel embarrassed and ashamed of that performance. Everyone in the country has been let down and most people won't understand it … The Egyptians are terrible, terrible; the English will do a job on them. We should be ashamed of the way we went about the game. It was shameful and depressing … I'm thinking of men like [Johnny Giles] and Tommy Eglington, the great players we produced, the Peter Farrells, the Liam Bradys, the David O'Learys and Ronnie Whelans. This is a great football country, to go out and produce that rubbish …'

Overall, Dunphy mentioned O'Leary thirteen times and Whelan twelve times. Both men were Dubliners, and both technical footballers in that city's best tradition. The latter, a 1990 league title winner with Liverpool, had broken a bone in his foot in late April and, despite returning to fitness, saw only 28 minutes' action in Italy. For O'Leary, the total would be 26 minutes.

In the case of the latter, Charlton had considered the defender responsible for the Ian Rush goal that beat Ireland in the new manager's first match. O'Leary then found himself excluded from the squad for a subsequent close-season tournament in Iceland. In the wake of several withdrawals – including the Liverpool trio of Jim Beglin, Lawrenson and Whelan, who attended an end-of-season trip to Spain – Charlton called O'Leary and asked him to join the squad after all. However, the player declined, citing a family holiday already arranged. Not until 1989 would he earn another cap.

Declan Lynch, in his superb account of the Irish experience of Italia '90, *Days of Heaven*, offers a supportive view of Dunphy's stance. 'What Jack did, with the results he achieved, was the popularisation of football in Ireland, beyond the hard core of aficionados which had always existed. And in so doing, with the primitive style which he favoured, he alienated the football men, the people who had always loved the game and kept it going.'

Charlton's initial response to Dunphy's words was to suggest he was as relevant as a fly on a window. Yet, when Dunphy flew in for his next press conference and tried to ask a question, Charlton refused, telling him, 'You're not a proper journalist', before walking out.

Colm Tóibín remembers it well, having been commandeered to keep an eye on his *Sunday Independent* colleague during a visit to Palermo which had been planned before the storm broke. Tóibín says, 'The editor of the paper calls me and says, "Dunphy's partner is going nuts because he is determined to go over to Palermo, and I'm worried about him that he may be in danger. I don't care what you do or what you write, but can you make sure that he's not left alone at any time?" So that was funny – my job was just to be with Dunphy.

'I was at the conference, and Charlton walked out once Dunphy stood up to speak. Dunphy wanted to ask him, "Why are you using this very primitive method of soccer that isn't working, and why are you leaving particular players off?" David O'Leary, for example. Charlton didn't rate David O'Leary, and Dunphy did. There were those arguments.

'What's important to remember is Dunphy could have gone to other press conferences and caused a similar fuss each time and, he didn't do that. He gets no credit for that. He said he was becoming the story too much, and he didn't want to stay being the story.

'I didn't know anything about soccer, I was just listening to him. The argument I'd have had with him, if I'd bothered arguing, was that it's like anything else – if something works, shut up moaning about it. It got us as far as Rome, so to try to talk about the niceties, the choreography as to how you actually play the beautiful game in the middle of a national eruption of emotion, seemed to me to miss the point. But Dunphy was trying to say that the journalists had become fans with typewriters – there's a need for somebody to speak the truth, and the truth is we're playing a form of soccer which we shouldn't be proud of.

'This is fine, but said in the euphoria of an entire nation where old ladies got to know about offside and people were screaming in the streets, and Dunphy just looked like he was the spoiler. If you look at Roddy Doyle's novel *The Van*, it's set in Dublin in 1990. They're selling fish and chips from this van, and if you want to buy a sausage, you ask for "a Dunphy" because a sausage was shaped like a prick, and Dunphy was a prick.'

EAMON DUNPHY WAS NOT ALONE IN EVERYTHING HE SAID. MARK Lawrenson, writing a column in the *Irish Times*, called for a defensive pairing of McGrath and David O'Leary. Instead, McGrath operated ahead of centre-backs McCarthy and Moran. This last-named argues, 'I remember people saying, "They're slow, you put a ball over and they'll get behind," but we never did get caught out. A lot was because of the way we played, with Paul [McGrath] in front of us – if one of us got pulled, Paul used to drop into the middle.'

Moran himself can empathise with Dunphy over his efforts to swim against the swollen tide of 'Olé, olé' elation. 'I know what people say, and I often thought, "Yeah, we could have played an awful lot more,"' he says. 'You'd look at it and it was a hell of a team – that team, you just wonder, if we could put the ball down and play, how much more could we have played? But in saying that, we didn't do badly when you consider where we got to even playing the way Jack wanted us to play. As a result of that, we started to have belief in what Jack's style was and go along with it. And we did – we got to the quarter-final of the World Cup, and at our peak were seventh in the world. We'd never got anywhere near that before.'

The first step was out of Sicily and, after their Egypt disappointment, they managed it thanks to a 1-1 draw with the Netherlands in their last group game. Gullit struck a smart early goal on a one-two with Kieft but the Irish ability to, well, put 'em under pressure meant Ronald Koeman had less space to pick his passes and the clever patterns of Dutch movement slowed down. With nineteen minutes remaining, Niall Quinn equalised with one of the scruffiest goals of the tournament following Bonner's long punt upfield. Berry van Aerle, in his eagerness to stop Cascarino collecting, miscued his volley and the ball flew back to Hans van Breukelen. The goalkeeper fumbled, and Quinn stretched out a long leg to score.

With news coming through that England led against Egypt, the draw would take both sides through. 'It was a hell of a game up until the last five or seven minutes when we downed tools a bit,' says Mick McCarthy. 'I said to Gullit,

"We're both going through here." That's true but we had it hammer and tongs for eighty-three, eight-four minutes. It was far from cheating. I'd say that was common sense at the end of the game with six minutes to go.'

That left just one thing to do: with Ireland and the Netherlands sharing identical points' and goals' totals, there was a drawing of lots to decide who finished second or third in the group. Luck was with the Irish who took second place, meaning they would avoid West Germany and face Romania instead.

The adventure would continue, but Kevin Sheedy, the man who had got the ball rolling on that rainy night in Cagliari, suggests it took a moment of comedy in a Palermo hotel lobby to lighten the mood ahead of their meeting with the reigning European champions. A smile creases his face as he recalls a mishap involving Mick Byrne, the squad's physio, and a beautiful model boat made from matchsticks.

'The morning after Egypt, we got lambasted by the Irish press, and we were all sat in the lobby. The main feature was this boat; it was a magnificent piece. Mick Byrne came down and saw the mood. Mick was a great character – he could always put a smile on your face. He said, "Come on, lads. We're still in this, we can beat Holland". He was trying to gee everyone up and for some reason started singing "The Lambeth Walk". He went, "Doing the Lambeth Walk ... oi" and he nudged his elbow and he just knocked the boat slightly. We're all looking and the boat started wobbling and we all knew what was going to happen and the next thing this boat just fell. Mick tried to catch it, which made it even funnier as he was never going to catch it and it just smashed to smithereens. The players were howling. The hotel manager came over and started kicking off. Mick was saying, "I'm so sorry", and we were laughing even more. It changed the mood of the camp.' Crash, bang, and then laughter. That was Ireland's World Cup in a nutshell.

Tico high, Tartan low

BORA MILUTINOVIĆ HAS A LOVE AFFAIR WITH THE WORLD CUP dating back six decades. It was a love affair born when, aged thirteen, he left Belgrade on a train bound for Sweden to watch his brothers, Milorad and Miloš, represent Yugoslavia at the 1958 World Cup. Milorad never left the substitutes' bench, but Miloš was there on the pitch in Vasteras for the 1-1 draw in their opening game against Scotland.

Their little brother Bora never made it to the World Cup as a player, but he made up for it as a coach by overseeing the fortunes of five different countries on global football's great stage. From Mexico '86 through to Korea/Japan 2002, Bora – easier to say than Milutinović in the various pidgins he has picked up – was there for each one, each time with a different nation: Mexico, Costa Rica, the US, Nigeria, China.

Of the stories he wrote with those countries, none was as remarkable as the Costa Rica chapter of 1990.

It is one thing taking two host nations – Mexico and the US – out of the group stage, or doing so with Africa's most populous country, Nigeria. Doing it with Costa Rica, a nation new to the World Cup with a population of little more than three million was another matter altogether. Not least after taking the reins only three months prior to the tournament.

'It was a marvellous experience, incredible really,' he says from his home in

Qatar. 'I wanted to go to the World Cup. For that reason I chose it. I had seventy days. They didn't have money.'

It would be easy to assume some blurring of Bora's memories given the sheer volume of World Cup pictures in his mind, yet the details of his 1990 venture remain intact.

He is still enthusing, for instance, about the tournament song, nearly thirty years on. '¡*Deputamadre!*' he exclaims, summoning a Spanish profanity loosely translatable as 'bloody great' for 'Notti magiche', a tune whose electro opening bars come straight from the Giorgio Moroder songbook.

There is another song, though, that captures rather better his eyebrow-raising adventure with Costa Rica – and the exertions along the way. It is not the squad's own tinny attempt at a World Cup tune, 'Lo Daremos Todo' – We'll give it everything – which might be described as a cruise-ship, Spanish-language interpretation of England's 1970 effort 'Back Home' with 'O Sole Mio' somehow stranded in the middle.

No, the song in question is Survivor's 'Eye Of The Tiger', the theme tune from *Rocky III*. After all, taking his raw bunch of players up into the mountains to begin their preparations, Bora did not just subject them to a gruelling training programme at a high altitude of 1,500 to 1,800m above sea level. He also showed them all the *Rocky* films.

'I think the Stallone films, especially *Rocky II* and *III*, are films that can serve as a motivation – especially for somebody coming from an environment like that and having to train like that,' he says. 'They have a lot of messages about making an effort, believing in yourself, having the fighting spirit. As Rocky says, "the eye of the tiger"!'

His players have not forgotten the brutal, thrice-a-day fitness regime – nor the video nights that followed. Hernán Medford, the squad's young forward who would score the goal against Sweden that confirmed qualification for the second round, recalls, 'It gave us a clear message, and those films helped us a lot – they gave us confidence. Bora spoke a lot to us about this because we still didn't believe we were at a World Cup.'

Alexandre Guimarães, the Brazil-born midfielder whom Bora would later mentor along the path to a career in coaching, adds, 'We trained three times a day.

He was putting us to the test, to see how much we could suffer, what our limits were. It was, "How far can they go?" And through this he could see the areas where he had to improve us.'

It was on 11 June 1990 that the Central American newcomers showed they might go further than anybody had anticipated. Genoa's Stadio Luigi Ferraris was the venue. And, as with his siblings' opening game with Yugoslavia in 1958, Scotland provided the opposition. Bora went one better than his brothers: Juan Cayasso's lone strike put Costa Rican football on the map.

It was the launch pad for a run to the last sixteen. In the process, they became the first nation from the Confederation of North, Central American and Caribbean Association Football (CONCACAF) to reach the World Cup's knockout phase on European soil.

SINCE 1990, COSTA RICA HAVE FEATURED AT FOUR WORLD CUP FINAL tournaments, culminating in a quarter-final appearance against the Netherlands in 2014, when *Los Ticos*, as they are known, came within a penalty shootout of the semi-finals.

I was there, at the Arena Fonte Nova in Salvador on the north-east coast of Brazil that night, as a small band of Costa Ricans in the main stand tossed red, white, and blue balloons into the air and the locals sang their support for the underdogs.

That 2014 squad had actually won their first-round group at the expense of Italy and England, both former World Cup winners and both sent home early.

It was a remarkable achievement. After their opening victory over Uruguay, one player in the group, Oliver Duarte, revealed that he and his teammate had prepared by watching a film about a little-fish triumph. Not *Rocky*, but *Italia '90* – the story of Bora's boys, the first Costa Rica team to leave a World Cup script in a thousand scraps of paper.

The maker of that film, Miguel Gómez, was eight years old when Costa Rica played at the 1990 World Cup. He worked as the art assistant on *Iron Man*, the first of the Marvel movies, but then had a wish to tell his own superhero story.

'When I thought about it, about who were my biggest heroes as a child, it was the players from Italia '90,' he explains. 'Some of them played for Saprissa which was the club I always followed, and I remember we were taken out of school to watch the games – against Scotland, against Sweden.

'I also remember when they flew home afterwards and people went out into the streets with mirrors. With the sun, they were making these signals – sending up flashes from down on the ground. It was something special.'

The Spanish word Gómez uses to describe that group of players is *artesanal*. Pre-industrial. When Costa Rica reached the quarter-finals at Brazil 2014, they had players based in eleven different countries. The 1990 squad was entirely home-based.

'Some of the players were part-timers,' he continues. One sold mix-tapes outside bars to supplement the income he received from playing football. Another drove a cab. Midfielder Róger Gómez, as his nickname *el Policía* might suggest, was a policeman.

'These players didn't go with this perspective of becoming millionaires,' Gómez adds. 'They wanted to do a good job – it was all that interested them. They had no other reference point. Now *Tico* players can go and play for Real Madrid as happened with Keylor [Navas]. These things can happen now, but it didn't exist then, that mentality.'

In Costa Rica then, the footballing infrastructure was minimal. There were no training grounds. Players trained on the pitch at their club stadiums. So too the national team, as Alexandre Guimarães makes clear. Later the *Ticos'* coach at the finals in 2002 and 2006, Guimarães says, 'The national stadium belonged to the government. It lent the team the stadium to train there and when they couldn't train there, when the pitch was really bad – and you have to remember, it rains a lot here – we trained on an alternative pitch in a really bad condition next to the national stadium. No club had a gym or anything like that – there was nothing, it was football, pure and simple. Nothing but the ball, the coach, the pitch and that's it.'

Up to the late 80s, training would be scheduled in the late morning allowing part-time players to fit their working lives around this window.

In the lead-up to Italia '90, though, change was afoot. The federation was placing more emphasis on its youth teams and a new generation of players had begun to gain international experience. Costa Rica participated in the football tournament at the 1984 Olympic Games. They sent their youngsters to the FIFA Under-16 World Cup in China where Hernán Medford scored the tournament's first goal. The fact the Costa Rican authorities had bent the eligibility rules to shoehorn the over-age Medford into their squad – despite a birth date seventy days outside the permitted age range – is something we will return to later.

The ultimate target was the World Cup. Before each of the eight final-round qualifying games for Italia '90 between March and July 1989, the team came together for a period of ten to twelve days.

The result was Costa Rica attaining their Italia '90 place as the winners of the CONCACAF third-round group. Mexico's absence, owing to a two-year ban for having fielded four over-age players in the qualifying rounds of the 1989 World Youth Cup, had presented a wider window of opportunity, and they jumped through it.

The coach who had overseen qualification was Marvin Rodríguez, who then took the team to Italy for a series of friendly matches against club sides, including Torino and Roma in October 1989. Yet, come February 1990, in the wake of a change of president and friendly losses to Mexican side Guadalajara and the Soviet Union, the Costa Rican Football Federation decided on a change. Talks with two Argentinians, Omar Sivori and César Luis Menotti, came to nothing and so, enter Velibor Milutinović, aka Bora – a name usually preceded by the word nomadic. Four years earlier, he had steered hosts Mexico to the World Cup quarter-finals. Now his nous would galvanise Costa Rica's greenhorns.

Alexandre Guimarães remembers, 'He had tremendous charisma. When he arrived, it really surprised us that he had so much information about us – and about us at that time, because 1990 was not like today. He had training methods that were different to what we knew in Costa Rica, and he had the power to convince you.

'We saw that he was a football man and he had international prestige – wherever you went, people knew him. It gave us confidence and security. We knew we had someone who could help us.'

Hernán Medford adds, 'We were very nervous. I was one of the youngest in the group. He worked a lot on the mental side with me. We set off two months before the finals and did a tour of Europe, and this really helped – being with Bora day after day in training, talking to him all the time, all of this helped us. He worked well on every detail regarding mentality and tactics.'

Gradually Bora's ideas began to sink in as the squad moved from the mountains of Costa Rica to Chicago – for friendly matches against the Mexican club Atlas and Poland's national team – and then on to Italy.

They were the first team to arrive, on 8 May, and Bora had the following message for them: 'I said, "Look, we've arrived first, but we're not going to go home first." It surprised a few people, but it became reality.'

It was not his only prescient comment. He continues, 'When we left Costa Rica, there weren't even family members there to see us off, so I said to the players, "Don't worry, it's better this way. There's no one here now, but when we get home, there'll definitely be a lot of people."'

For Juan Cayasso, the team's best attacking player, the long build-up abroad was significant. 'All the friendly games we played, we lost and when you lose three games, everything gets so problematic – but we were far away from Costa Rica, so they could do nothing. That gave us a chance to stay cool and talk together about what we were doing badly and what we were doing well.

'What was so good from Bora was he took us there a month before because it was all new to us. We went to Pisa, saw the Leaning Tower and were so impressed by all this culture. Then we went to Wales and saw everyone driving on the other side of the road.'

The trip to Wales was for a friendly at Cardiff's Ninian Park. It provided a taste of the challenges – aerial and physical – that came with facing British opponents. Costa Rica lost 1-0 but, as Guimarães recalls, they 'went toe to toe with Wales for the whole game'.

An incident afterwards highlights how different life could be for an international footballer in 1990. Back in the away changing room, a flustered federation official was horrified to see some players had swapped shirts with their Wales counterparts. 'Everything was so new for us, and we didn't have a shirt sponsor,' Cayasso explains. 'We didn't have enough. One or two of our teammates swapped shirts, and they were like, "No, no, no, that's not possible, you can't do it."'

It was not the only time they received this order. When it came from Bora, though, during a friendly match against Internazionale, it was another of the Serbian's psychological ploys.

Guimarães says, 'We'd not won a single game, but against Inter, you could start to see a few tactical tweaks he wanted us to do, and we showed signs we were on the right track. On top of that, he told us, "I don't want a single player to swap shirts with an Inter player. You're an international team. They're a club side. The important ones here are you, not them."

'We drew the game, and when we scored, our players celebrated. Bora said afterwards, "I want this to be the first and last time you celebrate a goal in a friendly against a club side. You're the Costa Rica national side." These messages might sound really simple but they gave us a lot of self-confidence.'

IN HIS BOOK ABOUT ITALIA '90, 'LA GRAN FIESTA', GUIMARÃES divulges that the Costa Rican federation's kit deal with Lotto was worth no more than $40,000 – one-tenth of what the Italian manufacturer was paying Ruud Gullit, star player for the AC Milan and Netherlands.

Even when it came to his team's kit, Bora had a rabbit in his hat. Once in Italy, he contacted Giampiero Boniperti, the president of Juventus, with an unusual request. 'I asked Mr Boniperti to give us twenty-two kits we could wear,' he says. 'Why? Our third kit was usually black and white, but we didn't have one. Black and white is Juventus, and we were going to be playing in the Stadio Delle Alpi against Brazil. This meant people would look fondly on us. On top of that, I'm Partizan Belgrade and that's their colours too.'

It was in these zebra stripes that they entered the terracotta-coloured home of Genoa and Sampdoria, the Stadio Luigi Ferraris, for their first World Cup fixture against Scotland. A fixture that no football lover in Costa Rica, where a half-day national holiday had been announced in advance, or Scotland too for that matter, has forgotten.

In the tunnel beforehand, Bora had told his players to make some noise and make their presence felt – a piece of psychology that had brought success with Mexico's Pumas, the club he coached to victory in the CONCACAF Champions

Cup. 'I wanted us to show them we were ready for the game and there was nothing that would hurt us,' he explains, though the really big noise came on the pitch.

Costa Rica had two heroes in particular that afternoon. One was matchwinner Cayasso. The other was goalkeeper Luis Gabelo Conejo. In a squad who carried with them a statue of Costa Rica's patron saint, the *Virgen de los Ángeles*, Conejo was the most devout of all. He took a Bible with him wherever he went. It was not the power of prayer but Bora's careful planning that helped him resist Scotland.

Using the contacts he had acquired during a spell as Udinese coach, Bora hired an Italian goalkeeper coach, Norberto Negrisolo, to work with Conejo. 'If there's any country that has capable goalkeepers, it's Italy – and he helped a lot,' reflects the Serbian.

Guimarães elaborates, 'Bora told him to with him on crosses, to batter him in training and work on coming out all the time. Seventy per cent of the work was on crosses.'

Conejo would end that World Cup as one of two goalkeepers in FIFA's squad of the tournament. He set the tone with a dominant performance in Genoa. Scotland had nineteen goal attempts to Costa Rica's four. They had fourteen corners to three. But they could find no way through.

To Scottish eyes, it was an unhappy revelation. 'We'd watched pictures of him before and he never really came out towards the edge of his box, but that day he came for every single cross,' former Scotland midfielder Murdo McLeod remembers.

Alex McLeish, his centre-back colleague, adds, 'We threw in cross after cross. We were told the goalie would drop every one of them, but he clutched every one of them.

'A lot of the boys were going around going, "I thought the goalkeeper was meant to be a dumpling – he caught everything." And Andy [Roxburgh, Scotland's manager] was kind of lost for words. [Assistant] Craig Brown had gone to see them and said, "He was a flapper, put him under pressure. Big Nally, get in there when the crosses come in."'

The Big Nally in question is Alan McInally, then a Bayern Munich player. His inclusion that day, at the expense of Rangers centre-forward Ally McCoist, warrants a digression. McCoist had initially, mistakenly, heard his name announced when Roxburgh read out the team to face Costa Rica, concluding with the forward pairing of 'Mo and Ally'.

In truth, it was Mo [Maurice Johnston] and Nally. McCoist just happened to be sharing a room with McInally and relates in his autobiography what happened when his delighted teammate returned to their room to take a nap. McCoist, by now aware he was not starting, writes, '[He] stopped and glared at me sitting on the bed, head disconsolately buried in my crossword book. "Oi you," he snapped at me. "Get that light out. Some of us have got a game today."'

The Scotland attackers who did start had opportunities. Conejo made a fingertip first-half save from Mo Johnston. Later, Johnston was in space eight yards from goal but Conejo beat away the shot and, on the follow-up, Paul McStay left fly only for Héctor Marchena to dive across and block.

During their few months together, Bora had instilled in his players a clear understanding of their game plan. Defend first, counter-attack second.

While their 3-6-1 formation became a 3-4-3 when the team attacked, once out of possession his players withdrew entirely into their own half. His attention to detail was evident in the second half against Scotland when, in a pause in play, he drew a tactical instruction on a piece of paper for forward Claudio Jara.

Put simply, he says, the plan was a case of 'not giving the ball away easily, and when we don't have the ball, knowing how to press our opponent.

'A lot of people were betting we'd be the team who conceded most goals in the tournament,' he adds. 'We had to be tactically right, with and without the ball – to press and be aware. And never forget that when you have a goalkeeper like we had, anything is possible.

'As for the goal we scored, it was a surprise – a lot of passes, first touches, changing flanks, good decision-making ... everything a team needs to have. Cayasso was very talented. He had great vision and timing.'

His timing was impeccable. Four minutes after half-time, the 28-year-old delivered the goal Costa Ricans are still talking about to this day.

Not that he'd be the type to lose patience as yet another middle-aged man comes up and asks for a photo or tells him just what he was doing at the precise moment the adidas Etrusco Unico flew past Jim Leighton.

Pura vida is the unofficial motto of Costa Rica – a verbal shrug of the shoulders, a placid call for cool, a don't-worry-be-happy philosophy – and Cayasso is a *pura vida* kind of guy.

Speaking via Whatsapp from his home in the Costa Rican town of Limón, where he works in sports administration for the local government, he tells me, 'You hear fathers say, "I want a photo with my son", but we really know it's the dads who want the picture.

'It's going from generation to generation. The best part is when someone sees you, remembers that moment and they thank you. I hear a lot of stories – what people were doing at that moment, how they were angry with their brother but got together again, or how someone jumped up, hit a wall and broke their arm!

'A lot of people ask me about this special moment. I wasn't prepared for it. We were thinking this was our first time in a World Cup and were trying to do our best, but I never dreamed of scoring a goal.

'When my teammate [Jara] did his back-heel [to put him in on goal], I never expected him to do that. It's a good thing it happened so fast as I didn't have time to think. If you remember Medford's goal against Sweden, he was fifty metres from goal and had a chance to think.

'Mine was so fast, I couldn't think so that was the best thing that could happen to me – one of the gifts God gave me is good reactions.

'What went through my mind was to put my foot under the ball and lift it, because the goalkeeper was coming out. He was so close to me that I didn't get to do it perfectly, like [Lionel] Messi, but it was enough. It clipped him and just kept on going.

'When the ball crossed the line, the first thing I did was to look back at the referee. I thought it was offside, because when Jara made the pass I was so alone and close to the goalkeeper. I turned around and saw he was pointing back to the centre-circle. It was crazy.

'You can see it on TV, and I'm still surprised when I look at it – see how I go to the corner and then turn around and give a smile. I know I'll never smile in that way again. A lot of sensations went through my mind. I couldn't believe it was happening.

'After the match, I remember people jumping around and celebrating, and I was in a corner. I was just sitting there trying to figure out what had happened. I lived with that a lot of years – I was always asking God why he picked me to be the first one. I think I was so blessed that I was the first one.'

✳

BLESSED IS NOT HOW SCOTTISH FOOTBALL FANS FELT WHEN THE final whistle blew on 11 June 1990. The next morning, the *Daily Record* begged, 'Stop the world we want to get off.' A cartoon in *The Times* showed a weeping Scotsman with a tam o'shanter on his head, a pint in his hand, and two tears rolling down a cheek, muttering, 'I didn't know Costa Rica even had a football team.'

When I meet Alex McLeish in search of a Scottish perspective, he delves into YouTube, fingers dancing across his mobile phone as he summons Cayasso's 49th-minute strike. 'Actually, a good fucking goal,' he declares. 'There's the back-heel, he's on his tod, and Jim Leighton has nae chance.'

We are in a pub on Wandsworth Common near his home in south London. McLeish, appointed Scotland manager for a second time in February 2018, allows his critical faculties to kick in as he takes a second look.

'Somebody allows this guy to come inside here,' he complains. 'He shouldn't be letting him come inside. Force him out there. It's too easy. Stewart McKimmie got dragged in. I've been done as well there. A little bit of good movement from Cayasso – he was a good player, and he drifted off me as I watched the ball. I used to always analyse goals I lost. I would tape *Sportscene* every week.'

McLeish, a defender in the great Aberdeen team of the 1980s, remembers a fatal air of apprehension in the dressing room. 'It was that old Scottish chip-on-your-shoulder thing: What if we don't win this? We were thinking the negatives. That was the way we played the game.

'I played against Brazil against Careca and Romário, and we never gave them a kick. With Cayasso, I can only explain it was a little bit of hesitancy. It was the unknown, plus the expectation level again weighing on your shoulders. When you think of the crosses and the shots we had, there was no conviction, not the way a player at his best would deliver.

'We didn't have the guile to penetrate them, and they were very well organised by a great coach. I met him [Bora] in Doha a couple of years ago, and he said there was a lot of noise coming from Scotland – it was more our press saying what we were going to do to them; it wasn't the players. When we lost, it was a national disaster.'

The *Scotsman* described it as 'not the worst display but the poorest result' for Scotland on the world stage. On reflection, there are other strong candidates. The 7-0 hammering by Uruguay in their debut campaign in 1954. The 3-1 loss to Peru and 1-1 draw with Iran which followed the folly of manager Ally McLeod's hubristic claim before the Argentina World Cup that 'You can mark down 25 June 1978 as the day Scottish football conquers the world.' Or the 3-0 humbling by Morocco at France '98, their last appearance to date on the global stage.

Defeat by Costa Rica was the cue for another hard-luck story for a nation which has never survived the group stage of the competition. In their second game, they overcame Sweden 2-1 on the day of a warmly remembered fan march to the Stadio Luigi Ferraris: Scots and Swedes together in a friendly conga of kilts and Viking helmets.

In the third, they held out hope of a point against Brazil, which would have secured qualification, before losing a soft goal to Müller with eight minutes remaining.

The Tartan Army could only dream of a such a near-miss today. In 1990, the health of the Scottish club game was such that Rangers, with four players, were the best-represented team in England's World Cup squad. Yet, if Italia '90 was a springboard for Costa Rica, Scotland have not won a World Cup finals game since. Indeed, with their absence from Russia 2018, they have missed five tournaments running.

It is a painful stat for a proud Scotsman like Andy Roxburgh. On the wall of the office at his home in Switzerland, he has a *Daily Record* cartoon featuring himself on a gondola; on the side of the vessel is the newspaper's masthead and the message 'Five in a row'. 'I wish you hadn't told me that,' he says when Scotland's modern five-in-a-row World Cup sequence is mentioned.

'Look back and think of the top international players Scotland had,' he laments. 'We still had some very good players, but we didn't have the Kenny Dalglishes, Graeme Sounesses and Joe Jordans of this world. Since then it's gradually slid away from that level. The question is, "Why is that?" I'd put it down to one word, and that's environment. I think the environment that was Scottish football changed and that means all the way from the streets to the youth teams to the schoolboy football. That diminished.'

Now technical director of the Asian Football Confederation, Roxburgh suggests different reasons for this diminishment: the weakening of the Scottish club game in correlation with the Premier League's power surge, and the accompanying narrowing of opportunities for Scottish players south of the border.

'Whether it's the development of the Champions League and Premier League, whether it's the change in the school football set-up, there are all sorts of reasons. You don't see the level of player now that they had there.

'With the Premier League in Scotland, you know the problems connected with that and the demise of Rangers. I saw a Scotland squad for a recent match, and there was not one of them from Glasgow Rangers. That tells you how the environment changed.

'It's not to be negative. Scottish football is doing its best to survive in the current climate, and the climate is difficult because of globalisation, because of the centralisation of money. Where I'm working now, people are up in the middle of the night watching games from England. It's taken over the world.

'There's another significant thing you forget about Scotland. You look at Germany and France, and immigration had a lot to do with what has happened there – think of the influence of Turkish immigration in Germany player-wise. Scotland was never part of that – it's never ever benefitted from that through its history because it was never a place that was part of such immigration. It's another element in the equation.'

Graeme Souness, one of Scotland's great players of the 1980s, touched on this same element in an interview with the *Sunday Times* in 2017 – 'Think of what it's done for the football prowess of the Dutch, the French, the English' – and in this, there is a case for a more sympathetic reading of the comment by now departed national coach Gordon Strachan, made after their Russia 2018 qualifying failure and mocked at the time, that 'genetically, we are behind'.

The search for answers is nothing new – in fact, it was under way even during the days Scotland were qualifying for World Cups. In 1976, the Strathclyde

Student Press published 'Banned! An investigation into the SFA and a look at Scottish football', while four years later, the *Scotsman* carried out a series of reports titled 'The pride and the poverty', which concluded that Scots were resistant to change and would always lag behind.

For Roxburgh, another factor worthy of comment is the shrinking of schools football, hitherto a rich seam of talent across Scotland, as attitudes changed within the teaching profession. He dates this to the teachers' strike of the mid-80s over pay and working conditions. Before this, any decent-sized Scottish school would have two teams per year group – and as many as three or four for the senior year. Afterwards, many disaffected teachers were less willing to commit to the extra-curricular activities of old. 'The strike killed all that,' John Watson, general secretary of the Scottish Schools FA, tells me.

Roxburgh, an old teammate of Watson at schoolboy level, expounds, 'It always stuck in my mind that there were something like forty-five thousand registered schoolboy players and it dropped to fifteen thousand. It took a long, long time to recover even modestly. Certainly during my period, the schools football had deteriorated. That's where I identified a lot of players who became top youth players and then internationals. They started in the schools programme, so schools football was very important in Scotland.

'It's funny now that China has decided to spend millions and millions investing in schools football because the Chinese realise their super league isn't enough. They need grassroots and want to do it through the schools. Everybody was a schoolboy player in Scotland. With every player of that era, I could tell you what school they played for.'

It is a fascinating detour, and Roxburgh is no less thoughtful about his Scotland team's shortcomings at Italia '90. They had qualified ahead of a Michel Platini-led France, beating them 2-0 at Hampden Park, and then overcame Argentina 1-0 at the same venue on 28 March 1990.

He recalls, 'We won one-nil in a very high-intensity friendly. Gabi Calderón [then an Argentina midfielder, now a coaching colleague of Roxburgh] said they hadn't experienced such intensity in a long time.

'Costa Rica, though, played this contain-and-counter game, and we got caught. These were the teams that caused us a nightmare. We were at our best when we played "off a tackle". What I mean is if it was competitive in the midfield and we won a tackle, we'd then accelerate forward from that position. If you gave us ball in a big space and we had to do the slow build-up, we were never comfortable with that.'

As it was, Scotland sprang back to life against Sweden, winning 2-1 through goals from Stuart McCall and Mo Johnston. 'You could describe it like a typical British cup tie, with Swedes being so tuned in to British football,' Roxburgh says. 'It was played with incredible intensity, and we were back to ourselves again that night.

'There were some elements I don't particularly want to go into, but we were not ourselves against Costa Rica. We had to respond against Sweden, and we did.' It seems fair to assume one such element would be the departure for home of centre-back Richard Gough, who had tried to play through the pain of a nerve problem in his foot, only to be withdrawn at half-time against Costa Rica – prompting a fall-out with Roxburgh. Gough accused his manager of not being open with the press about his injury, which meant the player became the subject of press suspicions when he then had to fly home.

On the success against Sweden, Roxburgh adds, 'Olle Nordin, who was the coach of Sweden said to me after the finals, "We killed each other on that Saturday in Genoa because we played that game as if it was our cup final," which it was for us, and neither of us recovered. There's a truth in that. We were shattered after that second game because we'd put everything into it – and so had they.'

'We just went at Sweden like a rat down a drainpipe,' is Alex McLeish's lively description of his country's last World Cup victory. That it proved the final roar – or squeak – of the Scottish rat, so to speak, is down to Jim Leighton's failure to hold on to an Alemão shot, or at least push it away from goal, eight minutes from the close of the final group fixture against Brazil. With a point Scotland, would have reached the last sixteen as one of the best third-placed teams.

Leighton had arrived at the World Cup carrying the hurt of his Manchester United manager Alex Ferguson's decision to drop him for the FA Cup final replay against Crystal Palace. McLeish, who had played with him at Aberdeen, attests, 'He wasn't the Jim Leighton that I knew in terms of his personality. He was very quiet in training and in the hotel. His training was brilliant, though, and he wanted to put it behind him. For the Brazil game Jim maybe gets criticised for the goal, but we all deserve a bit of blame. I wish I'd followed in; Maurice Malpas would probably say the same thing.'

It was Careca who slid in to beat Gary Gillespie to reach the loose ball after Leighton's fumble, yet the ball was still dropping wide of the far post when Müller, more alert than any Scotland defender, raced in to knock it over the line.

It was the knockout blow, though for one Scotland player, Murdo McLeod, his own had arrived already when he felt the full force of a Branco free-kick. 'It hit me on the side of the head and knocked me unconscious,' he chuckles. 'After a few minutes, I was back on my feet but still didn't know what was happening around me. I played on for a few minutes and eventually, I just went down.' Down and out.

Costa Rica, by contrast, were still climbing. Narrowly beaten by Brazil, they needed a draw against Sweden to progress but trailed at half-time to a Johnny Ekström goal. Conejo leapt around his goal, making acrobatic saves from Stefan Schwarz, Peter Larsson and Ekström, and the Central Americans still trailed after an hour when Bora sent an extra attacker, Hernán Medford, onto the field.

For Bora, the young forward's best role was as an impact substitute. 'He was the most talented player after Cayasso, but in principle, he played with the ball. I preferred to have a player up front who'd put in an effort without the ball. It was vital we played with discipline when we didn't have the ball.'

After 75 minutes, Schwarz's foul on Medford brought a free-kick which Cayasso delivered for Róger Flores to nod in. Twelve minutes later, with Sweden now in a desperate chase for a second goal, Medford struck at the other end. A Thomas Ravelli goal-kick was headed straight back in the opposing direction by Alexandre Guimarães, another substitute. With Sweden's defensive discipline vanished, Medford ran free to score.

Guimarães explains, 'We didn't realise it, but Scotland were already losing against Brazil, so we were through with a draw, but the excitement of having equalised was so big that we just went for it. This essence of Costa Rican football came out a bit – it's very free, very relaxed, unstructured.'

Medford adds, 'Ravelli was in a hurry, so he hit the ball up, Alexandre

Guimarães knocks it back and I go through on my own against Ravelli. It's hard to describe the feeling. You're twenty-one, and you're clean through in a World Cup game against a goalkeeper like Ravelli. I was pretty nervous.' He didn't show it.

The party that followed was not confined to Mondovi, the hilltop town in Piedmont where the Costa Ricans had their base. After a congratulatory telephone call to Bora, president Rafael Calderón, declared a public holiday. Amid the excitement, the *Gazzetta dello Sport* reported the deaths of three Costa Ricans – two men and one women – who had suffered heart attacks while watching the match on television.

In Mondovi, there had been a sense of fiesta – that *pura vida* again – throughout their campaign, according to Bora. 'The team spirit was extraordinary. For us, it was a fiesta. We'd go out dancing at night, enjoying the discos, and enjoying our participation. There was no military discipline. They'd go out most nights, and they won a lot of trophies because *Ticos* dance really well!'

'We were not *concentrados* in the sense of being shut away,' adds Guimarães. 'This was a hotel more or less in the centre of town, so we could follow what was happening in the streets. I don't think players have that today. In 2002, 2006, 2014, it was very different.'

FOR COSTA RICA, THE ROAD ENDED IN BARI AND A 4-1 DEFEAT BY THE Czech Republic in the round of sixteen. Conejo, their outstanding goalkeeper, had played through the pain of an ankle injury against Sweden but was now unavailable, his place passing to deputy Hermidio Barrantes. 'For us, it was a big loss we couldn't overcome,' says Bora. 'The best we played was the first half against Czechoslovakia.' With no Conejo commanding his box, however, the towering Tomas Skuhravý capitalised with a hat-trick.

All that remained now for Bora and his squad was a heroes' return to San José. After flying to Miami, the team took a charter flight back home. Before landing, the pilot did a tour of the country.

'He flew really low, and we could see the people down on the ground holding up mirrors to salute us,' remembers Guimarães. 'We went around the whole country doing this tour. When we landed, the airport was full, the president was waiting for us, and there was an open-top bus waiting to take us to the national stadium. It was about fifteen kilometres away, and we took three hours to get there. When we got to the stadium, it was full. What really excited us was the president had arranged with Toyota to give us a Toyota Corolla. We were saying, "Really? They're giving us a car?".'

They were indeed. The parameters had changed. Cayasso, Medford, Conejo, and defender Rónald González all left for clubs in Europe. Those who stayed at home began to earn more.

Cayasso illustrates the change by noting that in 1990, his club Saprissa would pay a maximum monthly salary of around $600. 'Ten years later, a player could earn ten thousand dollars a month,' he says. 'Now we have a lot of players playing in Europe, including a few in England, and this is a big change. Footballers began to earn more money. There were sponsors, the TV companies started to pay more money. Football began to evolve more. The players were more motivated to go to another World Cup because everyone saw this was an important thing for the country.'

For Hernán Medford, matchwinner against Sweden, there was one substantial hiccup soon after Italia '90 in the form of a FIFA ban, imposed on Costa Rica's under-age teams owing to his own illegal registration for the Under-16 World Cup in 1985.

'It wasn't an administrative error – they did it knowing my age,' admits Medford, whose real birth date of 23 May 1968 – rather than 23 August as written back in 1985 – had come to light only five years later when the player registered the proper date for the World Cup. According to *World Soccer*, the Costa Rican federation was spared a more severe punishment because 'they volunteered the fiddle themselves'.

Medford is one of several players from 1990 who, in conversation, marvel at the facilities now available in Costa Rica, after the building of a new national stadium and training centre – the latter constructed with the support of money from FIFA's Goal project.

Perhaps the best guide to this altered landscape is Alexandre Guimarães, given he played at Italia '90, coached Costa Rica at the 2002 and 2006 finals, and then saw his son Celso Borges represent the *Ticos* at Brazil 2014.

'The federation began to develop a more aggressive programme with their youth teams, a more aggressive programme with their international friendlies,' he says. 'Costa Rica now had more value. Teams entered this dynamic. A club like Saprissa, which provided the bulk of the national team, saw that if they had invitations to play in the US, they had a greater cachet now because five or six players from the World Cup were in their team. Private companies became more involved with sponsorship.'

Hermés Navarro, who took the reins as president of the federation in 1999, brought further impetus – 'They were much more aggressive looking for sponsorship for the federation, and to get the budget to develop plans with the senior and junior teams,' says Guimarães – and it was during Navarro's presidency that he coached Costa Rica at successive finals in Korea/Japan and Germany.

'When we qualified for Korea/Japan, straight away he [Navarro] got more sponsorship to give us the friendlies and the training camps we needed. In '90, the vast majority of friendlies were against club teams.'

Yet unlike in 1990, Guimarães's Costa Rica suffered first-round exits both times. 'Of course it was undoubtedly easier to surprise a team [in '90],' he reflects. 'Especially with Costa Rica being what they were – a complete unknown. In 2002 and '06, once the draw for the group stage was done, I went with some of my assistants to follow all the friendlies [their opponents] had and look for material from their qualifiers.

'In '90, it was Bora through his own resources getting information on Scotland, Brazil and Sweden. Against Czechoslovakia, it was a bit different, but those first three games, it was all Bora, showing us on a Betamax.'

Ironically, Guimarães's first match as a World Cup coach with Costa Rica, twelve years after that Italian summer, was against China.

The coach of China? Bora. And the result? A 2-0 victory for Costa Rica. 'It was a lovely moment for me personally – my first match in the World Cup as a coach against the man who became my mentor,' adds Guimarães, a member of a generation who will never forget what Bora did for them.

In the case of Juan Cayasso, he has a reminder wherever he goes of what Bora helped him to achieve – namely the red Toyota Corolla he received back in 1990 and which he still drives to this day. 'Anywhere I go, everyone asks me if it's the car from Italia '90. They all remember this. We had players in Costa Rica playing professional football at that moment who didn't have a car.'

Walls come tumbling down
Part 1 - USSR

'WE'VE LOST SOMETHING, THAT'S TRUE,' SAYS VAGIZ KHIDIATULLIN, leaning closer, his blue eyes suddenly serious. 'What we've lost is the idea that, before, we thought first about our country and after about ourselves. Today, people always think about money. We thought about our country first. I'm not a hypocrite: I understand a person has to feed their family and, of course, we also thought about money and wanted to live a good life, but the thing is we always had our job to do first. We always were taught that way in school. The system made us that way. We were a great country.'

Khidiatullin, a central defender in the Soviet Union's Italia '90 team, is sitting in his office on Marosejka Street in central Moscow. A short stroll away is Lubyanka Square, where the visitor's eye is drawn to a large, mustard-yellow, Neo-Baroque building: the former home of the KGB, the Soviet secret service. The ultimate symbol of a deeply repressive system.

Khidiatullin proffers another, contrasting, thought. 'In the Communist system, there were a lot of good things. Everybody, all the youngsters, were in sports clubs. Football, basketball, ice hockey ... It was free. That's the first thing. And there were some great coaches, the people who created our methodology. The line was vertical – not horizontal, like in Europe. The coach-player relationship should be like that. We're talking a little bit about a dictator. But if the results are good, it's fine. It works.'

It was a system that certainly gained results in the world of sport. The USSR won the inaugural European Championship in 1960 and finished runners-up in 1964. Two years later, they reached the semi-finals of the World Cup in England.

In the years leading up to Italia '90, Khidiatullin was a member of Soviet squads that reached the second stage of the World Cups in 1982 and 1986, and then the final of the 1988 European Championship in West Germany.

It was a system, moreover, that he paid into without a moment's pause. From 1988, he had been playing his club football in France, where each month, he would send most of his salary back to the Soviet Sport Committee.

'It was thirty thousand dollars a month,' he recalls. 'I gave twenty-nine thousand to my country. They allowed me one thousand dollars and told me, "You can't earn any more than that," because the salary of the Russian ambassador in France was around $1,200, and I couldn't earn more.'

By June 1990, though, the system was crumbling. Five years earlier, Mikhail Gorbachev had become leader of the USSR and embarked on a programme of glasnost and perestroika – meaning, respectively, openness and restructuring.

In the same week that Italia '90 began, the Soviet Communist Party Congress met for what would be the very last time. The 'Evil Nineties', as they are known today by many in Russia owing to the descent into grab-what-you-can anarchy, had just begun.

There was even a flavour of this abrupt paradigm shift within the Soviet World Cup squad. 'It was the time things started to go downhill,' says Khidiatullin, returning to his original theme. 'In our heads, it was the start of something else. Before, we had a team. You'd think first of your team, and then yourself. It wasn't the same team as in 1988 in Germany. I was now at Toulouse; [Rinat] Dasayev was at Sevilla, [Oleksandr] Zavarov and [Sergei] Aleinikov were at Juventus. There were lots of changes happening and the doors were opening to Europe. There was this idea of freedom in our heads. Before, it was, "Listen to us," and that was all you had to hear.'

Not anymore. The entire squad may have been kitted out in identical Adidas boots, but the collective fabric was fraying. For the first time at a major tournament, CCCP no longer featured on the team's shirts. Instead, they had a sponsor, Cititronics, whose logo adorned their training tops. It was an arrangement which sparked tensions between players and federation. Even before the finals, some players had voiced their unhappiness in a signed article.

After the team's first-round elimination – an unprecedented and deeply unsatisfactory outcome for a team considered dark horses beforehand – the players refused to take their scheduled flight home unless the federation shared with them the proceeds of this sponsorship deal. It fell to coach Valeriy Lobanovskiy and Nikita Simonyan, vice-present of the USSR Football Federation and head of the delegation in Italy, to negotiate with the country's central Sport Committee.

Khidiatullin recalls, 'We said, "Give us the money from the sponsor. If not, we'll stay here and call the press and tell them everything. So they gave us the money, thirty thousand dollars, which was shared out among the whole group – players, kit men, physio, administrator. We'd told them that if we were given the money, we'd divide it among everyone. It wasn't yet a revolution, but it was a beginning for truth.'

A beginning, but also – as Khidiatullin has already suggested – an end. USSR sat eighth in the all-time World Cup table entering the 1990 finals. However, this last participation under the hammer-and-sickle flag brought a first-round exit. In their next three World Cup finals appearances – in 1994, 2002 and 2014 – Russia's footballers won only two of their nine matches. Ukraine won just as many when reaching the quarter-finals on their World Cup debut at Germany 2006.

At Italia '90, the tone was set in their opening game against Romania in Bari on Saturday 9 June, where they suffered an unanticipated 2-0 reverse.

Rinat Dasayev, whose goalkeeping had once prompted comparisons to the great Lev Yashin, allowed a Marius Lăcătuş shot past him at his near post. Khidiatullin then saw his handball offence punished, unjustly, by Uruguayan referee Juan Cardellino's award of the penalty which brought Romania's second goal. 'It wasn't a penalty,' Khidiatullin says of an incident that occurred at least a yard outside the box.

In their second match, in front of a reported TV audience of 150 million back in the USSR, another handball decision went against them – this time when Diego Maradona handled a goalbound header by Oleh Kuznetsov, Khidiatullin's red-headed central defensive partner. Another 2-0 loss ensued, leaving the Soviets as the first nation eliminated.

That Maradona handball prompted an angry response in the Soviet camp. Simonyan, the delegation chief, aimed a shot at FIFA for the appointment of referee Erik Fredriksson, who had permitted two offside goals to stand when Belgium eliminated the USSR in the round of sixteen at Mexico '86. 'Evidently, our rubles aren't worth anything,' said Simonyan – a Spartak Moscow hero of the 1950s and, more recently, ball-picking assistant to Gary Lineker at the 2018 World Cup draw in Moscow.

Kuznetsov – interviewed for this book by Bohdan Buga, a Kyiv-based UEFA.com colleague – contributes his own recollection. 'I can't say he [Fredriksson] did it intentionally. Later, I heard the story that he reportedly said in Russian, "You'll never win anything until you have this red flag behind you," but it's total crap.'

Like Khidiatullin, Kuznetsov cites a deeper reason for the early elimination. The exodus of players had begun. The originally-permitted age restriction – 28 or above – for those seeking a ticket abroad now had the weight of a feather in the wind, and the rest were keen to follow.

Kuznetsov says, 'Perhaps the team was affected by the fact that many players wanted to leave [Dynamo Kyiv] to play abroad. Lobanovskiy [coach of both Dynamo and the USSR] understood that, but he called the players and explained, "I can't let you all go at once. I'll release you step by step." Of course, some guys felt aggrieved. We didn't feel the same level of unity.'

ANY KIND OF APPRECIATION OF THE QUALITIES OF THE LAST great Soviet Union side requires an understanding of Valeriy Lobanovskiy and his methods.

For a start, this was a team with a strong core of players from Kyiv. Khidiatullin was one of only two from Moscow, along with Dasayev, in the starting XI for the 1988 European Championship final.

With a grin, he rolls off some of the names of the Dynamo Kyiv contingent: '[Anatoliy] Demyanenko, [Volodymyr] Bezsonov, [Oleksiy] Mykhaylychenko, [Vasyl] Rats, [Oleh] Protasov, [Hennadiy] Lytovchenko ... Kyiv, Kyiv, Kyiv.' Ihor Belanov, the 1986 European Footballer of the Year, can be added to the list.

Khidiatullin's defensive colleague, Kuznetsov, provides a Ukrainian perspective on the regional balance within the squad. 'Sometimes Lobanovskiy even called some of the older guys and discussed with them whether we needed fewer Kyivans in the national team,' he says. 'Politics played its role in those times. It was good that we [Dynamo] had great results, otherwise there'd have been questions about why he didn't call up players from the Moscow clubs, or from Minsk, Baku etc. But Lobanovskiy was clever. He always made Dasayev the captain.'

For Kuznetsov, their peak years were from 1986-88. 'We became champions of the USSR for two years in a row, won the Cup Winners' Cup in 1986 and some top-level unofficial matches, like defeating Real Madrid at the Bernabéu – it was a friendly but still very competitive. In our heads, there were no opponents we considered unbeatable.'

This translated to the national team. 'Let's take the Euro '88 semi-final against Italy,' he adds, 'which I consider one of the best games in the history of USSR national team. We drove them hard through the whole game with our pressing.

'The key element was pressing. He put this concept in our minds and souls, and it shaped us as players and then as coaches.'

Such were the demands of Lobanovskiy's pressing game that he overlooked Spartak Moscow's iconic midfielder of the 1980s, Fyodor Cherenkov, for three successive major tournaments. Cherenkov, twice Soviet Footballer of the Year, was the symbol of the passing football beloved by Spartak, Moscow's best-supported club yet, as Vagiz Khidiatullin says of Lobanovskiy, 'He wanted pressing and Zavarov did that better.'

In a report on Dynamo's 1986 Cup Winners' Cup triumph for *Football-Hockey* magazine, Nikita Simonyan underlined this consideration, saying: 'In building another great team, Valeriy Lobanovskiy still considers speed and the highest fitness levels as his main criteria.'

Lobanovskiy, as a young man, had studied heating engineering at the Kyiv Polytechnic Institute. Kuznetsov recalls a quiet manner and scientific approach. 'He could motivate us just with his words and charisma,' he says. 'We could read everything in his eyes and gestures. He was a great psychologist.

As a defender, you can't avoid mistakes, and when you came to him, you could tell just by a look.

'A few years before I came to Dynamo, they started to watch games – ours and our opponents' – on those archaic video recorders. He'd also call you to his office and talk to you to explain things, showing you what you had to do with counters on the board or drawings on a piece of paper.'

Long before football's statistics revolution, there was a 'Dynamo Laboratory', devised by Lobanovskiy and his then co-coach Oleh Bazylevych in tandem with Professor Anatoliy Zelentsov, an early pioneer in statistical analysis of football, whom he had met in his first coaching job at Dnipro Dnipropetrovsk.

Zelentsov worked at the Kyiv Institute of Physical Culture where he (and Lobanovskiy in turn) found a source of inspiration and ideas in Valentyn Petrovskiy, the institute's head of track and field, and the strongly innovative coach of Olympic gold medal-winning sprinter Valeriy Borzov.

Remembering the lab, Kuznetsov says, 'It was based in an ordinary residential building, where four or five flats were equipped with computers, some sensors and other things. There were many video tapes and different analytical materials.'

It was not just science and systems – 'If Zavarov could beat a defender with his dribbling, or Belanov with his pace, or [Oleh] Blohkin with his intelligence, it was a case of "go for it",' he says – yet the emphasis on hard work was pivotal.

Physically, Dynamo were the strongest team in the Soviet top flight. Pre-season was a three-month slog. Kuznetsov recalls training camps beside the Black Sea in today's disputed territory of Abkhazia: 'I remember doing three sessions per day on waterlogged fields, knee-deep in mud, with a strong wind blowing in from the sea.'

The demand for physical toughness was a thread right through Lobanovskiy's career. Former Russia winger Andrei Kanchelskis, a Dynamo Kyiv player in 1989/90, recalls Lobanovskiy once showing his players a video of a Celtic-Rangers match and his purrs of approval at the resilience shown in the face of the flying tackles: 'He said, "Only go down if you've broken something."' According to Kanchelskis, defender Oleh Luzhny's response on completing his first training session under Arsène Wenger at Arsenal was 'At Dynamo Kiev, that's our warm-up.'

For another view of Lobanovskiy, I meet Evgeny Lovchev, one of Russia's leading football commentators. A Soviet international in the 1970s, he is a columnist with the *Sovetsky Sport* newspaper and also the 2018 World Cup ambassador for Sochi. 'Lobanovskiy calculated everything,' remembers Lovchev, settling into the welcome warmth of a Moscow coffee shop on a freezing December day. These words echo his newspaper's observation back in 1975 that: 'Every improvisation performed by Dynamo always looks like a set-play.'

Lovchev resumes: 'At Spartak, we'd often use the wall pass. Lobanovskiy would say, "Don't do it." He was a mathematician, and if the defender got the ball, there'd be two people out of the game.

'He had a medical team with him, and people would calculate how much physical activity you could do. Back then, we didn't have gyms but Lobanovskiy would set up twelve stations, each devoted to a particular muscle. It was fifteen seconds per muscle, then a whistle and fifteen seconds relax, and then fifteen seconds again. I blacked out because it was so intense, and my teammates pulled me out into the snow to regain consciousness. It was the way he saw football – physical.

'The Dutch would come to Russia and take notes and learn from him. When our coaches went to the Netherlands, the Dutch would say, "Why are you coming to us? We took our system from Lobanovskiy!" He was working on the body and the heart and pushing to the limits.'

Despite this wish to push to the limits, Lovchev insists that no doping went on in the 'Dynamo Lab', though he does allege that Lobanovskiy was responsible for the regular fixing of Soviet Higher League games.

'All [Ukrainian] teams would draw at home with Dynamo and would lose away. If there were five other Ukrainian teams [in the top flight], that's fifteen points. When Lobanovskiy was asked about this, he said, "What about chess players when they agree to draw? You don't punish them for that."'

Lobanovskiy had three spells overall as USSR coach: from 1974-76, 1982-83, and 1986-90. He would face regular criticism from the Moscow press for his obsession with winning, though for Lovchev, he warrants particular credit for the brilliant third Soviet side he built during his final spell as national coach, which began three weeks before Mexico '86 and ended with Italia '90.

Lovchev ranks this team above both his own 1970s USSR side (incorporating much of the Dynamo Kyiv team that won the 1975 Cup Winners' Cup), and the Andriy Shevchenko-spearheaded Dynamo that travelled to the semi-finals of the Champions League in 1999.

'The second was his child,' Lovchev explains. 'It was something he created. With my generation – when Dynamo won the Cup Winners' Cup and Blokhin was European Footballer of the Year – Lobanovskiy didn't have to build that team. He squeezed every last drop out of them for six or seven years. Then he took a step back and gathered a group of young players. I loved this team. In the [European Championship] final, they lost to the Dutch with that [Marco] van Basten goal, but we'd be proud to have a team like that nowadays. Lobanovskiy worked those players as hard as possible and took them to another level. Nowadays, it's all about money.'

FOR LOBANOVSKIY, ITALIA '90 WAS HIS PLANNED SWAN-SONG AS national coach following a heart attack in 1988. The defeat against Romania on 9 June dealt a huge blow to hopes of going out on a high. Romania had overcome the Soviets only once in seven previous meetings, albeit the Dynamo Kyiv contingent had not forgotten their loss to Steaua Bucharest in the 1986 UEFA Super Cup. 'In those times, Socialist countries were uncompromising opponents,' says Oleh Kuznetsov. 'There was a strong antipathy.'

Ioan Lupescu, a midfielder in that Romania side, concurs, 'Although we were fifty years a Communist country we never had a good relationship with Russia. This was from history, from the Second World War. We're a Latin country. We're more related to Italy, France, Spain, Portugal, than our neighbours – and definitely not to the Russian speakers.'

The key moments went Romania's way. Oleh Protasov and Oleksandr Zavarov, both well placed in front of goal in the first half, failed to beat Romania's Silviu Lung. At the other end, the off-balance Dasayev watched as a Lăcătuş shot flew over him. An erroneous penalty award then sealed their fate.

Dasayev, by now 32, was appearing in his third World Cup finals but Lobanovskiy had vacillated over starting him, owing to a loss of form. When he sought the opinions of his senior players, they gave their captain their backing, but Lobanovskiy would drop him for the second game against Argentina.

'We knew that if we beat Romania, we'd almost definitely qualify from the group, so the result against Romania hit us very hard mentally, but I must say we played well against Argentina, especially in the first half,' says Kuznetsov, moving on to the second group fixture in which he wore the captain's armband.

Luck was against them once more. Soviet forward Igor Shalimov had already missed a free header before Maradona's handling of Kuznetsov's near-post header from another corner. After Pedro Troglio's first-half goal, the sending-off of Volodymyr Bezsonov for a trip on Claudio Caniggia just after half-time was a setback too far in an eventual 2-0 loss.

If the two handball awards were a factor, there were others, including the absence of Oleksiy Mykhaylychenko. A driving force in midfield during their 1988 European Championship campaign, Mykhaylychenko sustained a broken shoulder in a warm-up match against Israel three weeks before the tournament began. Lobanovskiy decided not to gamble on his fitness – a decision not universally popular among his squad.

Another factor, according to Kuznetsov, was the impact of leaving their training base near Pisa for the heat of Bari down on the heel of Italy for that first match, where, as he puts it, 'We were out of breath there.'

Indeed, Lobanovskiy's faulty planning is widely cited. He had seen his team run out of steam at the previous World Cup in Mexico – they scored nine goals in the first round, and finished above eventual semi-finalists France, but then failed to match Belgium for stamina in the last sixteen – and so, he took a different approach now. It was, in mitigation, an approach which had borne fruit at the 1988 European Championship when the USSR reached the final.

Kuznetsov explains, 'Lobanovskiy made a mistake in planning the training loads. In 1986, we smashed everyone in the group stage but lacked the right physical conditions against Belgium [in a 4-3 defeat]. He learned from that, and at the Euros in 1988, we started still "under load" and were meant to reach our peak later in the tournament. In 1990, he seemed to have planned for the same – qualify from the group with our experience, character and individual qualities, and then peak in the knockout stages.'

Yet, this Soviet team was now two years older – to be precise, the second-oldest team of that World Cup behind the Republic of Ireland. And, as Kuznetsov observes, 'It's not a joke to say that one year under Lobanovskiy counted as three.' The 4-0 victory over Cameroon in their final group fixture counted for nothing.

THE HEALTH OF THE ENTIRE SOVIET GAME DETERIORATED IN the years that followed 1990, mirroring the wider effects of the Soviet Union's disintegration.

Indeed, the USSR team ended 1990 with a friendly match a week before Christmas, against Bayern Munich at the Olympic Stadium – scene of their 1988 European Championship final appearance – which raised over £400,000 for a relief fund organised by Bundesliga clubs to provide food parcels to stricken Soviet citizens.

By the start of the 1991 season, sixteen of the USSR's 1990 World Cup squad had moved abroad. Dynamo Kyiv, Soviet champions for the final time in 1990, lost nine internationals in the space of seven months. Clubs, suddenly deprived of state subsidies, had to generate revenue, and the appeal of western hard currency was obvious.

Kuznetsov was one of the ones to depart. 'I wasn't actually dying to go,' he recounts, 'but I went to Lobanovskiy asking if there were any offers, and he said, "Yes, it's time for you to go as well. There's a good offer for you." He told me that Graeme Souness and Rangers had spotted me at the European Championship in 1988 and followed me closely.

'I was sceptical about it as we knew almost nothing about the Scottish league in the USSR. Also, I knew Bayern wanted me and some Dutch clubs too – but Lobanovskiy convinced me, saying that this club really wanted me and had offered a five-year deal, which was the first time for a Soviet player. The other guys were mostly offered one or two-year contracts.

'I followed his advice, and he was right in the end. I had good years in Scotland though I never returned to my usual level after my knee injury [an ACL rupture sustained in his second match].'

The 1991 season was the last of the Soviet Higher League. Already in 1990, the leading Georgian teams, Dinamo Tblisi and Guria Lanchkuti, had quit, together with Lithuania's Zalgiris Vilnius. In November 1991, a month before the confirmation of the dissolution of the Soviet Union was confirmed, the USSR played their final match, a 3-0 European Championship qualifying victory over Cyprus.

Andrei Kanchelskis, who had signed for Manchester United eight months earlier, struck the third and final goal. 'When we went to Sweden for the European Championship, we had no anthem,' says Kanchelskis. 'We played as the CIS [Commonwealth of Independent States].'

Kanchelskis, in 1990, had been part of the USSR team that won the European Under-21 Championship, the country's final piece of football silverware. They beat Yugoslavia 7-3 on aggregate in the final. Kanchelskis had scored the final goal there too. Two of Yugoslavia's scorers over the two legs – Davor Šuker and Robert Jarni – would play in a World Cup semi-final eight years later for Croatia. Kanchelskis played in teams that finished bottom of their group in both the 1992 and 1996 European Championships.

'The system broke, the country broke, and it created problems,' he adds. 'Each of the different countries – Azerbaijan, Belarus, and so on – had two or three good players. Later, you see Ukraine had [Andriy] Shevchenko and [Serhiy] Rebrov, Georgia had [Kakha] Kaladze, Belarus had [Aleksandr] Hleb. If these players played together, you'd have a different story.'

Russia is a big country in its own right – 142.9 million was the count in the 2010 census – but Evgeny Lovchev says its football misses the breadth of quality and competition that existed in the Soviet championship. 'The Caucasus was like Latin American football. Ukraine was like Germany and Holland. There were very strong teams, and you were competing against them.

'When you had the government in Kremlin, they'd be teasing each other. Everybody wanted to win. It wasn't about the money when cars and apartments were given to the players. It was so at the next Politburo meeting they could say, "Hey, we're the best now."'

To illustrate the point, the success of Dinamo Tblisi, victors in the 1981 European Cup Winners' Cup, coincided with the football-loving Eduard Shevardnadze's time as First Secretary of the Georgian Communist Party. Such rivalries, adds Lovchev, were now lost. 'Suddenly, Ukraine had independence, and they were playing weak teams. Moscow was the same story. We didn't have a top league any more.'

Spartak Moscow, European Cup semi-finalists in 1991 after eliminating Napoli and Real Madrid, dominated the first decade of the Russian Premier League yet suffered, says Lovchev, for the lack of credible competition. 'Spartak could take young talent from the ex-Soviet Union, players from Ukraine like [Viktor] Onopko, but for a good level of football, you need rivalry.'

During my interviews with both Lovchev and Vagiz Khidiatullin, neither man expresses any consternation over Roman Abramovich's use of Russian resources to transform a football club in London – Chelsea – during the past fifteen years. 'Here in Russia, there's absolutely no profit from football,' is Lovchev's argument while Khidiatullin notes Abramovich's past investment in youth programmes in Russia. This includes the Konoplyov football academy, which received contributions from Abramovich's 'National Academy of Football' fund until 2013 and which produced current international Alan Dzagoev.

Where there is obvious regret from both is in the simple recollection of something more tangible to them that has been lost – the great Spartak-Dynamo Kyiv duels played out in front of 100,000 crowds, which were a highlight of the Soviet football calendar.

In the 2016/17 Russian Premier League season, the average attendance was 11,415. Only Spartak Moscow, the so-called 'People's Club' of Russian football, averaged upwards of 20,000 – 32,760, to be precise. The relative poverty of Russian club football was underlined in the week after the Kremlin's staging of the 2018 World Cup draw, as Spartak suffered the heaviest defeat by any Russian team in UEFA's club competitions when crushed 7-0 by Liverpool in a Champions League group fixture at Anfield.

Back on Moscow's Marosejka Street, under a sky thick with snow, Vagiz Khidiatullin points the way to the old Lubyanka Building with its KGB history.

Then the future intrudes into our conversation. 'I think it will help,' he says of the 2018 World Cup. 'That's normal. It'll improve the infrastructure of the cities, the logistics, the stadiums.

'We're finding ourselves,' he adds. 'We're getting stronger. There's always somebody who tries to stop that. It's time for people to stop telling us what not to do.'

If that suggests defiance, his tone is measured. He has a strong conviction that money does not hold all the answers. In his own life, as a USSR footballer, his motivation came from elsewhere. 'If you do what you love and don't betray that, all the good things will follow.' It is a philosophy taken from a different time, but a hopeful one all the same.

Walls come tumbling down
Part 2 – Romania

'HOW MUCH? IN ROMANIA I HAD A CONTRACT OF ONE THOUSAND dollars per year. There's no comparison. It was maybe four hundred times more – from a thousand dollars to four hundred thousand dollars, with a car and a house. They gave me an Alfa Romeo 164.'

Florin Răducioiu is responding to the question of just how much his life changed, materially, in the wake of the 1990 World Cup, a tournament which secured him and fifteen of his Romania teammates a new future in the west of Europe – in his case, with a transfer to Serie A side Bari from Dinamo Bucharest.

He calls over to his old friends in the lounge area of Cardiff's Copthorne Hotel to double-check his calculations. Parked at nearby tables are some of Romanian football's famous names from the early 90s: Gheorghe Popescu, Dan Petrescu and Ilie Dumitrescu, the last of these three catching the eye in a nightclub-owner ensemble of navy blazer, shiny grey slacks and blue loafers.

They have gathered here in the Welsh capital, scene of a decisive Romanian World Cup qualifying victory in 1993, to discuss old times and watch the evening's Champions League final between Juventus and Real Madrid.

Summer 1990 was a moment in time when a world of pinch-me

possibilities was opening up to this generation of footballers from a country suddenly stripped of the closed borders put in place by the freshly removed dictator, Nicolae Ceauşescu.

As a consequence, their team hotel in Telese – a town famous for its hot springs down in the Campania region of southern Italy – became a magnet for deal-makers.

'It was six months after the fall of Ceauşescu, and it was very difficult,' says Răducioiu. 'For us in the hotel, it was a disaster because many club directors and agents practically came to our rooms to make offers to us.'

Today, Răducioiu is a youthful 48: trim, tanned and gregarious; then, he was the second-youngest player to kick a ball at Italia '90 and sharing a room with Ioan Lupescu, a Dinamo teammate and latterly chief technical officer of UEFA.

'Lupo talked to Bayer Leverkusen in the room and I was on the other side talking to Anderlecht,' recounts Răducioiu, briefly a West Ham United player later in the decade. 'There was no control. We had a programme, but it was a mess. But even with that happening, we qualified and we played well. It's true, all the players wanted to go abroad to the west. Maybe we were more focused on signing contracts than playing football.' And in his case, getting an Alfa Romeo when he did not even know how to drive.

The sense of a football Wild West is underlined by Lupescu's contribution to this tale. Neither of the room-mates had an agent and their negotiating skills were rather rudimentary. Lupescu smiles, 'I was with Răducioiu in my room, and one day, the manager from Anderlecht came. Răducioiu said, "OK, I'll come to you, but we speak tomorrow".

'The guy came two days later with a contract but Răducioiu had changed his mind and said, "I don't want to come any more." The guy was shouting, so we kicked him out of the room. He was the manager of Anderlecht! It was fun to kick the manager of Anderlecht out of our room. I was twenty-one; Răducioiu was twenty. We didn't realise what we were talking about.

'I remember especially after the first match when we beat USSR, there was massive interest in our players. We had a different offer every day, but we didn't realise what it meant, to be honest. Reiner Calmund, a really great person [from Leverkusen], came to my training camp, and in fifteen minutes I signed a contract.

Just like that.

'It was for us really an adventure, and this is why '90 was something special for us. The country was starting a new direction, and we footballers as well. It was like a bazaar: everybody could join in. We didn't have a security guy. Today, if you try to go to the England or Germany team you'll find a couple of checks a kilometre from the hotel. With us, anybody could come.'

Another of their Dinamo teammates, Ioan Sabău, revealed to me that he reached agreement with Feyenoord by simply writing his demands, in Romanian, on a single sheet of paper and getting the Dutch club's president to sign it in front of him. Deal done, and not an agent or interpreter in sight.

The Bosman ruling was still five years away but, with the Iron Curtain falling, the westward flow of talent from eastern Europe had begun. Romania was an obvious target for prospectors and not just for their run to the round of sixteen in Italy. Steaua Bucharest had reached European Cup finals in 1986 and '89, winning the first via a penalty shootout against Terry Venables' Barcelona. Dinamo Bucharest were European Cup semi-finalists in 1984, losing to Liverpool, and reached the last four of the European Cup Winners' Cup in 1990. Universitatea Craiova got to the same stage of the UEFA Cup in 1983.

The exodus spearheaded by the transfer of Gheorghe Hagi, Steaua's star playmaker, to Real Madrid – a move confirmed before a ball had even been kicked in Italy – involved a crop of footballers about to flourish abroad, having grown up under a state-sponsored system about to break apart.

Lupescu explains: 'The best period of clubs in Romania was from '80 to '90, and only with Romanian players, only with Romanian coaches. These coaches never had access to education and information as we were closed, so something was good there. What was good? The education and dedication and payment for the youth structure under Ceauşescu was very good. We didn't have the nice stadiums and pitches like today. We played on an ash surface. The balls were a disaster. We never had heating. And we still produced better players. Now, we have better conditions and access to education, but no one invests any more in coaches and young talent. Was the previous system better?'

*

ROMANIA'S LAST PARTICIPATION AT A WORLD CUP LIES IN THE LAST century now, at France '98. Back in 1990, few would have foreseen the pessimism of today; not when the smell of freedom filled the air and unimagined opportunities knocked for the nation's footballers.

This is not to say there were no anxieties. 'To separate sport from politics is not easy,' read the introduction to Romania in the official tournament programme, and with good reason, with the country still feeling the tremors of the bloodiest of the Eastern Bloc's revolutions.

The previous December, mass protests across the country brought bloodshed, and then the fall of a dictator.

Ceaușescu was communism's King Canute, a centraliser opposed to the tide of reforms sweeping across eastern Europe. It was no accident that Romania was the last Warsaw Pact country visited by the Soviet Union's reformist leader, Mikhail Gorbachev, after he took office.

On 21 November 1989, he gave a six-hour speech at the start of the Romanian Communist Party (PCR) congress in which, amid 67 reported standing ovations, he urged members to maintain 'scientific socialism' in defiance of a carefully worded telegram from Moscow's Communist Party central committee. Yet the west's once favourite eastern European leader found his isolation deepening.

Three weeks earlier, he had seen East Germany's Communist government resign and the opening of the Berlin Wall. As the PCR congress ended on 24 November, he learned of the mass resignation of Czechoslovakia's Communist Party leaders. When he flew to Moscow for a meeting of Warsaw Pact countries on 4-5 December, he saw his call for an international debate on the communist movement rejected by Gorbachev.

His demise, when it came, was fast. Protests which began on 18 December in Timisoara, close to the borders with Yugoslavia and Hungary, had spread to Bucharest by the 21st. A day later, Ceaușescu – 'il Conducator', leader of the country since 1965, president since 1974 – fled Bucharest amid street battles. The helicopter carrying the 71-year-old and his wife Elena was ordered to land by the army. On Christmas Day, the couple were executed by a three-man firing squad after a hasty trial at the Targoviste military garrison.

In *Romania since the Second World War,* Romanian academic Florin

Abraham writes that 'the army abandoned its supreme leader, Ceauşescu, feeling humiliated by him and resenting being unwillingly turned into a tool of repression.' The chief of the Securitate, General Iulian Vlad, turned his back too. Yet the National Salvation Front which snatched power included former Communist Party officials, notably its leader, Ion Iliescu, while the new minister of defence, General Nicolae Militaru, had previously been exposed as an agent of the Soviet army intelligence service.

The Institute of the Romanian Revolution of December 1989 (IRRD) claims that 1,290 lives were lost overall in the chaos that continued until 31 December. Rumours swirled about foreign intervention and possible Soviet military aid even. Another theory is that rival army and Securitate factions contributed to the bloodshed.

Ioan Lupescu was in Cyprus with the Dinamo Bucharest squad when Ceauşescu's reign unravelled. The players could not go back until the restoration of calm at Otopeni Airport, scene of heavy gun fighting. And, as the club sponsored by the Securitate, Romania's secret police, they had no idea what to expect on their return.

'After two weeks, they opened the airport and, being the team of the Securitate, we expected everybody would blame us,' recalls Lupescu, who was Dinamo's captain. 'A lot of young army people died in the airport. They always say it was terrorists, but they never found any terrorists in Romania. There were some fights between the army and Securitate, and they killed twenty or thirty young officers.

'We thought we'd be blamed, so we brought food from Cyprus – chocolate and fruit – and when we got there and handed over these gifts, everybody was applauding us. We'd done nothing, and then you realise how important football is.'

Lupescu, speaking to me over a coffee in the canteen at UEFA's glass-and-steel headquarters in Nyon, adds, 'It was a coup d'état. A revolution. But I'd say also in this context, if you remember perestroika, I'm sure some forces from outside used this revolution to get rid of the regime. I'm pretty sure something was behind it, not only coming from [within] the population. We were the only country where we killed our dictators.'

The flow of troubling news continued after the squad's departure for the

World Cup. At the end of May, there were lives lost when an earthquake struck the town of Focșani in eastern Romania. On 13 and 14 June, there were more deaths as the security forces, with the support of miners, fought to clear Bucharest's University Square of protestors opposed to the presence of ex-Communist party members in the newly elected government – a story that the *Daily Mirror* headlined with typical red-top sensitivity: 'Bloody battles rage again in Dracula city'. After the group-stage programme's conclusion, the Italian press reported that between 200 and 250 Romanians had stayed on in the country to seek political asylum.

Yet alongside this, adds Lupescu, 'there was so much enthusiasm in the country when it came to football.' After all, this was Romania's first World Cup since 1970, and Lupescu did not need telling what it meant. His late father, Nicolae, had played in that team in Mexico, a team who returned home as heroes after a victory over Czechoslovakia and narrow defeats by England and Brazil. 'I remember they played old boys' games in front of full stadiums – one hundred thousand went to the national stadium in Bucharest just to see them play,' he says.

Two decades on, with a new Lupescu on the scène, Romanians had a new side to be proud of. In November 1989, they beat a strong Denmark team 3-1 in Bucharest to earn their World Cup place and make amends for missing out on the 1986 finals by a single point when Northern Ireland earned a 0-0 draw in their last qualifier away against an already Mexico-bound England. (An outcome, incidentally, that prompted pungent mutterings from Romania coach Mircea Lucescu, evidently unconvinced by Northern Ireland defender Alan McDonald's finger-jabbing assertion in a post-match interview that, 'Anyone who says that's a fix can come and see me.')

*

IT IS INTRIGUING REVISITING THE LANDSCAPE OF THE ROMANIAN game pre-1990, a place of government football factories and sinister machinations dominated by Bucharest's Big Two. Romania's World Cup squad included seven players from Steaua and ten from Dinamo Bucharest, making them the best-represented club at Italia '90.

'It was always decided between Steaua and Dinamo,' says Lupescu of the Romanian title squabbles. 'Dinamo were champions three times in a row from

'82 to '84. In 1990, we were so strong we won the double and played in the semi-final of the Cup Winners' Cup against Anderlecht. Five or six of the eleven were in their early twenties. Maybe if we'd stayed together we had a chance of getting to the final of the European Cup.'

As the team of the Securitate, Dinamo's players received privileges beyond public reach. They had ready access to US dollars at a time when possession of a foreign currency could lead to arrest. They jumped to the front of the queue for cars too – albeit the state-approved Dacia 1300. (Dacia, as Răducioiu explains to me, was the name by which the Romans knew Romania.)

Jonathan Wilson, writing in his illuminating book on football in eastern Europe, *Behind The Curtain,* said that the Securitate bugged Steaua's club offices throughout the 1980s. Steaua had their own power source in Valentin Ceaușescu, son of the the head of state. After his appointment as club president, Steaua won five successive league titles. He set up a sponsorship deal with Ford and, but for his father Nicolae, would have established another groundbreaking arrangement with Fiat. According to Wilson, '...had it not been for the intervention of Nicolae Ceaușescu, who decided the plan was too capitalistic, Steaua would have sold Hagi to Juventus in 1988 in return for funding to establish a Fiat car plant in Bucharest.'

It was in that same year, 1988, that Ceaușescu Jr brought the Romanian Cup final to a premature end by ordering his Steaua players off the pitch after the annulment of Gavril Balint's late winning goal for offside.

'We were one-one, and near the end we scored a goal,' recalls Miodrag Belodedici, the stylish libero of that Steaua side. 'Everybody was celebrating, but in the end, the assistant referee said it was offside. Valentin called the coach and captain over, and told them we had to leave the field and go to the dressing rooms.'

Ioan Lupescu offers a Dinamo perspective: 'The referee waited fifteen minutes according to the regulations, and they didn't come back, so he blew his whistle, and it finished three-nil to Dinamo. The funny thing is, the National Stadium had an athletics track, so now we're waiting for the officials from the federation to come. We were there, with one hundred thousand people in the stadium, waiting for a cup on a table, and nobody is there to give us the cup. For five or ten minutes, we stayed there like idiots, but then our captain and goalkeeper [Dumitru] Moraru took the cup. We did one lap, went to the fans and then back to dressing room.

'We took the cup to a restaurant to celebrate, and after midnight, we got the first edition of the newspapers, which said there was an edict imposed by President Ceauşescu that the cup had to go to Steaua.' Today the 1988 final stands in the record books as a draw.

Following the 1989 revolution, and the deaths of Nicolae and Elena Ceauşescu, Steaua forward Marius Lăcătuş sheltered their bereaved son Valentin in his apartment.

Speaking to me from Bucharest, Lăcătuş says, 'He was someone who was loved by us, and if you can help, you will do. He was like a big brother for us. You could talk to him without any pressure, and you'd never think for a minute he was the son of Ceauşescu. For us, he was a friend, he was always close to us. There were days he'd be at the training ground before us, and he'd go home last. He was always there watching training, listening to what was being said within the squad.'

Miodrag Belodedici notes, 'When he came to watch the game, the referees had to be careful. He helped us.'

Belodedici, whose easy manner matches the on-field composure he displayed at Steaua and later Red Star Belgrade, has some rich anecdotes of a period when he won the European Cup with both clubs. 'In that era,' he says, 'the countries from the east had good teams – the Russians, Romania, Yugoslavia. The military and police clubs had the chance to pick up the best players. We were lucky also in that the English clubs were banned.'

He recalls Steaua returning to Bucharest after their 1986 European Cup triumph and every player receiving an upgrade on their Dacia – in the form of a second-hand army SUV. 'They got them from military barracks, reconditioned them, and we all got one. Country people would drive them out in the fields and the military too, but it wasn't for the city, and every player sold his car – some in a week, some in three days – and we got a lot of money. This old fellow came with a bag full of money to the club, and we had to go with him to a notary to sell the car.

'We stopped in front of the notary to see how much money there was, and suddenly, two policemen appeared and opened my car doors, and it was,

"Get out of here! Hands up! Nobody moves!" At least until they realised who I was. I explained I was selling the car and we were sorting out the papers, but it shows you how vigilant they were. The Securitate functioned pretty well.

'Every month, I had my salary and you got a bonus if you played and won,' he continues. 'I had an apartment too – a one-room apartment, at first, paid by the state. We didn't have contracts but were happy we were playing football.

'What we had was we could go abroad. We'd buy trousers or a nice shampoo. Perfume was too expensive. We bought VCRs, and some players would buy two or three and sell them back at home. Some would buy cigarettes – Kent, Marlboro – and they'd sell them to get more money. We all had the same car. In the summer, we went to the Black Sea and in the winter to the mountains.'

For Belodedici, it was not enough. By the time Italia '90 came round, he was living in Belgrade following his flight into exile in neighbouring Yugoslavia.

He had grown up in a family of Serbian ethnicity in Socol, a village beside the Danube and close to the border with Yugoslavia. 'You'd get the *Pink Panther* and *Tom and Jerry,* whereas on Romanian TV, the Russian cartoons weren't as good,' he says, smiling beneath a mop of dark hair.

To adult eyes, there were more disturbing divisions. 'I left the country because I didn't like the system. I couldn't see the future. We played football, but if someone better came, they just got rid of you. We had no opportunity to grow. We could see they played good football in Spain or Italy or Germany, but they wouldn't let us go elsewhere. You couldn't make a business with your money or buy a flat and rent it. You couldn't open a restaurant.

'The Yugoslavians could go abroad when they were older, but not in Romania. You couldn't own two apartments. You'd go out to discos but at eleven-thirty or midnight you had to leave and they'd let in the foreigners who paid in dollars. Footballers who knew people could stay, but the normal Romanians had to go.

'We didn't have passports at home. They were in the club, and when we went through customs, they gave us them, and then got them back. I asked for my passport once to go with my family to Yugoslavia, and they wouldn't let me have it.'

Eventually Belodedici succeeded in persuading Steaua officials to give him his passport so he could accompany his mother – who had a permit to cross into Yugoslavia – on a visit to relatives. Instead, with his sister in tow, he escaped to Belgrade.

There, he went to a match at Red Star Belgrade and approached the club's technical director, Dragan Džajić. 'I explained I'd come to Yugoslavia with my sister and asked for political exile. He just looked at me, so I told him my name. "OK, you played in the national team and Steaua. What position do you play?" "Libero."

'He asked me if we had pro contracts in Romania. I said that we were just semi-pros. He said, "Good, but you're going to have to wait for the transfer."' FIFA rules meant a year's ban for breach of contract.

It was the fear of further punishment that precluded his involvement in the World Cup in Italy. Whereas Czechoslovakia's World Cup squad featured Ivo Knoflíček and Lubos Kubík, two players who had gone into exile before that country's Velvet Revolution, uncertainty over whether or not Belodedici had been found guilty of military desertion – having quit the army club, Steaua – thwarted his hopes. 'They came to speak to me from Romania and wanted to take me to Italy. but the authorities in Yugoslavia didn't want me to go as they said I had a military credential and didn't know if I'd been sentenced to prison. It could have been three, four, five years as I was technically a deserter and they'd not received the papers. In the end, they told me I wasn't guilty. I thought about it a lot.'

When Belodedici did play at a World Cup four years later, it was his penalty, saved by Sweden goalkeeper Thomas Ravelli, that sealed Romania's defeat in a quarter-final shootout in Pasadena, following a 2-2 draw. 'They say I missed the penalty but I tell them I didn't miss – the goalkeeper saved it,' he grins ruefully. 'That's a sad point for me. There were just five minutes to the end, and they got that goal for the equaliser, which was a mistake from our goalkeeper [Florin Prunea, who was outjumped by Sweden scorer Kennet Andersson], and then the penalties. We went into the history books in Romania, but we could have gone down in world history.'

*

THAT USA '94 CAMPAIGN, FEATURING A FAMOUS 3-2 SECOND ROUND victory over Argentina, was the apex for a group of players reaping the benefits of a now defunct system. Belodedici, a grateful alumnus of the Luceafărul school in Bucharest, explains how it worked.

'The state took the best boys, the most talented, brought them to Bucharest, and worked with them for a couple of years until the age of eighteen. We were fortunate as we had our team, at seventeen, competing in the second division, playing second division teams every weekend, only we didn't get awarded points. It helped us to grow up.

'During the week we got up at seven, went to school, and then trained every afternoon. Sometimes in the morning also. It was Soviet-style – physical and technical. I remember working with the ball, but I remember a lot of running too in the national stadium – up and down, up and down. The school was next door, and the canteen was five hundred metres away. In the centre, there were the gymnasts too, like Nadia Comăneci, and the weightlifters. All the sports people from the different national squads.'

This schooling, together with the experience gained in 1990 and during the intervening four years abroad, is his explanation for the team's success at USA '94. 'The players from '94 had gone through that – they'd gone through the long camps; they were used to going away for a month and working and working, so when they went to compete they were strong. It was like in *Rocky IV* – we'd go to the mountains and lift logs and go running in the snow with Steaua. We'd be there two weeks, us and the bears. Now, they don't do it. Now, we have the western system. We were like the Soviets.'

There was another reason for their success, a man in the year below Belodedici at Luceafărul, Gheorge Hagi. He was 25 at Italia '90; four years later in the United States, he would score exceptional goals in wins over Colombia and Argentina.

'I played with great players like [Franco] Baresi but I tell you honestly, Hagi was the best,' says Florin Răducioiu, beginning a brief Romanian rhapsody. 'It was everything – the way he could see what he should do with the ball before he actually touched it ... technique, fantasy, fantastic passing, amazing shooting, the biomechanics of his left foot. They called him the Maradona of the Carpathians. He was also our leader. Popescu was a leader too, but Hagi was our captain. When our team didn't play well, we needed Hagi to invent something. He was our joker. If he'd been born in Italy or England, he would have won the Ballon D'Or.

For me, he was a pure footballer. I exist thanks to him, really.'

With Romania, Hagi had the liberty to express himself in a free role behind the forwards granted him by Emerich Jenei in 1990 and later Anghel Iordănescu. 'That's probably why he was successful in the national team and maybe not so much in Barcelona and Real Madrid where he had to do the defensive part,' argues Ioan Lupescu.

Jenei, Romania's 1990 coach, had been appointed at the behest of Valentin Ceauşescu, following his success in leading Steaua to the European Cup. 'He was not a fantastic tactician, but he tried to create a good spirit,' adds Lupescu. 'I imagine it wasn't easy to get players from Dinamo together with players from Steaua.'

Marius Lăcătuş, scorer of one of Steaua's spot-kicks in their 2-0 shootout win over Barcelona in 1986, says, 'Mr Jenei was someone you wouldn't answer back to – any decision he took you couldn't dispute because he was a gentleman. He was a coach who liked technical players. He wanted to see us with the ball at our feet.'

Lăcătuş would play a pivotal role in Jenei's Romania winning their opening game in Italy, a victory achieved despite the absence of the suspended Hagi. Their opponents in Bari for that first Group B fixture on 9 June were Russia – a match-up that prompted a 'Perestroika and Freedom' headline in the *Gazzetta dello Sport* on the day of the game. It would be the final World Cup encounter between two nations of the Warsaw Pact prior to its dissolution.

If coach Jenei offered an optimistic pre-match declaration that his team had the qualities 'to get at least to the quarter-finals', Florin Răducioiu remembers anxiety among his players. 'It was like in '94 in the first game against Colombia. We thought we'd lose. I had the same feeling with Russia. They were a very strong team. Lăcătuş was the best player that day. We always played very well on the counter-attack – like the goals against Colombia and the United States in '94. We played direct to Lăcătuş. We surprised ourselves.'

It was a match where the Soviets would rue their first-half profligacy as three minutes before half-time Lăcătuş, released on the left side of the box by Ioan Sabău, drove the ball past goalkeeper Rinat Dasayev at the near post.

Lăcătuş's strongest memory is of the heat in Bari. 'What I can say is it was scorching hot. For the first half-hour, we started really, really badly. I don't know why but I personally didn't start well at all, but after scoring the first goal the confidence comes.'

Lăcătuş's second goal after 57 minutes was a penalty kick awarded incorrectly for a handball outside the Soviet box. 'I was expecting him to blow for a free-kick, but when I saw him point to the penalty spot I wasn't going to tell him the handball was outside the box,' Lăcătuş recalls.

His speed and aggressive running had forced Vagiz Khidiatullin into his handball; later the Fiorentina-bound player missed a clear opportunity of a hat-trick when teed up by Răducioiu in front of goal.

In a group of upsets, Romania had surprised themselves. Five days later, though, came another, less agreeable surprise. Hagi was back, but Roger Milla's Benjamin Button brilliance consigned them to a 2-1 defeat against Cameroon. This left Jenei's men requiring a draw from their final group match against Argentina. The venue? Naples.

'It was in the home of Maradona,' Lupescu recalls. 'From the hotel to the stadium it was twenty minutes, and on the bus, nobody spoke. I was sitting with Michael Klein, I tried to speak, but my mouth was blocked. It was something in my stomach, probably a bit of fear. With Romania then, when we were afraid we were very good. When we were optimistic, it wasn't very good. We were very afraid against Argentina.

'In Romania, all the nation was watching, everything stopped. I was with [Iosif] Rotariu, and we tried to mark Maradona in the midfield. You could feel he wasn't fit like four years before, but it was unbelievable how he touched the ball with his left foot. I never saw a player like this.'

Maradona crossed himself, sank to his knees, and held two clasped hands to the heavens after his corner kick led to Pedro Monzón's headed breakthrough in the 62nd minute. Romania had their own source of inspiration. Hagi's back-heel to Lupescu sparked the move which brought their equalising goal six minutes later. Lăcătuş crossed, Sabău headed the ball back across goal and Gavril Balint finished. 'We had our Maradona, Hagi, and he gave us confidence from the start,' says Sabău, source of the assist. 'He was the leader for our whole generation, on and off the pitch.'

*

TODAY, HAGI HOLDS THAT MANTLE ONCE MORE. IN 2017, VIITORUL, the club he established eight years earlier, won the Romanian league title. He invested €10m of his own money to develop the club, based in his home city of Constanța on the Black Sea. The first team was intended originally only as a finishing school for the academy, yet it gathered strength and momentum.

Viitorul means 'future' in Romanian and Hagi's wish was to do something no club had done in the post-Communist era: develop young talent. Some individuals have gained immense wealth in post-1990 Romania. Yet, the old collective enterprises – of which sport was one – have dwindled.

'Under communism, everything was the property of the government,' explains Răducioiu. 'I'll give you an example – 1984 in Los Angeles, Romania won twenty gold medals, sixteen silver, seventeen bronze [to finish second in the medal table]. Last year [2016] in Rio, one gold. What is the explanation? The government paid for all the infrastructure. The young people loved to do sport. We didn't have any other distractions.'

Răducioiu, now living back in Bucharest and working as a football agent, adds, 'Now I see more poverty than in those years. You can see nice hotels and nice cars, and the people dress differently. There is a huge difference between the rich and poor, and it makes me sad. Bucharest has changed a lot, but they don't know how to invest money, even with football. It's the same context as society and politics. We need good people to manage our football as with our economy.

'Hagi is the only positive in Romania at this moment. This crazy man invested his money in his academy. He won the Romanian championship for the first time. He started to sell good players to Belgium, Spain, Portugal. He told me, "I'm crazy, but I love football. I don't have only two kids, I have three hundred kids." It's a very romantic story.

'At Steaua, Dinamo, Craiova, nobody invested in youth teams. Many presidents brought, with respect, a lot of African players, second-class imports. It's not a nationalistic thought. He invested in our kids, and if two or three more club presidents had done this, the level would be better right now.'

It is a common complaint among his generation. In the communist era, every second division club, for instance, had the obligation to field one seventeen-year-old in their starting lineup and another on the bench. Today, the reduction of

Liga I from eighteen to fourteen clubs has meant fewer places than ever for Romanian prospects in top-flight squads.

Miodrag Belodedici has an ambassadorial role within the Romanian Football Federation but he adds his voice to the lament. 'What the state did was very good for us boys,' he stresses, recalling once more his Luceafărul days. 'In terms of sport, the country has lost out. In freedom we've won, we can go where we want. A lot of people have left Romania, though, and families have split up. In small towns and villages, you only see old people. All the young people have left. We have multi-multi-millionaires, but they've stolen a lot.'

Romania is the second poorest country in the European Union, and frustration over perceived government weakness in tackling corruption led to a series of mass protests in Bucharest in February 2017. Football, inevitably, suffers too. Belodedici adds, 'You've had people who took money from the bank and put it into the club. The money from the club they put in their own pockets. This has happened in important cities in Romania.'

During this past decade alone, Universitatea Craiova, Petrolul Ploieşti and Politehnica Timişoara – all three of whom were UEFA Cup qualifiers in 1990 – have had to start over under new names lower down the ladder. Rapid Bucharest have suffered both insolvency and bankruptcy in this time.

Perhaps nothing sums up the state of the club game more than the fact that the name of Steaua Bucharest is no longer found in the Liga I standings. Instead, there is a club named FCSB, owned by Gigi Becali, a controversial billionaire property magnate. Becali gained control of Steaua in 2003, five years after the cutting of the club's ties with the army sports association, CSA Steaua Bucharest.

In 2006, a drawn-out legal battle between the army and Becali began as the ministry of defence started to investigate the deal with which Becali had acquired the club. By 2011, a series of legal actions were under way which challenged both the sale and the use of the Steaua colours and brand. In December 2016, a court confirmed that the ministry of defence had the rights to use the Steaua brand and symbols related to it, prompting Becali to rename his club FCSB.

In 2016/17, Steaua were starting over in the fourth division of Romanian football, with the help of two of their heroes of 1986 – captain Ştefan Iovan as sporting director and Marius Lăcătuş as general manager.

'I felt it was time for me to give something to the club where I had my greatest moments as a player and which formed me as a person, so when they asked for my help, it was a pleasure to say yes,' says the latter.

This new/old club play their games at the original Steaua Sports complex, on a pitch flanked by small grandstands and sited in the shadow of the Stadionul Steaua, scene of European Cup semi-final victories over Anderlecht and Galatasaray.

Lăcătuş played in both of those matches. Today, he oversees more intimate affairs. 'There've been games with one thousand people, one thousand two hundred; but we've played midweek games too, on a Wednesday lunchtime when it's very hard for people to get there, so you'll get five or six hundred people. For a fourth division team, it's not bad at all.

'We have the fans who are very close to the club who've bought season tickets. Maybe a thousand people who are paying for those and contribute with their money. We have people who sponsor the team with small amounts. We have three grass pitches and one artificial pitch, so there's everything they need to little by little get up from the fourth division and get to where we want to be which is the first division – whether that's in three years or four, you can never say.'

Lăcătuş hopes this can be achieved with a youthful squad that includes more than twenty teenagers recruited in summer 2017 from Regal Sport Club Bucharest, a partner club of Spain's Atlético de Madrid. 'The oldest is twenty-six, so we are trying to build a team with quality but also a team for the future because we've got three or four big years ahead of us, and we don't want to be changing every year. They don't earn a lot of money, but their contract is for three or four years and if they keep climbing to the first division, when they get there, they can earn good money.'

Like Hagi at Viitorul, it is another glimmer of good news, at least, in a country whose football has shrunk in stature. Lăcătuş, the protagonist of that opening win at Italia '90, knows this as well as anybody.

Before our conversation ends, he relates how it felt to take the European Cup back to Bucharest in May 1986. 'It was only when we got to the airport in Romania that I realised what we'd done. I was twenty-two, and when we got home and saw the people, I felt like crying. They'd been waiting hours to see us and see the trophy. In those times people didn't have much enjoyment, and sport was where people could go and enjoy themselves and talk. When Ceauşescu came back from trips abroad, people would go out and applaud him, but that day, we had more people waiting for us.'

Lăcătuş had taken one of only two successful spot-kicks in that European Cup final in Seville in 1986. The pity for Romania four years later was that he was not around for the shootout that decided their fate in their round of 16 tie against the Republic of Ireland in Italy. He actually ended the group stage of Italia '90 with more shots on goal – twelve – than any other player.

Could he have made the difference? 'In football, you never know. You can never say, "If Lăcătuş plays, Romania win." Look, we lost on penalties against Ireland, but we also beat Barcelona on penalties in the European Cup. You never know in life.'

American dreamers

'I'M WALKING OUT OF THE TUNNEL RIGHT ALONGSIDE PAOLO Maldini and I'm like, "Oh my God." Behind him are Baresi and Vialli, and I'm thinking, "I cannot believe I'm in this situation about to go play these guys."' If Hollywood were scripting the tale of the United States' 1990 World Cup adventure, there would be no better place for the story to conclude than the Stadio Olimpico in Rome on the evening of 14 June. It was an evening when, to build on forward Bruce Murray's recollection above, the youngest team at Italia '90, a team with an average age of 24 years and two months, stepped out in front of seventy thousand screaming, flag-swaying Italians, and kept their heads, their nerve, and their pride intact against a host nation with more glitter than a 1970s glam-rock band.

Only three members of coach Bob Gansler's starting XI had played club football abroad. Gansler himself had never been to a World Cup before. A year earlier, a handful of these players had competed at the Five-a-side World Cup. And here, they were standing in a tunnel eyeing nervously Franco Baresi, Paolo Maldini, Gianluca Vialli, and the rest. When Giuseppe Giannini drove Italy into an eleventh-minute lead, the young Americans could have collapsed. Four days earlier, they had hit the canvas, falling 5-1 against Czechoslovakia. This time, as Murray adds, they stayed on their feet. 'It was a moment where we said, "You know what, even if it's just for this one night, we were actually okay today; we were deserving of being on the field with this team."'

Peter Vermes, his partner in the US attack, remembers, 'There were moments in that game where we realised, "Holy shit, these guys are at a different level," and then other moments where we surprised ourselves. You take a person from a place that never has seen something, and now, all of a sudden, they see it.'

For the United States, this was the summer that a forty-year World Cup exile ended. Against host nation Italy, the global spotlight burned and in the 67th minute, the door opened for a Hollywood ending.

Walter Zenga, Italy's goalkeeper, failed to smother a Murray free-kick, and the ball ran to Vermes on the corner of the six-yard box. It was the freeze-frame moment, the slo-mo shot at glory. The American underdogs upsetting the odds. Except they didn't: the shot bounced off Zenga's backside and was booted clear by a defender. Does it matter? Not according to the *Gazzetta dello Sport* the next day. Its message was clear: 'We've discovered America.'

VERMES, THE MAN WHO MIGHT HAVE SILENCED THE STADIO Olimpico, has gained enough perspectives to act as a perceptive guide through this American tale.

He played in the first season of Major League Soccer (MLS) with New York/ New Jersey MetroStars in 1996. He has served Sporting Kansas City, as manager or technical director, for more than a decade. On the day that we speak, his club has just cut the ribbon on a new twelve-pitch football facility, Wyandotte Sporting Field, for the use of some of its fifteen affiliated junior clubs which, between them, cater for up to 50,000 young enthusiasts from pre-school age to eighteen.

A brand-new $90m training centre for the first team, to be shared with US Soccer, opened at the start of 2018. For all the dismay over the national team's failure to qualify for Russia 2018, ending a run of World Cups that began with 1990, the bigger picture remains positive.

'That first year was amazing, the crowds were incredible, everything was incredible,' Vermes says, remembering the MLS's early days. 'The problem is the level of play didn't live up to what the interest was, and it fell away after that. It started to decline year after year. All of a sudden, it started to take a big jump in 2006, 2007, 2008. It just started to really progress.

'There's been incredible leadership behind the scenes, and also some incredible owners that have been the catalyst for sustaining soccer through very difficult times, and at the same time helping it achieve levels that people never dreamed it'd ever get to. Now, we're at such a fast pace, and the landscape is changing every year in a very positive way. It'll be amazing to see where the game is in ten years.

'It's the most popular sport among all of our youth in the United States, and when you see the amount of money that owners are putting in to be a new franchise in this league, you understand the popularity, the growth potential of the sport, is absolutely incredible, and it's not stopping. We've sold out ninety-something odd games consecutively as an organisation at home.'

It was a different world that Vermes grew up in as a young soccer player in the States. In 1985, the year he turned nineteen, the North American Soccer League expired. It had provided his first idols, and not just any old ones. 'I had heroes – Pelé, Johan Cryuff, [Franz] Beckenbauer. I saw George Best and [Téofilo] Cubillas, I saw them all in the NASL.'

Vermes's parents were Hungarian immigrants; his father, Michael, had played with Ferenc Puskás at Honvéd.

'I had a much different childhood compared to a lot of other kids because my world was soccer. It wasn't baseball, basketball, American football. It was soccer 24/7/365. I would go and watch Cosmos at Giants Stadium; I would also go and watch the Philadelphia Atoms play at Veterans Stadium in Philadelphia.'

With the NASL's demise, however, there were no more footsteps to follow in. 'We never really had anybody to learn anything from,' he adds. 'There was no high-level professional league in the country, so it wasn't as if we were going to professional teams and gaining that knowledge.

'We were rather like gypsies. It's a funny term to use, but we were trying to do whatever we could, trial anywhere, just to try to make our mark. I was the first player ever in the United States to go over to Europe and play in Division One on a regular basis. I did it in Hungary and Holland.'

This was an era of soccer pioneers. Paul Caligiuri in Germany and Chris Sullivan in France and Hungary were two other US squad members to sample the European game in the late 80s. Then there was John Harkes, who became the first American to play in English football's top flight with Sheffield Wednesday, the club he joined shortly after Italia '90.

Harkes, like Vermes, was the son of a soccer-loving immigrant father – in his case, Jimmy Harkes, a Scot from Dundee – and he recalls a boyhood in which professional football was a distant dream.

With the NASL no more, Harkes would marvel at VHS tapes of the English league, and his favourite team Liverpool.

'Once a week, you'd put the video tapes in and see the history of Liverpool and the success they had and you'd think, "Wow, that would be brilliant, I'd love to do that – imagine playing soccer for a living, that would be pretty cool."'

Harkes meets me at Sheffield's Jury's Inn hotel during a visit to the UK from his home in North Virginia to take part in his old club's 150th birthday celebrations. The fact the email confirming our interview reaches my inbox at 3.50am points to the success of an anniversary dinner featuring old faces like Ron Atkinson, his first manager at Hillsborough, and teammates Chris Waddle and Nigel Pearson.

Despite that late finish, the good looks which meant he even made a mullet look presentable in the Italia '90 Panini sticker album are still intact as the fifty-year-old greets me at the hotel bar.

'Seeing Big Ron again was fantastic, because he was the one that opened the door for me,' he says of the previous night. 'With the first manager that signs you, you have that special connection. You're in debt to them forever.' A dynamic midfielder, Harkes spent much of his first season at Wednesday, 1990/91, filling in at right-back but ended it with a piece of history as the first American to play in – and win – a major cup final in England after the League Cup triumph over Manchester United.

He shushed a few people in the process. 'For a lot of people looking at an American trying to play their game that they invented, it was, "Go back home." There was a lot of stick. I wouldn't say prejudice against me, it was just non-belief: "What's he doing here?"'

What those sceptics did not know is that Harkes came from a place steeped in football, Kearny ('Car-nee,' Harkes corrects me) in New Jersey. In the 1990s, a sign on the main strip read 'Welcome to Kearny. Soccer Town, U.S.A.', and its billing was well-earned. Three of USA's Italia '90 squad came from this town of 36,000 inhabitants, ten miles west of Manhattan.

It is a place where football soaked into the micro-culture – along with fish and chip shops – after the arrival in the 19th century of Scottish and Irish immigrants seeking work in the mills and factories opened by two Scottish companies, Clark Thread Company and Nairn Linoleum. 'Scottish, English, and Irish came over there for textiles work and ended up staying, so it was the culture in the town,' Harkes explains.

'My dad was from Dundee and had played. Everybody else's father was involved in soccer, so they ended up coaching us, and so you just grew up [with it]. It was a real club. We changed downstairs at the pub, and then you'd come up and go to the [junior] games, and you'd come back and see the big team play.'

Even the club's name harked back to the wave of Scottish immigration: Thistle FC. 'I grew up in that environment. The whole town was a culture of soccer – we were playing soccer on the Little League fields and getting kicked off because they had the better grass.'

Harkes attended the same high school as future national-team goalkeeper Tony Meola and played for the Thistle teams with Tab Ramos, a colleague in the US midfield whose own father had played the game professionally in Uruguay. 'Tab lived three blocks up the road from me, and Tony was on the other side of town. Tab was the oldest, and I was a year younger than Tab. Tony and I didn't play a lot together on the club teams, but we overlapped in high school.'

Kearny, for its size, was unique, but it was not the only soccer hotspot at that time. South California, birthplace of the American Youth Soccer Organization, was another – and the source of 1990 squad members Paul Krumpe, Eric Wynalda and Caligiuri. Wherever they came from, though, the question for all of these players growing up was, *where can we go to with this?*

According to Krumpe, one of the Californian contingent, the best option for most players coming out of college was the Major Indoor Soccer League (MISL) where a young player could earn a basic salary of around $30,000 with built-in performance bonuses.

After graduating from UCLA with an Aerospace Engineering degree in 1986, he did just that, joining an MISL club in Chicago. He remembers, 'The US indoor league was terrific for helping me develop quicker foot skills and for playing at absolute full speed for two-minute shifts, then getting off the field to recover before re-entering for another two-minute shift. It was not great at developing guys to play outdoor for a full ninety minutes.'

The first major international experience for many of the group that made it to Italia '90 was at the 1988 Seoul Olympics. Ten players involved in the States' opening fixture, a 1-1 draw against Argentina, would travel to Italy two years later.

By autumn 1988, the US Soccer Federation had corralled a group of sixteen players and put them under contract to ensure their availability for national-team duty.

'That same core group became a part of the qualification for the 1990 World Cup, and during that process, it became evident that that group of guys had an opportunity to do something that hadn't been done in forty years – qualify for the World Cup,' recalls Peter Vermes.

Sunil Gulati, who was president of the USSF from 2006 until early 2018, had a telling role as chairman of the international games committee, working with the then incumbent, Werner Fricker, and the number of official matches against international opponents rose sharply: from just three in 1987, they ended 1988 having played an unprecedented thirteen.

The decision by FIFA, on 4 July 1988, to award the 1994 World Cup to the United States intensified the urge for improvement. 'There's no question there was a lot of internal pressure,' vouches Bruce Murray.

During a US team trip to Italy in 1989 to play friendly matches against Sampdoria and Roma – the first a defeat, the second a victory – the organisers of USA '94 met their Italia '90 counterparts and Clive Toye, president of the New York Cosmos in their 1970s pomp, underlined the need for Gansler's players to deliver qualification.

'We're planning to exploit the World Cup occasion to the maximum,' he said. 'We have to first of all unify our leagues, and then we must absolutely qualify ourselves to the final phase of the Italia '90 World Cup.'

First, though, in early 1989 they played in a different World Cup – the first FIFA World Championship for five-a-side football in the Netherlands. Today, it is called Futsal. The US team beat Italy, Argentina and Brazil en route to a semi-final defeat against their Dutch hosts. The eventual bronze medal won was the first for any US men's team in a FIFA competition.

The wheels were turning, and the next step was the appointment of the German-born Bob Gansler, US Under-20 coach and a long-time federation employee, as national coach on a full-time basis. There were eight qualifying games still to play.

Bruce Murray recalls a coach who combined a disciplinarian approach with a wicked sense of humour. 'The players who played for him loved him, but at the same time, he wasn't always press-friendly. He closed the locker room after our qualifier in Costa Rica. We had the *USA Today* and *Washington Post* covering the game, and he closed them out of the locker room.'

Gansler's assistant coach in qualifying was Dr Joe Machnik, today Fox Soccer's refereeing expert.

'He'd played on the Olympic team, on the pan-American team; he was a very respected coach here in America,' says Machnik of Gansler, who had arrived in the US as an eleven-year-old. 'He brought a system of play, a professional attitude to training sessions, scouting programmes. But still the federation was short of funds, and in the qualification phase we were still meeting only two or three days before a game.'

Given his modest means, Gansler would often source VHS tapes of upcoming opponents from Jim Trecker, a football writer and former New York Cosmos press officer, who had assembled a huge video library at his home.

The setting for home qualifying games was hardly ideal either. 'The games at St. Louis were played at St. Louis Soccer Park which was owned in part by the Budweiser beer company,' explains Machnik. 'There was no atmosphere – it was a wide-open field with bleacher-type seating.'

It was at St. Louis on 5 November 1989 that the US team stumbled on the qualifying trail. Needing a victory against El Salvador to secure their World Cup finals place, they drew 0-0. El Salvador had arrived in disarray. Due to budgetary constraints, they slept four to a room. Indeed, a St. Louis business actually paid for their travel fares.

According to the FIFA delegate's report of the match, there were rumours of cash incentives to the El Salvador players – from Trinidadian and Costa Rican intermediaries – to get a result.

History was in the offing, but only 8,500 spectators turned up.

Bruce Murray remembers it well. 'It was a very cold day, a small venue, and it couldn't have been a bigger letdown. They had nothing to play for; we had everything to play for, and we were terrible. We came out, we were flat, and I had a terrible game. And I'm quoted as saying just that – I learned that day to never be as frank again, because in *Soccer America* the next day, the headline was, "Murray: I had a terrible game."'

✳

FOR THE UNITED STATES, ARGUABLY THE BIGGEST MILESTONE ON the road to becoming a credible football nation was the final qualifying match for Italia '90 in Trinidad and Tobago. They faced a home team on the brink of history themselves.

The Strike Squad, as they were called, included two young players who would shine in European football: an eighteen-year-old Dwight Yorke, later to sprinkle goals and smiles on the Premier League with Aston Villa and then Manchester United, where he won the Champions League in 1999, and Russell Latapy, who won the Portuguese title with Bobby Robson's Porto and became a crowd favourite at Hibernian, Rangers and Falkirk in Scotland.

Widely remembered as a more talented team than the 'Soca Warriors' who reached the 2006 World Cup finals, this T&T side had only to draw the game to qualify. They held the same points' tally as the US but a stronger goal difference.

Harold Taylor, vice-president of the Trinidad and Tobago Football Association (TTFA), declared the day of the game a 'Red Day', urging people to wear the national colours. Gates opened at 11am, long before kick-off.

From an American perspective, 19 November 1989 is remembered as a momentous, into-the-lion's-den day of triumph. Take the scene that greeted the squad on arrival in Port of Spain. 'We were on a Pan-Am charter plane, and the pilot came on and said to us, "I just want you to be aware there are thousands of people at the airport and they're waiting for you guys,"' Bruce Murray remembers. 'From the airport all the way into town, they were ten deep, everyone dressed in red.'

Paul Krumpe, who, at 26, was the oldest player in the starting XI, relates, 'I still get goosebumps thinking about that day. The only songs being played on the radio were songs written by local reggae artists, bragging about going to Italy and the World Cup.

'Our phones rang throughout the night in our hotel rooms until we took them off the hook – locals wanting to make sure we weren't getting a good night's sleep.'

The next day, a tide of red rolled through the surrounding streets and into the National Stadium. 'Going down the hill to the stadium that day the bus was only going four miles an hour because there were so many people on both sides of the road,' says Murray.

There was a malign hand behind this mass of bodies: Jack Warner, the then TFFA general secretary, who would become, the following year, the president of CONCACAF.

The *Guardian* journalist David Conn, writing in his book *The Fall Of The House Of FIFA*, explains that, 'Terrible overcrowding outside and inside the stadium led to the accusation that Warner [...] had had 15,000 too many tickets printed and sold, leading to a judicial inquiry which never reported.'

Lasana Liburd, the CEO and editor of *Wired868.com*, a Trinidad and Tobago-based online newspaper, says a day that could have brought a big leap forward for Trinidadian football, had entirely the opposite effect: 'A lot of football fans never really returned to support the team. They felt they were cheated. There are some taxi drivers who today still drive with their World Cup tickets inside their car – a stub under the rear-view mirror, which is the ticket they'd have gone to the ground with but been told they couldn't get in.'

A T&T player's perspective comes from Clayton Morris, captain of the home team. He recounts the suffocating pressure that built as they left their base in Forest Reserve, fifty miles from Port of Spain. 'The entire country was in jubilation,' Morris says. 'The moment we left the camp in a small village in Forest Reserve, the people were there partying. People stopped in front of the bus and the bus spent maybe half an hour before it could go through. We didn't have any security arrangement in place to give us an escort. It was just the bus driver, the players on the bus, and that's it.

'When we reached the stadium, we saw people outside with genuine tickets in their hands – the same amount of people that were in the stadium – so that too really put added pressure on us. People blocked the bus from entering the stadium because they felt they were cheated. The army personnel came and formed an honour guard to allow us to exit the bus. We couldn't go out with our bags as we had to fight off people who were trying to hold on to us to stop us from entering the stadium. The soldiers went back afterwards and took our bags when we were safe inside the locker room.'

Inside the stadium, the overcrowding was obvious. 'When you looked at the stands, you realised something was wrong because you're not seeing any staircase; you're not seeing the fire personnel or the security personnel who are supposed to take charge,' Morris remembers. 'All we're seeing from the middle was just red.'

This was the context for the ninety minutes that followed. US forward Peter Vermes adds, 'There's one big thing that will never leave my mind, and that's when we got in the tunnel and lined up. I remember looking in the eyes of their players, and there was so much pressure on them from their whole country that they were big-time nervous. All the pressure was on them.'

Today, Jack Warner refuses to look Clayton Morris, captain of that T&T side, in the eye. 'If he sees me he turns his face, he will never look at me,' says Morris, who believes there is one very obvious reason.

According to Warner's autobiography, the day after the USA game, he received a visit at his home from Chuck Blazer, the American former FIFA executive committee member who turned whistleblower in the FIFA corruption scandal. Blazer, then CONCACAF general secretary, suggested that Warner stand as president of the federation. The timing of that encounter, within 24 hours of the US achieving their World Cup place at Trinidad's expense, still gnaws away at Morris given the circumstances surrounding that fixture.

He alleges that Warner organised the ticketing scam to ensure that even if the hosts side won, the dangerous levels of overcrowding would have meant the result was overturned.

'Just before our game, there was a game somewhere in one of the African countries. The stadium collapsed, and they gave the game to the opposing team because they oversold the place just as we did in '89,' says Morris. 'I think Jack Warner couldn't come to the players about match-fixing because we weren't entertaining that, so the best thing is to do what he did – the valid tickets he actually triple-printed. The rules were you had to sell ten per cent less than the capacity. Our stadium was holding 28,000, and we had nearly 40,000 people.'

Walter Gagg, who was then the world governing body's technical director and later became a FIFA director, insists the timing of the two events was 'pure coincidence'. Sepp Blatter himself told me he had no knowledge of Warner's ticketing scam – 'Ticketing, I don't remember' – but did recall the home crowd's gracious post-match applause for the US victors, which earned a FIFA Fair Play award.

The FIFA match delegate's report of the occasion details the pre-match fanfare and small army of steel drummers but does not mention the overcrowded venue, nor the decision by the Argentinian referee, Juan Carlos Loustau, brought in especially to oversee the fixture, to ignore first-half Trinidadian calls for a penalty following a trip by John Doyle on Philibert Jones.

That was not the only grievance of home coach Everald 'Gally' Cummings. As a player, he had tasted an acrid injustice with the T&T team who lost out on qualification for the 1974 World Cup with a 2-1 reverse in Haiti in which the visitors had four goals disallowed. El Salvadoran referee José Enrique and Canadian linesman James Higuet would both later receive life bans from FIFA. Sixteen years later, Cummings asked for the sprinklers to be turned on on the morning of the match, in the event it did not rain, but his request went ignored.

Morris elaborates, 'We had rain for the entire week, and all our preparation was on a slushy field. We knew it would be an advantage for us against the US, when you're slipping and sliding, and we'd handle those conditions better than they would. When we reached the stadium, the ground was dry.

'When the final whistle blew, I took the result as a man, as a sports person – but then years after, when you hear these stories, it really broke my heart.

'As you say, age brings reason. I saw what people have done over at FIFA over those periods. It makes you wonder if there were things that were put there so that we wouldn't qualify.'

✱

THE GOAL THAT PAUL CALIGIURI, THE US MIDFIELDER, SCORED TO take his team past Trinidad and Tobago went down in American soccer lore as the 'Shot Heard Round The World'.

It came in the 32nd minute. Collecting a pass from Tab Ramos, he evaded one

Trinidadian and, as the ball skipped up off the dry pitch in front of him, the invitation was there: he lofted the ball goalwards on the half-volley from 25 yards. Up it flew and on it sped, before crashing down into the bottom corner of the goal.

It brought American soccer's most important victory since Joe Gaetjens' winner against England in Belo Horizonte at the 1950 World Cup.

Bruce Murray chuckles, 'When he hit it, I looked at it, and I'm thinking to myself, "What the heck's he doing?" Sure enough, it goes in, and you say, "My God, it's the greatest goal I've ever seen" but if you gave Paul a thousand balls, he wouldn't make one of those. He'd tell you the same.'

Caligiuri's only previous international goal had come five years previously. He had missed the last three qualifiers and was surprised to discover he would be starting the match in a defensive midfield role, ahead of his room-mate John Stollmeyer.

A few days later, Sonny Carter, a former Atlanta Chiefs footballer-turned-astronaut, kicked a World Cup football into space during a mission aboard the Space Shuttle Discovery. Wonderful PR, but it was Caligiuri's shot which shifted US soccer into a new orbit.

Without it, the US would have faced the awkward scenario of hosting the 1994 World Cup having not actually sent a team to the tournament for 44 years.

The US had first bid to stage the World Cup in 1983 after Colombia relinquished their status as hosts of the 1986 finals over a shortage of infrastructure for the staging of an enlarged 24-team tournament.

The three candidates were Mexico, Canada, and the United States. According to David Yallop's book *How They Stole The Game*, FIFA President João Havelange had agreed a deal in advance with Mexican TV mogul Emilio Azcárraga, owner of private network Televisana Americana and the Spanish International Network in the US, for his country to stage the event.

Yallop claims that Henry Kissinger discovered this while presenting the American bid to FIFA's Executive Committee in Stockholm on 20 May 1983. He wrote, 'Kissinger had just moved up a gear and into his second hour when an aide came and whispered in his ear. The Mexicans down below were apparently very busy organising a victory celebration. No one had ever treated Kissinger like this. He stormed out humiliated ... the entire morning had been merely empty ritual.'

FIFA made amends for that decision in 1988, awarding USA the '94 finals ahead of Brazil and Morocco. This time, the American bidders had delivered a considerably more substantial proposal, a 381-page document that cost $500,000 to compile.

Prior to the 1984 Olympics in Los Angeles, Blatter had been told by Peter Ueberroth, organiser of the LA Games, 'I don't want to see soccer in California.'

Now, a different tune was playing. Sepp Blatter told me, 'This guy who was in charge there, [Scott] Le Tellier, the chair of the organisation, said, "We'll do something in the United States that nobody has done so far – all seats will be occupied."' He was right.

In late 1989, that was all to come. All that Gansler's kids knew on that bumpy, dried-out pitch in Port of Spain was that they had a game to win, and they won it.

Bruce Murray says, 'By qualifying, it gave a little bit of credibility to the group, and it really took the heat off the organisers in 1994, I promise you that.

'We were all scared, because there were a lot of things that hinged on this. US Soccer was giving full-time contracts if we qualified. A six-figure salary at that time was a pretty good deal, and if we hadn't qualified, nobody would have got those. I was getting married in a week, so I was thinking, "I'm going to buy a house, or maybe I'm not going to buy a house". All that stuff goes through your head, and I don't know how much belief there was in that dressing room until the first goal goes in.

'The importance of that goal was getting us to the World Cup, and what that did was it brought in big corporations: it brought in Adidas, it brought in training centres, it brought in a Nike academy later. It allowed the money to flow and make it a credible sport within the United States.

'You can make arguments about MLS's standard of play, but there is no question the MLS is a solid league around the world in terms of attendance, television coverage, and players who are starting to come here. That goal started to precipitate all of this, and we all owe a great debt to Paul.'

The MLS average attendance for the 2017 regular season was 22,106

– a figure dwarfed by the NFL's 2016/17 average of 69,487 yet fractionally superior to Serie A's 2016/17 equivalent of 22,047 and bettered by only the Premier League, La Liga, and Bundesliga in Europe.

Peter Vermes, now a leading figure in the MLS as coach at Sporting Kansas City, adds, 'Have you ever seen the documentary on the 1980 US hockey team, *Miracle*? It's an incredible story, and there were similarities to that situation. He [Gansler] knew how to build a team. He knew how to get the most out of each guy, and he took a group of guys with very little experience and probably at times inferior talent, because of this lack of experience. And he got the most out of the group.

'He did it under incredible pressure when there should have been no pressure. No American team had qualified in forty years. We were a bunch of so-called college kids – he did it under a lot of scrutiny, and somehow, he maintained an incredible clarity of focus.

'One thing Bob always talked about was being the "best version of ourselves". The other thing he said was we needed to respect our opponents, but we needed also to understand that in any game anybody can beat anybody.'

They had done just that in Trinidad, though when Gansler's squad landed back at Miami airport afterwards, there was barely a soul there to greet them.

'I'M LIKE, "JESUS, I WISH I WAS MAKING WHAT YOU'RE MAKING," AND they're like, "Well, you got to play Juventus, you got to play AC Milan, you got to play Bayern Munich. How great is that?"'

Bruce Murray's recollection of a conversation with a current US men's national-team member is illustrative of how the friendly schedule used to look for an American international.

The summer before Italia '90, Gansler's team faced matches against six European clubs – Benfica, Sampdoria, Roma, Juventus, Dnipro, and Ruch Chorzów – and Mexican side Chivas. The crowd of 43,000 that watched the 1-0 win over Dnipro at Philadelphia's Franklin Field on 25 August 1989 was the largest for a national team home game outside of the 1984 LA Olympics.

When it came to European national sides, though, the US players had scant experience. In the four years since falling 5-0 to England in San Diego in June 1985, they had played only one official friendly game against opponents from the old continent.

That changed as the new decade dawned. With the World Cup draw having pitted them against three European sides in Group A – Italy, Czechoslovakia and Austria – it had to.

February 1990 thus brought home friendlies against the Soviet Union (1-3) and Finland (2-1). The next month, they flew to Europe to play Hungary (0-2) and East Germany (2-3).

For Peter Vermes, the first match provided a personal milestone: the fulfilment of a boyhood promise made to his Hungarian father. 'When I was eleven years old, I watched Hungary play the USSR in an international match. I used to go back every year as a little kid for about a month with my family, and I'd train somewhere like Honvéd. We watched the USSR play Hungary and I told my dad, "One day, I'm going to play against Hungary in this stadium". It came to fruition in March 1990. We played Hungary in that stadium, so my dad had the chance to watch me play there.'

Paul Krumpe wanted his own little piece of history when the squad arrived in Berlin to face an East Germany team playing one of their last-ever fixtures. 'I was aware of the Berlin Wall being dismantled and brought a hammer with me to bring a piece of the wall home. Bob [Gansler] was upset with me for not being focused on the job at hand.'

By now, US Soccer had provided the extra funds for Gansler to bring in another assistant for the World Cup, Ralph Perrin. The federation had some uncomfortable discussions with players over its boot deal with Adidas, though.

'We were all essentially forced to sign contracts that forbade us from wearing anything other than Adidas products, in uniform or on our feet,' explains Krumpe. 'Three of us – Hugo Pérez, Dave Vanole and I – had a Puma contract for two years and then the year prior to the World Cup, seven more guys did also. It was a significant contract, adding about thirty or forty per cent more to our existing national-team contracts. However, in order to play in the World Cup, we had to sign the new contract and wear Adidas. It was very contentious between Sunil Gulati and each guy who had to give up the Puma money.'

After victories over Malta and Poland, the Americans played one final, unofficial, friendly against Partizan Belgrade before departing for Europe.

Their first stop was Bad Ragaz in Switzerland. A victory over Liechtenstein and defeat against Switzerland marked the last acts of Gansler's preparation plan.

In one sense, Bad Ragaz was a bad thing. It gave the team a taste of the comforts of a smart Swiss hotel, which were largely absent at the team camp in Italy. The original plan had been to stay at the Italian Football Federation's facility in Coverciano. After the nations were grouped together, a plan B was required. This turned out to be the Italian National Olympic Committee's training centre in Tirrenia, sited on the coast close to Pisa.

Tirrenia has a curious history. A village established by Benito Mussolini with grandiose aims of making it a 'pearl of the Mediterranean' – and a hub for Italian film-makers – its villas became popular with American families after a US military complex, Camp Darby, was set up nearby in the 1950s.

It was less popular with the Americans who came to stay in June 1990. 'It seemed like we were in a military camp,' John Harkes relates. 'We were behind barbed-wire fences. To just go out and walk in town you had to ask for permission, and there were machine guns. I remember the rooms being so small, like a little cot like you were in the army. It didn't feel like the World Cup.'

'It reminded me of a sleep-away camp with bunk beds and a mess hall where you go in and have your buffet meals,' adds Bruce Murray. 'There wasn't a whole lot of television. There were some foosball tables and some ping pong, but we didn't get a chance to be out and be part of the community, and our families didn't get a chance to spend time with us. It got a little chippy in there, because the guys were stuck together for so long.'

One particular problem for the squad was the Italian breakfasts, comprising coffee and croissants, which led to the federation recruiting an army cook from Camp Darby to come in and serve up a full American.

'The federation really learned a lesson from that experience: at the next World Cup, the team stayed in a hotel, the federation hired a special play room for the children of the players, and they were allowed to walk in the streets and get a real feel of the Cup,' adds Joe Machnik. 'Whereas we were isolated.'

The atmosphere deteriorated in the wake of a deflating 5-1 opening loss to

Czechoslovakia in Florence. The US were already three goals behind when Eric Wynalda received a red card for a retaliatory shove on Jozef Chovanec following the Czech's sly stamp on his foot. Paul Caligiuri's fine individual goal was cold consolation. He intercepted a ball from Ľubomír Moravčík, exchanged passes with Murray and then eluded Ján Kocian, the Czech sweeper, before scoring. However, in the words of the *New York Times*, this was a team still 'humbled to the point of embarrassment'.

Joe Machnik offers his take on where it went so wrong in that first Group A fixture, starting with Tomáš Skuhravý, the 6ft 5in Czechoslovakia striker: 'We weren't ready for Skuhravý. When you play in CONCACAF, you play [opponents who are] smaller in stature, who don't play a game of crossing and heading.'

Then there were the Americans' own technical deficiencies. 'We didn't have a league where players could practise their technical skills in game situations, where without time and space you had to make quick decisions. So, our first touch often suffered because we were more worried about what we were going to do with that first touch – would we be able to control the ball as well as we should? The better teams have players thinking beyond their first touch.'

Allied to that was the Americans' naivety, as highlighted by Wynalda's reaction to Czechoslavakian gamesmanship. Machnik recalls attending a post-World Cup coaches' seminar at Coverciano at which he spoke about the need for US players to get cuter if they were to compete with the world's best.

'The point I made was that we were naïve and inexperienced. We didn't know how or when to foul, or how or when to receive a foul. It wasn't part of our game. The kids were playing in colleges, and you didn't have that pro league yet. We had a player sent off against Czechoslovakia because he didn't know how to receive a foul – he got challenged and came back at the player, and the referee obviously only saw the second part.

'If our player was smart, he'd have received the foul in a more professional manner, and we'd have had a free-kick – which would have been better than being sent off.

'I remember against Austria [in the final group game], they had a counter-attack against us. We had an opportunity to foul in the midfield and probably take a caution – a tactical foul – but no, we didn't. Then we had another opportunity before the player reached the top of the penalty area and no, we didn't again – and he scored, and we lost the game two-one. Sometimes, you have to take a tactical foul. Unfortunately, my speech got published later in a magazine here in the States called *Scholastic Coach,* and they got letters to the editor saying, "Joe Machnik is the most dangerous person in American soccer because he's teaching our players how to foul."'

The frustrations of that bitter Group A bow boiled over back at the squad base in Tirrenia when a tackle by Eric Eichmann on Bruce Murray sparked a brawl. The pair had been teammates at Clemson University. Now, they were trading punches on a training pitch at the World Cup two days before the big date with Italy.

'There were some extras in every tackle and it was really coming from the guys that weren't playing,' Murray remembers. 'That was disappointing. I'm like, "No, no, no. Just because we lost the first game, I don't think you can jump in here and take my job." I was always a fighter as a player.'

Yet, Peter Vermes recalls it as a turning point, a mass release of negative energy, which served the Americans well. 'That was a fantastic moment. It was basically an all-team brawl.

'What's funny is just when it ended, probably five or ten minutes later, all the dignitaries of US Soccer – the president, vice-president, the treasurer, the secretary, the board members – they all showed up to watch training. Thank God they missed that. But it got some of the frustrations out.

'The group was tight and strong mentally, so that was all left on the pitch and everybody had a good laugh about it later. We were a team of leaders. If you look at a lot of the guys, they're still involved in the game at a very high level, and it says a lot about the character and staying power.'

ANOTHER NOVELTY FOR THE US PLAYERS IN ITALY WAS THE LEVEL OF media interest – 'You can't believe these guys want to know what your hobbies are or who your girlfriend is,' remarks Bruce Murray – and it is intriguing to consider how much interest their fortunes were attracting back in the States. On Monday 11 June, the day after their opening game, the *New York Times*' front page did feature a story titled 'Now, the Czech reality', but the focus was politics and the weekend's elections in Czechoslavakia rather than World Cup football and the reality check of a 5-1 thrashing for Gansler's American team.

The match preview on the day of that historic first game 24 hours earlier, meanwhile, was found only on page six of the sport section.

Curiously, the 'Question Of the Week' on page ten of that same issue was 'Will Soccer Gain More Popularity in the US?' Not every response was positive. One suggestion, sent in by Susan Littlejohn from Summit, NJ, read, 'Soccer needs a five-minute clock. If the designated team does not score within this time, the other team is awarded a point.'

More constructive at least than the offering from Owen A. Murphy, The Bronx: 'Let this silly, boring "game" die a peaceful death.'

As for television coverage, while the Univision network transmitted the tournament into Spanish-speaking homes in the US – with an estimated 3.48 million households watching the final – not a single English-language network bought the rights for Italia '90. This represented a backward step after NBC's broadcasting of nine live games during Mexico '86; instead cable channel TNT screened the action and it did so with the help of Mick Luckhurst, the British former Atlanta Falcons player who had become the face of Channel 4's NFL coverage in the UK in the 1980s.

He had never commentated on football before but, as TNT saw it, was a Brit and could at least explain the offside rule to a US audience whose viewing was interrupted by ad breaks during the action.

'I hadn't seen a live game or even a television game in years,' laughs Luckhurst, 'because back then there was no football on television. But if you're born in England, whether you play sport or not, you know the rules of football. There was a large percentage of people, they were trying to capture that simply wouldn't have known what an offside was. They just wouldn't know the rule. It was a foreign thought. So we definitely did some stuff to help explain the game.'

Luckhurst was allowed an assistant and summoned a friend who had been working as an estate agent in St Albans, Geoff Shreeves, now a reporter for Sky Sports, Fox Sports and BT Sport. 'Geoff gave me the information he knew I'd need.'

It was a dream assignment. For Manchester United supporter Luckhurst, it got even better when he felt a tap on his shoulder one day from an NFL aficionado by the name of Bobby Charlton, and heard the Old Trafford legend ask, 'Are you Micky Luckhurst?'

Luckhurst's fellow TNT commentator, however, was rather less seduced by the spectacle taking place around them. 'My play-by-play was a guy named Bob Neal; he was a big baseball guy. We're at the final, and it's phenomenal – people are going nuts, and he looked at me and said, "I just don't see what all the fuss is about."' Bob Neal was not alone: TV surveys showed that only one per cent of Americans watched that World Cup final.

FOR THE US PLAYERS, THEIR OWN WORLD CUP FINAL ARRIVED ON 14 June. They still had to face Austria, a final group game which brought a 2-1 loss, but it is their assignment with the hosts at the Stadio Olimpico which provided memories to savour.

'It boggles the mind to think what might happen Thursday in Rome,' wrote the *New York Times*, while the Italian press focused their attention on the squad's two Italo-Americans: Tony Meola, whose Italian father had played in the youth ranks of Avellino, and Paul Caligiuri, grandson of Italian immigrants from Cosenza and Naples.

On the bus ride through the streets of Rome, there were Italians waving ten fingers at the Americans. It was a prediction of the humiliation they expected to see inflicted on opponents who had fallen 7-1 to the *Azzurri* when the nations met at the 1934 World Cup.

Yet, there were also Americans out there on the streets, as Peter Vernes remembers: 'Look, we used to play games in the United States, and we were the foreign team. If we played Honduras, there'd be more Honduran fans than Americans. As we were driving up the streets leading to the stadium, there were actually people wearing red, white, and blue and carrying flags. I get goosebumps telling you about it right now. It was something we'd never experienced, and was an incredible lift.'

It was an evening which suggested that maybe Planet Football was not so alien a place for US soccer players after all. Maybe Americans belonged there too – not that it looked that way after eleven minutes when, amid a blur of blue, Giuseppe Giannini struck the opening goal.

To the observer reviewing the goal today, the Italians are simply operating at a superior speed. Andrea Carnevale holds off John Doyle down the right and slides the ball inside. Suddenly, the pace quickens: Berti one touch, Donadoni one touch, Vialli dummy. Before you know it, Giannini is hurdling Mike Windischmann in the D of the penalty box. He's too quick for Desmond Armstrong too and flashes a left-foot shot into the goal before dashing away in a Tardelli-lite celebration, his arms making mini-windmills.

Things might have gotten worse, but a penalty, awarded for Nicola Berti's tumble at the feet of Caligiuri, did not bring a second goal. Instead, Gianluca Vialli drove his kick against the base of the post. The same player was then flagged offside after breaking clear on to Giannini's through pass.

As the game went on, the US players began to feel increasingly at home.

The America midfield of Caligiuri, John Harkes, Marcelo Balboa and Jimmy Banks worked ferociously to block Italy's passing routes.

'It was tough,' remembers Harkes. 'We were playing a diamond shape in a four-four-two; I was on the left side of midfield tucking in a little bit there; and I had to get around [Roberto] Donadoni as much as I could. He was quality on the ball, and his movement was great.

'We knew it was going to be tactically a challenge because they were such a high-level squad, but I think we impressed on that day. There was a sequence of passes, maybe twenty-three, that we kept the ball for. I remember being so proud of that and going, "I just kept the ball twenty-three passes against Italy."'

Striker Murray sensed the growing frustration of the home players. 'I was a really long, lean player and had a lot of arms and elbows, and Ricardo Ferri had a real problem with me the whole game. He kept telling me in really bad English that he wanted to fight me and then ended up giving me an elbow to the head.

'Two or three times too, I heard [Giuseppe] Bergomi, Ferri, Maldini, and Baresi yelling at each other and I thought to myself, "Ah shit, I don't care what the result is, I'm doing something right!"'

As Italy grew restless, the US came close to stunning the Stadio Olimpico with an equalising goal midway through the second period. It followed a free-kick awarded for that aforementioned Ferri elbow to Murray's head. Murray was the man who took the shot. 'It was about twenty-five metres, and I thumped it. Tab Ramos ran over it. He moves to the right, it creates a bit of confusion in the wall, and I really hammered this one. Zenga saw it late and got down. He blocked it right to Peter Vermes who is coming on it six yards out.'

The ball reached Vermes on the very corner of the six-yard box. The angle was tight, and he drove the ball back hard and low to the near post, where it went under Zenga but took a ricochet off his backside, squirming behind the goalkeeper and into the six-yard box where Ferri thrashed it away to safety.

'It could have [squeezed in],' says Vermes, 'but I always think about it and say to myself, "Honestly I don't think we deserved to tie the game." They were a great team, and we weren't. Of course, you always think differently in the moment.

'It would've been a lot worse if I'd roofed it and put it over the goal – that would've been really bad because everybody would've been talking about how bad I was in that situation. I thought I did pretty well with it. The fact it didn't go in is something I relived for a long time thereafter.'

One of the strongest shared memories of that night is what happened after the final whistle had blown. For Gansler's players, the response of their Italian counterparts has an etching in their minds.

'I've played a lot of games, and this never happened,' says Murray, 'but the Italy team came into the locker room to congratulate our team and to shake hands and tell us, "Congratulations, you should be proud." They did all this knowing they were going to get lambasted by their own people in the papers.

'So for us, it was a moment where we said, "You know what, even if it's just for this one night, we were actually okay today, we were deserving of being on the field with this team."'

They had succeeded where each of Italy's other World Cup opponents would fail, in stopping Totò Schillaci from scoring. And they came away with some decent souvenirs too.

'I had the number six of Italy, Ferri,' remembers Harkes. 'We'd exchanged jerseys, and then I was walking down the tunnel and looking at Donadoni and

Baresi and everybody and thinking, "We've just played against Italy and were unlucky not to draw with them" and Ferri said to me, "Shorts too?" I said, "Sure," so we get changed there in the hallway. It was all very surreal.'

WHEN THE UNITED STATES TEAM RETURNED FROM THE 1950 WORLD Cup in Brazil, Walter Bahr, the man who supplied the pass for Joe Gaetjens' winning goal against England, waited 25 years to do an interview.

Needless to say, their 1990 vintage received a different response, not least the three players from Soccer Town, aka Kearny, New Jersey. 'They had a parade afterwards, and they gave us a key to the city from the mayor at the town hall,' says Harkes of the honour bestowed on himself, Tony Meola and Tab Ramos.

And while Ramos departed for a five-year spell in Spanish football, Harkes was Sheffield-bound. 'In the January prior to the World Cup, I came to trial over here with Tony Meola, and Ron [Atkinson] asked me to stay on – I actually told him no at that time. I didn't think it was going to come up again but it did, and that's when I came over.

'It was a unique situation – I'd already played in a World Cup before I was really a pro player. It was like I'd done it the reverse way. Within seven months I'd scored goal of the year [against Peter Shilton, then of Derby County] and earned a League Cup winners' medal against Man United at Wembley.' In 1992, he became the first American to play in the newly inaugurated Premier League.

From afar, and on international trips, he witnessed the gradual growth of soccer back at home. It is fair to say the club game needed time. The 1991 American Professional Soccer League began with only nine of the 22 teams from the previous season involved.

The Portland Timbers, reborn today as an MLS club averaging over 20,000 spectators per game, folded at the end of 1990 after failing to reach the 3,500 mark for average attendance.

Not until 1996 would a proper professional league be up and running in the form of the MLS.

The national team's path was smoother. A year after Italia '90, they beat Mexico to win the inaugural Gold Cup under Gansler's successor, Bora

Milutinović. He would lead them, as hosts, to the last sixteen of the 1994 World Cup, a tournament of full stadiums whose final drew a US TV audience of 8.95 million viewers – quite a leap from the 1.07 million who had tuned into the Italia '90 final. (In Brazil 2014, the USA-Portugal group game on ESPN attracted 18.2 million.)

'I remember going back in the summers and playing US Cups, and we started getting some incredible results,' says Harkes. 'I scored against Italy, and we drew one-one. We beat Ireland three-one in the RFK Stadium in lashing-down rain, and there were over thirty thousand people in the crowd. The next year, we beat England two-nil. You could feel something's happening here, and people are starting to get behind it.'

It was Bora's team now, but Harkes, back on his old stamping ground in Sheffield, does not want to underplay the contribution of the man who started the ball rolling for him, even before Big Ron came calling with the dream ticket to the English game.

'I do give whole-hearted credit to Bob Gansler because he galvanised us as a young squad, he believed in us, and he got us there. He still doesn't get enough credit today for the development of the game.

'The '90 World Cup had such a massive impact on the game in our country, not just from the international global exposure, but domestically, the level of the game improved. Everybody wanted to find out what was going on, what was coming next, and the fact we got '94 back home, the timing of it was perfect. For us to have '94 on the back of '90 was needed. It had to go together for it to take off in our country and for Major League Soccer to take off. We were very fortunate it happened.

'I'm proud of it for sure as it's not every day you get to be a part of something pretty special, from a timing standpoint, in the history of the game.'

Arab adventures
Part 1 -
United Arab Emirates

'IT WAS FROM A LONG PASS. THOMAS HÄßLER WAS VERY SHORT, and he couldn't head it. I controlled it, and I focused on one area – the far post is always the best place to shoot. Every time, I used to shoot there. When I scored that goal, it was a surprise for me, and also for the Emirates.'

Khalid Ismail is sitting in the reception area at Abu Dhabi Airport's Premier Inn. He is dressed handsomely in the smart, full-length white garment that Arabs call the *kandora*. His friendly face is framed by a white headdress. Now in his early fifties, Ismail is the COO of a fire prevention company, and he has met me en route to a meeting with an army general.

Right now, though, he is back at the rain-sodden San Siro on the evening of 15 June 1990. The goal he is describing – a precise shot driven diagonally past West Germany's Bodo Illgner – marked a small piece of World Cup history.

Ismail straightens his left hand into the shape of an arrow as he remembers putting a swell in the net. There was no pretty preamble. Häßler, the diminutive West Germany midfielder, misjudged the bounce of a long punt forward, the ball spinning up off the wet turf and over his head, leaving Ismail in the clear. One touch to tee himself up and then *bang* – his name in the record books.

True, West Germany went straight down the other end and scored a third time themselves (with the scoreboard reading West Germany 5 United Arab Emirates 1 by the finish), but a nation that had only been in existence for nineteen years had its first World Cup goal, and Ismail his place in one of Italia '90's quirkier tales. It was the one about the UAE scorer receiving a Rolls Royce as reward for his goal. Ismail, like the world's press, believed it. Alas, it turned out not to be true.

He explains, 'One guy [reported at the time to be Sheikh Mohammed] said, "We'll give him a Rolls Royce car." They put it in the news, and I was dreaming about the colour – red, yellow – but in the end, nothing happened.'

At a time when Gulf states' petro-billions have shifted the balance of power in European club football, when the English football landscape features the Emirates and the Etihad as two of its leading venues, and Qatar is readying itself to host a World Cup, it is not easy to put the United Arab Emirates into the box marked 'plucky underdogs'.

In 1990, they were very much the outsiders – if not quite the romantics' choice – at the World Cup. In 1971, the year of its foundation, with the union of six sheikhdoms – and a seventh to follow the next year – the UAE had a population of 180,000. Nineteen years later, that population had risen to 1.8million, no more than twenty per cent of them actual citizens. Only two smaller nations – Kuwait and Northern Ireland – had reached the finals before. Not one of their players were full-time professionals. When Jürgen Klinsmann, the West Germany striker, was asked whether he knew any of their team before the match, he replied, 'Not a single one.'

The presence of a tented prayer area on the lawn of their Imola hotel was a curiosity to European eyes. Before that second Group D game against West Germany, a well-known Italian television presenter, Piero Chiambretti, followed the team in Arab robes and headdress, with a camel in tow. It led defender Yousuf Hussain to bite back, saying, 'We're a modern country. If you want to pray, there's a mosque. If you want to drink, there's a bar.'

IF ITALIA '90 BROUGHT A SENSE OF ARRIVAL, IT IS WORTH RETRACING the steps taken by Emirati football to reach the destination – and in Khalid Ismail, their history boy in Milan, they had a player with a connection to the man who began laying the path that led, eventually, to this World Cup participation. That man was Don Revie.

Long before Dubai became a popular playground for British footballers with their second homes on the man-made Palm Islands, Revie blazed a trail there. And it was the former Leeds United and England manager, Ismail explains, who gave him his break as a teenager during Revie's days with the Dubai-based Al Nasr, his second posting in the country following three years as UAE manager.

Revie had quit as England manager in 1977 to take the UAE role – a flight that earned him "Deserter!" headlines and a ten-year FA ban, later overturned in the High Court.

According to Richard Stott's book *Dogs and Lampposts*, it was a flight prompted by his discovery that the *Daily Mirror* was about to reveal allegations of match-fixing during his long Elland Road reign. The contrasting recollection of Revie's late son, Duncan, when speaking to me in 2010, was that 'he didn't actually run off to Dubai. He was going to get sacked with England and went to Dubai for what was then a king's ransom [a £340,000 tax-free, four-year contract], secured his family, and had six of the happiest years of his life out there.'

At Leeds, Revie had led a club with no previous major honours out of the old Second Division and to the pinnacle of the English game, collecting two league titles along with victories in the 1972 FA Cup and 1968 League Cup finals. His arrival in the Emirates – where a Rolls Royce collected him at Dubai Airport – was the first step by Sheikh Mana Al-Maktoum, then president of the UAE Football Association, to develop a competitive national side.

If the Gulf gaze had been traditionally drawn to Egypt as the main centre of influence for the Arab world, Sheikh Mana was now seeking lessons from elsewhere. On the field, there were heavy defeats in the 1979 Gulf Cup – 7-0 against Kuwait and 5-0 against Iraq – and though he was sacked the next year, Revie is credited with raising standards, both of his players' professionalism and the facilities available to them.

He had the foresight to suggest that the UAE would need ten years to have a competitive team – a comment much criticised at the time but perfectly prescient – and he even had a guiding hand in the development of the youngster who would become the nation's first World Cup goalscorer.

Ismail remembers how Revie fast-tracked him into the Al Nasr team. He was only a teenager but tall and strong already. It took some sharp practice, though, to ensure he was eligible to play. 'Revie said, "I need this player, Khalid,"' recalls Ismail. 'The club committee said, "He's young," and the coach said, "I need him in the first team." One member of the committee was chief of the immigration department for Dubai, so he changed my passport. They gave me two years more.'

At this point, he pulls out his blue-faced passport, opens it and points to the year of birth as proof. 'I'm 1967, but in my passport, it says 1965.

'Revie was a nice guy. He was my first manager. He was very disciplined. It was about respect. He was the first man to watch me and say, "This player has a good future." I remember Revie watched one of my first games, and he said, "Listen, we should work morning and afternoon. You have a good jump, you leap really well, and you should be scoring goals with your head." They call me "Golden Head" here because I practised and practised and practised, and I scored most of my goals with my head. Coaches would say, "Don't look for Khalid's feet but for his head."'

Ismail's early start meant that at as a teenager (passport age: 20) he was in the UAE team who were thirty seconds from the victory over Iraq which would have left them one step away from Mexico '86. A place in an AFC final qualifying play-off against Syria beckoned. Instead, their failure to defend one last high ball into the box led to an Iraq goal – and some broken hearts. 'We cried for three days after that,' says Ismail. 'If you mention Iraq to anyone our age, they'll remember this game. We were a better team than in '90.'

UAE's coach at that point was Carlos Alberto Parreira. He resigned in 1988 to take charge of Saudi Arabia, lured by a bigger salary and better team. Ironically, by the end of the final AFC qualification round for Italia '90, the Brazilian's Saudi side would be looking up at the Emiratis.

That final round took place in Singapore in October 1989. The UAE's opponents were North Korea, China, Saudi Arabia, Qatar and South Korea. Expectations for a side now coached by Mário Zagallo – Parreira's old boss in Brazil's 1970 World Cup coaching team – could not have been lower. A scandal caused by Al Jazira, one of the country's top-flight clubs, fielding ineligible players had led to the mass resignation of those running the game. All that was left, in their stead, was a small, four-man committee. 'Nobody set any target to go to the World Cup,' remembers Ismail. 'Why? We didn't have a football federation.

We didn't have a president. We didn't have anything.'

A different account comes from Abdulrahman Mohammed – a defender in that UAE side and captain for two of their Italia '90 matches – who insists that, amid the administrative disorder, the players kept sight of the prize at stake. 'We had a meeting on the night we arrived. It was just for the players, without the coaching team and management. Abdullah Sultan, one of my teammates, said, "If we get to the World Cup, we'll create history for UAE football and for ourselves." These were really important words for all of us. I felt that message in the match against China. We were losing one-nil and I saw the determination on the faces of my teammates.'

That 2-1 turnaround victory, achieved via late goals from Khaleel Mubarak and Adnan Al-Thalyani, proved pivotal. Their next match against Saudi Arabia – Zagallo v Parreira – brought a hard-earned point from a fixture delayed by an hour owing to torrential rain. It was a match memorable only for the sending-off of the Saudis' best player, three-time Asian Player of the Year Majed Abdullah.

By the time of their final fixture against the already qualified South Koreans, the door remained open for the team of part-timers, still unbeaten in Singapore with three draws and a victory. They needed only to match China's result against Qatar to make sure. When China took the lead against Qatar with a quarter of an hour remaining, Emirati hopes dimmed. Yet, two Qatari goals in the last five minutes floored the continent's most populous nation. UAE's 1-1 draw with South Korea was enough.

THE FINAL MOMENTS OF UAE'S QUALIFYING CAMPAIGN FOR Italia '90 are relived in a terrific documentary film titled *Anwar Roma (The Lights of Rome)*. It is a title inspired by the outpouring of joy by TV commentator Adnan Hamad who, on hearing about the dramatic finish to the concurrent fixture between China and Qatar, exclaimed, 'I swear, I swear, I swear; I see the lights of Rome now! I see the lights of Rome now!'

Ali Khaled, now editor of *FourFourTwo Arabia*, directed the film and suggests, 'Nobody believed in them, and by the sound of it, they didn't either. It was, "We'll just go and give it our best shot." A lot of them were quite young. They were all born in the late 60s, and the country didn't become an independent nation till December 1971. A lot of them worked in the civil service, some were policemen or firemen, and some were still in university as well. In fact, two of them had to defer their university studies to play in the World Cup qualifiers.'

The FIFA delegate's report of that last qualifier hailed 'Zagallo's tactical wizardry in getting this lot into the World Cup finals,' yet it was the Brazilian's last act as coach. Qualification prompted the installation of a new federation, and soon, they had the fresh task of finding a replacement coach after Zagallo's dismissal.

Yousuf Al Serkal, then the newly-appointed UAE FA general secretary, takes up the story. 'When we came to office, Zagallo was on leave in Brazil, so we had no coach to sit with and discuss how the preparation would be for the World Cup. We kept trying to contact Zagallo, sending letters, faxes, calls, but we had no answer. Every time we'd hear, "He's camping somewhere in the mountains, he's travelling somewhere." We had no chance to talk to him. We kept receiving letters from other qualified countries asking for friendly matches, but we couldn't answer as the coach had not given us a preparation programme. We couldn't get hold of him, so we decided to terminate the contract.'

According to Zagallo, a dispute over a bonus for reaching Italy was the reason for his departure. Either way, he was gone, and a Polish coach, Bernard Blaut, appointed in his place. But not for long. 'We appointed Blaut from one of the leading local clubs, Al Sharjah,' Al Serkal continues. 'Seven or eight of our national-team players were from Al Sharjah, but we had no idea that Blaut had problems with them. They were fed up with him, and that problem was transferred to the national team.'

Blaut's short reign featured a dismal Gulf Cup participation. Al Serkal had wished to rest the first-choice players and send a second string to the event – yet Sheikh Hamdan ordered otherwise after a request from the Kuwaiti football chief Sheikh Fahad al Ahmed. Sheikh Fahad, who was killed in fighting during Iraq's 1990 invasion of Kuwait, has his own place in World Cup lore: after stepping on to the pitch to protest a France goal against his team in an eventual 4-1 loss at the 1982 World Cup, he complained that a whistle from the crowd had caused his players to stop and the Soviet referee, Myroslav Stupar, disallowed the goal.

He had his way here too, albeit with unhappy consequences for the Emiratis. 'We went to Kuwait and had the worst-ever participation in a Gulf Cup,' Al Serkal remembers. 'We lost six-one against Kuwait. We brought back a team with so many problems, and [with] the players and [the] coach not on the same wavelength. So, we had to fire the coach and call Carlos Alberto [Parreira]. He said, "OK, I'm willing to do this, but I have to ask Zagallo first," because of his personal relationship. That was in March 1990.'

Parreira was a man who knew the UAE team. He was a man, too, who knew the World Cup. Aged 27, he had worked as Zagallo's physical trainer with the great 1970 Brazil team. The squad's conditioning was not his only concern; he would scout opponents and prepare slideshows for Zagallo on their strengths and weaknesses. More recently, he had taken Kuwait to that aforementioned 1982 World Cup campaign where, in between losing against France, they earned a 1-1 draw with Czechoslovakia and suffered a 1-0 defeat by England.

There is a sense from talking to those who worked with Parreira that his priority in Italy was damage limitation. The then 47-year-old set his team up with two defensive midfielders and demanded a more cautious mindset than Zagallo. 'I respect Carlos Alberto, but he never gave you the freedom to play,' argues Khalid Ismail. 'It was about defending and closing down. His philosophy was, "We don't want to lose, and a nil-nil would be good."'

In Parreira's defence, his players were not full-time professionals. Players at Al Nasr, Ismail's club, would earn around 2,000 dirham monthly (£320), together with win bonuses of 1,500 (£240). Their World Cup qualification had brought each of them 500,000 dirham (£80,000). A striking leap, and not the only one for the players as they arrived in Europe in their bespoke, light-grey Cacharel suits. 'We were quite innocent,' Ismail attests. 'We'd been away before, but this was different – a big, big, big difference because of the media, the journalists, the TV coverage.'

For these Emirati pioneers, there were one or two home comforts. 'We had a tent for prayer,' Ismail recounts. 'We all prayed together five times a day.' Thanks to the two cooks brought over from Sheikh Hamdan's palace, they also ate as if they were still at home – at least during the early days of their pre-tournament camp in Nimes in southern France. Yousuf Al Serkal explains, 'We took those cooks, and one week later, Carlos [Parreira] asked me to send them back. He was telling me he was training the players morning and afternoon, and they weren't losing any weight because of the food they were eating!'

THE UAE'S FIRST TEST IN GROUP D AT THE 1990 WORLD CUP WAS against Colombia in Bologna. This was the match that Sepp Blatter remembers as one of the spurs for his subsequent push to amend the back-pass rule. While the then FIFA general secretary dwelled on the Emiratis' repeated balls back to goalkeeper Muhsin Musabah – six inside the opening thirteen minutes – it is worth noting that René Higuita made saves in each half, the second a dive to smother the ball at the feet of Adnan Al Talyani in the second period.

At that point, UAE were already behind, trailing to Bernardo Redín's headed goal five minutes after half-time. Five minutes before full time, Carlos Valderrama drilled in a second goal following a counter-attack.

'Valderrama did not misplace one ball during the ninety minutes of the game,' recalls Abdulrahman Mohammed appreciatively, though it is when he talks about West Germany, the next opponents for the UAE, that a wide-eyed wonder really sets in.

'I used to watch AC Milan on TV, and it was my dream to play in that stadium. I was happy when I saw the schedule – Germany at the San Siro – and I was so pleased to be playing against Lothar Matthäus. The whole Germany team were superstars – and then you looked at the bench and saw Franz Beckenbauer!'

Abdulrahman goes on to provide a colourful aside about Matthäus, his fellow captain that night. The pair swapped shirts after the match and were reunited in 2001, when the German flew over to Dubai to play in Abdulrahman's farewell match for Al Nasr against Iranian club Sepahan. Matthäus even turned up in Arab garb. 'When he came to the stadium he was wearing the traditional Emirati clothing – *kandora* and headdress.'

On the occasion of their first meeting, a sou'wester might have been a more fitting choice of headgear given the biblical deluge that broke early in the contest, leading to the TV monitors shutting down in the press box. A similar deluge had been forecast on the pitch – at least by the computer which, according to Yousuf

Al Serkal, predicted a 12-0 win for West Germany. Had Jürgen Klinsmann and Rudi Völler taken all of their chances in the opening half-hour, they might have come close.

'We started very slowly,' adds Khalid Ismail. 'We were nervous – eighty-five thousand [the official attendance was 71,169] is not easy, it's a huge number of people. Of course we were scared.'

The West Germany strikers might have shared four goals inside the first half-hour, with Klinsmann coming closest when striking a post. By the 35th minute, the downpour had begun, and full-back Khalil Ghanim's slip on the wet surface let in Klinsmann to cross for Völler's breakthrough goal. Klinsmann added a second himself soon after.

The rather blunt recollection of their right-back, Thomas Berthold, is that, 'This was more a training match for us.' It produced the most shots on goal of any game in the first round (33), and just a minute after the restart, UAE had something to celebrate. By his own recollection, Khalid Ismail might have not been there to score it. During the pre-finals camp in Nimes, it took the intervention of UAE FA president Sheikh Hamdan to ensure he stayed with the squad after Parreira's preference for other players had left him wishing to quit. He had not featured against Colombia in the opening game, but now he took his chance.

That shot buried with precision into the side of Bodo Illgner's net did not spark an improbable comeback. Parreira had told journalists after the Colombia match that 'We can't hope for miracles,' and he was right: a minute later, a Matthäus volley made it 3-1. West Germany ended the match with five goals.

For Ismail, the Rolls Royce he was hoping for failed to materialise. The same happened, he divulges, with a putative transfer to Eintracht Frankfurt, which was blocked by Al Nasr's president.

As for his teammates, their bid for a World Cup bonus fell on deaf ears, as Al Serkal explains. 'We told them they'd get a bonus of 25,000 dirham [£5,000] if they won any game. I remember Ali Thani and some other players, after losing to Germany, came to me and asked me for the bonus. My question to them was, "You lost, why are you asking for a bonus?" and they answered, "The computer anticipated we'd lose twelve-nil, and we lost only five!"'

It was Thani who scored their second World Cup goal in the 4-1 defeat by

Yugoslavia which brought their Italian campaign to a close. After two early Yugoslavia goals, the Emiratis showed something of the freedom of a team suddenly seizing the moment. 'We released ourselves,' is how Khalid Ismail, no fan of Parreira's tactics, remembers it.

ITALIA '90 DID NOT JUST PROVIDE LESSONS FOR THE UAE ON THE football pitch. Yousuf Al Serkal has a noteworthy recollection of a conversation that took place with an official from the Emirati embassy in the country. Al Serkal, who was twice UAE FA president as well as vice-president of the Asian Football Confederation, says, 'I remember a friend who was working in the embassy told me that, before we qualified, it was so difficult for them to ask for appointments with the official authorities in Italy, and they'd get a response months later. Once we qualified, doors were opened for them in all of Europe for our consulate and embassy relationships. So it did have an impact for the country itself too.'

Here was an early lesson in the soft power of a sport which is now of such strategic importance to the UAE, its neighbour Qatar and other Asian nations, notably China.

In the case of the UAE, my flight over to Abu Dhabi offered a reminder of the transformation of Manchester City effected by the wealth of Sheikh Mansour, a member of Abu Dhabi's ruling family as well as UAE's deputy prime minister and minister of presidential affairs.

Etihad Airways' in-flight TV menu includes comedy, drama and football – and this last option is not just any football, but City Football. The cynic might suggest that once upon a time, before Sheikh Mansour's investment – which includes an estimated £1.2bn on players alone – comedy, drama and football all came together in a neat package at a place called Maine Road. A City fan back then – wearing, let's imagine, a baggy Stone Roses t-shirt and wielding an inflatable banana – would have looked at you with saucer eyes on learning that one day, travellers to the Gulf would hear the words, 'Arrive at your destination refreshed thanks to these on-board fitness tips demonstrated by Man City.' (Suffice to say, back in 1990, international travellers seeking advice on neck rolls and leg stretches from Steve Redmond, David White and Andy Dibble were few and far between.)

Sheikh Mansour's limitless riches have brought City super-club status – and raised Abu Dhabi's worldwide profile in a way his investment in local club Al Jazira never could. As Yousuf Al Serkal says during our meeting at one of Dubai's many malls, 'Spending on Man City is an investment. Spending locally here isn't an investment. There, whatever they spend will have a return, one way or another, but here, whatever you spend is going down the drain. If they spend more in Manchester City they are spending it under some sort of financial plan. Here, whatever you spend is only to develop the game for the community itself; it's not a business.'

That said, there is big money in UAE football too, not least for the players. The view of Khalid Ismail is that today's players are overindulged – a case in point is Omar Abdulrahman, 2016's Asian Footballer of the Year. Born into a Yemeni family in Riyadh, the Saudi capital, he became a UAE citizen owing to the willingness of Emirati officials to provide nationality for his whole family (including his brother Mohamed, who is also in the national squad). Omar, who once had a trial at City, has admirers in Europe – there was interest, most recently, from French club Nice in summer 2017 – but instead, he remains in a comfort zone where he earns an estimated 20 million dirham (£4.2m) tax-free annually.

Yousuf Al Serkal, with an amiable gleam in his eyes and a grey moustache on his lip, tells me, 'They're overpaid here. If they go abroad, they'll not get as much money. If I put myself in their shoes, I don't blame them – although I think I'd be more willing to take the chance because the financial gains if you make it abroad are much higher. But they're so relaxed internally – they have a good income, a good contract; they're among their friends and family, and in their local environment. What makes them want to go out? Only if they were under financial strain. The game of football, I'm sorry to say it, is for the poor. It's not for the rich. And our players are so rich.'

Al Serkal has a deep knowledge of the route taken by football in Abu Dhabi since Italia '90. He recalls how Ahmed Al Fardan, vice-president of the UAE FA, produced a report with ten recommendations for the future of the game in the wake of that World Cup. A key recommendation concerned the introduction of a professional league, yet not until 2008 – a year after the national team's historic first Gulf Cup triumph – did this materialise in the shape of the UAE

Arabian Gulf League. Saudi Arabia, by contrast, established its professional league in 1990, and sent teams to the 1994 and 2002 World Cups subsequently.

'At the time, the mentality was not ready,' he says, before suggesting that internal squabbling has stalled the development of the game at different junctures since.

'Unfortunately, I've experienced our football since 1990, from a general secretary to a vice-president to a president for two terms – and every time we raise the standard of football, another federation will come for four years and destroy everything which was built.'

BEFORE LEAVING THE UAE, I TAKE A TWO-HOUR BUS RIDE TO AL AIN to attend the country's final home qualifier for the 2018 World Cup at the Hazza Bin Zayed Stadium. Known as the Garden City, Al Ain is a smaller, less international place than Abu Dhabi and Dubai; a low-slung city spread out along broad, tree-lined avenues. It was here that Sheikh Zayed bin Sultan Al Nahyan, founder of the UAE, hosted the nation's football heroes after their qualification for Italia '90. Unlike Dubai – with its giant malls and gleaming towers – the only visible cranes here are those accompanying the quartet of sixty-foot minarets that stand surrounding the massive new Sheikh Khalifa Bin Zayed Al Nahyan Masjed mosque.

I pass it in a taxi en route to the stadium, driven by a Cameroonian who tells me he once played second division football back at home. 'There was no money in it,' he laments before informing me that I have a very English face 'like John Terry'.

Outside the stadium, men in long, white robes pour coffee from copper pots into paper espresso cups. The women in the small family enclosure to the right of the press box, by contrast, are clad uniformly in black *abayas*, loose garments covering everything but the face, hands and feet.

The Saudis have brought a sizeable following who occupy one end of the ground and maintain a steady rumble of noise. Despite free entry to three sides of the ground, though, this fixture is played out before a surprising number of empty seats. UAE's World Cup qualifying prospects may be purely mathematical, but they are facing the biggest team in the region.

Luring football enthusiasts out of their armchairs here is not easy, and league attendances during the hot summer months can drop to just several hundred. There is not the obvious passion for football found in Saudi Arabia where, as Carlos Alberto Parreira once noted, you find the true meaning of 'football as an escape valve for the people'.

In the UAE, there are plenty of other forms of escapism. 'Football isn't as attractive as it used to be,' says Yousuf Al Serkal. 'Why go to the stadium in the heat when you can watch the game sitting at home with a coffee and some nuts? There's also the effect of people watching the big clubs from the European leagues. Why would you go to watch a lower standard of football in the hot weather?'

It is 38 degrees as kick-off approaches, and the fans in the stand opposite – all clad in long, white robes – unfurl a banner underlining their feeling for the Saudi visitors: 'One nation, one faith.' If this sense of unity is less apparent on the field, where UAE prevail 2-1, off it they have a common enemy in Qatar: a state blockaded – at the time of my visit – by both these and other Arab nations amid accusations over Qatari support of Islamist movements.

This diplomatic row placed another question mark against the 2022 Qatari World Cup. According to Al Serkal, any positive feeling at the prospect of a first Arab World Cup has long evaporated.

'The majority maybe feel it should be withdrawn from Qatar,' he says. 'They can organise the game, but they can't organise the celebration because the World Cup is more than just a football match. It's a celebration, a festival. I think the majority of spectators will come and stay in Dubai, take a plane, watch the game, and come back here. All those that are financially capable of doing so will come and enjoy themselves outside of Qatar.'

Either way, for the more romantically-minded, those treasured lights of Rome will feel farther away than ever.

Arab adventures
Part 2 – Egypt

'LET ME SAY, THE HUNDRED MILLION PEOPLE IN EGYPT LOVE Mohamed Salah, and they respect him because nobody can believe how good a man he is. I'll tell you a story: a thief stole money from his [Salah's] father back in Egypt, and the police caught him. The thief said, "I'm sorry, I didn't know it was the father of our hero," and Mohamed Salah actually told his father to leave the money with this guy, to give him the money, and not to do anything against him with the police.'

It is a lovely illustration of a good heart in action, though there is a stronger reason why Egyptians love Salah, and it owes less to his heart than to his feet: namely, his conversion of the injury-time penalty kick against Congo on 8 October last year which opened the door for the Pharaohs' return to the World Cup finals.

Magdy Abdelghany, the man telling the story about Salah, will have had a better idea than most of his compatriots of just how the Liverpool winger felt as he stood beside the penalty spot that evening. In fact, probably a better idea than any other watching Egyptian.

After all, it was Abdelghany who scored the only goal of Egypt's last World Cup finals campaign, 28 years ago. In the 82nd minute of their first Group F fixture at Italia '90 against the Netherlands at Palermo's Stadio La Favorita, the then thirty-year-old faced a test of nerve as he waited by the penalty spot with Hans van Breukelen, the Netherlands goalkeeper, standing close by, muttering some unsympathetic words.

Undistracted, the bearded midfielder directed the ball, low and sure, beyond the right hand of the tall Dutchman a few moments later to earn Egypt a 1-1 draw with the reigning European champions.

Abdelghany and I are speaking at the Crowne Plaza World Trade Centre in Moscow on a grey December morning. It is the morning after the draw for the 2018 World Cup finals. He meets me fresh from breakfast, clad in a red sweatshirt bearing the Egyptian Football Association logo, with matching beanie hat. As a member of the EFA delegation, he has been in Moscow to plan ahead; over the next hour, though, he will be busy looking back – beginning with that goal in Palermo, which, as he tells me, inflated in value the longer his country's World Cup exile endured. 'My goal is my jewellery,' he grins.

'Nobody talked about this goal until around fifteen years afterwards. Nobody talked about it, nothing. But suddenly, I don't know what happened, it was like a miracle from God. Everybody was talking about my goal and me.'

Although reruns of the national side's three Italia '90 matches had already become a staple of the TV schedule during Ramadan, Abdelghany is referring in particular to the Italia '90-themed Vodafone commercials he appeared in earlier this decade, taking viewers back to his moment in the sun.

In one of the ads, he plays himself as a 1990 World Cup bore, forever harking back to his penalty kick. It begins in a pharmacy where he is showing the penalty on his smartphone to a couple of white-coated assistants, explaining to them the mechanics of his shot. 'A little to his right, and he was gone,' he says.

Next, he is chiding his nephew for not mimicking Uncle's technique in a park game. Then comes a shot of a weary Dutchman – a Van Breukelen lookalike – complaining about Abdelghany's pestering messages on WhatsApp.

And finally, the punchline as his phone provider calls and informs him, 'We loved your goal, Captain. But really, Egypt needs a new one.'

THERE WAS AN APPEALING SYMMETRY ABOUT EGYPT'S PRESENCE at Italia '90. Their previous participation at the World Cup had been on Italian soil back in 1934, when they qualified 'by beating Palestine – then officially the

British Mandate for Palestine – in a Middle East play-off. Facing an all-Jewish Palestine team playing under the auspices of the Eretz Israel Football Association, Egypt triumphed 7-1 in Cairo, then 4-1 in Tel-Aviv. A month later, in Naples, in a World Cup with a straight knockout format, they played just a single match, falling 4-2 against first-round opponents Hungary.

With that appearance, Egypt became the first African, and Arab, nation to appear at the World Cup finals. As the most populous and progressive Arab state, Egypt was a cultural lodestar throughout the 20th century: a hub for films, music, media and television – and the source of a soft power unrivalled in the region until the past decade or two.

As Abdelghany notes, they led the way in football too. 'We had a big community from England; they started to bring football to the English colony, so we started a long time ago. You can see the dates. The first club in Egypt was for the train company.' It is called El Sekka El Hadid Sporting Club and was founded in 1903 by British and Italian railway engineers.

Al Ahly, Egypt's most decorated club, entered existence four years later in 1907. Their great rivals Zamalek followed in 1911, with the initial moniker of Qasr El-Neel Club. 'We started our championship early, more than any other Arab country,' Abdelghany continues. 'Especially in the Gulf in this time, there was no development. They hadn't discovered petroleum yet. They lived a simple life and didn't think about sport and things like that.

'There's no comparison between Egypt and the UAE,' he notes of the other Arab nation that featured at Italia '90, 'even if UAE paid a lot of money for players and big names played there, just like in Qatar. Qatar has a professional league, but if you're looking at the national team, they have very few inhabitants, and they can't do anything.

'Before, we were a reference point in all things – in sport, music, education, civilisation. If you talk about Arab countries, Egypt was very advanced. You had roads and could travel from Cairo to Aswan by car, and from Cairo to Alexandria by car.'

The EFA's year of birth was 1921; FIFA affiliation followed two years later. In 1957, Egypt became a founder member of the Confederation of African Football (CAF). It was no surprise when they won the first two Africa Cup of Nations tournaments, then an event featuring only two other teams in Ethiopia and Sudan.

Yet, progress slowed. A closer affinity with the Middle East meant a lack of engagement with the game south of the Sahara. The economic pressures brought by two major conflicts – the 1967 Six-Day War and 1973 Arab-Israeli War – were another factor. Egyptians watched on as Tunisia, Algeria, and Morocco all won their first World Cup matches between 1978 and 1986.

It was in 1980s that the country's big club sides finally began to assert themselves in CAF's club competitions, with Abdelghany's Al Ahly and Zamalek each winning two continental crowns as part of a combined haul of ten trophies in that decade.

Success came to the national team too, with a 1986 Africa Cup of Nations triumph attained on penalties against Cameroon in Cairo. Abdelghany was among the players to convert his kick in the 5-4 shootout victory after a goalless draw.

As the Nineties approached, a return to the World Cup loomed at last. To secure it, Egypt had to overcome Algeria in a two-legged play-off. After a goalless first leg in the Algerian city of Constantine, Kamel Lemoui resigned as coach of the Desert Foxes, and a four-man emergency committee took charge for the decider back in Egypt on 17 November 1989. The FIFA delegate's report estimated that there were as many as 120,000 crammed inside the Cairo International Stadium, a huge bowl constructed by Werner March, architect of the Berlin Olympic Stadium. Those sardine-tight spectators saw Hossam Hassan deliver the only goal with an early header – though FIFA's aforementioned delegate singled out Abdelghany for praise as the pivotal man in midfield, 'usually to be found waiting in areas that potentially creative Algerians wanted to go'.

It was a high-emotion occasion with an ugly postscript in the form of a hotel brawl in which Egypt's team doctor, Ahmed Abd El Moniem, lost an eye. Algeria forward Lakhdar Belloumi, a former African Footballer of the Year, was alleged to have struck him in the face with a vase and became the subject of an international arrest warrant. Only in 2009 was that warrant rescinded. When I spoke to Belloumi in 2010 in a conversation over a crackly phone line to Mascara, his home city, he was reluctant to discuss the incident, stressing simply that, 'The most important thing to say is I'm innocent.'

*

IN THE LEAD-UP TO ITALIA '90, EGYPT EMBARKED ON A LONG preparation programme. There were training camps in France, West Germany, and England, and seven friendlies against European opposition alone between February and May. 'They stopped the championship, and all the people in Egypt were looking to the World Cup and only the national team's games,' Abdelghany remembers.

Such was the focus on the World Cup that the Egyptian FA sent only a B squad to the Africa Cup of Nations in March 1990 and lost all three games. The A team were faring rather better; notable results included victories in Czechoslovakia (1-0) and Scotland (3-1). This latter match is remembered well – if not fondly – by Alex McLeish, Scotland captain for the afternoon owing to the staging of the fixture at his club Aberdeen's home ground of Pittodrie.

'They were sharp, they were fast, they were aggressive – not in a tackling way but the way they attacked us,' McLeish told me.

'We got caught on the counter-attack with a goal, and I broke my nose. I jumped behind the centre-forward, Hossan Hassam, headed the ball, and he cracked his head right into my nose. He went down screaming like a pig, and I was the one with the nose bust. I said, "Wait a minute, it's your *heid* against my nose!"'

Under Mahmoud El Gohary, the coach who had led Al Ahly to their first African Champion Clubs' Cup, Egypt conceded only two goals in eight qualifying matches for Italy. El Gohary had been a captain in the Egyptian army for ten years after a back injury ended his playing career. Defence became the priority after he replaced Englishman Mike Smith, a former Wales manager, as national coach in 1988.

Adelghany says, 'We had a good coach whose philosophy was to not let the other team score, and then look to score ourselves. "Even if you don't score, just don't lose" was his philosophy. The national team at this time was like a club, because the players stayed together more than six months.' Abdelghany was an exception as the first player of his generation to be based abroad. In 1988, the year after finishing fourth in the vote for African

Player of the Year, he left Al Ahly to join Beira-Mar in Portugal.

This was an era when a move to Europe involved rather more machinations than Mohamed Salah would have required when departing for Basel aged twenty. In his eagerness for an opportunity, Abdelghany had assembled a video montage of himself and presented it to Arabic-speaking *France Football* journalist Patrick Godeau, then resident in Cairo, to show to clubs in Europe. 'I made the video by myself,' he remembers.

By this point, he was already nearly thirty. 'I began my professional life very late because in Egypt at this time, nobody knew anything about professionalism. It was an amateur league then. We were semi-professional. Football gave you some money but you had a job on the side. I was a student. I was studying philosophy at Cairo University, and after I finished, I worked in a bank.

'You played at a certain club, and you stayed at this club until you ended your career. You didn't know what the FIFA regulations were. We had no knowledge. But I was dreaming of being a professional player. We had two TV channels, and they transmitted the FA Cup final on Egyptian Channel 1 every year. When I saw it, I said, "I want to be with these players."'

He had been part of the Egypt side which survived the group stage at the 1984 Olympic football tournament. There he played against an Italy team in Pasadena that included Franco Baresi, Ricardo Ferri, Aldo Serena and Pietro Vierchowod – all future Italia '90 participants too.

Though his job title was defensive midfielder, he managed to get a goal in a victory over Costa Rica. 'When I started to play in Egypt, they didn't look at a player who was running, and playing tough, and cutting out passes, which was my position – defensive midfield. They wanted dribblers. They liked the players who scored goals. When I started, I didn't score goals.'

By 1990, he was one of his country's pivotal players and underlined this on their opening night in Italy – from striving to contain Ruud Gullit to striking the penalty that secured an historic point.

The venue was Palermo, and if Dutch fans coloured swathes of the stadium in orange, Egypt's players were not alone. They had the backing of the locals and, moreover, of hundreds of white-uniformed sailors from the Egyptian navy ship now docked in Palermo's harbour. 'A boat came from Alexandria to Palermo for the first game just to watch and support us,' Abdelghany remembers. 'Our president, Hosni Mubarak, and our defence minister knew there'd be many Dutch supporters in Palermo and so for that he sent this ship.'

With 54 per cent of the possession, Egypt played with imagination and effervescence, producing some fine one-touch football and troubling the Netherlands defence with the pace of Hossam Hassan. The early Dutch threat, by contrast, was all in the air, as a Gullit header and acrobatic Marco van Basten volley flew off target.

Yet, after Ahmed El Kass had stretched Hans van Breukelen with a volley from twenty yards, Egypt lost a goal to Dutch substitute Wim Kieft after 58 minutes. Though Frank Rijkaard failed to connect with a Van Basten cross, the ball ran on to Kieft, whose improvised flick took a deflection and wrongfooted Ahmed Shobeir, the African side's goalkeeper.

The unmarked Gamal Abdelhamid ought to have equalised with a far-post volley but shot over, and instead, it fell to Abdelghany to earn the parity the Egyptians' efforts warranted with a penalty awarded fortuitously when Hassan fell in the penalty area after a Ronald Koeman shirt tug outside the box.

'I became the first Arab player to score in the Olympics and the World Cup,' says Abdelghany.

'Holland weren't interested in Egypt. They thought they could beat us any time. I think what happened was Holland didn't respect us, even though we'd played many friendly games.'

'Pyramid men one of the wonders of the World Cup,' said *The Times*. 'Don't joke with Egypt,' declared the *Gazzetta dello Sport* which quoted Arrigo Sacchi, then coach of AC Milan, saying they had 'impressed me even more then Cameroon with their individual technique'. For his part, Pharaohs coach El Gohary noted the success of his man-marking tactics against van Basten.

He would send out a less open, less adventurous Egypt for their second Group F match against the Republic of Ireland, however. Ahead of the game, El Gohary said, 'Allah smiles on Egypt now,' but Ireland manager Jack Charlton, for one, wore a distinct frown after the teams' drab goalless draw. 'I hate teams like that. I deplore them,' fumed Charlton.

Abdelghany has not forgotten. 'He [Charlton] was angry with the way we played, but let me tell you what happened. When we played against Ireland, they were a very strong team. They played typical English football: they didn't use the midfield, they played from behind, and they had a striker, [Tony] Cascarino, who was very tall and played long balls. For two years, they'd hardly lost a game and when our coach studied all these things, he said, "We can't play with Ireland like we played with Holland, in an open game. We must defend well because we don't want to lose. We have a point, and if we can get a second point and then also get one against England, then we have an opportunity to qualify.'"

Facing England in Sardinia in their final fixture, they remained in qualifying contention at the interval after a scoreless first half. Ahmed Shobeir did not make a save until the 45th minute when palming away a Paul Parker shot. 'The Egyptians are defending very well, they're working very hard, let's see what's going to happen,' said David Pleat in the ITV commentary box as the second half opened. What happened next was an England set-piece goal after 58 minutes: Shobeir stepped out to collect Paul Gascoigne's inswinging ball but Mark Wright leaped high and reached it first, nodding into an empty net.

'We were better than the England team,' Abdelghany argues. 'They had very famous players like Gary Lineker, Paul Gascoigne, Chris Waddle, but we were competitive. The first half was very tight. We closed down all the spaces.' He fails to mention the booking he earned for time-wasting in that opening period.

'They scored from a free-kick, and I still remember the mistake from the goalkeeper,' he continues. 'I remember Gascoigne too. When we attacked, Gascoigne was saying, "Slow it down; Holland are beating Ireland," because he wanted us to take it easy. He tried to tell us we'd qualify together. I didn't believe him.'

*

THE ENDEAVOURS OF SOME OF EGYPT'S MORE IMPRESSIVE performers at Italia '90 did not go unnoticed in Europe. Prior to the tournament, only Abdelghany and midfielder Magdy Tolba played top-class football abroad, the latter with PAOK in Greece. That number rose in the immediate aftermath with twin brothers Hossam and Ibrahim Hassan – striker and full-back respectively – joining Tolba at PAOK, and centre-back Hany Ramzy signing for Swiss side Neuchâtel Xamax. Goalkeeper Shobeir had a trial at Everton but was unable to get a work permit.

At home, meanwhile, the EFA introduced professionalism and increased the size of the top division from twelve to eighteen clubs. Ian Hawkey, in his excellent history of African football, *Feet of the Chameleon*, writes, 'Professional football, with salaries for full-time players, was introduced to the Egyptian league in 1990 at the behest of the national coach, Mohammed El Gohari [sic]. Led by Al Ahly and Zamalek, the wealthier clubs began to recruit from across Africa, particularly west Africa.'

Today, the presence of an Egyptian club in eleven of this century's first eighteen African Champions League finals – with seven victories posted, six of them by Al Ahly – underlines the strength of the Egyptian Premier League in relation to its African rivals.

For Magdy Abdelghany, though, there are sizeable sticking points, starting with the fact Egypt had to wait so long to return to the World Cup finals. 'We take a long time to change,' he laments. 'In '90, they changed the league and [introduced] professionalism, but it's not proper professionalism. Let me say the Egyptian people know there's professionalism in the world and you must be professional, but they don't know exactly how to do it. They do it their way.

'Look at the clubs – there are no owners up to today,' he adds, citing the fact that the Cairo-based Big Two are both state-owned. 'At Al Ahly, there's no owner. At Zamalek, there's no owner. You select the committee of the clubs, and they have an election every four years to select the board members.'

Alex McLeish, the Scotland manager, had a 65-day spell in charge of Zamalek in 2016, and he points outs a major problem faced in that brief period: 'They find it hard to pay. My coaches were not paid for two months. I tended to feel a lot of players were still kept waiting on money as well, which made me think did they have money problems. I don't know how the system works. You have to manage players that are unhappy about not being paid, and coaches as well.'

Another significant blemish is the ban on away supporters. 'You can hear your own voice throughout the stadium,' McLeish notes.

This ban dates back to the Port Said stadium riot of 2012, which caused the deaths of more than seventy Al Ahly fans. They were killed when attacked by fans of the home side, Al Masry, although the Ahlawy – the Cairo club's ultras –

claimed subsequently that the violence was the work of the security forces, avenging the group's involvement in the protests that ousted President Mubarak from power.

If there are patches of gloom, Abdelghany, Egypt's Italia '90 hero, finds light in the generation of players he got to know as head of the EFA delegation at the FIFA Under-20 World Cup in Colombia in 2011. That Egypt squad included Mohamed Salah, Ahmed Hegazy, and Mohamed Elneny, all current Premier League footballers. They reached the round of sixteen where Salah scored in a 2-1 defeat by Argentina.

'I remember when I met him,' he says of Salah. 'He'd come to the Egyptian federation to register his contract with his agent. He was very small and didn't look like a player. I asked his agent who he was, and he told me, "He's going to be the best player in Egypt." This was the day before El Mokawloon El Arab [Arab Contractors], Salah's old team, played against Al Ahly. Salah, he scored a goal. He was eighteen years old.' It was Salah's first senior strike.

'I'm very close to him,' adds Abdelghany. 'I play ping pong with him, and I beat him. He tells me, "I'm a good player," so I say, "Come on, then." He's very young, and I don't like to lose. Plus he talks too much. I don't gamble but I told him, 'If I beat you, I'll take two hundred dollars."

'Every time I see him, I ask him where my two hundred dollars is.' Salah should have known better. As the world saw at Italia '90, when the stakes are high, Abdelghany knows how to be the man on the money.

KNOCKOUT

Boys from nowhere
Part 1 – Totò Schillaci

'SOMETIMES I ASK MYSELF, "HOW DID IT HAPPEN? DID IT REALLY happen to me?" I really do ask myself, because for me, it was something totally unexpected. It was difficult to come to terms with. I didn't speak Italian well, and I didn't know how to explain it all.'

If there was ever a look that spoke all of these words and more – a look melding joy and amazement and sheer how-the-fuck – it was the wild-eyed look of Salvatore Schillaci during Italia '90.

Forget the green, white, and red stickman Ciao; after all the promotional efforts, the real Italian symbol of their home World Cup turned out to be a Sicilian with a crazed countenance called Totò.

Schillaci, then 25, had played only once for Italy before the start of the World Cup. He would hit only one more international goal afterwards. Yet, he ended the 1990 tournament with both the Golden Boot for his six goals, and the Golden Ball as its best player. 'Who was the bigger surprise, Schillaci or Cameroon?' asked *Il Giorno*, the Milan daily, in its World Cup post mortem. Of the 75 goalscorers at Italia '90, only Cameroon's Roger Milla rivalled him for the impression made on the global audience. Schillaci's eyes had a story to tell.

'Everybody asks me to do that wild look,' he adds with a grin. 'In reality, that look said many things. It was an expression with a lot of meaning from a boy who had so much hunger to do well and be successful, and it went into homes across the whole world.'

Today, as we sit in the office of his football school in Palermo, those same green eyes are friendly and bright – and probably the most recognisable feature on the face of a man much changed since his 1990 goal rush.

After a handful of hair transplants, and rumoured plastic surgery too, the fiftysomething before me looks little older than his sallow-eyed 25-year-old self, the mongrel among the *Azzurri*'s lustrous-headed thoroughbreds.

'I've changed my look,' he says, reiterating what the wave of dark hair and Mexican-bandit moustache have spelled out already. 'I like to look good for my work today.' This is the Schillaci who has appeared on reality TV – he finished third in *L'isola dei famosi,* a celebrities-on-an-island show, in 2004 – and played a mafia boss in a TV series.

'After I stopped playing, I wanted to pay more attention to myself physically,' he elaborates. 'I like to do things for myself and not for others. I want to feel well in myself. I don't love visibility and publicity – I'm quite reserved – but if you want to get ahead, you have to do this and not hide away.

'The physical aspect is another string to your bow, and it's nice when people tell you you look younger.'

In a sense, Schillaci has come full circle, back to the place of his youth. The Scuola Calcio Totò Schillaci is found at the Centro Louis Ribolla, where he played football for six years from the age of eleven with a local club, AMAT. After leaving Japan, his final staging post as a professional footballer, he returned to his home city and, in 2000, established this school. It now has a full-sized all-weather pitch, two smaller football courts, and caters for boys aged from five to seventeen.

Outside the office stands a stout palm tree. In the club house next door, his father – short, bald and arguably looking more like Totò Schillaci (the one the world remembers) than Totò Schillaci himself – is behind the bar.

A line of shirts hang on the wall behind Schillaci Sr, most of them bearing the names of forwards: Cavani, Miccoli, Klose, Giovinco, Milito. (The two shirts carrying the lesser known name Di Mariano belong to a graduate of Schillaci's school now at Serie B side Novara, Francesco Di Mariano.)

The walls around the bar are alive with memories of Schillaci's career: photographs with Pope John Paul II, with Roberto Baggio, with Juventus's UEFA Cup-winning side, in the blue and black of Inter, and in the light blue of Jubilo

Iwata, the club he represented for four years in Japan's J-League.

'If you tell my story now, it seems like a fairy tale,' he reflects. The football world is a place of hyperbole, but not in this instance. When Italy won the World Cup in 1982, he was just leaving AMAT for his first professional team, Messina.

'I was eleven when I started playing in this sports centre here,' he explains. 'When I got to seventeen, in June, around the start of the 1982 World Cup, I was signed by Messina who were in Serie B. I celebrated Italy winning the World Cup with my friends in the city centre – I was on the roof of a bus with the Italian flag, risking my life.

'I'd have never thought of being able to achieve all this. Ultimately, I just liked playing football. I was quick, and I could dribble – I liked taking on defenders and scoring goals. Messina bought me for eighteen million lire, which was about nine thousand euros.'

If emulating Paolo Rossi, Italy's 1982 Golden Shoe winner, had seemed a pipe dream then, even in the lead-up to Italia '90 he was taking nothing for granted. 'The TV and the newspapers were starting to say my name, but I wasn't sure,' he recalls. 'That year Juventus had signed me, and I had a great season, winning the UEFA Cup and Coppa Italia, and scoring twenty one goals – fifteen in Serie A. I was the last to be called up, though, and the only player to have been playing in Serie B the year before.

'When the season ended, one of the directors at Juventus came in and read the names who'd been called up. He said, "[Stefano] Tacconi, [Giancarlo] Marocchi, [Luigi] De Agostini," and then he left the changing room. Then he popped back in and said, "Oh, I forgot, there's also Schillaci!" I told him, "*Vaffanculo*! [fuck off]"

'I shouldn't have even been on the bench but in the stand. During the training sessions, though, I gave the manager a problem, and he put me on the bench. For me, that was massive in itself. During the first match against Austria, the game was goalless. I was on the bench, and in the 76th minute, [Italy coach Azeglio] Vicini called me and I went on and I scored from a [Gianluca] Vialli cross. It was a lovely ball in; I was in between two big central defenders, and he really fired it across and I headed it in. The joy was immense.' It was his first touch of a football at Italia '90.

One of the remarkable aspects of Schillaci's World Cup exploits is that he did not win his first senior cap for Italy until March 1990. Indeed, when Italy met England in a friendly match in November 1989, Schillaci was being tried out, as an overage player, in their Under-21 team.

Just as remarkable, with hindsight, is the fact Paul Gascoigne was with England's second string for that match at the Goldstone Ground in Brighton, and it was Gascoigne who ended Schillaci's involvement in his first-ever international after 44 minutes. 'He gave me a kick on the instep, and I needed three stitches,' Schillaci remembers.

'I liked Gascoigne a lot because he saw football as a spectacle,' he adds of a man who, like himself, was an instinct-driven footballer who flowered at the perfect time. 'There were extraordinary players then. They played for the spirit of the game, for the hunger, for the shirt. It's no longer like that today. They're not as good technically as before. Now, football's based more on running, on speed, and on physical power.

'Today, pure strikers no longer exist. They all share in the tasks. They all go back; they all defend; they all join in the attacking, in the pressing; and a lot of players get tired. You no longer have the out-and-out striker. I was like that – sometimes I'd go missing, but other times, I'd win the match.'

Schillaci had the capabilities required to flourish at international level. Juventus president Gianni Agnelli told him on his arrival in Turin from Messina in the summer of 1989, 'You've got goals in your blood. Do what your instinct tells you and you'll achieve great things.'

His instinct during Italia '90 was a simple one: just go for goal. He had the most goal attempts – 21 in all, a total matched only by Jürgen Klinsmann – and the most shots on target (12).

Italy's captain at Italia '90, Giuseppe Bergomi, relates, 'With Totò, I played with him at Inter, and he was all about instinct, with not much reasoning. You couldn't cage him in schemes and formations, you had to let him play. You know those boys who always want the ball, who are unpredictable, who shoot from thirty metres and get you a goal – that was Schillaci. He was carefree, cheerful, and it was good to be in his company.'

Aldo Serena, his fellow forward in Italy's 1990 squad, proffers a similar thought: 'Schillaci was an anarchic player who you couldn't integrate into a collective game, but he was incredibly fast, he always shot, and this was his golden moment. He had the support of the public too because he played for Juventus, and they have fans all over Italy.'

Now was his time to shine. He began the second game, against the United States, among the substitutes, but as he took the field in the 52nd minute, Napoli striker Andrea Carnevale, the man making way, mouthed '*vaffanculo*' to the Italy bench.

Although Schillaci did not score against the US, Carnevale's outburst and Gianluca Vialli's penalty miss in that game meant neither forward featured in the third group fixture against the Czech Republic. Instead, for the first time in a competitive international, Schillaci was in the starting XI, supported in attack by Roberto Baggio, an unused substitute in the first two matches. In 1989/90, they had finished as the top two scorers in Serie A. Nine minutes after kick-off, Schillaci had another goal. Baggio, with a dazzling run and finish, completed the 2-0 victory that ensured first place in Group A.

'We were the "goal twins",' says Schillaci of Baggio, who was making his first World Cup start too.

'We had a great understanding, a great feeling between us. We were always looking for these little combinations, in training and in the matches. He played less than me but he should have played a lot more in that World Cup because he always made the difference. He was a great athlete, a great pro and for me one of the best Italian footballers ever.'

As for Schillaci's goal that evening, it owed everything to his powers of anticipation. When Giuseppe Giannini volleyed a Roberto Donadoni corner into the ground, the ball span up to the right edge of the six-yard box, and Schillaci, having read its flight expertly, applied the headed finish. Off he sped down the touchline to leap into the arms of Tacconi, the reserve goalkeeper, who had told him in the dressing room that he would score.

Afterwards, Schillaci urged reporters, 'Don't call me the new Paolo Rossi,' but the comparison was inevitable, and he underscored his status as Italy's man of the hour in the round of sixteen against Uruguay on 25 June, a match in which he and Serena contributed the goals.

As before every Italy match that summer, Schillaci prepared to face the South Americans by watching the *Rocky* films and listening to the soundtrack. By now, as he observes, his own story had the beating of the Italian Stallion's. 'The music helped me get psyched up and focused, and ready to go out there and battle. Then, when I went out on the pitch, I wouldn't look anybody in the eye. I compared myself a bit to Rocky – like him, I had to make the most of that moment of going from a nobody to a somebody. That was a film, though, and this was reality.'

Schillaci's breakthrough strike against the stubborn Uruguayans came after 65 minutes and was stunning for its speed and simplicity. Baggio met goalkeeper Walter Zenga's falling kick with a sumptuous flick to Serena, and he touched the ball on through an opponent's legs towards Schillaci – who, reacting before the two defenders in his vicinity could reach him, unleashed a wickedly dipping shot from the arc of the penalty box, sending the ball zipping past the raised right hand of Fernando Álvez, Uruguay's goalkeeper. 'He's hit it that early, the keeper hasn't expected it,' said Trevor Francis, commentating for ITV.

It was the cue for a brief shot of Schillaci's wild eyes before his disappearance beneath a mound of blue shirts. 'It was an instinctive thing,' he remembers. 'I didn't think. The ball came and like strikers have to do, I hit it with my left foot and scored a great goal. Even the TV commentator was taken by surprise.'

'Totò, the fable continues' declared the *Gazzetta dello Sport*, which informed its readers afterwards that the Sicilian had now overtaken Franco Baresi in a poll to find the most-loved *Azzurri* player.

THE FIRST WORDS OF SCHILLACI'S AUTOBIOGRAPHY, 'IL GOL È TUTTO', are 'You've killed Falcone.' They are the words of Giovanni Trapattoni, his then coach at Juventus. The Falcone in question was Judge Giovanni Falcone, the prominent anti-mafia investigator murdered, along with his wife and three police escort officers, by a bomb on the highway from Palermo airport (which now bears his name along with that of another murdered judge, Paolo Borsellino). The date was 23 May 1992.

Recalling that conversation, Schillaci tells me, 'He said that because he was upset about what had happened. He would've said it without thinking too much.

I didn't take it too strongly. In fact, I said to him, "*Mister*, I was with Baggio, you can ask him. I've not killed anyone today."

'Palermo was a city on fire, where so many things were happening. I don't like it that people link Palermo with the mafia. There are good people here; it's a great place, an extraordinary city, and there are positive and negative sides. At that moment, I felt really bad for Palermo.'

As a Sicilian playing in the north, Schillaci faced regular insults. Fans would chant, 'Schillaci steals tyres' – a reference to his brother Giuseppe's arrest after he lent friends a spanner and they did just that. There was graffiti daubed on the wall of his apartment building. 'In Turin I lived in an apartment, and the graffiti said, "*terrone*" [the insult for people from the south of Italy who live off the land] but I was very proud to be a *terrone*. I understood this was within the football context. There's always this rivalry between Torino and Juventus, and I said, if they were insulting me, it's because they're afraid of me.'

Adding another layer to his response, he adds, 'In Italy, there's always been this racism or antagonism between north and south. Consider that a lot of Sicilians emigrate all over the world, like to the USA, and they get ahead, people who didn't have a penny and left with a cardboard suitcase.'

For a month in the summer of 1990, though, Italy had a Sicilian hero. Amid his flood of World Cup feats, left-wing satirical weekly magazine *Cuore Mundial* ran a feature titled 'Schillaci resolves the southern question' – a reference to the divide between the prosperous north and poorer south. (A divide that still endures – in 2015, the lowest average annual household income in Italy was the €21,950 recorded in Sicily; in Piedmont, the region where Turin lies, the figure was €30,260.)

Schillaci received a reminder of the world he had left behind on the eve of the match against Uruguay on 25 June, when he called an old friend back in Sicily and learned of the death of a boyhood associate, shot dead by the police.

'He had problems in his childhood, but when we played together, he used to always encourage me because he saw my abilities, and he'd always tell me that if I didn't become a footballer, he'd kill me,' he remembers. 'Life in our neighbourhood wasn't easy. There are good people and bad people, and a lot of lads went down a very different route.'

Schillaci had barely attended school and instead was out working from the age of eleven. 'Every day, I'd work with my grandfather. I liked working: I wasn't interested in going to school. It wasn't my strong point. I did all types of job.'

His first was collecting pitchers of wine for the bar where his grandfather worked. Another was for a milkman, rising at 4am to help on the morning round. No wonder he looked knackered at 25.

'Living in a very poor neighbourhood is like that,' Schillaci continues. 'With its problems, you can go off the rails, but football changed my life.' Indeed, it probably saved it: in his autobiography, he recounts the occasion a teenage rival turned up in the neighbourhood looking for him with a gun. Fortunately, Schillaci was at the football club – the same club where we are sitting for this interview – doing extra shooting practice.

Palermo today is the perfect city for a weekend break: history, architecture, food, sea, sunshine. As if to illustrate the point, Sarah Greene, the former *Blue Peter* presenter, walks by singing 'Volare' at one surreal moment a few hours before my meeting with Schillaci.

A ten-minute walk past Palermo's opera house, Teatro Massimo, moving away from the centre of town, is Il Capo, the market district where Schillaci spent the first five years of his life and in whose narrow streets he began working with his grandfather. There, he would join other boys for kickabouts on the cobbled square adjoining the parish church, the Chiesa della Mercede, drawing the priest out to complain about the thud of the ball against the large brown door that served as a goal.

The raised square looks down on Via Cuppicinelle, a sloping street lined by market stalls. Two men stand washing fish in plastic bowls. Next door, a stall displays nine varieties of olive. A man with white hair and a mouth of missing teeth pauses from selling brushes to point and tell me, 'When he was little, he played there.'

A short walk up the street leads to Bar Casisa, an unfussy place with an entrance obscured by scaffolding and sheets of corrugated iron. Inside, on the tiled wall, I spot an Italia '90 sticker. Behind the bar is Salvo. His grandmother, he tells me, was a Schillaci, making Totò a distant cousin.

'I played with him,' says Salvo, beginning a time-worn lament. 'I was better than him. At sixteen, I went to Varese in Serie B. I broke my leg in three places.' The chubby, balding man beside me nods in agreement. '*Ci vuole fortuna,*' he says. You need luck.

This tight maze of streets was awash with Italian flags in the summer of 1990. One of their own had become the luckiest of them all. And Schillaci gained a sense of the excitement back on his home island via the new toy he had received as a member of Italy's World Cup squad: a mobile phone. 'All the players were given a mobile, and it was something quite unusual in that period,' he smiles.

The first call he would make after each match was back home to his parents. There, he heard the wave of noise and excitement breaking on the streets outside the family home in the CEP, the estate where they lived on the north-western fringe of Palermo.

'You could hear the enthusiasm, and they were singing songs comparing me to Pelé.' To the tune of Mozart's 'Eine kleine Nachtmusik', he sings the one in question: '*Noi abbiamo un siciliano che/ Gioca al calcio meglio di Pelé.*' It translates as, 'We've got a Sicilian who plays football better than Pelé.'

'My father lives in a district near here,' he adds, 'and when I scored a goal, he wouldn't go down to the square to celebrate like the rest. He'd go and stand on the balcony, and there'd be all these people on the street below, waving to him. He was like the Pope.

'It was very emotional seeing people's affection towards me and my father. It's true, I cried tears of joy.

'It's as if it was all predestined. I lived at number nineteen Via La Sfera in Palermo. *Sfera* means ball, and that was my shirt number for the World Cup. I was born prematurely, after seven months, and my shirt at Messina was number seven.

'My story's like a film, but it's the reality because in a year my life changed completely. There was even the birth of my son Mattia during the World Cup [a birth he missed having played in the Italy-Uruguay match just hours earlier]. From Serie B with Messina, I go to Juventus and then to the national team, and become the star player. I think it's impossible to repeat a story like this.

'I found myself in a different world. I was the hero of the World Cup; the Golden Boot, the best player at the World Cup, second in the Ballon D'Or.

I was in a situation I couldn't explain. If you were writing a film script, you'd say it couldn't happen.'

✱

'PLEASE DON'T WAKE ME UP,' WAS THE *GAZZETTA DELLO SPORT*'S headline after his quarter-final strike against the Republic of Ireland, but the dream did come to an end. While further goals followed against Argentina and England, the latter, from the penalty spot, came not in the final but in the third-place match.

On a positive note, it ensured that he surpassed Czechoslovakia's Tomáš Skuhravý as the tournament's top scorer. 'We won third place, and it allowed me to win the Golden Boot, which was huge for me, but I'd have given that up to play in the final,' he admits.

A surreal summer concluded with him spending a holiday in the palace of Vittorio Emanuele di Savoia, the Prince of Naples and son of the last king of Italy, Umberto II. After that, reality bit. 'It was a disastrous year,' he observes of the post-World Cup descent.

'It felt like a building had come down on top of me. It was hard to come to terms with it, as it wasn't in my expectations – I'd just wanted to be part of the group, not to get that far. During the World Cup, all these journalists, media, TV were around me, and I thought, 'What's happening to me?" It was harder to handle that than actually going out to play in the World Cup.

'I'd feel embarrassed when they called me to speak on TV, as I'd not had much of an education. So, becoming famous around the world was the hardest thing to handle.

'After the World Cup, I was no longer "Schillaci from Messina" but "Schillaci from the *Mondiali*" [World Cup], and everybody expected me to do things differently than before – you know, outstanding performances, the key player, the man to make the difference – and it was also very difficult because defenders were looking at me differently too, not like before.'

Schillaci's autobiography lays out a year of missteps on and off the pitch. In a fixture against Bologna in November 1990, he earned himself a one-match ban for threatening opposition forward Fabio Poli with the words, 'I'll have you shot.' A difficult relationship with Luigi Maifredi, who had replaced Dino Zoff as

Juventus coach in the close season, did not help, and after a six-month scoring drought, he ended the 1990/91 campaign with just five goals. His seventh and last goal for Italy arrived at the season's end, in a 2-1 European Championship qualifying loss in Norway on 5 June 1991.

With his marriage collapsing, meanwhile, Rita, his first wife – who later began a much-publicised relationship with Gianluigi Lentini, subject of a world-record £13million transfer to AC Milan in 1992 – had him followed and even put a mini-microphone in his sweater when seeking evidence of his serial cheating.

A transfer to Internazionale offered a fresh start, but there was no salvaging the spark of his annus mirabilis. It is possible here to draw a parallel with Paul Gascoigne, another free spirit from the 'other' end of a country; two players who touched the sky in the Italia '90 bubble but then fell to earth. 'At Inter, I started really well, scoring five goals in three games, but then I got injured – a serious groin tear – and was out for more than six months. It got me down as every time I recovered, I pulled up again.'

In 1994, aged 29, he left Italian football for Japan, where he became one of the biggest names in the fledgling J-League – a move made, he admits, 'thinking more of my wallet'.

Thanks to his four years in Japan, he could set up the school where I find him today, and it is not his only current involvement in the game. 'I do some work with the Juventus legends and for RAI [the Italian state broadcaster] on their Sunday football show *Quelli che il Calcio*.

'In the end, I'm happy with what I do. I don't have any ambition to earn more money: I'm more curious about visiting as many places as possible, something you don't get to do when you're a footballer.'

When not off travelling and exploring the world, Italy's 1990 hero has days like this one, back on the same patch of Palermo whence he once set out on his improbable journey. 'When I see that desire to play in the eyes of the boys,' he says, 'it does fill me with joy, as I see myself reflected in them and remember when I was a boy.' In the eyes. It always was in the eyes with Totò.

Boys from nowhere
Part 2 – Roger Milla

IT IS ONE OF THE WORLD CUP'S GREATEST STORIES. MAN GOES into semi-retirement on a volcanic island 1,300 miles off the east coast of Africa. Man comes out of semi-retirement on the whim of his country's president and scores four goals at Italia '90. Man wiggles his hips down by the corner flag. World swoons. Man is 38 years old.

Twenty-eight years on, it still sounds too outrageously good to be true. The man himself, Roger Milla, can only conclude there was a divine hand at work, from the goals he struck to the dance that put a smile on the world's face.

'Everything I did there, it's God who told me what to do because I can't imagine myself scoring goals at that World Cup,' he says. 'Really, I couldn't imagine it. And when I scored that goal, he led me to the corner. I'd never done that.

'It wasn't planned, no, no, no. I've never done that – go to the corner to do that dance. It's like the dances we have in Cameroon, but it's not the makossa [a popular musical genre] as people say. It's like all our dances. I'm proud, I'm happy, Cameroon's happy that this dance got Cameroon known everywhere and got people everywhere talking about us.'

They certainly were talking about them, and about Milla in particular. '*Milla, che polpacci*' – literally, Milla what calves – was the headline of one *Gazzetta dello Sport* feature investigating the secrets of his success in the wake of his deeds in the round-of-sixteen victory over Colombia. The article analysed his 'shorter than normal' calves which contracted more quickly, and his 'longer than normal' Achilles which 'allows the foot to "work" better'.

Milla is happy to highlight his physical gifts. 'I was the junior champion at high jump,' he remembers of his schoolboy prowess. 'It's genetic, and when you talk about genetics, you're talking about God. When my mother was pregnant, it's God who said, "This boy's going to be like that."'

If that was God, it was his mother Ruth who, when local clubs came to the family home asking for young Roger to appear for their team, would negotiate, in return for each run-out, a domestic helper to assist her with household tasks.

Even before the first kick at Italia '90, Milla had given journalists a wonderful story to write with his return to the national squad on the orders of President Paul Biya, Cameroon's autocratic leader.

After the story came the sensation. Here was a man who had been African Footballer of the Year in 1976, the same year that Franz Beckenbauer had received the European prize. When Milla struck twice against Romania in Cameroon's second match, he became the World Cup's oldest scorer, surpassing the 37 years and 236 days of Sweden's Gunnar Gren. He broke his own record with two more goals against Colombia aged 38 years and 34 days. He would repeat the trick four years later at USA '94, by which time he was 42 years and 39 days old when scoring against Russia.

*

NOW IN HIS MID-SIXTIES, ROGER MILLA IS A ROVING AMBASSADOR for Cameroon. His home in Yaoundé, the capital city, is a large, peach-coloured bungalow on a long street of smart government villas. Towering coconut trees line the side of the road. Beyond the black security gate, manned by a yellow-uniformed guard, is a driveway where a man in a Liverpool away shirt washes the flagstones.

I am with Martin Etonge, a local journalist, and we are led inside, into a long reception room, where we settle into woven wicker chairs and wait for Milla. On the wall is a painting featuring two images of the man himself: one as the elder statesman, the other as the Cameroon centre-forward. Between the two images of Milla is a lion, looking out from the canvas with a vigilant eye. The inscription beneath reads 'Cœur d'Afrique' – Heart of Africa.

When Milla appears, he is wearing a long-sleeved gingham shirt that hangs loosely over his still-slim frame. On those famously productive feet is a pair of black sandals. His thin, grey moustache and clear-framed spectacles signpost the passing of the years, yet there is no mistaking the gap-toothed smile which once lit up television screens across the planet.

His ambassadorial role means he has recently returned from an overseas trip with a Cameroon under-age team. It also means that I should address him not as Roger or Monsieur Milla – but as '*Excellence*'.

He brought joy to an entire continent at Italia '90, and if he quibbles over the notion that he was a standard-bearer for all of Africa, this is precisely how it panned out. 'I can't say it's a role I had, it was simply a duty as an African and a Cameroonian footballer. It's normal that with God's grace, I did what I could do for the African continent, for football in general and for Cameroon.'

The best place to begin Milla's World Cup story is on Réunion, the French colonial outpost in the Indian Ocean, 500 miles past Madagascar. 'I was tired, as I'd given a lot playing professional football in France, getting up at seven each morning, in the middle of winter, to go and train,' he begins. 'My heart wasn't in it any more. I asked the president at Montpellier [Louis Nicollin] if he'd let me go and stay with a friend in Réunion to take a break. It was the best place to rest – nobody would know where I was; I could switch off properly there. It was an island, the air was fresh, and so off I went.

'My friend hadn't told me he was the general secretary of a team there, Saint-Pierre. Straight away, he took me to their training ground. It was, "Come, let me show you something." So, he took me to the ground, and I thought, "Great, I'll take advantage of this to do some running and keep myself in shape." Next thing, the club's president turned up. They told him, "That's Roger Milla training, the Cameroonian who used to play in France." He said, "No way, that's not him."

'I remember, my friend then called me over and introduced me to the president. He said, "Is that really you?" I said, "Yes, it's me." I carried on with my training, and that evening my friend called me and said the president had called him to ask if I could help them in their championship.

'I said, "I don't know yet if I'll still be capable of doing it; I need to see how I am physically first." I told him I'd gone there for a rest, but he convinced me.

I played for almost a year, and we won the league and the cup.'

If Milla was the catalyst then, it was not the first time, nor would it be the last. From winning the inaugural African Cup Winners' Cup with Tonnerre Yaoundé in 1975 and scoring in the 1981 French Cup final for Bastia, to shooting Montpellier to the French second division title in 1987, Milla was an on-field energy source for players around him, even if this did not always make him popular.

In fact, his nickname was Gaddafi, after the former leader of Libya. 'Jean-Paul Akono, the former national coach who was Olympic champion at Sydney [in 2000], was the one who called me Gaddafi,' Milla explains. 'It was because I was always boiling over. I was dynamic, I didn't know defeat. On the pitch, I always wanted everything to be perfect – just like with other great players. I wanted my teammates to be perfect so they could win. So, I was always behind them telling them, "Why are you doing that?" A lot of them thought I was having a go at them, but it's my way of talking as I stammer a bit. I'd push them to the limit.'

The opportunity to drive forward a new generation of Cameroon footballers in summer 1990 arose unexpectedly. He had just begun a coaching diploma on Réunion when the call came to play in the testimonial match of an old teammate, Théophile 'Doctor' Abega, in Douala in December 1989.

'When the public saw me, they were in uproar, saying I'd tricked them and hadn't retired after all. That's how word got to the ears of the president, who demanded that I join the Lions squad for the World Cup.'

There was displeasure among a significant portion of the Cameroon squad at the veteran's return. 'I went to a training camp with the national team and a lot of my teammates said, "No, we don't want this,"' he explains. 'It was really, really tough. But I knew my strength, my technique. I wasn't worried.

'I told Thomas Nkono that it was on the training ground where you show what you can do, and from there it's the coach who decides. We had some training matches and I scored five goals.

'When I got to Yugoslavia [for the squad's pre-finals camp], the next morning we went jogging. I'd not run for a while, and I felt my chest was going to explode. I got through the first jog, I got through the second. The third, the fourth, I was holding my own. The players behind said, "Take it easy", but I said, "You didn't want me here, and I'm going to show you that I'm physically ready."'

Nkono, a long-time national-team colleague, as well as sparring partner in derby matches with Canon Yaoundé against Milla's Tonnerre, remembers debating his inclusion with the squad's younger members. During an interview in Barcelona, Nkono tells me, 'For Roger, I had to fight with more than one. The tasks that the coach gave us, he couldn't do them all, as he was thirty-eight. If there were eight repetitions, it would've been five or six, not eight. So, if there was a young player wondering why Roger was doing five, I'd have to say, "Look, you're not the same age as him."'

With a chortle, Nkono adds of Milla, 'He was very competitive. I remember one derby with Tonnerre, his last derby I think before he went to France. Our coach decided to man-mark him. The whole game he went out wide, and the lad just followed him. In the end, he gave the defender a punch and got a red card.'

Milla arrived in Italy carrying a grievance from Cameroon's first World Cup in Spain appearance eight years earlier. 'Yes, the goal against Peru,' he says, recalling an effort ruled offside despite there being two Peruvians between him and the goalkeeper. Cameroon, unbeaten with three draws, would have qualified ahead of Italy, the eventual World Cup winners, had that goal stood.

Given that performance and their two African titles in the intervening years, Milla, a proud man, scorns what he regards as condescending European views of Cameroon at the outset of Italia '90.

'I'm a bit disappointed with all these coaches and connoisseurs of football, because you can't tell me it was a surprise. In 1982, we were at the World Cup and produced a really good performance. We had draws with Italy, with Poland, with Peru. We had some of the same players in 1990. I don't understand this talk of a surprise. People overlooked us.

'Between '82 and '90, we had a high level. We won the Africa Cup of Nations in '84 and again in '88. In '86, we reached the final. The country had worked eight years for that, and we had an intelligence on the pitch.

'We had a great team. Our clubs had won the African Champions' Cup and the African Cup Winners' Cup several times. In Africa, we were already ready, and now we were prepared for the international stage – and when I say international, that means the World Cup.'

Argentina, their opening opponents, he says colourfully, 'took us for rabbits'.

They paid the price, and Cameroon could have won by a bigger margin after Milla's introduction after 81 minutes.

It is instructive watching again his first cameo of the 1990 finals. His passport name of Miller – he preferred Milla as it looked more African – pops up on the TV screen as he takes the field, and what stands out at once are his ability to hold on to the ball and his awareness of players around him. In injury time, Milla picks up possession thirty yards from his own goal, turns, and darts between two Argentina defenders before releasing Émile Mbouh down the right. Breaking down the middle, Milla is clear, but his teammate shoots and misses. Milla punches the air in frustration.

That summer, Valeri Nepomniachi, Cameroon's coach, said of Milla, 'He spots problems, and when he gets on the pitch, he works like the coach – organising, adjusting positions . . . I believe he has some kind of computer in his head and knows what to do in any situation.'

Milla, in his own words, knew what it took to 'change the face of a match' and in Cameroon's second group fixture against Romania, he exploited this ability to stunning effect. After 59 minutes, he stepped on to the pitch in Bari. By the 86th minute, he had two goals.

'Two miracles,' he affirms. 'These were the goals of a centre-forward, a great centre-forward, because not just any centre-forward can do what I did in that match.'

For the first, he sensed the opportunity as defender Ioan Andone let a long ball bounce. As the ball came back to ground, Milla challenged, hustling the defender off balance, kept his own footing, and lifted a left-foot shot past Lung.

For the second goal, he even provided his own assist. 'Nobody in the world had seen anything like it – a player playing himself in on his own,' he enthuses. 'It deserves consideration. If I wasn't black they'd talk more about that goal. No other player in the world has done that.'

He lifted a ball to the head of François Omam-Biyik and when the tall striker, jumping with Michael Klein, failed to get a touch, Milla had the speed and awareness to move round the back of him, easing past a yellow shirt with those light, feline strides, and then thumping the ball high past Lung.

'You know in football, the one-two, whether it's on the floor or in the air, you follow the action. So playing that ball up, I followed it. Even Pelé, the King himself, said that nobody had done what I did there. So Cameroon deserve to be respected.'

'Technically it was outstanding,' adds Thomas Nkono. 'That's in your genes. If that goal was scored today, it'd be all over the television.'

It was in Cameroon's second-round meeting with Colombia nine days later that Milla scored the most readily recalled of all his World Cup goals. He had already shot Cameroon in front sixty seconds into the second half of extra time, hurdling a defender's leg and sweeping the ball past René Higuita at his near post.

It was his second effort, though, two minutes afterwards, which became an iconic World Cup moment. This owed everything to the action that preceded it, involving Milla and the Colombia goalkeeper.

It is a moment that conveys the 'speed of thought' that Pelé identified when talking about Milla in the preface to his autobiography. 'You can't get that intelligence from going to school,' Milla remarks. 'You have to react in a split-second to understand what your opponent's going to do in order to get the better of him.'

'Roger's a good observer,' says Nkono, and in this instance, he watched as Higuita collected a pass thirty-five yards from his own goal and then pounced at the sight of the goalkeeper's loose first touch. Though Higuita sought to avert danger with a drag-back, Milla was too swift for the 23-year-old, stealing away with the ball and running free. Higuita made a futile feet-first lunge as Milla advanced and rolled the ball into an empty net.

A cartoon of Milla leaving Higuita in the distance appeared in the *Cameroon Tribune*, accompanied by the following imagined quote: 'I don't like insolent goalkeepers. After twenty years operating in opposition defences, I'm the one who dribbles around goalkeepers and not the other way round!'

IF 23 JUNE 1990 WAS A DAY TO REMEMBER FOR MILLA AND Cameroon, it is intriguing to wonder how it was for the man on the receiving end, '*el Loco*' Higuita. I find out late one December night in Moscow.

It is the evening of the World Cup draw, though already past midnight when I step out of the ankle-deep slush and into the splendour of the Radisson Royal, FIFA's base for the occasion. My WhatsApp calls and messages to Higuita have gone unanswered, so it is now or never. I have been told he has an early-morning flight to catch.

The Hotel Ukraina, to use its original name, was one of the seven Stalinist-Gothic skyscrapers that rose across Moscow in the late 40s and 50s. Up in the bar on the 31st floor, set in the hotel's spire, snowflakes dance outside the windows, embellishing the Moscow-by-night panorama. Laurent Blanc and Marcel Desailly are in conversation at a table, but there is no sign of Higuita.

Back downstairs in the lobby, I bump into Sergio Goycochea, Argentina's 1990 World Cup goalkeeper, his face framed by a big Sherpa hat. 'Higuita? He's in the FIFA Club, but he's leaving in an hour.'

The FIFA Club is a cordoned-off microclimate inhabited by heroes of World Cups past: a name-dropper's paradise. Dimly lit but star-bright. Ronaldo (the Brazilian one), Miroslav Klose, Fabio Cannavaro. Gary Lineker in conversation with Gianni Infantino and Zvonimir Boban. And there, at a corner table, with surely the most luxuriant poodle perm ever seen on the head of a man in his sixth decade, the fabulously hirsute René Higuita. It is a feat of tonsorial longevity to match Milla's footballing one at the World Cup.

After introducing myself, he hands me a glass of rum and coke. Moscow might be too cold for the man from Medellin – 'I've only been outside to smoke,' he tells me – but, thankfully, it has not cooled his generosity towards journalists he has never met before.

First things first – the Milla moment in Naples. 'It was the kind of mistake those of us who play football make; those of us who love the ball, those who want to keep the ball inside the pitch and not just hit it out,' he tells me.

'Football is a game of mistakes, and taking advantage of the mistakes that happen. If we lose two-nil, it's not a problem, nobody sees Higuita's mistake. You see the Higuita mistake when Bernardo Redín scores for two-one.'

And afterwards? 'Everyone accepted it. All of us know who makes a mistake at a given moment, we don't need people to point it out. I can hold my hand up and say, "I made a mistake."'

If the fall guy then, Higuita sees himself as a torchbearer for today's goalkeepers, a custodian who 'did not just play with his hands but his feet' and who was a catalyst for change in a way that 'neither Pelé nor Maradona nor Messi' managed.

'It was a way of expressing yourself,' he argues. 'We showed the world. It was something the world saw, and other footballing figures then took hold of it. [Pep] Guardiola took it, and he won everything.

'If it were today, Barcelona would sign me, and I'd be playing there. It's what they need in football now – goalkeepers who come out and play. Goalkeepers today have to know how to use the ball. There are different ways of protecting your goal – some play between their posts, some inside their eighteen-yard box, others outside. I was a complete goalkeeper. I could play in any system and I did, but today, I'd be in a team like Barcelona.'

It is Higuita's view that Francisco Maturana, Colombia's coach at Italia '90, was a visionary. 'He was a strategist, a wise man. He was ahead of his time.'

A year before the World Cup, Higuita had played in the Maturana-led Atlético Nacional team who became the first Colombian winners of the Copa Libertadores (in a final in which he saved four penalties in a shootout and scored one).

In that same year – and it may not be entirely coincidental – Pablo Escobar, head of the Medellin drugs cartel, was ranked by *Forbes* magazine as the world's seventh richest man. Andrés Campomar's book *¡Golazo!* relates that the Argentinian match officials for the Copa Libertadores semi-final against Uruguayan club Danubio received a visit on the eve of the match in Colombia from a group of men carrying machine guns, a bag of money, and the message 'Nacional wins or you're all dead meat'. Nacional won 6-0. In November 1989 the domestic championship was cancelled after the murder in Medellin of referee Álvaro Ortega. (The whole football world would later feel a quiver of horror at the killing of Andrés Escobar, Higuita's old teammate with club and country, after Colombia's premature return from USA '94.)

Back in 1990, Colombia's presence at their first World Cup since 1962 gave people reason for cheer, says Higuita. 'We were thinking about the problems of the country [notably a fast-rising murder rate in Medellin owing to drugs wars], and the best that could happen at that moment was to watch the national team winning and getting through to the World Cup after twenty-eight years.'

In Carlos Valderrama, the playmaker with the blond afro, they had 'a reference point', Higuita adds. 'The only player we had with experience on an international level was Valderrama. The rest of us, we were looking out there and seeing giants. We didn't believe it, but we had everything it needed. We always had fifty per cent – the pure talent – and the rest comes through experience. If we'd had a bit more knowledge, if we'd got up earlier in the mornings, if we'd had television and seen European football, bloody hell . . .'

Against West Germany in their final group game, they held the champions-elect 1-1 thanks to Freddy Rincón's 92nd-minute equaliser, a result that set up their meeting with Cameroon. The next time Higuita faced a team in German shirts, incidentally, was when the Nacional players took on Pablo Escobar's prison XI inside the Catedral jail in Medellin and found them kitted out in the white and black of the *Nationalmannschaft*. 'We gave a masterclass,' he says of the game against Franz Beckenbauer's side.

Pierre Littbarski, scorer of West Germany's goal, has clear recollections of the Colombians on that afternoon in Milan. 'They had that short passing and weren't stuck in a tactical system,' he tells me. 'They just played how I would play when I was ten or eleven years old and playing on the street – just enjoying it. They were difficult to play against, because you never knew what they'd do in the next situation.'

Higuita was nearly caught out by Rudi Völler after one dash outside his penalty box, and Littbarski remembers the flash of *schadenfreude* from his room-mate Andreas Köpke, West Germany's back-up goalkeeper, when his shot flew past the Colombian. 'He hated that goalkeeper Higuita, because he did some things which were not usual for a goalkeeper – he went out far from his area. He said he'd be really happy if I scored – and when I scored, he ran on the pitch to congratulate me!'

Most reacted positively to Higuita's showmanship. Gary Lineker passes by and tells him with a friendly grin, 'I was there,' in reference to his presence at Wembley on the night in 1995 that Higuita produced his astonishing scorpion-kick save in a friendly against England. 'I enjoyed myself,' Higuita declares when asked about his box of tricks. 'When I saw the players weren't doing their bit,

I'd come out, and it gave them confidence – "If Higuita can do this and he's the goalie, how can I not do this as a defender or a striker or a midfielder?"'

*

BACK AT HIS HOME IN YAOUNDÉ, ROGER MILLA IS REFLECTING ON his own role as a confidence-giver, in his case to the whole of African football. 'To reach the quarter-finals and be on the cusp of the semi-finals of a World Cup, that was something the African continent had never seen,' he says. 'All African countries became Cameroonian at that moment. You asked a Senegalese, an Ivorian, a Tanzanian, which country are you from? And he'd reply, "Cameroon". So, it was pride for the African continent, a real pride, and I think the African continent deserved that because for a long time, Africa had sent out very good players to Europe, but nobody took the African continent seriously. It took us to do that in '90 for people to say, "We have to pay attention, there are very good players there."'

It is something that Milla touches on more than once during our conversation, the fight to earn respect. The history books show that he was not the first Cameroonian to have shone in European football, and for all his own trailblazing, he wishes to highlight those who travelled the same road before him. 'I had the chance to go to France in 1977, but before that, there were other Cameroonians playing there,' he says, citing individuals such as Jean-Pierre Tokoto, a forward at Bordeaux and Paris Saint-Germain, and defender Michel Kaham, both teammates at the Spain '82 World Cup. 'I was just following in their footsteps.'

In fact, there were Cameroonian success stories in French football as far back as the 1950s: Zacharie Noah, father of future French Open tennis champion Yannick, was a French Cup winner with Sedan; Eugène Njo Léa scored prolifically for league champions Saint-Etienne in 1957 before helping to establish the French professional footballers' union (UNFP).

The difference with Milla, of course, is that the impact was now global. In a survey of African footballers in Europe twelve months after Italia '90, *World Soccer* emphasised the 'ever-increasing number' earning contracts with European clubs – and counted 267 in total. In the season before, 1989/90, only two full African internationals, Liverpool goalkeeper Bruce Grobbelaar and

Queens Park Rangers forward Dominic Iorfa, had appeared for top-flight clubs. (In the first six months of 2017/18, the equivalent number in the Premier League was 43.)

If Milla and his Cameroon teammates shone a light on the quality of African footballers, it is another thing whether they dislodged deeply-fixed attitudes. Milla is unconvinced on this matter.

In the summer of 1990, *L'Équipe* carried a cartoon of Milla meeting the Pope and the pontiff urging him not to eat any Englishmen – '*Cameroun gentil, pas manger anglais*' – while Margaret Thatcher cowers in the background. If such blatant racism would be unthinkable today in any mainstream publication, it is worth noting that a decade and a half after the World Cup, Milla was moved to devote a passage of his autobiography to arguing that referees should take players off the pitch in instances of racist abuse, such when his compatriot Samuel Eto'o threatened to leave the field during a game for Barcelona at Real Zaragoza in 2006.

'Did we change attitudes?' Milla ponders. 'I don't think so. Perhaps we changed the profile of Cameroonian players.'

Thomas Nkono, who broke new ground as an African goalkeeper in Spanish football in the 1980s with Espanyol, has a more sunny interpretation, suggesting that he, Milla, and others of their generation led by their example.

'Truth, is we were pioneers. We opened up paths by what we did and the way we conducted ourselves, and from there, people have been able to profit,' he says. 'Our conduct was important in helping us earn respect. We were professional, and if you're professional, people can say nothing to you.'

There is one other person Milla wishes to mention during our interview – and does so several times – and that is Sepp Blatter, the former president of FIFA.

Milla served as a member of both FIFA's Technical Committee and Technical Study Group under Blatter and holds the unfashionable view that 'things were better' at the football governing body under the man who took the World Cup to South Africa in 2010.

It was Blatter who in 1976, at the CAF Congress in Addis Adaba, introduced Project 1, the first Coca Cola-sponsored development programme in Africa (and start of the company's long-term partnership with FIFA).

For Blatter himself, Milla's exploits in 1990 were a measure of the progress taken in the intervening years. 'For Africa and especially with the dancer [Milla],' he tells me, 'it was very much for them confirmation that the job that had been done was really bringing something to those countries.'

Milla grumbles more than once about new FIFA president Gianni Infantino, whose ascent to power coincided with the fall of Issa Hayatou, the Cameroonian former CAF president who served as acting FIFA president after Blatter's departure and supported Infantino's rival candidate, the Bahrain royal Sheikh Salman bin Ebrahim al-Khalifa.

'The president of FIFA, Mr Infantino, should read Pelé's preface,' he says, referring back to his own autobiography. In this preface, Pelé describes Milla as one the greatest footballers of all time and 'the man who opened the doors of the world to African football'.

His legacy is just that. The Mozambique-born Eusébio in 1966 might have been the first Africa-born footballer to occupy headline-writers across the globe during a World Cup finals, but he did so in the colours of Portugal. Milla did it wearing the green, red, and yellow of Cameroon.

He ends, just as he began, with a grateful nod to divine destiny. 'I think that God wanted me, at thirty-eight, to play a World Cup, and that's why he sent me. At thirty-eight, lots of players can fall over and die in a stadium, but he sent me there, and I held my own.'

Bilardo and
the wild bunch

IT IS MIDNIGHT AT RADIO LA RED IN BUENOS AIRES. THE EYES OF the two security guards manning the reception desk are fixed on a flat-screen TV mounted on the wall, which is showing the World Cup qualifying play-off between Peru and New Zealand. Another TV displays a sequence of publicity shots of the radio station's presenters. Among them is Carlos Bilardo, Argentina's coach from the 1986 and 1990 World Cups, who is pictured grasping the stand of a vintage steel microphone.

His hour-long weeknight show, *La Hora de Bilardo*, has just concluded, and the man they call *el Narigón* – big nose – will be on his way down shortly. During the wait, the words of one of his former players swim around inside my head: 'He was always mad, and now even more so.' Bilardo was famously obsessive, an insomniac with an eye for the smallest detail. A qualified doctor, who practised for a period as a gynaecologist, he was, at the same time, a master of football malpractice who stopped at nothing in the quest for success.

Perhaps the most egregious example of all came at Italia '90, and it came during the biggest fixture of all for his country: Brazil v Argentina, the South American *clásico* in the round of sixteen in Turin.

The murky incident occurred moments before half-time as Diego Maradona lay ten yards from the corner flag, deep in his own half, receiving treatment for a shoulder injury. Several Argentina players took advantage of the pause to swig from a water bottle. So too did Branco, the opposition's left wing-back.

After the match, following Argentina's against-the-odds 1-0 victory, the Brazilian complained to reporters that he had unwittingly consumed a spiked drink, handed to him in a separate bottle by a member of the *Albiceleste* backroom team. 'I asked the Argentinian physio for a drink,' Branco said. 'They gave me a bottle of a well-known saline supplement drink. When I took a swig, I tasted something strange.

'I then became suspicious when the same physio, asked by one of their own players for something to drink, yelled at him not to drink from that bottle but from another. At that point, I tried to get the bottle and take it over to our physio, so he could analyse it, but a couple of Argentina players took it away from me.'

TV footage of the moment shows Branco complaining to the referee's assistant. Back in the changing room at half-time, he complained of weak legs and a spinning head.

In December 2004, Maradona reignited the controversy when he said in a TV interview that he had encouraged the Brazilians to drink from the bottle. Another member of Argentina's 1990 team, Julio Olarticoechea, does little to deny the chicanery when telling me, a few hours prior to my encounter with Bilardo, 'I always say there are things that should stay in the group. Some people have spoken – [José] Basualdo and Maradona – and for me, it's not good they've spoken about something like that. If mistakes were made, they should stay in the group.'

What can be said with confidence is that four years after Maradona's 'Hand of God' goal, this alleged skulduggery at the Stadio delle Alpi confirmed a certain perception of Bilardo's Argentina as a team who did not so much cross the line of legality to win games, as leap over it with two feet raised and both sets of studs showing.

At twenty past midnight, with Bilardo settled into the seat opposite me, the opportunity arises to ask whether this anti-football image was fair or not.

'For me, it was wrong,' he begins. 'If it's in the laws, then you have to change the laws. If you steal, it's different to steal with a revolver than steal with your hand. It's a shame. We played well, and we played within the laws of the game. We did nothing strange.'

And the Branco incident? When asked about it in the wake of Maradona's

2004 revelation, he refused to deny it. Now, breathy laughter punctuates a reply which, like rather a few of his answers, leads off in a different direction. 'No, no . . . these are things . . . People would say everything about me . . . I didn't complain. I studied medicine, and here they said I played with a needle and I'd jab players. If I jabbed a player, they'd check him and see ... I never played with a needle. These were things that were invented.'

There are so many tales about Bilardo, and the needle one dates back to his days as a midfield enforcer with Estudiantes de La Plata's great team of the late 1960s.

There is a straight path between Bilardo's Argentina reign and his days as standard-bearer of that Estudiantes side, and it is worth a brief detour down it to understand the methods of the man who did not just guide Argentina past a superior Brazil side at Italia '90 but took them, contrary to most expectations, all the way to the final.

With his baggy V-neck sweater and the unruly wisps of dyed-brown hair on his head, Bilardo, in person, looks every inch the 78-year-old grandfather, but he was once the embodiment of a brilliantly methodical, if sometimes brutal, winning machine created by his coach and mentor, Osvaldo Zubeldía.

An unfashionable club whose only previous league title had come in the amateur era in 1913, Estudiantes became champions of Argentina in 1967 and followed that up with three straight Copa Libertadores successes between 1968 and 1970.

'Zubeldía influenced me very much,' he acknowledges – repeating the word '*mucho*' seven times for emphasis. 'I came from a very hard-working side at Estudiantes La Plata. We were a team who studied our opponents.

'We played Manchester United, and we knew everything about them. We played against Milan, and we knew everything about them. We knew how they played, we got videos, we had everything – right down to the smallest detail. Zubeldía, who was coaching Estudiantes in those years, was like that, and he taught me a lot.

'He said, "You can't leave anything to chance. You have to pay attention to everything." He'd go and look at the pitch in the morning, to see if the grass had been cut. He'd see the journey the bus would have to take to the ground. For every match, there'd be a car in front of the team bus and one behind, because there were some countries where they threw stones at us.'

On the field, their game plan included a man-marking system and highly effective offside trap. Bilardo had the job of destroyer. In his book, *El Miedo Escénico Y Otras Hierbas*, Jorge Valdano – a member of Bilardo's 1986 World Cup-winning side – described him as 'an expert in immobilising his opponent', and he did just the same as a player.

'I would mark their best player,' Bilardo recalls. 'It was always the number ten – the best from Peru, from Uruguay, from Brazil, I marked them all. I knew how I liked to mark, and I knew how I liked to get away from my man.' Such were his destructive tendencies that Manchester United manager Matt Busby, referring to Bilardo in reference to the 1968 Intercontinental Cup encounter with Estudiantes, said, 'Holding the ball out there put you in danger of your life.'

The 1968 meeting with United is notorious for the thread of violence that ran through both ties. It featured the sending-off of Nobby Stiles in Estudiantes' 1-0 first-leg victory in Buenos Aires, then red cards for George Best and José Hugo Medina following a flare-up near the end of the 1-1 second-leg draw at Old Trafford.

Five decades on, however, nostalgia's soft–focus filter is in force.

'How much did the little one kick?' he says of Stiles. 'And he talked too, but I didn't understand English then. But what players! Stiles, Pat Crerand, Bobby Charlton, Georgie Best ... I loved them. Seriously. I thought what great players these are.' He had a funny way of showing it.

Before the second leg, Zubeldía wrote on the blackboard in the visitors' dressing room, 'You don't get to glory through a bed of roses.' The perfect maxim for Argentina at Italia '90.

*

IT WAS ANYTHING BUT A BED OF ROSES WORKING UNDER BILARDO, an intense figure from the opposite end of the spectrum to the man he had replaced as Argentina coach, César Luis Menotti. The long-haired, chain-smoking Menotti – architect of his country's 1978 World Cup triumph – was the cavalier to Bilardo's roundhead.

If working today, Menotti would have been the hipster's choice, a socialist who strove for expressive, attacking football. Bilardo met Menotti only once after replacing him, and the conversation was brief – hardly a surprise given Bilardo's contrasting philosophy, outlined in his autobiography as follows: 'Professional football is about winning, and only winning.'

Julio Olarticoechea was in Menotti's squad at the 1982 World Cup in Spain and then worked with Bilardo at the next two tournaments. Of the former experience, he remembers, 'We were by the beach near Alicante. We could see girls sunbathing topless. It wasn't a place to concentrate. That's not a small detail. Bilardo would never take us somewhere like that. They were totally different in their way of life, in their way of thinking football, in their tactics.'

The cheery kind, Goycochea may be best remembered by England fans as the man who somehow denied Gary Lineker an equalising goal in a tumultuous 1986 World Cup quarter-final in Mexico City, stealing in front of the England striker just as he shaped to head in from John Barnes' cross and diverting the ball away with his neck. 'You have to take me to England, and get Lineker and me together for a chat,' he grins. 'I don't know how I got it clear. There's a film I was watching yesterday in which Lineker says that when he's about to put it in the net, I appear and the ball's no longer there. He doesn't name me – he doesn't even remember who I was. I call it the "Nape of God"! It was incredible.'

Had it not been for Bilardo's *locura*, or madness, Olarticoechea would not have been on the Azteca Stadium pitch that afternoon. He had originally rejected a call-up for that 1986 World Cup finals campaign but changed his mind after agreeing to a roadside meeting with Bilardo while driving back to his home city of Saladillo from Buenos Aires. There, Bilardo picked up a stone, scratched a football pitch on the side of a building and detailed the precise role he wished Olarticoechea to fill.

It was in Mexico, Olarticoechea tells me, that Bilardo prohibited any excessive goal celebrations because of the potentially sapping effects of running even fifty metres at high altitude. There are countless other examples, and Olarticoechea – sitting in a quiet café on Avenida Córdoba, one of the many tributaries running into Buenos Aires's central Avenida 9 de Julio, famed as the world's widest boulevard – remembers one particular occasion when he brought his players together to study a video.

'He'd say, "There's a mistake in this move," and we'd have to spot it. We got together one time, and it was our attack and then a counter-attack by the other team.

'"There's a mistake," he says, so we're looking at our positions.

'He stops. "Can you see the mistake?" "No, no no." We watch again. "Can you see the mistake?" No, again. We watch this ten times, until [Ricardo] Giusti raises his hand. "What's the mistake?" "Caniggia." Caniggia was wearing a hairband, and when we were dropping back, you could see in the right corner of the screen that he was going back without watching the ball and adjusting his hairband instead. This was the mistake! I wanted to kill him. We'd all dropped back okay, but it was the hairband!

'Bilardo practised everything. When we had to stop play and kill some time, the doctor would come on the pitch, and we'd stand in the way of the stretcher. Giusti was in charge of that. He'd stand between the stretcher and the player who was down, and wouldn't let them past. So, they'd run on the pitch but then couldn't get to the player!

'Some things about Bilardo I didn't like. He was too obsessive. But tactically he could find an advantage everywhere, in the tiniest detail. He knew everything about the opposition – the changes they might make depending on the score. He got information about how they played, their weaknesses. All of his *locura*, the pressure he had to get the team to perform, he passed on to you, and that's why we performed.

'He didn't sleep. At two in the morning, perhaps if you couldn't sleep and were reading or listening to music, he'd come past and look to see if there was a light under the door, and he'd come into your room and sit down and start talking, and he'd fall asleep in the chair. Then he'd wake up and carry on talking! It was always about football.

'At mealtimes, he'd sit there and watch us eat. He'd sit watching players' faces, to see their attitude and whether they were nervous or not. He sat sipping water and was constantly watching. He was so stubborn too. There was a big screen they put against the wall of the dining room so we could watch the matches. It was set up behind him, but he didn't want to move, so in order to watch without changing his place, he put a mirror in front so he could watch the screen behind.

There are a million stories like this.'

One of the best Bilardo anecdotes comes from the man himself in his autobiography, and it concerns Diego Maradona's wedding celebration in November 1989. After spotting Careca, Napoli's Brazilian forward on the dancefloor, Bilardo instructed his wife Nancy to dance with Oscar Ruggeri, one of his centre-backs, and lead him close to Careca.

'I needed to know how tall he was, as I didn't trust the stats I'd got hold of,' he wrote. 'Often, the official documents tell you a footballer is 1.80m, and when you see him on the pitch, the guy is 1.90 … I was able to establish a fact that proved essential: they were nearly the same height.'

Ruggeri ended up marking Careca in the last-sixteen triumph in Turin.

'TERRIBLE, TERRIBLE,' MUTTERS SERGIO GOYCOCHEA, THE Argentina goalkeeper at Italia '90, as he remembers life in the Bilardo era. Smiling, he says, 'We had a play where I'd put the ball down and signal for everybody to push up and I'd shape to take it, but then somebody would run halfway down the pitch and I'd give it to him, he'd give it back to me, and then we'd do it all over again. Is it the best spirit of the game? No, but it was a situation we used to our advantage.

'Bilardo had every detail covered. He understood that a high-performance athlete under maximum pressure at a World Cup had to be in the best state possible – with diet, with rest, emotionally. He'd look at the bills for each room to see how many phone calls we'd made, because if you had to be shut away for forty-five days at a World Cup, you had to be able to control your emotions and not miss your family, and you had to eat what everyone else ate. He always based his decision on talent, but if there were two players, he'd choose the one who was better equipped that way.'

Indeed, Bilardo has admitted to selecting one player for Italia '90 – Néstor Lorenzo – after he had proved resourceful enough to talk his way on to the team's flight to Glasgow for a friendly match against Scotland having arrived at the airport without a passport.

There was nobody more resourceful than Bilardo himself who flew to Paris to acquire video footage of Argentina's opening opponents, Cameroon. 'Today with the forms of communication there are, it seems normal to know so much, but we watched videos at a time when it wasn't so common among coaches,' adds Goycochea.

It was in the wake of that Cameroon game, and the shock of a 1-0 defeat, that Bilardo faced his first big challenge of Italia '90: to summon an instant response from his players. There were strong words spoken.

Julio Olarticoechea recalls, 'That night, Bilardo knocked on our bedroom doors and says, "Meeting." He said to us all, "We're not going out of the World Cup like this," and called us cowards.'

Holding two imaginary testicles in his hands, Olarticoechea, a keen mimic, continues: 'He said we didn't have the balls for it, and that if we lost against Russia and went out of the World Cup, he didn't want to go back to Argentina. He said he'd rather the plane crashed.

'The day before the game against Russia, we were at the table – Goyco, me, Diego, and someone else – and Goycochea started to talk about our meeting with Bilardo and him saying he wanted the plane to crash. Goyco started to say that if we lost, Bilardo would take over the flight cabin with the pilot's cap on, and he then started to imitate him: "Good evening, I'm Captain Bilardo. Our flight time to Buenos Aires will be forty-five minutes." We all started laughing, and Bilardo looked over but couldn't understand why. We were imagining him crashing the plane!'

As it was, an Argentina side featuring five changes from the opening match revived their hopes with a 2-0 victory over Russia, though it came at a cost. Olarticoechea collided with goalkeeper Nery Pumpido, his knee cracking his room-mate's right leg, causing a double fracture.

'I'm broken in bits,' cried the stricken goalkeeper as he departed on a stretcher. Not until after the match was Goycochea told the severity of his colleague's injury. 'When the first half finished nobody wanted to tell me so as not to affect me psychologically,' he says.

Goycochea, newly introduced to the World Cup, had Maradona to thank for keeping his goal intact, with the second coming of the 'Hand of God', as he stopped a goalbound header from Oleh Kuznetsov. The score was 0-0 at the time.

Clarín noted, 'And so, it was proved that Maradona can score a goal with his left hand and prevent another with his right.'

Goycochea breathed a huge sigh of relief. 'I'd just come on. It was the first attempt I faced.'

Argentina went on to prevail through goals from Pedro Troglio, a header from Olarticoechea's cross after 27 minutes, and Jorge Burruchaga, who struck from close range eleven minutes from the end. They had showed spirit and determination, though their former coach César Luis Menotti moaned, 'Argentina have got the players to play a different game. This "little" approach is down to [Bilardo].'

Olarticoechea had mixed feelings too, given Pumpido's terrible injury. 'When I went back to the room and saw the empty bed, it was awful. We had so many problems – injuries, sendings-off, our performances. It was quite the opposite to '86 when we had no injuries and all arrived there in top condition.'

The team had the same image of the Virgin Mary – Our Lady of Luján, from the Argentinian shrine of the same name – on their team bus as in 1986, but little else was the same. Aside from the excluded Valdano, two other pivots were missing in defender José Luis Brown and midfielder Héctor Enrique. Others were barely fit. Centre-back Ruggeri had pubalgia and had deferred the surgery that his club, Real Madrid, wished him to undergo. Jorge Burruchaga, who had barely played for three years owing to a series of knee injuries, was struggling now with a thigh problem.

Then you had Maradona. 'He came into the finals very tired,' says Olarticoechea. 'Diego played that World Cup at fifty per cent or less. He virtually didn't train which was totally different from 1986 when he was perfect.'

Even a semi-fit Maradona remained vital to Carlos Bilardo.

His first major act as national coach had been to meet Maradona in Barcelona and, as the plates were being cleared away after lunch, offer him the captaincy of Argentina. This occurred during the player's period of recovery from hepatitis, at a time when he had not worn the *Albiceleste* shirt since the 1982 World Cup. 'I said Maradona was going to be the only guaranteed starter and the captain of the team,' Bilardo remembers. 'A lot of people didn't want that. Maradona was thrilled about it, and he delivered.

'I'd known Maradona since he was fourteen or fifteen years old. He played for a club four or five blocks away from my home, Argentinos Juniors.' Today the club's stadium – rebuilt and renamed, inevitably, the Estadio Diego Armando Maradona – features murals of him on its walls. A building opposite is split by two different colour schemes, half of it painted in the sky blue and white of Argentina, the other half in the red and white of Argentinos Juniors. There are murals of Maradona as man and boy. Painted above are the words '*El amor de un país, Orgullo de un barrio*' – the love of a country, pride of a district.

'It was a very small pitch, but he'd dribble there and beat one, and then another and another,' Bilardo recalls of that young Maradona. The thirty-year-old with him in Italy was a different player, but still vital to his team.

'His ankle hurt him so much, but he was Maradona,' says Bilardo. 'A lot of teams were still man-marking and they'd put a man on Diego. We'd then put Diego on top of another of their players, so in effect, there were two taken out.'

Inside the camp, Maradona was a central figure too. Together with his father, 'Don Diego', they continued the tradition from four years earlier in Mexico of preparing the occasional *asado* – Argentinian barbecue – for the squad. 'They brought the meat over from Argentina,' says Olarticoechea. And Maradona being Maradona, he would not hesitate to call his favourite pizzeria thirty minutes away in Rome either. 'They'd bring it for him – typical Diego,' Olarticoechea grins.

ACCORDING TO INFLUENTIAL FOOTBALL MAGAZINE *EL GRÁFICO*, Argentina had entered the second round 'through a window shouting, "help"'. Next they faced Brazil. Argentina had never beaten their biggest footballing foe in a World Cup finals match. After a 2-1 victory for Brazil in the second group stage in 1974, the teams had drawn 0-0 at the same stage of the 1978 finals.

The consequence of that stalemate was a controversial final group fixture against Peru in which Argentina – who entered it with a goal difference of +2 to Brazil's +5, and just two goals scored to their rivals' six – earned a stunning and decisive 6-0 victory.

Brazil, who had already played their last game, were out, and Argentina through to the final. A vapour trail of suspicion followed that result into the record books, and not just for the fact Peru's goalkeeper, Ramón Quiroga, had been born in Argentina. The *Sunday Times* claimed in 1986 that Argentina had shipped 35,000 tons of grain to Peru as part of an arrangement for the home team to win.

In 2012, a former Peruvian senator, Genaro Ledesma, cited the Condor Plan – whereby Latin American dictators co-operated in the repression of dissidents – as he told a Buenos Aires judge that the match had been fixed. Ledesma, giving evidence against Peru's former military president, Francisco Morales Bermúdez, said that Argentinian dictator Jorge Rafael Videla had agreed to take thirteen Peruvian prisoners – for torture – on the condition that the World Cup hosts got the result required in that key match in Rosario. 'Videla needed to win the World Cup to cleanse Argentina's bad image around the world,' Ledesma told the court.

José Velásquez, a member of Peru's 1978 side, rekindled the controversy in March 2018 when pointing the finger at six teammates who 'sold themselves' in that match.

Jonathan Wilson, writing in *Angels With Dirty Faces*, his comprehensive history of Argentinian football, says, 'Whatever the circumstantial evidence of a fix, from the match footage itself it looks as though Peru are guilty of nothing more than not fancying it very much once the goals started to fly in.'

When the teams met again at the 1982 finals in Spain, once again in the second group stage, it was a flying kick from Maradona, into the midriff of Brazil midfielder Batista, that provided the defining image: an eruption of frustration from the 21-year-old, which earned him a late red card as Argentina exited the tournament with a 3-1 loss.

Eight years later, Maradona had yet to get the better of Argentina's arch-rivals, with a record of three defeats and a draw.

He arrived in Turin for the round-of-sixteen tie suffering with an ankle swollen to the size of a ball. He was the most-fouled player of the first round – 28 (thirteen more than the next players on that list) – and after taking a heavy kick against Romania, team doctor Raúl Madero had sought Maradona's removal at half-time during that final group game. Maradona insisted on carrying on.

Three days before facing Brazil, he walked slowly on to the training pitch and, wearing a pair of slip-ons, sat down and did keepie-ups with only his right foot. The medical diagnosis had been less than encouraging – revealing a 'strong direct trauma to the bone' and tendon damage – yet his message to the crowd of journalists around him was defiant: 'I believe in miracles.'

Sergio Goycochea remembers: 'He was our leader, by actions and words. He actually administered his own injection before the Brazil game. The doctor didn't want to give him any more.'

Midfielder Pedro Troglio adds, 'Only a player like Maradona could play with that pain, withstand a swollen ankle in every game and express himself, despite the pain. But that was the gift Diego had.'

If Argentina's World Cup campaign had turned into an obstacle course, Brazil had anxieties of their own. They had arrived in Italy promising a different approach. Dunga, the then Fiorentina-based midfielder, said, 'We're not the samba team anymore. We've got a more European mentality, and we hope to cause a sensation.'

After the failure of their magnificent 1982 team to win the World Cup in Spain, Brazil had stepped gradually away from the *jogo bonito* model. Coach Sebastião Lazaroni had introduced a libero, switching from the favoured 4-4-2 system to 3-5-2. In 1989, they earned their first South American title for forty years.

According to David Goldblatt, writing in *Futebol Nation*, Lazaroni came from the 'military school of obsessive physical preparation and muscle building', and his methods were not popular.

He writes, 'It was not a happy camp in Italy, where the application of military-era discipline could no longer work with players newly enfranchised by wealth and European experience. The Brazilian press feasted on stories of internal rows and huge drinks bills that no one would pay.'

In Group C in Italy, they had won their three games narrowly, following up a 2-1 success against Sweden with 1-0 victories over Costa Rica and Scotland.

Even after that first game, Pelé, in a syndicated, Seiko-sponsored newspaper column, complained, 'This team that's here in Italy has nothing to do with the Brazilian teams you know', and added that 'only with the speed of Muller and the cunning and experience of Careca did they come close to the true Brazilian football.'

FIFA's post-finals technical report observed a reliance on creative midfielder

Valdo, suggesting that the absence of other skilful midfielders to distract defenders and create space for the strikers meant that 'a third man was often missing in the opposition penalty area' – a pertinent point for a team who had 56 chances to score at the World Cup and took only four of them.

This profligacy cost Brazil dearly at the Stadio delle Alpi. The date of the game, 24 June, was the feast of St. John the Baptist, patron saint of Turin. To Argentinian eyes, the surprise that unfolded was nothing less than a footballing miracle.

The first half was a story of Brazil's total supremacy. In the first minute alone, Careca wrong-footed two Argentina defenders, but, slipping as he shot, failed to stretch Goycochea. Müller, well-placed in the box, then angled a shot high and wide. Dunga headed against a post. Balls flew across Goycochea's goal. Brazilian boots were an inch or two away from connecting.

Back in the Argentina dressing room during the interval, Carlos Bilardo stood silent. 'At half-time, you wait for the coach to say something – to explain or correct something,' Julio Olarticoechea remembers. 'Bilardo didn't say a word. The bell rings for us to go out and because he'd still not spoken, we set off down the tunnel.

'Bilardo then shouts to us, "Lads, just a second – I have to say one thing. If you keep giving the ball to the ones in yellow, we'll lose." That was all he said, because in the first half, we'd made a lot of mistakes with our passing and Brazil took advantage. They had a lot of dangerous situations which were our own fault. Brazil pressed us and we gave the ball away, but we were better in the second half. It wasn't total domination.'

There were still scares. Goycochea flapped at a Careca cross and palmed the ball against the crossbar. Sixty seconds later Alemão drove the ball against the goalframe once more. That was in the 52nd minute. Then Careca flicked a header narrowly over. Yet, eventually, Giusti and Burruchaga helped Argentina establish a midfield presence.

Asked what he remembers of that afternoon, Sergio Goycochea responds with a chortle. 'The noise of the goalposts! This is a clear example of why football is football. We could have played that game ten times and won once and lost the other nine. And it was just the one we had to win and it was in the World Cup.

'They made mistakes too, because it wasn't a case of me stopping everything.

Not taking your chances is a mistake. It's all well and good creating chances, but you have to finish them. They outplayed us. The best thing we could do was hang on and realise we were being outplayed.

'In the second half, it wasn't such a siege, and we controlled things a bit better. I had to work quite hard, and when I wasn't working, the ball was hitting the post or flying wide, but that's football. Our main sporting rival is Brazil. It's Brazil, England, Italy, Germany, in that order. Uruguay too, but our big rivalry is with Brazil – and for us, it was fantastic. Beating Brazil buried the bad start.'

In the first half, Caniggia had run repeatedly into a yellow wall. Only once, freed by Maradona, did he get behind Brazil's defence, but the offside flag was raised as he rolled the ball into the net.

Now, the pair combined once more. Maradona's point of departure, as it had been for his astounding Azteca Stadium slalom against England, was Argentina's side of the centre circle.

He turned away from Alemão, his Napoli teammate, and entered Brazil's half. Next, he held off Dunga and was suddenly running at three defenders. Ricardo Rocha came across, but he drove past him as well.

Crucially, the other two central defenders, eyes drawn to Maradona, allowed Caniggia to cut between them in a dash from right to left. Though falling, Maradona was still able to angle a perfect dream of a pass to his teammate. The striker, a blur of Ben Johnson speed and Heather Locklear hair, was in the clear.

If you freeze the image as Caniggia collects, there are three Brazilians united in a cold, hard panic. Captain Ricardo Gomes and sweeper Mauro Galvão actually bump into one another. Ricardo Rocha casts a desperate glance across at the linesman.

Maradona, now on his knees, hands gripping the turf, watches. He declared before the opening game that 'Caniggia will be the revelation of this World Cup'. Here was payback for that faith in a player who, like him, would later face a ban from football after a positive test for cocaine. The Atalanta forward rounded Cláudio Taffarel and buried the ball into the net. Maradona stood for a few moments with both arms raised to the skies, then sank to his knees and held his hands together in a prayer of thanks.

Clarín described it as 'the revenge of Maradona against another stadium that was hostile to him from the start', while Bilardo hailed his captain's spirit. 'Maradona is playing because he's got a heart of iron,' he said.

For Maradona himself, it was a victory that thrilled him like few others. He might have spent Italia '90 listening to a Lambada tape given him by Careca, his Napoli teammate, but Brazil's football was less to his liking than its music.

'Brazil have sold the world this idea that they're the only ones capable of the *jogo bonito*, of playing beautifully . . . bollocks!' he said. Back at their Trigoria base, the Argentina players ended the evening up on the tables, singing their battle songs and swinging napkins above their heads like ultras' scarves.

Understandably, there was a different response from Branco, the Brazilian who had drunk water laced with tranquillisers, as Maradona would later claim. He left the field gesticulating unhappily to the Argentina players. Five years later, when Sergio Goycochea joined him in Brazilian football, Branco was still talking about it. 'He said, "They put something in it" and I said, "No." He felt bad, but a lot of players had a drink, so lots should have felt bad. We didn't win that game because Branco got sick.'

There are smirks on the top table as Sophia Loren delves into Pot 1 at the draw ceremony.

'The referee really got it wrong' – Cameroon's Benjamin Massing on André Kana-Biyik's red card, though Claudio Caniggia would beg to differ.

Cyrille Makanaky departs with a smile and a clenched first after Cameroon's stunning opening win.

Italia '90 general manager Luca Cordero di Montezemolo with then FIFA general secretary Sepp Blatter.

'He seemed to be talking as if everyone was going there to cause trouble' – England fan embassy leader Craig Brewin on UK minister for Sport Colin Moynihan (second from right).

'No football please, we're British' – *Gazzetta dello Sport* headline after England's draw with the Republic of Ireland.

'The Irish fans simply had no interest in being hooligans' – Irish writer Colm Tóibín.

'He had tremendous charisma. When he arrived, it really surprised us that he had so much information' – Costa Rica coach Bora Milutinović, as described by Alexandre Guimarães.

Austria's Klaus Lindenberger adds fashion crimes to excessive time-wasting on the charge sheet against 1990 goalkeepers.

'We never paid attention to physical power – technique was the number one' – Dragan Stojković (left) on Yugoslavia's secret.

'I shouldn't have even been on the bench but in the stand' – Totò Schillaci prepares to take the pitch against USA.

'I heard Bergomi, Ferri, Maldini, and Baresi yell at each other and I thought, "Ah shit, I don't care what the result is, I'm doing something right!"' – USA's Bruce Murray, pictured challenging Giuseppe Bergomi.

West Germany full-back Thomas Berthold takes a tumble against the UAE.

'Rijkaard's a quiet guy. I don't know what happened to him. He lost his mind' – Thomas Berthold on the Dutchman's dismissal for spitting.

René Higuita is left flat on his back as Roger Milla outwits him to score.

'I was a complete goalkeeper – today, I'd be in a team like Barcelona' – Colombia goalkeeper René Higuita.

Packie Bonner smiles after saving Daniel Timofte's spot-kick.

'Andy Townsend and Tony Cascarino ran from the halfway line into the penalty box and jumped on top of me, and there was still another penalty to be taken' – Republic of Ireland goalkeeper Packie Bonner.

'I remember falling on my knees, thinking "What's just happened?"' – David Platt, the man at the bottom of the pile of England players after scoring against Belgium.

'My agent said, "You didn't score a goal, but at least everybody will remember that moment." It's true – nobody forgets your red card!' – Czechoslovakia's Ľubomír Moravčík on his quarter-final dismissal.

'We went there totally relaxed – we went out and laid on the pitch before the game watching Argentina play in the other quarter-final on the big screen' – Ireland captain Mick McCarthy on the pre-match scenes before facing Italy.

'If you ever see it, he's got a black eye, and I think that one's down to me' – Mick McCarthy on Totò Schillaci.

Jack Charlton bids farewell to Italia '90 after Ireland's defeat in Rome.

Cameroon goalkeeper Thomas Nkono is booked for protesting the award of Gary Lineker's winning penalty.

'Diego in our hearts, Italy in our chants' – The message on the banner promising the Naples crowd's support for the *Azzurri* against Argentina.

'It was the most important save of my life – it changed my relationship with the world' – Argentina's Sergio Goycochea on his semi-final penalty save from Aldo Serena.

'There was a black hand at work' – Diego Maradona's lament at the end of Argentina's campaign ... and the strain is already showing on semi-final night.

The England dressing room at the Stadio delle Alpi.

'We actually played the best football of the tournament in that game' – England captain Terry Butcher leads his team out in Turin.

'He'd express himself. That's what Gazza did in that 1990 World Cup. He just expressed himself. He wasn't afraid of the competition. He just went out and enjoyed himself' – England midfielder Bryan Robson.

Bobby Robson watches from the bench as England's fate is sealed.

Rudi Völler and Jürgen Kohler celebrate with an embrace.

'The Argentina players started from the first foul in the opening minutes to say they'd been told FIFA didn't want them to win the World Cup' – Referee Edgardo Codesal on the mood even before he sent off two Argentinians.

In a nod to the future, the closing ceremony had fireworks – and toga-wearing models.

'With players from the East joining, the German team will be unbeatable. I'm sorry about that for the rest of the world' – West Germany coach Franz Beckenbauer's famous post-final quote.

Luciano Pavarotti and Italy coach Azeglio Vicini play the role of spectators on final night.

Legends in their own living room

PIERRE LITTBARSKI DID TWO THINGS IN 1990 THAT HE HAD NOT dared dream possible; one was to lift the World Cup trophy. Eight years after playing in the West Germany side beaten by Italy in the final, and four years after watching from the bench as Argentina prevailed, he finally got to hold a prize that had twice eluded him.

'All the frustration over eight years came out,' he remembers of the feeling on 8 July 1990. 'I was thinking it was impossible. For me it was not only joy – I was really relieved after twice falling into a deep hole after the World Cup.'

For a full appreciation of the new mood surrounding the West Germany team and their supporters in Italy that summer, though, it is worth dwelling first on the other thing that Littbarski did that year.

It was a simple act, nothing at all like a football match in the glare of the global spotlight. It was just a stroll across a patch of his home city, but it meant the world. It was the first time he had stepped through the Brandenburg Gate, the great neo-classical monument next to which the Berlin Wall rose in the early 1960s but which, as 1989 morphed into 1990, was now, all of a sudden, a symbol of newfound unity.

In November 1989, Littbarski had sat in front of his television watching Berliners chip away at the blocks of concrete which had divided their city and nation. The Berlin Wall was coming down. He watched the news again two days before Christmas when Helmut Kohl, the West German chancellor, walked through the Brandenburg Gate to be greeted by Hans Modrow, the East German prime minister.

Eight days later, as Germans celebrated the arrival of 1990, the Gate was even the backdrop for televised festivities that featured David Hasselhoff, the *Baywatch* actor, singing 'Looking for Freedom', a song the American had taken to the summit of the German charts the previous spring. Hasselhoff performed it from a bucket crane, wearing a jacket sparkling with electric lights.

Littbarski's own Brandenburg Gate moment was rather more intimate, and it brought home to him the meaning of the profound political events that were unfolding. 'The happiness came much later when I passed the *Brandenburger Tor*,' he recalls, using its German name. 'That gave me a really strange feeling because at the time of the border, you could see it from a distance and see some parts of East Germany. We never thought we could actually walk through this.'

Littbarski had experienced the meaning of that wall as man and boy. 'I was born in '60, and the wall was built in '61. Putting up a wall to keep people out creates something in everybody's mind. It was really like we were shut out. This was really unbelievable in a modern world. We were growing up and actually hating everything that was behind the wall on the east side. We never, ever thought that this wall would fall one day. This is only an experience that people who were living there have.

'I travelled a few times to the east side of Berlin, as we had some relatives there and it was really stressful just to cross the border. They checked your car, they checked your luggage. We passed Checkpoint Charlie, and when I travelled with my grandparents, I had situations where we had to step out, and [the authorities] took out the back seat because many people would smuggle things into the east like coffee or food. I had an aunt in East Berlin. When we arrived there, my Aunt Anne would tell me every time, "Don't speak so loud, don't say anything about the system." We were happy to see the relatives, but actually the general feeling was not really positive.'

These negative sensations would stir whenever, as a player, he drove back to visit his family in West Berlin. Even in the first few months of the 1989/90 season, he was still enduring the fraught car journey through East Germany.

'Every second week, I was driving back to my family and every time, I had to pass through the east,' he recounts. 'It was two hours of being really afraid. In a German country, as a German, I was afraid that they'd catch me for speeding or check my luggage. If you travelled from Cologne to Berlin, you had to cross the border, and they gave you a time stamp so that they can see how fast you travel and how long you were staying on the east side. That made you really nervous, because if you stayed longer than three hours, when you came into Berlin, they'd do a more detailed check.

'It usually took two hours, but if you took three hours they'd ask, "What did you do?" because some people from the west would find a parking spot and sell things in the east. There was a fear. I always tried not to stop, because you never knew what kind of people might be coming to you.

'The second thing was speed traps. They had bridges, and although there were no road works, you had to reduce your speed in about five seconds from one hundred to sixty, and right after the bridge, they'd be standing there and take the fine directly.

'They wanted the Deutschmark, so they took it in cash – there was no chance of paying with a credit card. These fears made it very complicated. I was all the time praying my car wouldn't break down and I'd have to stop. This was like you travelling from England to Scotland and being afraid to go. That was a wall you thought would stand for ever. Opening it in '89 was like a miracle happening.'

It is an arresting testimony, and it has a place in the story of West Germany's 1990 campaign. After all, this was the last World Cup for the West Germans, who had already triumphed in 1954 and 1974, and reached three other finals too. On 3 October 1990, the official stamping of German reunification took place.

ON THE AFTERNOON OF MY INTRODUCTION TO LITTBARSKI, AT THE FIFA Museum in Zurich, he has just been reacquainted with the World Cup trophy. Now head of scouting at Bundesliga side Wolfsburg, he is still slender, and that bow-legged gait conjures an instant image in the mind's eye of a slight, twinkle-toed winger in a white shirt and black shorts.

Along with Lothar Matthäus, he was one of two survivors of the 1982 tournament in West Germany's Italia '90 squad. He has a rare perspective, therefore, and it is worth listening when he describes a special atmosphere for players and supporters, quite unlike at his previous two World Cups.

'Just travelling to the San Siro was better than any speech the coach could give,' he says. 'Before the game, we travelled through the supporters – everywhere, it was white shirts and the German flag, and coming into the stadium, it was like we played at home.'

It was at the San Siro that Franz Beckenbauer's side had their first five matches of the finals, and Milan's relative proximity – Munich is a five-hour drive away – meant a flood of fans each time.

Bodo Illgner, the goalkeeper in that West Germany side, has a similar testimony. 'People were very happy and more confident than maybe before. The feeling to be German and proud was not as badly seen as it might have been before due to our history. We had great, great support in Italy. We had a lot of Germans coming over because we played a lot of games in Milan, then the semi-final in Turin close to the border.

'It was the start of a modern Germany after the Second World War with all the misery that happened there. The bad image of Germany turned from that moment. Fans were behaving very well, and they weren't shy to show the Germany flag – all those things that were maybe a little bit awkward and that we'd felt a little bit strange and shy about because of our bad history. I think that was the change of it – the World Cup in 2006 completed this development, and let Germany shine in a much brighter and better light than before.'

Thomas Schneider remembers the sight of German jerseys all around too. 'It was the first time I saw masses of Germans wearing national shirts,' says Schneider, head of fan engagement for the German Football League (DFL), who attended Italia '90 to observe a group of West German football hooligans. 'Before, they came casual in the colours of their club – it was not so fashionable to wear the shirt of a football team. So, it was really astonishing when you got to the Piazza del Duomo [Milan's cathedral square] and for the first time, you saw so many white shirts.

'Never before had so many Germans gone abroad,' he adds. 'We have a special relationship with Italy. It's really easy to travel there. Fantastic weather, beautiful sky, and add successful football and the nice shirt – these are the reasons, not the political thing.

'It was too fresh, the German reunification. I was in Hamburg on the night reunification was celebrated, and there was a big street fight on the Reeperbahn – right-wing against left-wing people. The atmosphere was difficult. When you live on a higher level you look at it as a phenomenon and think "wonderful", but economically it was not so easy for Germans at the time. The mainstream point of view is maybe it had to do with the "hooray" feeling that we were unified, but this was the official, political attitude and nothing to do with the life of the normal people.'

*

WHATEVER THE MOTIVES, THE TRAVELLING MASSES HAD A TEAM that Germans could warm to. Although West Germany sides had reach the World Cup final in 1982 and 1986, this bunch were different.

In 1982, Jupp Derwall's side had a run to the final soured by controversies: the so-called *Anschluss* match with Austria, in which a contrived 1-0 victory over their neighbours in front of a whistling Gijón crowd ensured both countries' progression to the second round at Algeria's expense; and then a spellbinding semi-final against France, marred by goalkeeper Harald Schumacher's brutal, unpunished assault on opposition defender Patrick Battiston.

In 1986, they fought their way to the final once more and found the courage to retrieve a 2-0 deficit before eventually falling 3-2 to the Diego Maradona-inspired Argentina. Across Europe it is probably only Germans who would decry as 'bad' a World Cup in which their team reached the final but this is something that surfaced more than once in interviews for this book.

Jörg Jakob, chief editor of leading German football magazine *Kicker,* says, 'This team was more loved than the other ones before. We had a lot of personalities who were loved not only by their own team's fans – [Rudi] Völler, [Jürgen] Klinsmann, [Guido] Buchwald, [Andreas] Brehme.' As a result, they generated a hitherto unseen excitement at home as people gathered in bars and restaurants to follow the progress of Franz Beckenbauer's side.

'I remember they closed the streets around the university in Giessen where I was working,' adds Jakob. 'This was the first time people were out in the streets having a fiesta together.'

Outside his office on the third floor of the *Kicker* building in Nuremberg is a wall mural in honour of that 1990 team. It features a photograph of Lothar Matthäus on his haunches, holding the World Cup. The accompanying quote reads, 'We were the most deserving of German World Cup winners. In 1990, everything went perfectly.'

It certainly did – not least the group stage, which West Germany eased through after scoring nine goals in their first two matches, against Yugoslavia and United Arab Emirates. Yet, when German football lovers look back today on the road to the Rome final, arguably the biggest source of satisfaction comes from a victory eked out against their greatest rivals. It may dismay England fans, but this means the Netherlands, the team West Germany met in the round of sixteen. When *Kicker* produced a special issue to mark the centenary of the national team in 2008, it included this encounter with the Dutch – and not the semi-final against England – in its list of greatest Germany games. 'Our arch-rivals in football' is how Matthäus describes the *Oranje*. 'Perhaps we are very similar in many aspects.'

West Germany and the Netherlands had last met on the world stage in the final in Munich in 1974 when the hosts, captained by Beckenbauer, prevailed 2-1 against Johan Cruyff's Dutch. By 1990, their rivalry had gained a new dimension: the German camp featured the Internazionale trio of Matthäus, Klinsmann and Brehme, while the Dutch squad included the AC Milan threesome of Ruud Gullit, Frank Rijkaard and Marco van Basten. In short, a dash of Milan-derby spice added to the long-fomenting mixture of prejudices and resentments, footballing and otherwise.

By the time the second round approached, West Germany were already firmly in their stride – helped, without doubt, by their presence at the San Siro throughout the group stage. Even the squad's base at Erba on Lake Como was close enough to captain Matthäus's home to allow him to take teammates out on his motorboat. 'San Siro was my living room,' he recalls. 'It was a massive advantage to play in a stadium you know very well and in front of a friendly crowd with three *interisti*.'

In this 'living room', Matthäus displayed his complete ease as he dominated Dragan Stojković with his energy and determination in the middle of the pitch and struck two goals in the 4-1 opening win over Yugoslavia. The second was a goal-of-the-tournament contender, the skipper driving upfield and unleashing a twenty-yard strike into the net.

Sky Sports commentator Martin Tyler, then working for Australian television in Italy, recalls, 'I did the West Germany-Yugoslavia game and I came back to the office, and said, "I've just seen the world champions" and I don't think I've ever done that in any other World Cup.'

Matthäus struck again in the subsequent 5-1 thrashing of the UAE five days later as strikers Klinsmann and Völler featured on the scoresheet as well for the second match running.

Klinsmann and Matthäus had a troubled relationship when teammates at Bayern Munich later that decade, yet today, Klinsmann acknowledges his old colleague's huge influence. He tells me, 'He brought many important pieces to the team – leadership, total commitment, fearlessness, and ability to change a game in a split-second with his amazing runs. He was at his peak at Italia '90 and the best player in the world at the right time.'

The bond of trust between Matthäus and Franz Beckenbauer was integral to this. Where Beckenbauer, as a player, had had an unstable relationship with his own international coach, Helmut Schön, owing to the strength of his own influence, this was different. Matthäus says, 'Franz was like a second father to me. We had a very close relationship, and we still do.'

Always a dynamic presence, Matthäus had acquired leadership qualities, as Pierre Littbarski explains: 'When we started in '82, we just played football, but now, he took responsibility. He was thinking for the whole team. Beckenbauer's personal goal was to teach him to be not only an outstanding football player but also an outstanding leader.'

Beckenbauer had changed too. During his first World Cup as a coach at Mexico '86, he was an intense figure at times, but now, at 44, he brought a lighter touch. Littbarski adds, 'One of Beckenbauer's qualities is he never showed what he was doing. Many coaches are saying, "I'm doing this and that." He never acted like this, but he was a very hard worker; he was very detailed. One time I went to his hotel room, and he had all these video tapes, and we never thought he'd be watching videos, but he studied every opponent very closely. He never showed it to us that he knew everything. So, beside an aura as a player, he'd improved very much [as a coach] from '86 to '90, and he gave us the right words, not only before the games but during the whole week.'

It helped that Beckenbauer had a tighter squad than four years earlier when there were separate dining tables for players from Cologne and Bayern Munich owing to a rift between goalkeeper Schumacher and forward Karl-Heinz Rummenigge (the latter based with Inter but previously of Bayern Munich). This led Beckenbauer to leave at home one or two players he regarded as potentially disruptive, including Bayern midfielder Hans Dorfner.

There were still flare-ups – Matthäus and Völler came to blows on the training pitch one day – but no grudges borne. 'It was a team full of different characters but focused, with the only goal in mind to win the World Cup,' Klinsmann remembers. 'We could have had arguments, but in the evenings, we cleared the air.'

It helped too that they had a settled starting XI. 'We had a better structure when you compare '86 and '90,' explains Littbarski. 'We had seven or eight players who were decided for the starting XI – seven or eight leaders – and there was a lot of respect from numbers twelve to twenty-two. That was actually the key to winning the World Cup.'

When Littbarski scored in the 88th minute of their final Group D fixture against Colombia – a game that finished 1-1 after Freddy Rincón responded in stoppage time – it meant Germany had finished the first round with ten goals scored. The second-most prolific group winners, Spain, had five. A team who had qualified as one of Europe's two best group runners-up – the others were England – had found a smooth, swift stride in Italy. Their reward, though, was a dubious one: a round-of-sixteen meeting with the Netherlands, the reigning European champions.

It was not what Beckenbauer had envisaged when, on 21 June, he hopped on and off planes and helicopters to take in both Belgium-Spain in Verona and England-Egypt in Cagliari during a twelve-hour scouting trip of prospective second-round opponents.

Yet, the Netherlands' failure to beat the Republic of Ireland in their last group match – their third straight draw – meant the Dutch and Irish, level on points, goals scored, and goals conceded, had to be separated by a drawing of lots by FIFA general secretary Sepp Blatter. Third place went to the Dutch, and a mouth-watering derby appeared on the schedule.

MOUTHWATERING FOR MANY, BUT FOR THOMAS SCHNEIDER A source of anxiety. Today the man in charge of fan engagement for the DFL, Schneider had travelled to Italy with a group of football hooligans, in an initiative every bit as groundbreaking as the endeavours of the English Football Supporters' Association's fan embassy in Sardinia documented elsewhere in this book.

Prior to West Germany's opening game against Yugoslavia, Schneider witnessed a rampage by German fans in the streets around the Piazza del Duomo which led to around thirty injuries, the expulsion of six hooligans, and an apology from the government in Bonn to the city of Milan.

A decade and a half later, he would be responsible for organising the entire fan and spectator programme at the World Cup in Germany, and his earliest lessons of fan behaviour at a big tournament came in the wake of the violence in Milan with his efforts to avoid a repeat in the match against the Netherlands.

He begins by explaining how he ended up travelling around Italy with a group of hooligans: 'I organised a trip to Italy, four and a half weeks, for thirty-five people, from Hamburg and Bremen – all hardcore supporters and fighters – because my belief was Germany, the national team, was more important than the club rivalry and so we wouldn't get violence within the group, and in the end, it worked like this.

'It was funded by European money, so it was a cheap trip for the fans – they paid one thousand euros each for tickets, accommodation, everything. It was a special programme named Youth for Europe. For a cheap trip to Italy, they had to fulfil some tasks. We had a photo lab where they learned to develop film, and they had to describe football fan culture. On the streets, they were interviewing fans from all over the world.'

Schneider and his fellow activists had staged the first fans' congress for German football supporters in autumn 1988, having previously lobbied unsuccessfully for an alternative approach to policing at the 1988 European

Championship in West Germany. 'We wanted to invite all the fans coming from Europe to Germany with the slogan "Culture instead of police sticks",' he remembers.

Describing the violence in Milan on 10 June, Schneider says the spark that lunchtime was the arrival in the city centre of a busload of Yugoslavian fans, but holds the view that trouble would have ignited anyway. 'The Germans had come with an attitude that today something must happen because there were so many of them. The conflict really started because they realised there were only thirty policemen. They caught four or five people and tried to arrest them, in a gallery near the Duomo, and that was when the attack on the police started.

'They threw things at windows, they tried to upturn a tram. They were like barbarians.

'The police force were doing their security work surrounding the stadium, and the problem was they had something like thirty or forty policemen on the Piazza del Duomo, and the others couldn't get to where their colleagues needed them because of a traffic jam. It took them two hours to come.'

The *Gazzetta dello Sport* the following day said that the disorder had lasted for four hours from 2pm. FIFA's Organising Committee reported afterwards that, 'Only in Milan were the security forces unprepared for the hooligans.'

Schneider's group actually filmed the mayhem with the video camera brought along for their cultural activities, and watched it back later. 'We made the movie, and in the mind of the hooligans, we were fighting and winning all day long,' he explains. 'Rumours travel fast, and the rumour was we had a video of their victory, and we had to give it to them [the hooligans]. I said, "No way." We had a very big debate within our group, in our campsite close to Rimini.

'In the end at two in the morning, I said, "Before you fight me or rob it, or others come – because the pressure was not within the group but surrounding us – let's put the video in the tape recorder and look at it." It was very interesting because the so-called victory wasn't a victory – on the tape, they could see most of the time they were escaping from one policeman, who was driving around the Piazza del Duomo.'

Given the potential for another eruption of violence on the day of the Netherlands game, Schneider arranged an alternative activity for his group.

'We learned that we had to organise an alternative to the inner city where all the hooligans are coming together,' he explains. 'For the match against Holland, everybody had it in their minds there'd be a big fight, but we said, "OK, you have it two ways – one you go into the city on your own and it's your own responsibility, or together with the German ambassador we go to the municipal head office in Milan, and we have a discussion about violence in football." We said, "It's your choice," and in the end, everyone accompanied us on the bus to this special debate.'

Inside the stadium, there would be racist monkey noises directed at the black Dutch players, but outside, there was no repeat of the disorder from a fortnight earlier.

Schneider's work brought him to the attention of the German media, and, in turn, led to a call from a government office back in Bonn which he received at the campsite in Rimini. 'I'd gone to Italy with a deficit of fifteen thousand euros, and they said, "Don't worry about the deficit. This project is so prominent, we'll support you no matter how much it costs." It was a special European office in the youth ministry which normally funded Oxford students or Wagner musicians – high culture.'

By summer 1992, Schneider was responsible for organising the first-ever fans' embassy for German football supporters, at the European Championship in Sweden. There, he witnessed another significant step forward in the way football supporters attending major tournaments were viewed.

'Because they had such small stadiums – we were playing in Norrköping and it had a capacity of eighteen thousand – we said to the Swedes that many people would be coming and they should think about using big screens. The German football body was very angry with me because they said whoever didn't have a ticket had nothing to do in Sweden. Their argument was that big screens would bring all the criminals, so if you don't have them, you don't have problems. But if you look at the German World Cup, they were saying, "You don't need a ticket because we have fantastic fan miles, and big video screens, and so on." The event outside the stadium nowadays is as important as the football match itself. If you remember, when England played Sweden in Cologne there were one hundred thousand English football fans and fifty thousand Swedish football fans.'

*

ON THE PITCH, ONE OF THE MOST INTENSE EPISODES IN THE
German-Dutch football rivalry had taken place only two years before Italia '90
at the 1988 European Championship semi-final in Hamburg.

As in the 1974 World Cup final between the nations, each scored a penalty,
but this time, it finished 2-1 to the *Oranje*. West Germany had led through
a Matthäus spot-kick, awarded after Rijkaard's rash challenge drew a dramatic
fall from Klinsmann. Ronald Koeman equalised from the spot after an even
more questionable penalty award, this time for Jürgen Kohler's challenge on van
Basten. Eventually, the Dutch went through thanks to Van Basten's 88th-minute
sliding finish. There was a simmering intensity in the stands too. Dutch fans
chorused, 'Give us our bicycles' – a reference to the confiscation of bicycles
during Germany's Second World War occupation of the Netherlands.
'*Ein Reich, Ein Volk, Ein Gullit*' read a banner parodying a Nazi slogan.

At the finish, Ronald Koeman stood in front of those Dutch fans and pretended
to wipe his backside with the German shirt he had swapped with Olaf
Thon. 'Revenge!' declared *De Telegraaf* the next day, as the Dutch celebrated a
first victory over their neighbours in 32 years.

As Beckenbauer recalled, when speaking ahead of the Milan rematch, 'There
were fifteen thousand Dutch against forty-five thousand Germans, and yet it
seemed like we were in Holland.'

Pierre Littbarski remembers, 'They outsmarted us in '88. I knew everybody in
their team and am good friends with Ruud Gullit. Usually, you go out before the
game and shake hands. I went to Gullit and the other players I knew, and they
didn't shake hands – they just walked away. At that moment, they outsmarted us
already – we starting wondering what was happening but that was their plan.
We didn't play at our top level.'

When the countries met again in qualifying for Italia '90, they drew 0-0 in
Munich, then 1-1 in Rotterdam, where the West Germans had their sleep
interrupted the night before by a bomb alert. Those results helped the undefeated
Dutch finish above West Germany in their qualifying group, but by the time Italia
'90 came round, there were clouds over the *Oranje* camp. Thijs Libregts, the

coach who had replaced Rinus Michels after the European Championship triumph, had lost his job after a vote of no confidence from his Dutch players.

Gullit had a prominent role in the push for a change of coach. His explanation in his autobiography dwells on the memory of an earlier fall-out with Libregts over an allegedly-racist comment that his then Feyenoord manager had made in a newspaper interview.

Yet, after the Royal Dutch Football Association granted the players a vote on the matter, they only had their wish half-granted. Out went Libregts, but their preferred replacement, Johan Cruyff, did not take his place. Instead, Michels, head of the committee charged with appointing the coach, handed the reins to Leo Beenhakker, the second choice in the squad's poll, and allocated himself an advisory role.

It was the former Real Madrid manager's second spell in the post – the first had ended with failure to reach Mexico '86 – and, as coach of Ajax, he could only begin his work at the start of May. Beenhakker would later reflect in David Winner's book *Brilliant Orange,* 'I had no chance. I knew it before the tournament.'

Gullit's own chances of a good World Cup were another source of anxiety owing to longstanding fitness problems dating back to August 1988 – less than six weeks after his goal in the European Championship final win over USSR, when he damaged his right knee in a pre-season friendly with Milan.

He underwent meniscus surgery, and though he returned in time to score two goals in the 1989 European Cup final against Steaua Bucharest, he soon required two further operations. As a consequence, he only returned to the Milan first team on 22 April 1990, seven weeks before the start of World Cup. The West Germany game would be his first at the San Siro since 20 May 1989.

A computer glitch had provided an unhappy omen when Gullit's tournament pass arrived without pitch access, and his team's underwhelming display in the 1-1 draw with Egypt – in their first World Cup match since the 1978 final – brought his frustrations to the surface. He uttered an expletive to an autograph-seeking ball boy and told journalists, 'The draw against Egypt was the result of two years of bad work, bad football, and bad coaching.'

*

THERE WAS CONSIDERABLY MORE SERENITY IN THE OPPOSITION camp judging by Thomas Berthold's description of Franz Beckenbauer's standard match-day meeting. 'You know, before the matches, we met five minutes before lunch for the line-up,' the former West Germany defender tells me. 'Everybody was coming in, sitting down, and he put the line-up on the table and said, "Guys, enjoy the match, play football, and then nobody can beat you, just yourself. Enjoy your lunch." Nothing about your opponent, if he's left foot or right foot, strong, quick, no video, nothing.'

Whatever cool *Der Kaiser* exuded at lunchtime on Sunday 24 June, there was a different temperature inside the San Siro that evening. 'This was the only match where the stadium was split between Dutch and Germans,' remembers Berthold. 'The other matches were eighty per cent Germans and ten or twenty per cent the others.'

The mercury continued its climb once the contest had begun, culminating in the oft-remembered moment, after 22 minutes, which brought the sendings-off of Rijkaard and Völler by Argentinian referee Juan Loustau.

There was a first spark of trouble in the 20th minute, when Rijkaard caught Völler as the striker ushered the ball past him down the inside-left channel. Loustau cautioned the Dutchman and Rijkaard, as he ran back past Völler, turned his head, and sent a globule of spit flying the striker's way.

Völler's reaction – he approached Rijkaard jabbing an angry finger – earned him a booking too, despite his attempts to explain to Loustau the indignity suffered by pointing to his hair.

The main flashpoint followed moments later. TV images show Völler getting his head to Andreas Brehme's free-kick into the box and then leaping towards goalkeeper Hans van Breukelen – however, he pulls out as the Dutchman catches the ball, and falls to the floor behind him. With Rijkaard leaning over him aggressively, he rises to his feet, and squares up to both the defender and Van Breukelen, at which point Loustau steps in flashing his red card. Rijkaard's response? Another shot of saliva aimed at Völler's head as he passes him on his way off the field.

Looking back, Berthold, Völler's room-mate with both AS Roma and their national team, recalls his bemusement. 'He was a quiet person,' he says. 'He was my room-mate in the national team for ten years. Also, Rijkaard's a quiet guy. I don't know what happened to him. He lost his mind. Nobody knew why Rudi was sent off.

'He was standing there, and Rijkaard was passing by and spat. He did nothing. And then, the referee came and red, red. For Rudi, it was not a really good World Cup. Red card against the Dutch team; suspended against the Czechs; and the game against England, he got injured.'

For Rijkaard rather more than Völler, it was not a good World Cup. Indeed, it led to a self-imposed, fifteen-month exile from the national team. He had been unhappy about his allocated role in central defence, rather than in midfield where he had just won the European Cup with Milan.

Nor did he appreciate Gullit's strong influence over – and loud pronouncements on – the Netherlands side at a time when he was still rediscovering his best form; this was a thorn which pricked the relationship between these two boyhood pals.

As for his surrender of his senses Rijkaard would later deny claims made by some Dutch players afterwards that he was responding to racist abuse by Völler. 'The main reason why I spat is that he deliberately got me a yellow card, which would have cost me the next match,' explained Rijkaard, who apologised at half-time to Van Breukelen. 'He comes running at me, and while I made a sliding tackle, he kicks the ball past me. I see that, and I pull my leg back – but even so, he deliberately runs into me and drops theatrically, although I don't touch him at all. And then, he stands up and gives me an annoyed push, as if to say, "Why did you do that?"'

The Dutch certainly missed both his playmaking abilities and the mobility he had brought to their defence. A feature of the second half was the quick, direct running at the Netherlands defence of Matthäus, Littbarski, and Klinsmann, in particular.

'It was the best game of my career,' was Klinsmann's post-match verdict, following a thrilling exhibition of pace and power which brought the breakthrough goal after 51 minutes, swept in at the near post from Guido Buchwald's cross. 'My finish was much easier than Guido Buchwald's assist,' Klinsmann tells me, looking back. 'His step-over got him the nickname Diego.'

It was Klinsmann who took the man-of-the-match honours. He spent the evening dragging Dutch defenders to and fro with those high, galloping strides that were a legacy of the extra speed training undertaken in his late teens with one of his brothers, a decathlete.

Before left-back Brehme curled in a fine second goal with his right foot to secure victory, Klinsmann had nearly made certain himself by rattling the post with a terrific half-volley.

Littbarski recalls, 'He was capable of running two or three hours. He never stopped and we had more space now, and that was perfect for him. We had two excellent forwards, but they were taking away space from each other. Having Klinsmann alone up top, he had the speed advantage over the Dutch defenders, and they could never catch him. It was a reason why we won that game. We had a little bit more space, and without Rijkaard in the game, they weren't as compact as before.'

For Klinsmann, it was his third goal of a tournament in which his hunger was highlighted by an angry response to his 71st-minute removal from the group match against the United Arab Emirates. According to one eye-witness account, with Beckenbauer muttering, 'He thinks he's the white Pelé,' Klinsmann stormed off to the dressing room and flung his boots at a window, smashing a pane of glass. 'I was quite happy he did that,' remarks Littbarski, 'because I knew if he was angry, and Beckenbauer knew this as well, that'd motivate him for the next game.'

The contrast with Van Basten, top scorer at the 1988 European Championship but now a listless figure, was striking. When Gullit told reporters that '[Beenhakker] took over the team on 7 May with seven players in really bad shape', the Milan striker was near the top of many observers' lists.

'I really played badly' was his own appraisal in the direct aftermath, and the perfect illustration came in the second half at the San Siro when he misdirected a pass to Gullit, with his teammate stood no more than eight yards away.

In truth, it was Gullit – awarded the *Gazzetta dello Sport*'s highest rating for a Dutch outfield player – who carried the fight for this side, summoning his strongest display of the finals, yet Ronald Koeman's 88th-minute spot-kick came as cold consolation.

Beckenbauer had approached Beenkakker before the game and told him, 'The one who wins this game will be the champion.' That prediction would be borne out.

Nothing compares
to youse

'THE COUNTRY HAD GONE SOCCER MAD. OUL' ONES WERE explaining offside to each other; the young one at the check-out in the cash-and-carry told Jimmy Sr that Romania hadn't a hope cos Lăcătuş was suspended because he was on two yellow cards. It was great. There were flags hanging out of nearly every window in Barrytown. It was great for business as well. There were no proper dinners being made at all. Half the mammies in Barrytown were watching the afternoon matches, and after the extra-time and the penalty shootouts there was no time left to make the dinner before the next match. The whole place was living on chips.'
Roddy Doyle, *The Van* **(1991)**

'What has it been like, though, to come this far and to do this now?' The question comes from George Hamilton, the match commentator of Irish state broadcaster RTÉ.

He is standing with Packie Bonner and David O'Leary, the freshly-stamped heroes of the Republic of Ireland's penalty shootout victory over Romania on 25 June 1990.

They are somewhere inside the Stadio Luigi Ferraris in Genoa. There is no sponsors' backcloth; just a grey curtain, a figurine of Italia '90 mascot Ciao, and a plastic cup of champagne in each man's hand.

It is an obvious question to ask – 'What has it been like?' – though with an afternoon like that, the more interesting answers can come years later, once the aftershocks have ceased.

As Bonner can attest, they continued for some time. In 1991, there was the publication of Roddy Doyle's *The Van*, the Dublin-based novel about two unemployed friends who, scenting an opportunity during World Cup month, go out and buy a chip van. When the film adaptation came out in 1996, Bonner could watch himself stop Daniel Timofte's spot-kick on the big screen, albeit this time with a quick cut to a woman wearing a chunky Irish tricolour earring and screaming, "He's fucking gorgeous!"

After that came the times Bonner's children, Andrew and Melissa, came home from school with *The Van* on their reading lists and some questions for Dad. 'My daughter and my son were shocked when they were doing the Roddy Doyle books, and doing *The Van* as part of it, and reading up about that,' he remembers. 'I suppose the whole thing about that particular period – and everybody still talks about it from our age group and beyond – was it had an emotion around it, it had real emotion for our country.

'We'd never been in the World Cup before. We had the taste of the European Championship, which went well for us, but without qualifying from our group. This particular time was the first time, and how it affected our country [is something] nobody will understand unless they lived through that – not even my wife and kids to a point. They went to the World Cup, but unless you were in Ireland and lived through it, you don't know how it affected everybody. Everybody has a story around that particular time. It's very hard to describe that to a young person nowadays.'

Bonner and I have met at the Hilton hotel in Manchester, a thin, glass skyscraper that is the United Kingdom's tallest building outside London. He has travelled here from his home in Scotland to attend a meeting with fellow UEFA course instructors.

In 1990, he was thirty years old and had already played more than 450 games for Celtic. But that sweltering afternoon in Genoa was one of those rare moments in life with a visible line marking before and after.

'There's no question,' he confirms. 'I had my career at Celtic and was there seventeen years, but what happened there [in Italy] allowed me to do things I'd never have done if that hadn't happened. I argue with people that I made more than one save, because people only remember that save, but for a small country like Ireland, it did certainly change the way people thought about me.'

And not just in Ireland. 'There were so many people who came down to Donegal, where I live, to visit – people from Italy, from Sweden, from all over, coming to my mum's house, and my mum welcoming them and making them a cup of tea.'

On a wall in Gracie Bonner's house in the fishing village of Burtonport, they will have seen a souvenir of her son at Italia '90 – a photograph taken of the Ireland squad's visit to the Vatican to meet Pope John Paul II. 'My mum had that photo of myself, the Pope, and some of the players round the back of us,' he says. 'It was in the house, up in a frame.

'It was the same family home I grew up in. There was a lot of recognition after that, and I suppose people's perceptions of me changed, but our home didn't change and my mum didn't change. I loved that with my mum. She died a couple of years ago at ninety years old. She kept everything very balanced in the house – when you're from Donegal, from that part of the world, you don't get carried away in life.

'We grew up in a Donegal where we had to be self-sustainable. We had a small country croft. We had animals, we had potatoes. We grew up learning all of those skills. Very seldom do people do that now – some might go back to it more as a hobby than anything else. We grew up working on the sea, and I loved all that.'

It is a picture of a rural, traditional Ireland, though in 1990, this was just one of two Irelands, and the two did not get on. 'Hibernian versus Cosmopolitan' is how David McWilliams, the Irish economist, lecturer and broadcaster, defines it in his book *The Pope's Children*. For McWilliams, 'the three central pillars of Hibernianism were Catholicism, nationalism and the GAA' [Gaelic Athletic Association].' Cosmopolitan meant liberal, metropolitan, and looking past those three pillars to Europe (whose agricultural spending on Ireland, incidentally, rose from €500m in 1980 to €2bn on average each year from 1990-2010).

Journalist Declan Lynch, in *Days of Heaven*, his book on Italia '90, calls it 'rural Ireland' versus 'Dublin 4'. The latter, a postal district for an area containing RTÉ's studios and University College Dublin, is shorthand for Ireland's upper middle class. Yet, as Lynch wrote, the beauty of the World Cup in 1990 was that it brought the two factions together: 'You couldn't go far without encountering this cultural split between the old Ireland and the emerging one, [but] as the big matches got bigger, it felt like everyone was on the same side for a change.'

They were never more on the same side than on the day that Jack Charlton's side found a way past Romania and into the quarter-finals of the 1990 World Cup.

In the lead-up to the game, opposition Labour leader Dick Spring had called for a national holiday. That call was ignored, though the Dublin Chamber of Commerce did advise businesses to start and finish early to enable employees to watch a match that kicked off at 4pm Irish time.

Charles Haughey, the Irish Taoiseach, suspended a press conference following a summit of European leaders at Dublin Castle so that he could watch the climactic shootout. John Healy, a well-known political journalist, burst into tears. Con Houlihan, the late Irish sports writer, would declare subsequently, 'I missed Italia '90, I was in Italy at the time.'

Irish historian and blogger John Dorney suggests it was a near-unique moment of national unity, symbolised by a ubiquitous colour scheme of green, white, and orange. If there had been reluctance among some Irish citizens to fly the flag in the 1970s and 1980s owing to widespread disgust at the IRA's atrocities, this was a moment to embrace the tricolour once more. 'What the World Cup did was people could express their nationalism or patriotism in a way that was non-threatening, in a way that included everybody, and it was a celebration,' says Dorney.

Every single shot of the crowd inside the Stadio Luigi Ferraris during that round-of-sixteen tie seems to feature an Irish flag or two. Packie Bonner concurs: 'During that period, people weren't embarrassed to wear the shamrock and the green. In the past, there were a lot of people in Ireland that wouldn't bother with that stuff, but suddenly, they were supporting Ireland. You'd be surprised by the type of people that were actually celebrating Ireland and celebrating the greenness.'

According to Bonner, even the contentious style of play – anathema to Charlton's critics like Eamon Dunphy – helped seduce the non-traditional soccer fan. 'The way he played the game probably fitted in a little bit with the neutral supporter, the ones who weren't going to watch soccer on a weekly basis, the rugby guys, and the GAA people,' he reflects. 'They quite liked that "up and at it", high pressure, playing it forward early, and it dragged a lot of them in to support the team. When you had success, then they were all coming in to support. And he almost united the whole of Ireland behind that.'

FOR JACK CHARLTON'S SQUAD, THERE WAS A SHARED FEELING OF relief when they reached their base on the Italian mainland, the pastel-pink Grand Hotel Bristol in the splendid harbour town of Rapallo, close to Genoa. 'You put the shower on, and the water was yellow in Palermo,' says Tony Cascarino. 'The lads went mad, but Jack didn't care. We didn't have any air conditioning in the room either, so it was boiling hot.'

Mick McCarthy describes the reaction as the squad decamped at this exclusive spot on the lovely Ligurian coastline. 'We walked into the foyer of the Hotel Bristol overlooking Portofino, and it was the usual football banter – "Fucking hotel, look at this, this is where Scotland have been staying". And Jack said, "Yeah and that's why they're fucking going home!"'

To prepare for Romania, ITV provided Charlton with videos of Romania's matches. Bonner was even able to study Steaua Bucharest's 1986 European Cup final penalty shootout. 'It wasn't easily accessible,' McCarthy says of those VHS days. 'Even when I got the job [of Ireland manager in 1996], it still wasn't that easily accessible, not like we do now – I say, "Just get me some details of this French or Egyptian player" and they'll have something on Wyscout.'

Over in the Romania camp, meanwhile, the focus was not as sharp as it could have been. 'Everybody was focused then on signing a contract somewhere, and this cost us,' says midfielder Ioan Lupescu of his team's imperfect preparations. 'First of all, we celebrated getting out of the group. Everybody was in our training camp: people I knew, people I didn't know, celebrating and eating and drinking with us – families, friends, agents, clubs; anybody and everybody.

'Maybe this was because it was the best performance in our history to get out of the group stage, and then there was this mentality problem. Normally against British or Irish teams, we don't have a problem – they play long balls and aren't so good in possession and technically, but we were probably too optimistic. Maybe also we played too individually. They managed to play how they wanted to play, so we couldn't impose our game – we didn't have our combination and possession game.'

Lupescu adds with a giggle, 'I told Packie [Bonner], who's working with me now, that I remember when I jumped for a long ball and I headed the balls of [Niall] Quinn. He was something like two metres [tall], and instead of heading the ball, I headed his balls!'

Lupescu's comments about the individual holding sway are borne out by the statistics. Playmaker Gheorghe Hagi had nine of their eighteen attempts on goal. With one, he drew the save of the match as Bonner palmed over his fizzing twenty-metre drive just before the hour. 'Hagi was just amazing,' McCarthy remembers. 'Packie Bonner played very well in that game, made some saves from shots from thirty yards, when he [Hagi] would just twist, turn, come in, and shoot.'

Bonner recalls, 'I've spoken to Lupo [Lupescu], and he said Hagi was allowed to drift. They allowed him to be the spare player. The rest of them worked very hard, but he then had to go and produce – and, to be fair to him, he did. He played predominantly on the right, cutting in on to his left. He had quick feet and a powerful shot.'

Romania made the stronger start, keeping possession well and attacking with speed as they created an early opening that midfielder Ioan Sabău rolled wide after Hagi's explosive surge down the right and pullback.

Yet, gradually, Ireland's midfield gained a foothold, shepherding the ball around the Romanian half in neat triangles. With the interval approaching, chances arrived. Kevin Sheedy lunged to meet Tony Cascarino's flick across goal, but goalkeeper Silviu Lung smothered the close-range shot. Quinn, finally free of his man-marker, was off target with a header.

Cascarino, an early replacement for the injured John Aldridge, went close next during a positive opening to the second period – 'I headed one over the bar I could have scored with,' he recalls – before Bonner found himself tested at the other end, stopping a Florin Răducioiu snapshot and the aforementioned Hagi strike. In extra time, he denied Hagi again down low to his left.

'That did seem a long extra time,' says McCarthy. 'It was a red-hot day in Genoa, and we were both just knackered' – knackered and fortunate to finish the match with eleven men after a flare-up between Hagi and Paul McGrath. As they fell to the turf in a tackle, Hagi gave McGrath a dig in the ribs, and the Ireland man caught his opponent with an even stronger elbow in retaliation. 'He'll do well to get away with a sending-off there, will the big man,' said ITV commentator Ron Atkinson of his former Manchester United player. Instead, both men, already booked, got nothing more than a ticking-off.

In the stands, the Irish fans chanted, 'Ceauşescu is a wanker' though their recurring cry of 'Olé, olé' will have had a greater resonance with the TV audience back in Romania. After all, the same song had echoed around squares across the country the previous December: '*Olé, Olé, Olé, Olé, Ceauşescu nu mai e*' – Ceauşescu is gone.

And so, to penalties. Bonner was in a positive frame of mind. 'I'd played well, and I felt this was the game, this was the moment for me,' he says. 'Confidence is a big thing, and you know when your eye is in – you're moving quickly and are into the line of the ball very quickly. Other days, you've maybe got a fraction of a second when you're not quite there.

'At penalties, I'd take a slight step to my left and then push off to my right-hand side, so the timing of that is absolutely critical, and if you're off in any way, you look a fool. But my timing was spot-on that day.'

It helped the Irish that the penalties were taken at the end occupied by their supporters. Their flags and banners adorned the tall, orange stadium towers at either side of the bank of green bodies.

Ireland's five takers were Kevin Sheedy, Ray Houghton, Andy Townsend, Cascarino and O'Leary. Neither Houghton nor O'Leary had taken a competitive penalty before. O'Leary, an extra-time substitute hitherto ignored by Charlton in Italy, had been thrown on to help contain Hagi. He and Ireland's four other takers would all score.

Romania's five were Hagi, Dǎnuţ Lupu, Iosif Rotariu, Lupescu, and Daniel Timofte. Bonner got a hand in vain to Lupescu's kick but succeeded in denying Timofte with another dive to his right. The rest is a history best retold in their own words:

Tony Cascarino: 'Ray Houghton went, "Are you going to take a penalty? Are you a man or a mouse?" And Andy Townsend just went to me, "Pass the cheese, Ray." I said I'd take one, and then O'Leary became the fifth because McGrath didn't want to take one. We wanted Quinny [centre-forward Niall Quinn] in goal because he was our best goalkeeper from penalties. All through the trip, he'd do three penalties at the end of training sessions – if he saves one, you have to give him a tenner; if he lets in three, he has to give you a tenner. He cleaned everybody out.'

Packie Bonner: 'I went over to Kevin Sheedy and said, "Kevin, are you taking a penalty?" and, very directly, he said, "Yes, I'm taking the first penalty, and I'm going to smash it right down the middle." Minutes later, that is exactly what he did. That showed how focused he was.'

Kevin Sheedy: 'As soon as the whistle went, I thought, "Right, I'll take the first one, there's no point saving your penalty until the fifth as you might not get that far." I made my mind up: I was going to go straight down the middle, because I thought the goalkeeper's got to dive – first penalty he's not going to stand there and look a fool. I made sure I kept it high down the middle, got my head down, and hit it as hard as I could. Fortunately, the goalkeeper dived.'

Packie Bonner: 'You know when you have a thousand people behind the goal and you pick one guy out and you see him – he was from three miles up the road, from my local village. I remember walking down after the third or fourth penalty, and to pick him out of the crowd was quite incredible. Jim Boyle. Big Jim as they called him.'

Tony Cascarino: 'Obviously I've never walked the plank on a boat, but I remember walking and thinking, "Everybody I know, my family and friends, anybody who knows me, they're thinking: *No, walk back!*" I remember thinking, "Just low and hard, don't blast it over." Jack loved people hitting the ball hard. If you'd placed it in the corner and just side-footed it, Jack would have gone nuts. So, I put it on the spot, and I just kept thinking, "Low and hard, low and hard", and just ran and drilled it as hard as I could, and it went in. It took a bit of a divot, and the keeper gets close to it [the ball creeping beneath him], but the way I took the penalty was the only way I felt I could score. I didn't feel comfortable trying to pick a spot in the bottom corner. Sheeds was telling me with his eyes, "You lucky fucker." I got a lot of stick afterwards. I think we got a seven grand bonus for getting through. Andy Townsend is running around at the end going "Seven!", and everyone is thinking, "Seven?" and it was the seven grand bonus.'

Packie Bonner: 'You could see the indecision in his [Timofte's] walk-up actually – as a goalkeeper, you've time to look and see how the guy is walking up, and it was a slow walk-up. I always knew it was going to my right-hand side; that was the feeling I had. It wasn't a great penalty, it was a yard off the ground, perfect height and position for a goalkeeper to save it. What was quite incredible was that when I saved the penalty, Andy Townsend and Tony Cascarino ran from the halfway line into the penalty box and jumped on top of me, and there was still another penalty to be taken.'

Ioan Lupescu: 'Dănuţ Lupu, another colleague who'd scored, went to Timofte and told him to shoot there. That was a mistake, because you should never interfere with a player, but leave him alone. That match, we played for three thousand dollars if I'm not wrong – probably a big bonus then, though four years later, we lost to Sweden, and we were playing for fifty thousand dollars.'

Packie Bonner: 'Lupo keeps saying to me, "I lost him a fortune," and I said, "You made me a fortune." I spoke to Daniel Timofte not so long ago. A guy from the *Irish Independent* was going out, and he asked me would I speak to him and I said, "Yes." He said he'd opened a bar out in Romania called "The Penalty", and the reason he opened the bar was if anybody gave him stick, he could chuck them out.'

Kevin Sheedy: 'I said [to O'Leary], "Dave, a piece of advice – pick your spot, hit it cleanly, and don't change your mind." I'd taken a couple of penalties for Everton and missed them from changing my mind at the last minute. You have to stay true. I know Jack heard me saying that afterwards, and he tried to make out he'd said it!'

The final word should go to O'Leary himself. George Hamilton had provided Irish football lovers' favourite line of commentary – 'The nation holds its breath' – in the long split-seconds that it took O'Leary to stride forward and send Silviu Lung the wrong way with his kick. Down in the interview room, the defender, long ignored by his manager, told Hamilton, 'I'm just so delighted to be on the pitch, particularly for my mum and dad watching now. I hope they're happy at last and I've done them some good.'

*

IRELAND'S NEXT STOP WAS ROME FOR THE QUARTER-FINAL AGAINST Italy. On arrival, there was an appointment for Jack Charlton's squad at the Vatican. 'We'd been granted an audience with the Pope, and in our heads we were thinking, "Oh great, we're going to meet the Pope and we'll be in his inner sanctum,"' says Mick McCarthy, 'Well, it was the inner sanctum, but there were ten thousand other people. I was introduced to him as the captain, and I gave him the shirt. We were on the stage, all sat in our white tracksuit tops that were far too warm and inappropriate for that bloomin' weather.'

It was Pope John Paul II's weekly Wednesday morning audience. 'It was a big occasion being Irish, being Catholic, being all those things,' adds Packie Bonner. 'We spoke about [the Pope] having been a goalkeeper when he was young in Poland, and he knew what I'd done – he was obviously well briefed.'

While the pontiff had a genuine interest in the game, the Ireland bandwagon was picking up plenty of new passengers.

'The entire island of Ireland became obsessed with this,' remembers author Colm Tóibín, who was reporting in Italy for the *Sunday Independent*.

Tóibín had observed in Sicily and Sardinia that the majority of the Irish gathered there were 'traditional soccer supporters' – urban and from Dublin. Now, they were joined by the newbies. In an article published on 1 July, titled 'Days of Miracle and Wonder', he wrote, 'This was the week when fans coming to Italy brought their tennis racquets with them, and managed a game in their posh hotels in the afternoon before the match.'

Whether old or new, authentic or plastic, they had quite the night in Genoa, as Tóibín relates: 'That same night, Italy had won somewhere else, and the Italian fans were out on the streets. This is downtown Genoa, where the Irish fans and the Italian fans are just going nuts. I remember people running in and out of bars, hugging each other, waving things, getting into fountains. It really was something to see. What happened then was everybody went to try to get planning permission from their wives to go to Rome.'

In Rome, it was not so much yuppies as politicians that Tóibín encountered.

'Everyone around me was a politician,' he says. 'I was sitting beside Jim Mitchell, who'd been minister for justice, and Jim just kept shouting, "Watch

[Totò] Schillaci, watch Schillaci!'"

According to journalist and author Declan Lynch, Charles Haughey, the prime minister, had previously refused invitations to soccer internationals, owing to the association with 'foreign' games.

At 10.30am on Saturday 30 June, wearing a shamrock-patterned tie, Haughey departed for Rome on a government jet. By day's end, he would be on the Stadio Olimpico running track with a tricolour in his hand.

In total, more than forty flights left Dublin for Rome that day, carrying 6,000 expectant Irish spectators. At home, cinemas closed, and buses made their last trip from the city centre at 7pm. Ireland was in a state of wild anticipation.

Jack Charlton's public mood could not have been more different. On the eve of the match, he arrived an hour early for his briefing with reporters, sent away Tony Cascarino and Paul McGrath when they turned up to join him, and was so opaque in his responses that an Italian journalist stormed out, shouting, 'This is not a press conference!'

His players saw a different side. His instruction after gathering them for a meeting that evening was, 'get some Guinness down you.' Tony Cascarino remembers, 'Jack said, "Right, lads, we're going to have dinner at seven-thirty, and after dinner, you're going to have a couple of kegs of Guinness delivered, and you're going to have a pint or two. You'll sleep well tonight. You're playing Italy in their own backyard, you're going to get beat, so have a couple of pints." We ended up having a good few pints.

'I asked him years later why he said what he did. He said, "Look, you were playing Italy in Rome, and the referee was going to give you nothing, and I wanted you to sleep on the night but didn't want you taking sleeping tablets and being all groggy." In the end, we played the best we did in that tournament that night.'

Mick McCarthy adds, 'We went there totally relaxed. We went out and laid on the pitch before the game watching Argentina play in the other quarter-final on the big screen. The Italians came out, and they couldn't believe it.'

Italy were on a ten-match run of clean sheets, yet coach Azeglio Vicini, concerned by Ireland's aerial threat, tweaked his defence, as home captain Giuseppe Bergomi explains: 'They had such tall, physical players like Cascarino, Quinn and Aldridge, so Vicini changed things around. He played Maldini as the left centre-back, as we needed height in there.'

Bergomi himself, normally a centre-back, was switched to the right-back slot and tasked with shadowing Kevin Sheedy. 'We had to stop Sheedy's supply of crosses. We then had to surprise them with our speed, through Schillaci and [Roberto] Donadoni. The Irish at the back were very strong physically, but we could hurt them with pace. They were our tactics, but they were some team. It was a tough, tough match.'

Ireland began with composure. Paul McGrath disrupted the Italians' flow in midfield, and his cross brought an early attempt on goal as Niall Quinn out-jumped Riccardo Ferri and forced a save from Walter Zenga.

It was actually Italy, not Ireland, who had gone into the game with the most headers on goal in the tournament. Schillaci, with a glancing effort, and Paolo Maldini, meeting a corner with force, soon both went close.

The decisive moment came instead after 37 minutes. Following a Roberto Baggio surge from the halfway line, Schillaci and Giuseppe Giannini worked the ball on to Donadoni, 25 yards out in the inside left-channel, whence he unleashed a strong, swerving shot. Although Bonner got his hands to the ball, it spilled out to Schillaci who rolled it into the goal.

'When Donadoni hit the ball, it was going to my right-hand side,' Bonner remembers. 'I'd moved my feet, but during the flight, the ball started moving back into my left-hand side. I couldn't catch it, because it was almost away from me. I couldn't redirect my body to get back into the line of the ball. I had to take it with me, back out to the way I was going. But when I knocked it out, it fell straight to Schillaci's feet. No other player but Schillaci, who'd finished almost everything when he had a sight of goal, and now I was outside the post, and the goal was vacant. Looking back, I don't think I could have done anything else.'

Schillaci recalls, 'I managed to hit the ball flat and low, even if it was really difficult to control it, and I put it in the corner of the goal.'

A goal was not the only thing Schillaci collected in the first half. 'He was a tough little sod – he threatened me with the old knife, he was giving me that,' relates McCarthy, with a cut-throat gesture. 'If you ever see it, he's got a black eye, and I think that one's down to me.'

Back in the dressing rooms, Jack Charlton would focus his frustration on

Sheedy, who had attempted a pass into the feet of John Aldridge moments before Schillaci's strike. Sheedy elaborates, 'Coming off at half-time, I was walking in with Aldo and he said, "Jack's going to give me a bollocking here." I said, "Quite right as well as you should've got hold of it." We got in the dressing room, and Jack just slaughtered me: "What are you doing playing into him? I've told you, get it in behind!"'

During that interval, Graham Taylor, speaking on ITV, suggested that Ireland's efforts meant, 'Baresi doesn't look so clever in this game,' and they caused their hosts further anxiety on the resumption, with Paul McGrath arrowing a half-volley not far wide.

Eamon Dunphy, writing in the *Sunday Independent,* described McGrath as 'our most heroic player'. Dunphy was less pleased, though, by Charlton's decision to leave Ronnie Whelan on the bench and send on John Sheridan instead. 'This is what was missing, despite the courage, last night,' he wrote.

Still, Vicini's changes highlighted the trouble Ireland were causing as he replaced his playmaker, Giannini, with the more defensive Carlo Ancelotti, and then introduced a robust target man, Aldo Serena, in place of Baggio.

The clearest openings were still Italy's, though. Schillaci had shot over from close range in the first half, and now, he drove a fierce thirty-yard effort against the underside of the crossbar. Serena spurned two opportunities when alone in front of Bonner. Schillaci, like Baggio in the first half, had a late goal ruled offside – in this case, when clearly onside.

It was Ireland's first defeat since 16 November 1988 against Spain. The feeling in the dressing room afterwards was that the Portuguese referee, Carlos Silva Valente, had made their night doubly difficult.

'I was broken-hearted,' says McCarthy. 'We'd had a Portuguese referee, and I don't think he gave us a chance of competing. Our game was very much put-it-on-'em, get-after-'em, high-energy-'em. I thought he stopped the game so often, he broke our rhythm. I should watch it again to see if he was as bad as I thought, or was I just bitter and twisted and full of resentment because we'd lost? I don't think so.

'Baresi swapped shirts with me. I was marching up the tunnel and he called after me. I was in tears because we'd lost. I didn't cry too often. I actually missed the players celebrating with the fans.'

Bonner recounts a comment Charlton passed in the aftermath, that Ireland could have gone all the way had they overcome the host team. 'Jack always felt if we got by Italy, we had a real chance because we were going to go against Argentina. I always remember him saying that we can beat Argentina because they play one-touch, two-touch football, and we'll close them down, and nail them high up the pitch. We had a really strong, physical, competitive team, and nobody liked playing against us.' This had been only their sixth defeat in 43 games under Charlton.

*

'THERE WAS A SING-SONG GOING ON, AND CHRIS DE BURGH GOT UP and sang "Lady in Red",' smiles Kevin Sheedy, sharing his memories of saying goodbye to Italia '90. The best bit, with due respect to Mr De Burgh, had yet to come. This happened more than three hours after Jack Charlton's squad had landed at Dublin airport on the evening of Sunday 1 July.

'We got to the bottom of O'Connell Street, and looking back, there were about 250,000 people,' he adds. 'That moment of looking back down O'Connell Street will live with me forever. It was a sea of people. You realise you've been part of something special.'

Since Italia '90, Ireland's national teams have played at major final tournaments in 1994, 2002, 2012, and 2016. Nothing has been so special since. They advanced from their group on three of the four occasions, with the help of memorable victories over Italy at both USA '94 and Euro 2016. Yet today, that victory over Romania in Genoa remains their only success in a knockout tie on the big stage.

Even that, technically, was not a victory, notes Tony Cascarino wryly. 'We were hailed as heroes coming back to half a million people, and we hadn't won a game. We got through on penalties. Most of our performances were crap – we didn't play particularly well against England; we were shocking against Egypt; we were alright against the Dutch, and alright against the Romanians.'

None of it mattered a jot as Cascarino and his teammates experienced a homecoming unmatched in the history of Irish sport. It was a celebration of something beyond sport: of a nation acquiring a new confidence, a fresh sense of self.

'Thanks a million . . .' was the *Irish Independent*'s front-page headline the next morning, above an aerial photograph of two open-top buses snaking through a sea of people, estimated at half a million, en route to a civic reception at College Green. There had already been 50,000 waiting at the airport – more than for Pope John Paul II's 1979 visit – when the squad's Aer Lingus Boeing 737, renamed 'St Jack' for the occasion, touched down at around 6.30pm. Charlton stepped off the plane holding a new carbon fishing rod, a gift received from his players during the flight home. He was off to catch some fish in Connemara.

Not long before, a less happy homecoming had taken place. Eamon Dunphy's flight had landed an hour earlier, and, as he relates in his autobiography, his car got caught in the great swell of people outside the airport. Some spotted Dunphy and started shouting abuse and rocking the vehicle. Two middle-aged women emerged from the mob and asked him to wind down the window for a photograph. When he obliged, one of them responded by spitting out an altogether different World Cup verdict: 'You're a fucking little bastard.'

The Lions' last roar

'WE DIDN'T APPRECIATE THAT WE WERE IN THE QUARTER-FINALS and just eight minutes from the semi-finals. It didn't register. We carried on playing naively.

'It reminds me of the film *The Gods Must Be Crazy*. It's the story of an African who leaves his village and goes to the city, continues behaving like he was in his village, and continues looking at people the same way. They take him to court, and he goes in there with a smile, and says hello to the people there, when they're going to send him down.

'We were like that. We were playing for an important prize, the World Cup semi-finals. Everybody in the world is watching, but we didn't realise the stakes, and we carried on playing naively, doing back-heels. And we lost. We cried, we did our lap of the stadium and saluted the crowd, and we didn't realise the moment had gone and we'd missed an important crossroads.

'The goal was there in front of us, and even today, no African team has reached it. Again, if we'd got to the semi-finals, anything was possible. That was a unique opportunity for Africa to reach another level.'

History tends to be written by the winners. In the case of the Cameroon-England quarter-final in Naples on 1 July 1990, the other side of the story, as the reflective testimony above indicates, is well worth hearing.

The man speaking is Eugène Ekéké. His World Cup was only two minutes old when he lifted Cameroon into a 2-1 lead over England. Cameroon, a nation whose football association had been established only four years before England's 1966 triumph, led the creators of the game.

The first three quarter-finals of Italia '90 had produced two goals between them. Now, the watching world had some big-dipper football to enjoy: twists and turns, five goals, and three penalties. It ended with the neutrals' favourites bound for home.

Cameroon have never been so far since – have never survived the first round, in fact – and today, as he looks back, Ekéké knows that it could have been so much more. It is not only Europeans who talk about African footballers' naivety. They can do it for themselves, and with no little eloquence.

Ekéké was the man who put Cameroon on the brink of the semi-finals. For eighteen minutes after he left behind England's frozen defence and lifted the ball high over the outrushing Peter Shilton, the Indomitable Lions stood on the threshold of the semi-final.

YouTube highlights of the game show England on the ropes. François Omam-Biyik could have – should have – put them on the floor. With only Shilton to beat, he tried to back-heel the ball past the goalkeeper, who made the block.

That would have been 3-1. It is a moment that Ekéké returns to once more. 'When the match started, we realised we had an opponent we could handle. We realised it was an even game. I remember that after I scored, we had some chances. Omam-Biyik does his back-heel, and it was there that we didn't grasp we had our destiny right in front of us, because if you get to the semi-finals, you never know what can happen. No, it was us that lost the match, rather than England winning.'

Ekéké and I are talking at a table in the garden of his residence in Bonassama, a small village sited on the estuary of the river Wouri. On his head is a panama hat. Over his shoulder is the bridge into the port of Douala, Cameroon's largest city and commercial capital.

The road travelled over that bridge offers a white-knuckle rush of sights: a battalion of motorbike taxis straddled by dust-faced, beanie-headed riders weave in and out of traffic, carrying everything from mothers with small children to a man with a wriggling, market-bound pig. Vehicles pass with slogans such as 'Prudence, please' and 'God's grace'. On roads like this, there seems no harm in invoking a greater power.

Ekéké's residence is both his home and his business. Tables are spread across the lawn from a recently-finished celebration. Behind the coconut trees is a two-storey building currently under construction as a wedding venue, rising with the proceeds of a playing career spent largely in France.

It was back to this western corner of Cameroon, back to his home village, that his mind raced as his shot flew high into Shilton's net, only two minutes after his introduction to the heat of World Cup action. And, specifically, back to the mother who had died two months before.

'I'd lost my mother that May,' he explains, 'and I didn't really want to go to the World Cup.' A visit from two community elders – '*grands frères*' as he calls them – prompted a change of heart. 'As your elders, we're telling you to swallow your anger and go there,' was their message – which is how he came within eight minutes of putting an African nation into the World Cup semi-finals.

He talks through his goal, the product of a one-two with Roger Milla which slices through a static England defence.

'I've got the ball, and I go forward, and when I make the pass, I see Roger, and I see the space too. I set off, and Roger, with extraordinary timing, puts it right in my path. I lower my head, because when a forward lowers his head, that's the moment a goalkeeper comes out. As I lift my head, I see his position, and I shoot.

'When the goal went in, I ran off thinking above all about my mother. I thought, "I'd have so loved for you to be there for this moment." It was a strong moment because when we played, she'd be in front of the television with the whole neighbourhood. She'd have been very moved.'

Ekéké, as mentioned in an earlier chapter, was known in the Cameroon squad as 'the Pastor'. He is articulate and brimming with conviction as he explains the ripples across Africa following the Indomitable Lions' feats in Italy.

'Straight away, there was a great feeling of identification. People identified Cameroon as Africa. Cameroon had something that appealed to people. We were this naive David in the world of football and business that was starting. A little African who turns up from who knows where and brings something fresh to remind people that football is a game and everybody has a chance. We said something interesting and put a smile on faces.

'It also gave others cause for hope. If Cameroon can do it, why can't the others? And all of Africa was proud. At the time, you saw images of Africa and it was Ethiopia and starving children. For once, a different image came out of Africa, a winning Africa, a proud Africa, a more positive Africa than was in people's heads. It was another image of Africa, and I think we surprised the whole world. That's why I say you could have one thousand diplomats working thirty or fifty years, and they won't do what football has done for Cameroon in terms of public relations.'

*

CAMEROON ENTERED THE NAPLES QUARTER-FINAL MISSING A quartet of suspended players in André Kana-Biyik, Jules Onana, Victor Ndip, and Émile Mbouh. 'Cameroon, the bench rises' was the headline of the *Gazzetta dello Sport*'s match preview. Benjamin Massing, absent since his red card in the opening game, would return in defence.

The defender sensed no fear in the ranks. 'We knew that it'd taken England a lot of effort to get this far. We knew they'd be a bit tired. That was an advantage for us, because we had players who were a bit fresher, players like myself coming back from suspension. We knew they'd feel the fatigue, and there'd eventually be the odd moment when they'd switch off a little. That's what we were counting on, and that's what happened. We played our best match at the World Cup, technically and tactically.'

Goalkeeper Thomas Nkono concurs: 'That game was our best match of the World Cup, and it was the subs [that helped].'

If Cameroon had become the darlings of the tournament, England's own climb to the uplands of the World Cup was gaining its own compelling momentum. Against an attractive Belgium team in the round of sixteen, they had conjured their most dramatic World Cup victory since the final of 1966.

With his exceptional swivel-and-volley, David Platt had become the first Englishman since Geoff Hurst to win a World Cup game for his country in extra time. In this case, in the 119th minute.

Belgium's *Le Soir* newspaper asked, 'How could it happen?' while Red Devils playmaker Enzo Scifo noted ruefully, 'We gave them a lesson in football movement.' Even Ron Atkinson, providing analysis in the ITV commentary box, turned to commentator Brian Moore following the end of the broadcast and muttered, 'We could be the worst team ever to win it.'

England captain Terry Butcher concedes it was a tight contest. 'I remember Scifo hitting the post. He was elusive, had great technique and hit some great shots.' Jan Ceulemans struck a post too.

'It was a real hard-fought game, really tough,' Butcher adds. 'We didn't quite get our game going. David Platt came on, and we were thinking, "My God, it's going to go to penalties." Then, up stepped Gazza with a free-kick and David Platt with that wonder goal.'

In fairness to England, John Barnes had seen a fine volleyed strike incorrectly ruled offside in the first half. Instead, it was Platt who seized his World Cup moment superbly. The Aston Villa midfielder had not scored an international goal before. He had only made his debut against Italy the previous November and had begun just one match for his country.

Yet, he came to Italy fresh from earning the Professional Footballers' Association Player of the Year prize after scoring nineteen league goals for Villa. And, after replacing Steve McMahon in the 76th minute in Bologna, he became the hero of the hour. By the tournament's end, he would have another two goals to his name – and his feet on football's fast track.

'I didn't expect to be going, so was delighted to be in the squad,' he remembers. 'These were the days when you named five substitutes, and I didn't expect to be on the bench, but I was. I never expected to get on the pitch, but I did. Now I look back as a coach and can understand why. I've been with the [England] Under-21s myself and have had to piece squads together – you might get to sixteen, seventeen players who are shoe-ins and with the rest, you start asking, "What can he do?". I had the benefit that I could play midfield and I could play up front so I had an advantage over another midfield player who missed out. My goalscoring record helped me, because you can fill two spaces.

'I got on against Belgium, but if I don't score that goal or I score it ten minutes earlier and they equalise, I don't know whether I play in the next game or not. But I managed to play in the next game, so I'm now into a quarter-final of the World

Cup playing against Cameroon and score again after twenty-five minutes. And before you know it, when the team's being named, Bobby Robson isn't going to leave you out. It happened so quickly. I don't know what the time span was between me scoring against Belgium and us going out in the third and fourth place play-off. I bet we're only talking two weeks maximum, but it changed my life. I got back, and there were five commercial deals waiting for me.'

Platt's moment came after Gascoigne, attempting one last forward surge, carried the ball forty yards before tumbling under a push from Eric Gerets, in a position central to goal. Gascoigne lofted the free-kick over towards the far post where Platt, spinning on to the ball seven yards out, caught it flush on the volley and sent it flashing past Michel Preud'homme.

'I guess if you turned around and measured the adrenalin surge, I'd put money on that being the top one,' he says. 'I drifted into the box, and Gary Lineker was on the other side, so you find some space. It came over my shoulder, and I was just trying to direct it towards goal. I hit it so sweetly, and that's what took the goalkeeper by surprise. I remember falling on my knees, thinking "What's just happened?"' Cue the happiest pile-on in England history.

Gascoigne had earlier responded to his first booking of the tournament by holding up an imaginary card at the referee and then waving a dismissive hand. Now he played on a mock-violin in front of the Belgium fans, while Terry Butcher and Chris Waddle sang along with the supporters who filled the night air with the cry of 'Let's all have a disco', the terrace anthem of England's summer.

'The celebrations afterwards were just sensational,' remembers a smiling Butcher. 'Me and Chrissie Waddle doing the disco – that was an image that will live with me for a long, long time. He had a Belgium shirt on [swapped with his ex-Tottenham teammate Nico Claesen], and I had an England one. I didn't like giving my England one away.'

With that song, England fans were showing their good face: they actually had a sense of humour. It was their own rebellion against the Mexican wave, as Craig Brewin, one of the Football Supporters' Association volunteers from the England fan embassy, recalls: 'Because the stadiums were bowls and the games quite dull the Mexican wave would always start and whenever the wave hit the England fans they'd just stop it and rather than not put their hands up they'd make hand gestures, jeer and then start dancing, singing "Let's all have a disco". That's what started it, and I have to say it looked magnificent. I thought it was really funny. It was, "We're English and we're not joining in," and at the time, that was the culture of the England fans.

'I remember someone saying to me, "I wish they didn't do that," but I thought it was just a bit of fun and a small group of England fans in a big bowl not wanting to join in with everybody else, and I think you've got an absolute right not to join in. Nowadays when I go to Wembley Stadium, they do the bloody Mexican wave, and when it's coming around, I sometimes think, "I really want to stand up and sing, 'Let's all have a disco'."

The lyrics of another song were on Paul Gascoigne's lips in the post-match scramble of media interviews. In a corridor of the Stadio Renato Dall'Ara, he began quoting lines from 'World In Motion', New Order's World Cup song, during an interview with an Italian television reporter. Not surprisingly, it is a stunt that his palpitating interpreter, Giacomo Malvermi, the team liaison officer, has not forgotten.

'It was about midnight, and this bloke says, "Hi, are you the interpreter? You're on Rai Uno news now." All of a sudden, the guy starts asking, "How do you feel?" and something just clicked in his brain, and he started 'World in Motion'.

'All of a sudden, he starts quoting. I'm trying to interpret, and he's coming out with words from a song, and he's laughing at me because I'm on the spot in front of God knows how many millions of Italians who were watching live on television.'

It was not Malvermi's only task that evening. 'The reason why the England team did so well was because they had fun,' he smiles. 'These were lads in their twenties, and they were there to have fun. When England beat Belgium, there was a ban on alcohol being sold in Bologna, but some of the players wanted a few beers on the coach after the game. I asked around, and in the end I pulled a few strings, and I was a hero to them. I got them their forty-eight cans of beer. I remember they were on the bus chanting my name – I remember, "Giacomo Giacomo, Giacomo". Because I got them beer, they were happy.'

With Cameroon next, the sunshine mood was forecast to continue. Not least after Howard Wilkinson, then manager of Leeds United, produced a scouting report on the African team which suggested England had little to fear. Terry Butcher says, 'Howard Wilkinson did his report, and it came back to Bobby, and Bobby read it out to us, which he shouldn't have done. It said, "If you don't get through this game against Cameroon, then you don't deserve it, this is yours for the taking."'

For Thomas Nkono, the notion that England might have underestimated Cameroon draws a sympathetic response. 'I remember in 1982, Enzo Bearzot [coach of Italy] came to the Africa Cup of Nations in Libya and he said he'd seen nothing – Cameroon had individual talents but Italy would win easily. But with African teams, you can't say, "They play like this" because everything can change. You have to expect anything might happen, good or bad. It's the good thing about African football – it's more a question of inspiration.

'From an organisational viewpoint it's not like today, where they study the opponent a lot and know exactly how they can hurt you. We played a more imaginative game. The only plan we had was ours – basic organisation, and from there, try to invent things when we have the ball. That's always been the strength of African football – in the last twenty-five metres, you invent. If we're inspired, our opponent has a problem.'

That evening in Naples, they were inspired. And England had the problem. The mere sight – and sound – of the Cameroon players in the tunnel told Terry Butcher that a considerable obstacle lay in their path.

'I was captain of the team,' he recounts, 'and we were quite early in the tunnel. I've got the England crest – because England don't have a pennant, but a crest which is gorgeous – and Bobby Robson is ahead of me and we got to the steps that go up [to the pitch] and are lining up. Cameroon aren't there. We were there a few minutes, and then we hear them coming along the corridor: "*Nous allons gagner, nous allons gagner*" [We're going to win]. They're jumping up and down and you're thinking, "Oh my God – what specimens. Massive boys."

'I remember Bobby saying to me, "Well, they could sing but they can't play." I remember thinking, "Wrong thing to say, Gaffer." They came alongside me, and the captain heard him, and he passed it down the line. He tried to say it the way Bobby Robson said it. I was mortified.'

These war cries are an integral part of the culture of Cameroon football, as

Benjamin Massing explains: 'If you get on the bus of any African team, you'd think there was a disco going on because the players all sing to get in the right frame of mind for the match. Singing and dancing helps you deal with the stress. We used to sing a lot and pray a lot.'

Roger Milla adds, 'It was to galvanise us and then to let the English know we were ready to fight it out with them.'

THAT EVENING, THE NAPLES CROWD WAS WITH CAMEROON. IT WAS England, though, who struck first. Platt, starting instead of McMahon, scored again, this time with a far-post header. 'I clipped it down to Stuart Pearce, and he ran down the wing, crossed it, and David Platt scored,' recalls Butcher. 'We got one-nil up so early in the game, first attack really, but they came back very strongly and smashed us.

'They were big guys, but they were quick as well. Some of their movement was just sensational. They were strong, they'd hold the ball up and in the air were aggressive. When we got the ball, we seemed to give it away pretty easily, and then we couldn't get it off them. We'd win the ball, then give it away. They knocked us right out of our stride – literally knocked us out of our stride.'

Even before Platt's goal, François Omam-Biyik had a clear sight of goal, but Shilton blocked the shot with his fists and Louis-Paul Mfédé's rebound strike swerved wide.

'What they had was not just the physical capacity but also some ability,' adds Platt. 'There's no doubt about it, we were very, very close to going out. I think the reason we won is they showed naivety. Now with the African players playing in Europe, if you'd replayed that game twenty years later, they'd have probably run out the game two-one and wouldn't have got beaten.'

Brian Glanville, the esteemed British football writer, would suggest afterwards in a column for *World Soccer* that England's much-applauded sweeper system did not help on this occasion. 'There were those who felt, with some reason, that the situation was created essentially because there was no midfield "filter", that the midfielders simply did not pick up and intercept the attackers steaming through from the Cameroon midfield,' he wrote.

This was certainly the case for Ekéké's goal. At the moment he played a vertical pass ten yards upfield to Roger Milla, he had two England midfielders ahead of him but cut straight through Paul Gascoigne and Platt as he drove up to meet Milla's return pass.

Milla, a half-time substitute, had already won the penalty with which Emmanuel Kundé had equalised, stealing half a yard on Gascoigne to draw a trip. With eight minutes remaining, though, referee Edgardo Codesal signalled the second penalty of the night at the other end. From a half-cleared Gascoigne free-kick, Paul Parker headed the ball back towards the penalty box, Mark Wright flicked on and Lineker, after a touch to bring it under control, went to ground under a challenge from Massing.

England had not had a penalty for four and a half years. As Lineker sought to compose himself, into his mind came thoughts of his brother Wayne at his bar in Tenerife who 'always worries about me when he's watching on television'.

Bobby Robson's son, Mark, was watching at home with equal anxiety as he imagined the next day's papers in the event of defeat. 'I can remember thinking, "If we lose this, this is really going to kick off and get nasty."'

These fears began to ebb when Lineker lifted his kick into the left corner of the net as Nkono went the wrong way.

As Espanyol's goalkeeper, Nkono had faced Lineker in Catalan derbies during his Barcelona days. 'I knew where Gary was going to put it because I'd seen him take penalties in Spain, and he always went to the goalkeeper's left,' Nkono recalls ruefully. 'I was saying to myself, "Left, left, left," and at the last moment, I changed to the right. I thought, "I'll change because he knows me". It was stoppable if I'd gone right.'

With another Lineker penalty, England won the game. As against Belgium, Gascoigne – still alert in extra time – had a central role. From just inside his half, he threaded a sublime pass into Lineker's path and the striker's collision with the outrushing Nkono had the Mexican referee pointing with two outstretched arms to the spot once more. This time, Nkono did go left. Lineker drilled the ball to his right. The England striker lost a stone in weight that night and, as he quipped, 'Half of it must have been over those penalties.'

'We were so, so lucky to go through,' says Butcher, echoing the *Daily Express* back-page headline 'You lucky lot!' 'I remember being taken off in the game, and I was sat next to Chris Woods, who was my room-mate, and we were two-one down with ten minutes to go and I said, "At least we'll be home tomorrow". Then of course, Gary pops up with a goal for extra time and scores a winner in the end, and we're through, and you're thinking, "How did that happen?" We didn't play well at all. We got smashed by them really, absolutely beaten up by them, but we got through.'

In the BBC studio, Jimmy Hill noted that the introduction of Trevor Steven in place of Butcher – which meant Parker stepping infield – had helped England hold on to the ball better. Butcher had struggled with the explosive pace of Cameroon, while Parker brought speed and agility and flexibility.

In his post-match briefing, Bobby Robson admitted, 'Their movement and their strength and their running for the ball surprised us, and they punctured us, and we had to dig in there desperately for many periods of the match.'

Not surprisingly, Roger Milla still regards this as the one that got away. 'I said to the players, "There are ten minutes left, get the ball up to me in the attack and I'll hold on to it for as long as I can." But unfortunately, we wanted to carry on playing like we played, to please the public and perhaps get another goal. Sincerely, for me, the game was won.'

From a Cameroon perspective, a sense of injustice lingers even today over the penalty awards which turned the game on its head. Nkono remains sceptical, telling me, 'The first one wasn't; the second one is possible.'

Massing is more forthright. 'You know, in all sports, they protect the stars, and Lineker benefitted from the referee's largesse. There was no bad contact. For a long time, I suffered with this – I knew that we were in the penalty box and I knew the stakes. So I knew I couldn't do that. But with his experience, he tried to influence the referee, and perhaps the referee was only too happy to go with it.

'He's engraved in my mind – Codesal Méndez was his name. That's him. He blew for two penalties as if he couldn't wait to do it.' The video of the incident suggests that while Lineker knew how to draw contact, Massing erred in extending a long leg after the ball had passed.

It is intriguing to learn the perspective of Codesal, the man who awarded the kicks. The Mexican-Uruguayan says that by this stage of Italia '90 a series of high-profile refereeing mistakes – and accompanying public criticism from Sepp Blatter – had created 'a lot of nerves' among the match officials.

Moreover, he recalls 'a strong media campaign' from the Cameroonians who were suggesting that 'it would be very difficult for them to overcome England with everything they represented in the world of football – football speaking and politically speaking'.

Entering the quarter-finals, Cameroon had committed the most fouls –115 in four matches at a cost of twelve yellow cards and two reds – yet, as Benjamin Massing's words imply, with the sanctions came a sense of persecution.

Codesal adds, 'At our base in Rome, you could feel the tension before this game. FIFA's refereeing committee sounded us out, asking us one lunchtime how we saw the game. I said I'd come here to referee and had had fourteen days more or less without refereeing, just running the line. I said I wanted to referee to show I could do any game.

'The England manager said, and I remember him saying this clearly to the press, "Let's hope this referee from the third world knows the rules well enough to handle a game as important as this one." For me this was an extra motivation to do well.

'I have to say, the first penalty I gave was in their [Cameroon's] favour. They were leading, and they had the chance, with a one against one against Peter Shilton, and the forward missed it. And England came back. We always try to blame the referee for our own mistakes. Without any doubt, in the review of the three penalties by FIFA, everybody said that in their view that they were all clear – and this helped me get the final.' He might also have said that moments before awarding Milla a penalty he had ignored the sight of Nkono hauling Platt to the ground.

*

'INVENTORS OF FOOTBALL REMOVE JOY FROM THE CUP.' THE headline in Brazil's *Folha de Sao Paulo* was a reasonable summing up of how most of the world viewed the outcome in the Stadio San Paolo.

The Neapolitans were the first to express it, as Thomas Nkono remembers. 'The thing that stood out most was the Italian public and the send-off they gave us – it was as if we'd won the trophy,' he says. 'The whole stadium were on their feet. We'd lost, and the stadium was celebrating.'

Amid the overflow of emotions that followed their lap of honour of the stadium, Nkono himself felt a deep frustration. 'I remember some lads saying they were ready to go back home. I said to them, "You don't know the opportunity we've missed."'

The homecoming was no less spectacular for it. First, they stopped in Douala. Next day, it was Yaoundé's turn as the players left the airport and embarked on a three-hour tour of the city. 'Even when Pope John Paul II came to Cameroon, there weren't that many people on the streets,' Nkono explains. 'Every player had a military jeep and toured the whole city. People were so happy they were throwing water at us, and I was in bed for two days with a temperature after that!' At the palace of President Paul Biya, the squad received the nation's second-highest honour, the medal for the Commander of the National Order of Bravery.

The *Cameroon Tribune* gave the following, rather wordy, verdict: 'They transformed the Italian pitches into a vast diplomatic display whereby numerous nations of the world, of which some, until now, would have been unaware even of our basic existence, came to discover, with curiosity at first, then, respect and admiration, the Cameroon people, and what we offer in dynamism, faith, determination and talent.'

Elsewhere in Africa, Ivory Coast's *Fraternité Matin* said, 'Thanks, Cameroon. No one on the African continent could remain indifferent to the battle waged by the Indomitable Lions against the English. Their valour is recognised across Africa. Roger Milla and his comrades have permitted us to vibrate to their rhythm for three weeks, taking us on board with them for this wild adventure.'

FIFA's response to Cameroon's feat was to award Africa a third World Cup place for the next finals. Suddenly, Pelé's prediction, made back in the 1970s, that we would see an African World Cup winner by the end of the century, felt plausible.

Yet, though Cameroon won gold in the Olympic football tournament of 2000, following the example of Nigeria four years before, we are no closer to an African World Cup winner. Senegal and Ghana followed in Cameroon's tracks to the last eight, but each fell short – in the latter case after Asamoah Gyan's penalty scraped the crossbar in the last breath of extra time in 2010, after Uruguay's Luis Suárez had handled a goalbound effort. Cameroon's own record since 1990 has been dismal: one victory and ten defeats from fifteen World Cup finals games.

Massing says, 'In reality, African teams, even today, lose matches through naivety. Africans know how to start a match but afterwards they don't know how to finish it. It's a Cameroonian problem because it's a problem coming from the organisation and the way that football in Cameroon is organised. It means, grosso modo, that we're not very professional here. This is why victories don't always follow. Even when we've got players who are capable, who have talent and can do something. The organisation always comes and strikes a false note in our preparations.'

Not long after the bunting came down on Italia '90, there were press reports of £400,000 worth of profits going missing at FECAFOOT, the Cameroonian Football Federation. A sorry tone was set. According to Martin Etonge, a Yaoundé-based journalist, 'The 1990 World Cup made people aware that for Cameroon to get to the World Cup was a money-making opportunity for corrupt officials – it opened the floodgates for corrupt officials to come in, and instead of using that newfound dynamism to build something, it became a beehive and people were attracted to the honey.

'We don't manage well. Not because we aren't intelligent enough but because of corruption. We say in pidgin that "chop broke pot". It means the guy eats and destroys the pot because he doesn't care about tomorrow.'

A striking example is the farce of the fundraising drive for the squad's USA '94 participation. *Opération Coup de Cœur* was a nationwide effort to collect money for team costs, and there were even collections taken in prisons according to a fascinating study of the social and political significance of football in Cameroon, *Visions of a Better World*, written by Bea Vidacs, a Hungarian cultural anthropologist. More than $1.25 million was raised but Vidacs writes, 'Despite the enormous amounts of money collected through *Opération Coup de Cœur*, the players remained unpaid until after the match against Brazil (their second match in the competition). And even then, they were only paid when, under the threat of a strike, Augustin Kontchou Koumegni, the Minister of Information, was hastily dispatched as the Special Envoy of the Head of State to pay them.'

Thomas Nkono was goalkeeper coach for Cameroon's 2002 campaign in Korea/Japan and he cites the problems encountered then: a delayed departure from Paris after a players' strike over money meant a late arrival in the Far East, and the dominos kept falling from there.

'I always talk about the organisational aspect,' says Nkono. 'I've been in Europe for over thirty years, and organisation within a short tournament like that is important – travel, preparations, food.

'I was lucky to coach one of the best generations of the Cameroon national team. We had Samuel Eto'o, Lauren, [Patrick] Mboma, and that team could have got further than we did. But how is it possible that a national team who are going to play the World Cup have to travel fifty hours to get to Japan? There were stops in different countries. That was us losing before we'd even boarded the flight. That World Cup was a big fiasco. When do the players recover?' Even at the 2014 tournament, the squad arrived in Brazil a day late.

THE GLOBALISATION OF FOOTBALL HAS MEANT MORE opportunities for individual players from a country like Cameroon to earn wealth and prestige abroad, but the domestic game is little better off today than it was in 1990. Journalist Graham Turner visited Cameroon for the February 1991 issue of *World Soccer* and was told by Bonaventure Djonkep, one of the Indomitable Lions team, that 'there are no decent facilities for training'. Nearly thirty years on, nothing has changed.

The bare and bumpy training pitch in Yaoundé where Nkono once worked out as a Canon player is still there, set against a sprawl of orange-roofed slum housing and the verdant hills that encircle the city. Canon's reserves are out training: bring-your-own-kit, no bibs, and just the one ball.

On the same day, I look on as players from APEJES Academy, a top-flight club, get changed beneath trees flanking the rectangle of red earth on which they have just completed a training session. The president of the club,

Léon Aimé Zang, tells me, 'We rent the pitch from the school. No club has their training ground.'

He speaks with envy of ASEC Mimosas, the Ivorian alma mater of Kolo and Yaya Touré, among others, and a club previously partnered by Belgian side Beveren. 'We played ASEC, and it's extraordinary, the infrastructure – there are dormitories, a canteen, a training ground,' he says. When another Belgian team, Lokeren, sought to work with Canon Yaoundé, the collaboration was short-lived. 'It's the Cameroon environment at fault,' adds Zang bemoaning what he calls loose management.

Roger Milla tells me, 'The heads of state talk a lot about young people, but they were neglected. There was a moment when people really let things slip. For ten or fifteen years, we had no youth football.'

The few successful academies in Cameroon have private backing: Les Brasseries du Cameroun – source of such players as Geremi Njitap, Rigobert Song and Eric Djemba-Djemba – have the support of an eponymous brewery. KADJI Sport academy, where Samuel Eto'o once played, is another brewery-backed venture. Coton Sport, the now serial league champions, are owned by the Cotton Development Company.

If APEJES have no training ground, they have no stadium either. I watch them in action during a double-header at the Stade Militaire in Yaoundé. This is one of two stadiums in the capital that serve eleven first and second division clubs. In Douala there is one pitch for nine teams. 'For now, we have only five or six pitches like this in the whole country,' says journalist Martin Etonge.

A report in the *Cameroon Tribune* during my stay in Cameroon said that 'teams are complaining about the quality of match planning', as this mass sharing of facilities means it is not uncommon for club officials to only receive confirmation of their kick-off time with a text message the day before games.

The Stade Militaire had a facelift ahead of the 2016 Women's Africa Cup of Nations – where it was used as a training pitch – and today, it has two identikit, single-tier stands, the roof of each painted in the red, yellow and green of the national flag. Both goalmouths are bare and so too is the centre circle.

A woman wearing a fake Germany football jersey passes with a basket of drinks on her head. A peanut vendor tosses small bagfuls up a dozen rows to a spectator. As there is no home team, there are no local kits on display. Instead, the stands are a patchwork quilt of polyester displaying the colours of European clubs and countries: Paris Saint-Germain, Real Sociedad, Ajax, Croatia, England, Real Madrid, Atlético Madrid, Manchester United, Marseille, Borussia Dortmund.

It is the same all across Cameroon: every fourth or fifth person in a football jersey. In Mutengene, a town in the Anglophone region of the country, I see several hundred students, male and female, from the town's police physical training college, on their march back to base. All wear combat trousers and black boots, and each has a football shirt on.

This passion once had a purely local focus. When the likes of Milla and Nkono played in the 1970s, there would be attendances upwards of 100,000 at the Stade Ahmadou Ahidjo, Cameroon's national stadium. Then, of course, there was no television (which arrived only in 1985). The photographs of Tunisian sports journalist Faouzi Mahjoub, on display at the FIFA Museum in summer 2017, offer a glimpse of a now-lost world: black-and-white images of spectators squeezed on to every possible vantage point – some standing on concrete pillars at the back of an unfinished grandstand, others perched bird-like on floodlight pylons.

Life has changed. The country's economic strife – the currency was devalued in 1994 – did not help. The cinemas began closing in Yaoundé in the 1990s, and the football crowds started to shrink. The Stade Militaire's two stands hold only around 3,000 spectators. 'Two thousand francs [£2.70] is the maximum ticket price,' says Etonge, offering some context. 'Canal Plus [the primary source of televised European football] is around ten thousand per month.'

The view of this generation of players is that there has been something gained and something lost.

Defender Victor Ndip reflects: 'It's very disappointing to see a club like Canon Yaoundé, who gave people public holidays in this country because of victories. The head of state would declare public holidays. That spirit is no more. It's money now.'

Thomas Nkono, another Canon old boy, says, 'People identified with players in the past. Now, if you go to a league or a national team game, there's not many people who identify with the player. They go abroad very young, so it's difficult. You go to a game and say, "I saw this great player." You go the next week to see the same player, and he's no longer there.

'What we've got is the world leagues are now available for the so-called underdeveloped countries, you can now see every league in the world. And what happens? It means people don't go to the stadium. I like my team, but if Real Madrid are playing I won't go if they're on at the same time. This is what happens in Africa. I stay at home and watch Madrid. This is what has happened. Technology has brought us good things, but we've lost in other ways.'

Back on the terrace of Eugène Ekéké's residence, he takes me back to that other time, the time before Italia '90. 'When there was a Cameroon match, the streets were empty. In the morning, everybody would be making noise, and when there was a goal, the whole city would shake. When I came out of the tunnel, I'd lift my head, and there'd be one hundred and twenty thousand people – people on the floodlights. It's like a bull being thrust into the arena. You come out and "whoa" – all that energy just hits you.

'Where are the emotions today? Today, people don't go to the match. They watch a lot of football on television, which means they know the entire Barcelona team but don't know a single team in Cameroon. Ask me who is the best player in Cameroon today, and I couldn't tell you – and I'm a former player.'

Across the water and past that bridge with its mad drivers and motorbike riders was a city with a football culture that meant something more, at least in Ekéké's eyes. 'I think that's why you miss the past times a bit because when you see a city like Douala, it had at least four grounds, and that's not including the school pitches. Today these have disappeared.

'We had a team called the Léopards. When the Léopards played, all of Douala was at the ground. Matches would start at two o'clock, but there were times the stadium would be full by eleven. Today, we have clubs here like New Star and Les Astres [both founded this century], which are the fruit of the efforts of individuals, who don't live in the area. Money doesn't create a club. You can buy players, but that doesn't give you soul.'

Soul. Ekéké, the man the Indomitable Lions called 'the Pastor', can certainly talk about soul. And before he bids me goodbye, we return to something that stirs his, still: Italia '90. When the Cameroon squad flew home from Naples after the drama of defeat by England, they carried with them all manner of souvenirs. In the case of defender Victor Ndip, son of a polygamous father, his bounty included fifteen pairs of Italian shoes for his many siblings.

For Ekéké, there is one specific item that still brings out the goosebumps. It is the record with which he returned home: 'Notti magiche', the official tournament song.

'The day I die, when they're lowering my coffin, that's what I'd like as the piece of music to say goodbye to the world with.' A reminder of those precious minutes when he had a whole country, nay a whole continent, dreaming.

Before the divorce

IT IS FRIDAY LUNCHTIME IN PRAGUE, AND I AM SITTING IN THE FRONT passenger seat of a Ford Fiesta. The man at the steering wheel is wearing a black Slavia Prague top and shorts and is driving us back into town from the small, homely stadium out on the city's eastern edge where he has just overseen a training session of his club's Under-19 squad. The driver's name is Ivo Knoflíček, and he is a member of the Czechoslovakia team that reached the quarter-finals of Italia '90.

Right now, though, he has another team on his mind: oddly enough, the Derby County side of 1989. Knoflíček is digging deep into his store of memories, trying to retrieve a few of the names from the English team that he fled his country for, but for which he never actually played. Gradually, they come back to him: 'Peter Shilton, Dean Saunders, Mark Wright ... Ted McMinn ... Nigel Callaghan.'

The effect of being taken back to the Baseball Ground nearly three decades ago is enhanced by the fact Knoflíček's hair is a magnificently intact 1980s mullet. It calls to mind actor Ian McShane's mane during his days as the eponymous, roguish antiques dealer in the BBC TV series *Lovejoy*.

'Did you like Derby?' I ask.

'Prague is very beautiful,' he responds, his brown eyes smiling.

The story Knoflíček has to tell leaves all of Lovejoy's adventures in the shade. It is a saga featuring a British newspaper tycoon, a fake Bolivian passport, and a year and a half lost in limbo. It is a tale that has even been turned into a play, by supporters of Slavia, titled simply *Knoflíček. An Evening with Gary Lineker* is not the only piece of theatre inspired by a 1990 World Cup footballer.

Knoflíček's story belongs to the days just before the Velvet Revolution which swept across Czechoslovakia in November 1989, bringing to power the country's first non-communist government for more than four decades. But for that revolution, Knoflíček, top scorer in the Czechoslovakian top flight in 1984/85, would almost certainly have never got to play at the World Cup.

This, after all, was a player who had spent almost eighteen months banned from the professional game after going in search of the liberties every European footballer takes for granted today.

It was thirty years ago, in the summer of 1988, that Knoflíček, then 26, and Slavia teammate Luboš Kubík, 24, left a club training camp in West Germany and embarked on a journey that led them to Spain and then the Low Countries before their arrival in the East Midlands at the end of the year.

Knoflíček had first come to the attention of Derby scouts by scoring against Wales in home and away qualifying fixtures for the 1988 European Championship. The effort in Prague, a shot thrashed high past Neville Southall from the edge of the box after he had left Pat van den Hauwe on his backside, was Goal of the Season in Czechoslovakia in 1987. It even featured in the titles for the main sports bulletin on state television – at least until his flight into exile.

Representatives from Derby, then in the old English First Division and owned by the Czech-born media tycoon Robert Maxwell, a major figure in the deal, visited Prague and began negotiations with both Slavia and Pragosport, the communist party organisation which owned the rights of every player in the Czechoslovakian system.

Knoflíček explains what happened next. 'Slavia weren't against it, but the problem was the Czechoslovakian federation official [Rudolf] Kocek who didn't want to allow it,' he begins, his words interpreted for me by Ondřej Zlámal, a respected Czech football journalist and author of several books on Slavia Prague.

'The negotiations led nowhere, as they didn't want to allow me to leave officially. In July 1988, we went to a training camp with Slavia to Hannover, and on the last day, when we were supposed to return home, the attaché from London came to see me and told me they wouldn't let me go, and the only solution was to leave with him to England. He said I'd have to go through a period without football but they'd take care of my family.

'I didn't want to leave alone. Luboš Kubík was my room-mate, so we agreed that he'd join me. He was expected to go to the army for two years' national service, and he felt the prospects weren't good for him, so we jumped into the car, still in our shorts and with no passports as these were with the team manager, and we left for England.'

Knoflíček had not even had time to forewarn his wife, who was left at home with their two young children. It was not an easy phone call. 'She said, "Stop joking, finish your beer and come home!"' he recalls. 'She thought I was just drinking somewhere and messing around. She began to cry when she realised I was serious. It was a hard decision, as you can imagine. My son was six months old, but I hoped they'd soon join me.

'I explained to her that Mr Maxwell had promised he'd arrange for our families to join us, but it was complicated. We didn't have passports, so we had to stay in Spain for half a year. Officials from Derby told us that they'd get the passports for us from Latin America, and that took virtually six months. Finally, we left for England using Bolivian passports they'd sorted out for us. They'd bought us Bolivian citizenship for forty thousand dollars. I still have it.'

During the wait for their passports, Maxwell, the *Daily Mirror* owner and chairman of Derby, sent money to Knoflíček's wife each month. Calling to mind the reaction of his other family members, he goes on, 'Our family were farmers and landowners in Moravia. An old family tradition. They lost all their property after the communist coup. When I escaped, my parents were crying, but my grandfather, who had tough experiences with the communists, shouted, "I'll break him in two if he returns!" So the family were a great support. When my father went to his pub, they told him, "You can't sit here, you're the father of an émigré," but later I sent him some *Playboy* magazines, which were banned here. He lent them to people in the pub in return for free drinks!'

There were attempts made to persuade the Slavia duo to return home – Czechoslovakian FA secretary Rudolf Bata met the pair in Brussels – but Knoflíček was wary of the potential repercussions. 'I refused immediately. I'd made my mind up. Luboš Kubík told them that a return would mean two wasted years in the army for him, so they left not achieving anything.

'In Spain, we were staying as guests of the Guinness family and slept in a chateau for five months in Figueres where Salvador Dalí was born. We were there when he was dying. The Guinness family took care of us. They'd lent money to Maxwell for him to be able to take over the *Daily Mirror*. Eventually, we travelled from Barcelona down to Gibraltar and a week before Christmas from Gibraltar to London.'

✱

ON 6 JANUARY 1989, THE BACK PAGE OF THE *DERBY EVENING Telegraph*, in a story headlined 'Search for Freedom', carried news of Knoflíček and Kubík's unveiling as Derby players in a press conference at the Connaught Rooms in London alongside a bow tie-wearing Robert Maxwell.

The report said the pair had work permits but now faced a wait for FIFA clearance. Maxwell himself declared, 'Their status as refugees is recognised, as is their status as amateurs in Czechoslovakia. Ivo is a locksmith and Luboš a fitter and engineer.'

While this was technically true – players at Slavia were classed as employees of an engineering company, while goalkeeper Jan Stejskal over at Sparta Prague, for example, had a contract classing him as a plumber – it would fail to sway FIFA, whose regulations stated that a political refugee must wait twelve months to play in the association of their choice after being declared a defector.

'On 1 January, we started to train with Derby,' Knoflíček relates, but his subsequent introduction to the Baseball Ground crowd before an FA Cup tie against Southampton was the nearest that Derby followers got to seeing him and Kubík.

'We played friendlies but were banned from playing by FIFA. This complicated things even more. I didn't know this, but the Czechoslovakian federation then contacted Kubík again saying Fiorentina were interested in signing him and that if he came back, they'd let him go to Italy.

'He didn't tell me, I just found a letter in the hotel room where he said he was going back to Czechoslovakia. The reason was his family. So he returned, and the Derby representatives then came saying that we'd been presented as a duo and that I had to leave England as well within a month, so that was it.' (Kubík, incidentally, would finally experience English football briefly during a fifteen-match spell as Torquay United manager in 2006/07.)

Knoflíček's next stop was Italy. There, he spent a couple of weeks training with Czech coach Zdeněk Zeman's Foggia side before going to Verona. 'I trained for three months with them. We met with the communist official Kocek again in Frankfurt. He said he wouldn't let me play, and I refused again to return.

'When the Italian transfer window closed in August, I took my Bolivian passport and left for Germany. I played in an amateur league as a non-registered player. Nobody knew me, so I played for an Italian team. In every game I'd score two or three goals, so they kept telling me to slow down.

'Ján Kocian [his national-team colleague] was at St. Pauli, and contacted me in the October. Then the Velvet Revolution happened on 17 November. Just a few days later, it was confirmed I could play, so I went to Prague and got all the papers.'

His debut for St. Pauli, the Hamburg-based club, had the sweetest of endings for a player who had not tasted competitive football for so long. 'On 15 December 1989, I played my first game against Borussia Mönchengladbach and scored the winner in the eighty-fifth minute,' he smiles. 'It was simply fantastic.'

It is ironic, given his fruitless stay in Derby, that four months later, he should find himself back in England, playing for his national team at Wembley and showing to Czechoslovakia's coaching team of Jozef Vengloš and Václav Ježek why they should take him to the World Cup. This was the match where Paul Gascoigne made his own irresistible case for inclusion in Bobby Robson's starting XI, scoring one goal and contributing to England's other three in a 4-2 victory.

'When Ježek and Vengloš called me up for the friendly against England, my first thought was that someone was pulling my leg, but it was true,' says Knoflíček. 'We both played. I set up [Tomáš] Skuhravý's goal, Kubík scored from a free-kick, and we were named in the squad for Italy.'

Six minutes before Gascoigne's superbly-scooped ball for Steve Bull to score England's first goal of the evening, Knoflíček had angled a pinpoint cross to the giant Skuhravý for the visitors to open the scoring. It helped to settle an intense debate within the squad over the merits of a recall for the pair.

'They were so good that they took the place in the starting line-up of other players, and for those who'd played in qualifying, this was hard to swallow,' says Michal Bílek, a midfielder in the Czechoslovakia team and a future coach of the Czech Republic.

'There was tension at the beginning. The coaches came to us and asked, "What do you think about this?" and it wasn't an easy situation.' After the team's 1-0 home loss to Egypt on 4 April, media pressure grew on Vengloš to restore the pair. The England game three weeks later confirmed their importance to a team struggling to click.

'We were out of sorts going into the World Cup,' explains Bílek, moving on to their final warm-up game, a 1-0 defeat against West Germany. 'We'd not played well, and after the game, we had a meeting with the coaches and the players. People had the chance to talk about what was going wrong. There were too many of us trying to play, and nobody prepared to work hard and run. That was the problem. But we cleared the air, and it was different from then on.

'Vengloš didn't get too emotional. He was clear-sighted, he'd think about football and talk to players. He left a real impression on me. As a player I thought his approach, this human approach, of talking to players, of communicating well, was the best way to be.'

Bílek had been the two-goal hero of a decisive home qualifying win over Portugal in October 1989, which took Czechoslovakia, playing 73 minutes of that game with ten men, to the brink of their eighth World Cup finals. Remembering the late free-kick which won the match, he says, 'After I scored, I went out of my mind. I still don't know how I finished the game. The emotion was so much. I lost it for the last seven minutes.'

It was a moment of joy too for goalkeeper Jan Stejskal, whose mistake eight minutes earlier had given Portugal an equalising goal. 'He saved the team, and he also saved me,' he acknowledges. 'It was the worst moment of my career – think about it, you are in a full stadium and need to win to qualify for the World Cup, and it was my mistake, and nobody else's.'

ON 17 NOVEMBER 1989, SIX WEEKS AFTER THE WORLD CUP qualifying win over Portugal, a peaceful demonstration in Prague to commemorate

International Students' Day drew a brutal police response. It was the spark for a series of protests across the country from workers' unions and other civic groups. By 20 November, in the biggest demonstrations since the 1968 Prague Spring, state TV estimated there were 200,000 out on the streets.

Václav Havel, the dissident playwright imprisoned more than once by the ruling regime, became the head of Civic Forum, an umbrella organisation of influential civil and human rights groups assembled hastily on 19 November to demand the resignation of the leading communists, an investigation into the police action and the release of all political prisoners. The following Friday, 24 November, witnessed the mass resignation of the politburo. By Christmas, the country's communist president, Gustáv Husák, had resigned. Havel held the reins of power.

Jan Stejskal recalls a sea of people on the streets of Prague. 'I went out to celebrate in Wenceslas Square. There were half a million people. It gave you goosebumps. You knew something was happening, something historical. We didn't know what was going to come, but at least it was ending, and you had so many expectations. There was the hope something better would come. We'd been able to travel for football but no other reason so I'd come home from football trips with washing powder and yoghurt – even a TV and radio.'

For the present-day visitor to Prague, glimpsing the expensive elegance of Pařížská Street, with Prada and Bulgari stores posited on opposite corners, it is difficult to imagine a time when a can of Coca-Cola was a rare treat brought back from abroad.

Some shoppers may still cross the border for the supposedly creamier version of Milka chocolate bars on sale in Germany, but the past that Michal Bílek remembers was a darker place. Sitting in a Costa Coffee outlet in a shopping centre outside Prague, he says, 'I never thought communism would end, I never thought that I could live a year of my life outside of communism, and it suddenly ended and we were free. You can't describe that.

'In communist times, I'd go to Germany for yoghurts and bananas, and when I tell this story to kids today, they can't understand it. I remember going to training camps, and the custom office checks when we came back into the country were unbelievable – it was a horrible time.'

With restrictions on the media, speech, and travel lifted, this became the first World Cup where Czech and Slovak fans could go and support their team. 'We'd never had this before,' Bílek continues. 'After the revolution and the opening of the borders, it was the first time we'd had this kind of support. In Florence, there were fifteen or twenty thousand people, it was fantastic.'

The Stadio Comunale was the venue for their first Group A match against the United States on Sunday 10 June. Goalkeeper Jan Stejskal says, 'What I remember as the most emotional moment was when the kit man, Václav Jez, saw all these people as we were on the bus arriving at the stadium, and he started crying.'

To enhance the sense of new possibilities, this was the weekend of the country's first democratic elections, and captain Ivan Hašek would dedicate the victory gained to Civic Forum, party of the now officially elected Havel.

Before the match, a group of fans had carried a banner through Florence which declared optimistically '1934 Finale, 1990 Finale'. It was in Italy in 1934 that a Czechoslovakia side playing football of the 'short-passing "Danubian School"' – as Brian Glanville described it in *The Story of the World Cup* – reached their first World Cup final, losing to the hosts in Rome.

They were runners-up again in 1962 in Chile, where a team led by Josef Masopust, that year's European Footballer of the Year, fell 5-2 to Brazil in the final. Two World Cup finals on foreign soil and one European Championship crown, attained in 1976, is a record demanding respect – yet, entering Italia '90, they had not won a game on the world stage for 28 years.

The *Gazzetta dello Sport* went so far as to describe them as 'slow, monotonous and lacking flair', yet, everything changed with their opening 5-1 rout of the US.

'The World Cup was such a success for us because of the first game,' observes Bílek. 'We'd been lacking self-confidence beforehand but we got it back in that game. During the whole campaign, we didn't play a bad match. We had a team based on technical skills, Skuhravý's finishing, and the speed of Knoflíček. Lubo Moravčík had a great tournament, and I loved playing with him. At the back, Kocian was experienced and in great form. We didn't have weaknesses, and we all got on off the pitch too.'

Soon to join Genoa from Sparta Prague, Skuhravý recorded the first two of his five World Cup goals – including the first of four headers – that afternoon.

'It was like a fairy tale,' says Knoflíček of his partnership with his fellow long-haired forward. '[Assistant coach] Ježek came to me right at the first meeting and said, "Skuhravý will be the forward, you'll be the winger."'

Also on target against the US was Bílek, who scored a penalty. He failed to convert another, when scooping the ball weakly into the arms of US goalkeeper Tony Meola.

'At the final whistle, the Americans confronted me because they thought I'd tried to humiliate their goalkeeper, but that wasn't the idea,' he recounts. 'The only person embarrassed was me. They were really annoyed. I thought I'd give it a try, we were four-one up, but it was a stupid thing to do.'

Bílek made amends swiftly with the penalty that earned a satisfying victory against Austria in a hammer-and-tongs second Group A match against their wealthy neighbours to the south.

'I remember Vengloš was looking at the other players, and nobody looked back. I was a bit nervous because of what happened against the US, but I looked at Vengloš, and he nodded his head. My teammates told me I was mad to take another one.

'I wanted to be [Antonín] Panenka,' he adds of the Czechoslovakia midfielder whose famously dinked spot-kick won his country the 1976 European Championship final against West Germany. 'That's why I tried that stupid penalty. I always liked players with great skills. Panenka would take corners from the left side with his right foot and the right side with his left. There were players with good skills and imagination who could produce the unexpected. This is what I miss in today's game.'

Bílek, who was Czech Republic coach at Euro 2012, continues: 'These players today learn things in training and do them, and there's a lack of creativity and surprise – the ability to find finding unexpected solutions. There's less free thinking. Times have changed.

'When I was growing up, I'd be out playing, and my parents would have to come out and drag me back into the house. Now, they spend two hours training, and when you play a bit and do something good, agents appear and they get control of you. They promise you things and get into your head. The taste for football and the enthusiasm is diminishing.

'Our football used to be a technical school. I wouldn't say that now. In the past, when you were asked who was a good set-piece taker, you could list the names – Panenka, Knoflíček, etc. Now, you don't have the names. There's Dočkal, but he's in China now.'

This last-mentioned is Bořek Dočkal, former Czech Under-21 captain, who moved on to the MLS in February 2018, after a year in China. 'Now, footballers think more about money. I don't understand how a player, when he has the chance to go to play in England, will go to China because of the money. I can't get my head around that.'

And yet, he and his 1990 teammates were the very players who began the exodus abroad. By the end of that year, Bílek himself was at Real Betis in Spain.

'Under the old rules before the revolution, you had to be thirty and have a certain number of international caps before you could go. Now, it changed. It was the first time players had the chance to go, and everybody wanted to leave.'

Captain Ivan Hašek made no secret of this at the time, telling reporters, 'We've got a team full of people who want to take profit from this World Cup to put themselves in the shop window.'

JAN STEJSKAL WAS ANOTHER CZECHOSLOVAKIA PLAYER ON THE move after Italia '90, in his case to Queens Park Rangers in England. Speaking to me in a café in Jevany – a lakeside, forest-fringed hamlet an hour from Prague where he serves as mayor – he grins at the memory of the Panasonic TV set he received from his national federation on returning from Italy. The real riches came with his move to west London.

Stejskal, who made 108 league appearances for QPR, would be one of the thirteen foreign players in action on the inaugural weekend of the Premier League in 1992. A decade earlier, he had been playing for Cheb, a Czech army club which, like Dukla Prague, would recruit young footballers for the two-year duration of their military service.

'There was a recruitment camp in the city of Tabor,' he explains, 'and once a year, all the players scheduled to go to the army went there, and the coaches from the army clubs arrived and selected the players they wanted. You had a number, and you played a tournament, and the coaches sat in the stand and selected the players they wanted.

'For me it was a bit easier because I'd gone through the national youth teams, so the coaches knew me, but it was still strange going along to the camp not knowing where I was going to end up.'

Not as strange as his early days in England. 'It was a shock at first. Everywhere we went the stadiums were full. When I played for Sparta we'd have home crowds of around thirteen thousand. You had the running tracks around the grounds too, and when I came to England, it felt like the fans were sitting in the goal. My first game was Leeds away. We were two-nil down after twenty minutes, and I didn't know where I was. In the end, we came back to win three-two.'

The conversation returns to Italia '90 and Czechoslovakia's third group fixture – and an atmosphere more intimidating than Elland Road. Italy were the opponents at the Stadio Olimpico, and first place was at stake.

'To step out against the host team at the World Cup in front of eighty thousand people was a shock. Of course, once the game starts it's different, but it was a big thing. At Sparta, we'd played one or two games like this in the European Cup but otherwise, we never had an experience like this. Now it could be different with the Champions League, but for us, it was something completely new.'

Ivo Knoflíček proffers an extra detail: 'My teammates [Miro] Kadlec and [Jozef] Chovanec who played in the Czech league were really nervous. When they were leaving the tunnel and saw the crowd, they stepped back and pushed all the line of players back.'

It was a match embellished by Roberto Baggio's brilliance, that liquid slalom which made dummies of four Czechoslovakia defenders, and showed why Juventus had just paid a world-record £8 million transfer fee to prise him away from Fiorentina.

Beauty is in the eye of the beholder, though. Stejskal grins when he thinks about facing Baggio: 'I think Miro Kadlec could have fouled him. He didn't want to commit another foul, though, as he'd have missed the next game with a second booking. Baggio was all alone on the penalty spot. I had to gamble by diving to one side, and I guessed wrong.'

A different view of that match comes from Lubo Moravčík, the creative midfielder who emerged as one of Czechoslovakia's brightest lights in Italy.

Citing a legitimate-looking headed goal by Stanislav Griga, he says, 'The referee disallowed a goal that would have made it one-one. I don't know why. An imaginary offside? It's politics. If Italy drew, we'd have been first in the group and stayed in Rome.'

Moravčík is at an outside table in Café Lino, a bar on the main street in Nitra, the town in Slovakia where he grew up. At regular intervals, a car horn sounds or a hand rises in acknowledgement of an acquaintance passing by.

Moravčík was one of nine Slovakians in that 1990 squad. He was one of two from Plastika Nitra, his hometown club.

'Coming to the national team from Nitra was not usual,' he reflects. It helped that Nitra had proved uncomfortable hosts for the big Prague clubs and Moravčík had shone in those matches.

It was a club, he explains, supported by the town's plastic factory. 'This was the system in Czechoslovakia. The factory paid the players as employees, and the players were free for football. I never worked, because I was a student. I studied agricultural engineering at the University of Nitra. Six months before I left for France, I finished, in December '89.

'Ivan Hašek, our captain, studied Law and we finished at the same time. That was a speciality of a communist country – when you play football, you have a nice life and better money but afterwards, what? You need to go to work. Now, with millions in your account, you don't need to go to work. At that time, we didn't earn a lot, especially in Slovakia. When I went to France, I earned one hundred times more than here.'

Moravčík's move to French club Saint-Etienne was agreed before the quarter-final against West Germany, by which point he had earned the praise of the great Internazionale and Italy defender Giacinto Facchetti, who wrote in the *Gazzetta dello Sport* that 'speed, dribbling and fantasy are his gifts'.

'Of five of Skuhravý's goals I gave the assist for three,' he elaborates. 'I was very proud of the first goal against the USA. I got the ball and went from right to left – I could have shot because it was about fifteen yards out, but I feinted to shoot and put the ball into Skuhravý for an empty net. The goalkeeper was waiting for my shot and he just had to put the ball into an empty net. I wasn't a greedy bastard, you see! It was a pleasure for me to give that pass because that pass was very clever and the first goal was very important.'

It was Vengloš's tweaking of their system – a switch from the 4-4-2 seen most commonly in qualifying to a 3-5-2 to incorporate Knoflíček as a second striker, playing off centre-forward Skuhravý – which helped him to flourish.

'After Knoflíček came in, Mr Vengloš put in Kocian as a libero with two stoppers, and two wing-backs in Hašek and Bílek. Me and Kubík were in the middle supporting the attack. I changed side from left to the right. The first time was against [the] US, as all the time in qualifying I'd played on left. But I'm originally right-footed, so everything was perfect.'

Vengloš, then 54, had been the assistant to head coach Václav Ježek in Czechoslovakia's 1976 European Championship triumph. Now, they reversed the roles.

'There was a good balance,' Moravčík says. 'Mr Ježek was like a grandfather who took us into the hotel and said, "Don't be scared, be calm, play the way you know, be confident because you are good players." Mr Vengloš was the tactician, he found this new system.

'He always told me, "If you have good players, you have to find the system to let them all play. It's a mistake to leave good players on the bench." And he found a system to play the best.'

It would be Vengloš who later took Moravčík, his fellow Slovakian, to Celtic in 1998. By then, 'Dr Jo' had become the first coach from outside the British Isles to manage a top-flight club in England with his year at Aston Villa in 1990/91.

A quiet, thoughtful man, he was an alien object on the English football landscape with his doctorate in physical education and advocacy of curious 'Johnny Foreigner' practices like post-match warm-downs for players hitherto used to heading straight for the bar. The experiment ended after a season which Villa finished 17th in the table.

'He was the first non-English coach, and it wasn't easy for him,' Moravčík argues. 'It was a lot of responsibility, as he was more a coach than a manager – and in England, you have to be the manager, you have to sign the money, and take control of everything. It's a lot of responsibility. It's a completely different job.

'For example, at Celtic, Martin O'Neill was never at training. He came only once on the Friday before the weekend, but he had head coach Steve Walford, along with an assistant head coach and goalkeeper coach.'

Approaching the quarter-final in Milan on 1 July, Czechoslovakia were the team with most shots on goal at Italia '90: 67 to the 61 recorded by West Germany. They were fresh from a 4-1 victory over Costa Rica in the round of sixteen in which hat-trick hero Skuhravý terrorised Hermidio Barrantes, the reserve goalkeeper deputising for the injured Luis Gabriel Conejo.

Moravčík, who provided two assists, had turned 25 the day before the game. A memorable celebration came afterwards. 'We had a big party in the hotel swimming pool with champagne everywhere. The owner of the hotel wore a Czechoslovakia shirt. He said, "You can drink what you want, I'm paying for everything."'

At the San Siro, in their quarter-final against West Germany, the fizz went flat. It was an afternoon that ended early for Moravčík with a red card in the 70th minute, following an accidental show of dissent with a flying boot.

'It wasn't deliberate,' he remembers of an incident that began with him jostling Pierre Littbarski for the ball deep in the German box. 'Littbarski came across me,' he continues. 'I wanted to go down the byline, and Littbarski took a step on my heel. My boot slipped off. He stepped on my heel, and I think it's a foul if someone steps on you, so in the penalty box it should be a penalty. The referee ... nothing.'

Frustrated by the referee's inaction, he lashed out with an angry air kick – and inadvertently sent flying the left boot that Littbarski had dislodged.

'I had no chance to put my shoe back on. I showed him "Look at that," and my shoe came off. It wasn't me who did that. The referee came to me and gave me a second yellow for ungentlemanly conduct. I said, "Look, my shoe is off." [The] Littbarski [foul] was unintentional but he still did it. But the referee was from Austria.'

His foot today is wrapped in an adidas basketball boot which, thankfully, does not fly off as he mimics his motion in Milan all those years ago.

It was not the Czechoslovakians' only grievance with match official Helmut Kohl (a name shared – unhelpfully in the circumstances – with Germany's reunification chancellor).

The penalty Kohl awarded West Germany for the only goal after 24 minutes followed a dramatic tumble in the box by Jürgen Klinsmann. The replays of the incident show him cutting a path between two defenders. There is some degree of contact with František Straka, who dangles out a leg, yet Klinsmann's exaggerated dive was – to British eyes back then – something out of the ordinary.

Indeed, in the BBC's review of the Italian World Cup, broadcast at Christmas 1990, a caption appeared at the top of the screen as that sequence of play unfolded, asking the question, 'When you hear the name "Klinsmann" what do you think?'

Klinsmann's own take on the incident is unequivocal. 'It was a one-thousand-per-cent penalty,' he insists. 'Otherwise, I'd have scored directly.'

Moravčík is more inclined to agree with Michal Bílek's observation that 'Klinsmann put the ball between the two players and just dived.' He adds, 'I remember Ivan Hašek twice headed the ball away on the line, and we were under pressure – but who knows, without that penalty it might have been zero-zero, and maybe on penalties, we'd have gone through.

'There was no chance to get [match] tickets, as the Germans bought everything. It was seventy-five thousand Germans against five thousand Czechs and Slovaks. With a referee from Austria. Everything was done before the game. No chance for us.' With that, the eighth and final World Cup campaign of Czechoslovakia was over.

ON 1 JANUARY 1993, THE 'VELVET DIVORCE' OCCURRED: THE FORMAL dissolution of a country that had been born at the end of the First World War. Some 2.5 million people had signed a petition demanding a referendum on the split. However, the will of the respective leaders – Czech prime minister Václav Klaus and his Slovakian counterpart Vladimír Mečiar – was to chart a different course.

Since the split, the Czech Republic have played at only one World Cup, in 2006, but have featured in six consecutive European Championships, reaching the final in 1996 and the semi-finals in 2004.

Slovakia have also reached the World Cup once – advancing to the last sixteen at South Africa in 2010 – and progressed to the same stage on their Euro finals debut in 2016.

'The Czechs are more pro-west,' says Moravčík, reflecting on the two countries today. 'Slovakians are more nostalgic. I consider Czech Republic as a western country like Germany or Austria. I feel we're more like an ex-communist country.

'Czech Republic have a better league with better organisation now, with clubs like Sparta and Slavia who are able to buy players for good money. We miss those confrontations. When Sparta and Slavia came here, it was a big occasion and the stadium was full. Bohemians Prague had a good team and Dukla Prague too, and when teams from the capital came, it was a good occasion for players to show what they could do against the best.

'We'd average seven or eight thousand, maybe ten thousand people. This season in the top division, they'll get one thousand at best. I played at a time when people didn't have a chance to watch European leagues. The only football they could watch at the weekend was their local team. Now with the internet and TV, it's difficult to get them to watch football at this level.'

As an example, the best-supported club in Slovakia in 2016/17, with an average attendance of 4,112, was Dunajská Streda, a club based in the south-west of the country where the majority ethnic-Hungarian population ensures a sense of local pride and committed fanbase.

Slovan Bratislava, the club with the most Slovak titles, have spent eight years playing at the home ground of Inter Bratislava, their local rivals, after delays in the redevelopment of their own stadium. 'How do you want to build up a club without a stadium?' asks Moravčík despairingly.

Over to the west, in the Czech Republic, there is at least some light, he argues. 'In twenty-five years since the separation, they've made more progress than Slovakia. Players are choosing Czech Republic before the Austrian league or Belgian league maybe. It's a big success. Slovakia is a level below. They built stadiums ten years ago. The licensing is stricter. Now, we've started that in Slovakia but ten years late. That's the difference.

'With Slavia and Sparta, it's like Rangers and Celtic, and they have Plzeň too who've built a good club. It's about sponsors and TV rights, no longer about support from [the] government.'

Moravčík is a cheerful soul, and before leaving, he returns one last time to that summer when freedom carried a box-fresh scent.

'We had liberty, and people could go and watch the World Cup – the timing was perfect,' Moravčík says, as he puts on his crash helmet and walks over to his moped. And even his sending-off on that final afternoon at the San Siro had a silver lining, it seems. He grins, 'My agent told me afterwards, "You did well. You didn't score a goal, but at least everybody will remember that moment." And it's true – nobody forgets your red card!'

The Brazilians of Europe

'WE LIKE BEAUTY ON THE PITCH. IF YOU SEE THE HISTORY OF OUR players, technically they were very strong. We never paid attention to physical power. Technique was the number one. Our nickname was "Brazil from the East".'

It is not a bad attempt to sum up the essence of the Balkan footballer, though Dragan Stojković might have been better off simply directing me to a YouTube clip of the 78th minute of Yugoslavia's second-round victory over Spain at Italia '90.

It was a special afternoon for Stojković. The then 25-year-old playmaker delivered both goals in his side's 2-1 victory in Verona, and the first of them was particularly wonderful. It was the act of a footballer operating in a seemingly different dimension, with a singular swiftness of mind and lightness of touch.

When a cross from Yugoslavia's captain, Zlatko Vujović, looped up off the head of Srečko Katanec and dropped beyond the far post, Stojković could easily have connected with the falling ball. Instead, he waited. He let the ball land at his right foot, saw Spain midfielder Rafa Martín Vázquez – blocking the volley that never came – fly past him, steadied himself with a second touch and then with his third, rolled the ball calmly past Andoni Zubizarreta. 'If someone who plays at the World Cup has a dream, this is what exactly happened to me,' he says from his home in Miami. 'This was a game I'll never forget. To score two goals against Spain and to send them home is a really big achievement – personally, and also as someone who fights for their country.

'Of course, the way I scored the first goal was absolutely fantastic, and this goal showed all of my capacity, all my technical skills, all my talent. I had two choices in that moment. One was to kick the ball direct, which ninety-nine per cent of players will do. The other was to stop the ball and do a really magic thing. I did the second. It was an absolutely fantastic feeling.'

His second goal – a thirty-yard free-kick to win the game three minutes into extra time – was a more straightforward kind of spectacular which, 27 years on, does not even get a mention from him.

These moments certainly embodied the beauty the Balkan footballer can conjure. They illustrated too why Stojković, now a coach in the Chinese Super League, became such an icon in his homeland. They have a greater significance, though, as the last goals scored by Yugoslavia at a major tournament before the country's fragmentation and the terrible conflict that accompanied it.

After the beauty, the truly beastly was just around the corner.

THE DATE OF YUGOSLAVIA'S MATCH AGAINST SPAIN IN VERONA was 26 June 1990. Almost a year to the day, on 25 June 1991, Croatia and Slovenia would declare their independence from Yugoslavia. The fighting that had begun to break out did not end until 1995. By the end of it, more than 100,000 people had lost their lives.

Already in 1990, tensions were simmering. A decade had passed since the death of Josip Broz Tito, chief of the war-time Partisans who became the principal architect and leader of the 'second' Yugoslavia, the socialist federation established in place of the Kingdom of Yugoslavia at the end of World War Two.

Prior to Yugoslavia's next game at Italia '90, the quarter-final against Argentina four days later, coach Ivica Osim suggested that a victory for his team could have broader repercussions for a country that comprised six socialist republics – Bosnia and Herzegovina, Croatia, Macedonia, Montenegro, Serbia, and Slovenia – together with the autonomous provinces of Kosovo and Vojvodina within Serbia.

'Yugoslavia is split with so many problems,' Osim said. 'If we could beat Argentina, football could help the country find a measure of national unity.'

With the game goalless after 120 minutes, Yugoslavia were a successful shootout away from the third World Cup semi-final in their history. They lost. Stojković, one of their three players who failed from the spot under a fierce Florentine sun, downplays Osim's declared wish that day.

'Personally, I don't believe that, because it was nothing about football; it was nothing about sport, it was politics,' he says. 'Maybe, emotionally, Osim [felt] it like that, but even if we'd been champions in Italy I think nobody could have stopped everything that had been prepared.'

While that is the opinion of Stojković, Faruk Hadžibegić, the man responsible for their fifth and final penalty, holds a different opinion. Ever since that July afternoon when he saw Argentina goalkeeper Sergio Goycochea stretch across his goal and snuff out a dream, he has had a question, tiny but tenacious, in his mind: could it have made a difference?

'Football supporters in Yugoslavia all loved the national team,' he reflects, 'and we can all imagine the scenario, whether it's true or not. If we'd got past Argentina, we'd have felt we were destined to win the World Cup. It was a very talented generation, a great generation. You can imagine the euphoria if we'd been world champions.'

As a son of Sarajevo, the Bosnian capital which was besieged for 1,425 days, Hadžibegić has insights worth hearing. His first sense of the dangerous fissures forming came in Yugoslavia's final warm-up match before departing for Italy.

The date was 3 June, and the opponents were the Netherlands at the Maksimir Stadium in Zagreb. The home crowd greeted the Yugoslavian anthem with a wall of whistles. Some turned their backs. Later, chants of 'Holland, Holland' filled the evening air. A TV microphone picked up Hadžibegić saying to his teammates, 'There are eleven of us, and 22,000 Croatians.'

'It was the hardest match and the hardest moment for all of us, because it was the first time the public weren't with their national team,' he says, looking back. 'We players, the players on the pitch, we never felt any tension within the group – whether it was sport or politics – it was a group who got on. We'd never spoken about Serbs, about Croats, about Bosnians, about Montenegrins or Slovenians or Macedonians. We spoke only about Yugoslavia. That match for us was a very, very bad surprise. It really unsettled us.' It was just the beginning.

Indeed, a startling detail from Hadžibegić's own experience of the conflict that followed is that the former psychiatrist at his first club, FK Sarajevo, would become one of its most notorious figures. Radovan Karadžić, the Bosnian Serb warlord found guilty of genocide for the massacre of eight thousand Muslim men and boys in Srebrenica in 1995, was actually a one-time source of pep talks to Hadžibegić and his teammates.

'In the period where he was involved in football, he never showed the thread of any aggressiveness,' Hadžibegić recalls. 'He was working in his role of psychologist, motivating us. I remember him showing all the great speeches of Tito. He was inspired by what Tito had done. He wasn't around all the time, but in different periods, if things weren't working, the club would bring him.'

When Karadžić, who had cultivated an image as poet-psychiatrist, was imprisoned for fraud, Hadžibegić was among the players who visited him in jail.

He laughs a bitter laugh. 'He was in prison for a time in that period, and we had to take cigarettes to him. Karadžić should feel shame, even if he wouldn't say it publicly. He lived a part of his life in Sarajevo; he benefitted from the way of life here. He committed unforgiveable atrocities. When I learned what he'd done, it was a terrible surprise. I don't think he deserves that we even talk about him.'

WHEN IT COMES TO YUGOSLAVIA'S 1990 WORLD CUP STORY, IT IS NOT easy to separate football and politics. The two become frequently tangled. Yugoslavia's qualifying campaign was the strongest of any European team. The first qualifiers from the UEFA section, they accumulated the most points too – and their most impressive result en route was a 3-2 victory over France in Belgrade in November 1988.

In the visitors' first match under new coach Michel Platini, they led twice. It was Yugoslavia who took the points, though, after Dragan Stojković converted a Dejan Savićević cross eight minutes from time.

'The tide of Yugoslavian attacking football was irresistible,' is how FIFA's match delegate described the on-field events. Yet his official report touched also on the small crowd, which was a consequence of happenings elsewhere in the capital: 'A series of mass political rallies had been enveloping the city . . .

People had stayed away from the ground, in the light of the aforementioned civil uncertainties.'

Tomislav Ivković, Yugoslavia's Croatian goalkeeper, adds some extra detail: 'There were only about six or seven thousand there. Everybody expected a full stadium, but in those days, there was a big meeting for Milošević in Belgrade, and here the problem began.'

Ivković is referring to Slobodan Milošević, a fomenter of Serbian nationalism and the soon-to-be-central figure in the mayhem of the Balkans conflict, who for a time became 'the most dangerous figure in post-cold war Europe' according to his obituary in the *Guardian* newspaper.

He had become president of Serbia in 1989. In June of that year, he addressed one million people at a rally to mark the 600th anniversary of Serbia's defeat by the Turks at the Kosovo Polje battlefield in 1389, and to tell them they were 'facing battles'.

At the same time, the Croatian nationalist movement was gaining strength. In April 1990, multi-party elections established the ardent nationalists of the Croatian Democratic Union (HDZ) as the largest party. At the end of May, their leader Franjo Tuđman – once a Communist general and, in the 1950s, president of Partizan Belgrade – became president of what was then still the constituent Socialist Republic of Croatia. (Among his many nationalist flourishes, he would remove the Cyrillic script that accompanied Latin script on street signs, and adopted the red-and-white chequerboard shield, the *šahovnica* – one of Croatia's oldest symbols but, in the eyes of many Serbs, associated with the fascist Croatian Ustaše regime of World War Two.)

Another significant date earlier in the month of Tuđman's election – May 1990 – was the 13th. It was the day when violence erupted before a league game between Dinamo Zagreb and Red Star Belgrade at the Maksimir Stadium. There were 132 arrests made after 79 police officers and 59 fans were injured in fighting between the Bad Blue Boys – Dinamo's ultras – and the Delje, their Red Star counterparts. In the midst of it, Zvonimir Boban, the nineteen-year-old home captain, aimed a flying kick at a policeman who had been striking a Dinamo supporter. It cost him a four-month ban from football, closing the door for him to Italia '90.

Boban is now FIFA deputy secretary-general. I meet him one spring morning during a visit to the underground archives at the world governing body's headquarters in Zurich. For the visitor to the Home of FIFA, there is a sense of entering a Bond villain's lair as the huge black entrance door slides open and beckons you into a vast, granite-floored foyer.

Behind the welcome desk is an ornamental pool (free of any Blofeld-style piranhas). On one wall a row of clocks offers the time in New York, Rio, Zurich, Johannesburg, Hong Kong, and Sydney. On another, a line of World Cup balls, starting with the 1970 Telstar and including the Italia '90 Etrusco, provide an instant nostalgia hit.

The good-looking, multi-lingual Boban would make a decent international man of mystery. The evidence of that kick which fractured a policeman's jaw is that he can look after himself. He can charm, too. Dressed in a checked suit, his professor's goatee enhancing a natural air of authority, he chats about BBC comedy series *Only Fools and Horses,* which was hugely popular in 1980s Yugoslavia – 'Del and Rodney,' he grins, remembering the two main characters – and about a trip he once made to Liverpool, incognito, to fulfil a dream of watching a match from the Anfield Kop.

Unfortunately, his position within FIFA means he is reluctant to discuss that day in May 1990. Yet, if today he would not wish to be considered a hero, as a younger man, Boban spoke freely about the afternoon he struck a Bosnian Muslim policeman called Refik Ahmetović, in an interview for a documentary film made in 2000, titled *The Last Yugoslavia Team.*

He said then, 'That was an important date in my life, because I didn't only get involved in the sporting life but also the political life of my country. It happened that hooligans that came from Serbia were smashing up our stadium and the police got involved.'

In the film, the camera pauses on a statue of a band of soldiers outside the Maksimir Stadium. Its plinth carries the inscription, 'To the fans of this club, who started the war with Serbia at this ground on 13 May 1990'.

Boban is quoted later in the film as saying, 'I always gave everything when I played for Yugoslavia, but then when you play in the Croatia shirt, it's a different thing ... I would die for Croatia.'

The opposing captain that day was Dragan Stojković. 'I remember we started to warm up for the game,' he recalls. 'We got in a circle and started stretching, and at that moment, I saw the bar collapse behind the goal, and people started running to the pitch. I told my teammates to get back to the dressing room, and we started to run. The game was in the afternoon, and we stayed until maybe midnight. We stayed in the dressing room, and through the small windows, we saw huge numbers of people outside waiting for something – I don't know what.'

In the streets outside, seven trams and hundreds of cars were damaged. A central figure in the violence was Željko Ražnatović, the notorious Serbian gangster better known as Arkan. A former bank robber and alleged hitman for the Yugoslav State Security Service (UDBA), he would spend the bloody years that followed as leader of a paramilitary group, the Tigers, who formed part of the Serb Volunteer Force and carried out some of the most brutal ethnic cleansing in Bosnia.

Prior to his assassination in Belgrade's Intercontinental Hotel in January 2000, Arkan had been indicted by the international war crimes tribunal in The Hague. His alleged atrocities included the massacre of approximately 260 men in the Croatian town of Vukovar in 1991. The victims – including hospital workers, patients, and civilians – were taken from a hospital and executed on farmland a few kilometres away.

In May 1990, Arkan was leader of the Delje. The night before the explosive Dinamo-Red Star encounter, he sent his thugs out to stick false Belgrade number plates on cars around the Maksimir Stadium, prompting Dinamo fans to smash up some of their own compatriots' vehicles.

Arkan – who later took over a smaller Belgrade club, Obilić, and oversaw an unprecedented Serbian title triumph in 1998 – was well known to the Red Star players. 'His house was just twenty metres from the stadium,' says Stojković. This was a time, according to Miodrag Belodedici, Red Star's Romanian international defender of the time, when many of his teammates would carry a pistol. ('After big victories, someone would pull out a gun and bang, bang, bang, shooting in the air,' he says.) Stojković plays down the connection, though. 'When somebody comes to you and says, "Hello, how are you?" you're polite to them, but we never had a dinner together, or coffee or lunch. The players didn't get involved too much with him.'

*

IT WAS IN THE WAKE OF THE MAKSIMIR STADIUM RIOT THAT THE Yugoslavia team met the hostile reaction that so shocked Faruk Hadžibegić when facing the Netherlands at the same stadium before travelling to Italy.

The crowd's chant of 'Boban, Boban' underlined their objection to the ban imposed on their club captain. Yet, according to Branislav Ivković, the squad remained calm and united at their base in the northern town of Sassuolo, close to Modena. 'Nobody talked about the political situation,' says the team's goalkeeper. 'In that moment, it wasn't as bad as one year later. We'd been together many years as players in the national team – with the under-age teams, the Under-21s – and had a very good atmosphere in the team. Osim was a very good coach, and we were like a family. In the squad, we had many nationalities, but we were big friends.'

Ivković describes how, after a 4-1 opening defeat by West Germany in Milan, players of different nationalities visited a Roman Catholic church to pray together ahead of their second match of the group stage against Colombia. 'We had Muslims, we had Serbs, I was Catholic,' he says. This group included the captain, Zlatko Vujović – who was born in the Bosnian capital, Sarajevo, to a Montenegrin father and Croatian mother and grew up in Split – and his Paris Saint-Germain teammate Safet Sušić, a Bosnian Muslim.

Mirsad Baljić, another of the Bosnian contingent, was not among them. He has less positive memories. 'I grew up with communism, and so we didn't have too much religion,' he says, offering a cynical take on 'certain players who suddenly believed in religion'.

After Baljić was dropped from the team following the West Germany match, the full-back complained to a FIFA media officer that his exclusion was politically motivated. His view remains the same today. 'The coach was under pressure. There were Serbian journalists who exerted enormous pressure on him. He had to react and so put in different players. We were closer to the Croats, and often, the Serbs would stay apart.' Dragan Stojković is dismissive of this – 'We were never involved in the politics,' he insists – and so too Hadžibegić, Baljić's fellow

Bosnian: 'If he told you there was a political problem or pressure that he shouldn't play for political reasons, it's because he hasn't got the courage to accept he wasn't at the level of colleagues who were starters. I can say that to you and to him too. That's the truth.'

According to Vladimir Stanković, the press officer for the Yugoslavia team, the discord lay outside the camp, not inside. 'Political tension existed, and journalists from different parts of Yugoslavia were looking just for their players from their republic,' he notes.

Osim had included in his squad three members of the Yugoslavia side that won the 1987 World Youth Championship in Chile: that tournament's Golden Ball winner Robert Prosinečki, along with Robert Jarni and Davor Šuker. (Boban, a scorer in the final in Chile, might have featured too but for his ban.) All three would help Croatia reach the semi-finals of the World Cup eight years later, with Šuker earning the Golden Boot. However, Osim was cautious about using them and kept faith in thirtysomethings Vujović and Sušić.

Stanković adds, 'Probably Osim preferred the experienced players because Prosinečki was twenty-one, Šuker twenty-two, Jarni twenty-two. They were very young players. He tried to make some combination between experience and young talent. Sušić was a surprise for many people because he was thirty-five at the time, but he'd had a great season in France [with Paris Saint-Germain]. Osim believed he could help and he was right because Sušić played very well.'

As a deft, drifting ball player, Osim had appeared in the Yugoslavia team which lost the 1968 European Championship final. He had a life outside of football and taught mathematics at the University of Sarajevo. In 1990, he was 49 years old, and the cultured, creative footballer had morphed into a highly-pragmatic coach. He had to be.

Speaking to Jonathan Wilson in the *Blizzard* magazine in 2013, he said, 'You had to be careful about the name, about religion, about the club, about the region of the country a player's from. You had to calculate everything. Everything is politics. Every club was politics, and especially the national team was politics. Let an Englishman try to pick the national team of Britain and Ireland. So you choose two from Scotland, three from England but nobody from Ireland, it would be a riot...'

Osim went on to claim that Srečko Katanec, his Slovenian midfielder, actually asked to be excluded from the quarter-final against Argentina because of threats to his family back at home. 'I had a case with one player who said a few hours before the game, "Please, don't pick me, because I received a threat in my city, so I am afraid to play for the national team." That was Srečko Katanec, who was a really, really important player for us. He was afraid to walk around in Ljubljana because of threats. I can understand that's not a nice position. How can he play? If he goes to play in Italy and his family stays in Ljubljana, then they are under threat.' For his part, Katanec declined an interview request for this book but let it be known that he denies Osim's version of events, insisting he had an injury.

TO REACH THE LAST EIGHT, YUGOSLAVIA HAD FIRST SHAKEN OFF their heavy loss to West Germany by beating Colombia and then the United Arab Emirates. Osim had accused his players of lacking courage and aggression against the Germans, but it would be their only defeat in five matches. Lift-off came against Colombia. After Sušić had struck a post, Davor Jozić, a central defender playing in an advanced midfield position, volleyed the only goal – his first in sixteen years.

Sušić, Darko Pančev twice, and substitute Prosinečki then secured a 4-1 success against the UAE, and the last sixteen beckoned.

As the media criticism continued, Osim was by now refusing to conduct his press briefings in Serbo-Croatian, speaking instead in the French he had acquired during eight years as a player in France. His view was that his critics 'have motives that have nothing to do with sport'. He added, 'I admit that we've not been perfect, but I can see other teams like Holland and Argentina, to give you two examples, who've not been better than us.'

Fortunately, against the Spain of Míchel and Emilio Butragueño, Osim had a man inspired in Dragan Stojković. Nicknamed Piksi after one of the twin mice in the Hanna-Barbera cartoon *Pixie and Dixie and Mr Jinks*, he had arrived in Italy with a billing to match the £5.5m transfer fee Marseille, then one of the continent's wealthiest clubs under owner Bernard Tapie, had just paid for him.

Thwarted in his attempts to sign Diego Maradona the previous season, Tapie had turned to Stojković, taking his private jet to Belgrade one day the previous November. Stojković remembers receiving a call at home from the technical director of Red Star, Dragan Džajić. 'He called me around five in the afternoon and said, "Come to the office immediately." I was surprised. I said, "What's happened?" He said, "I don't know, but somebody told me Bernard Tapie's in the office waiting for us."

'I took my jacket and went there, and it was true – Bernard Tapie was there. He said simply, "To be champion of Europe, I need him. He's my favourite number ten, and he's the last piece of my puzzle." We signed some kind of pre-contract. It was not an official contract, but a promise. I agreed to go, as I knew the team and the power of the team, and my dream was to be the best player in Europe officially – and to do that, you must play the final and be champion of Europe.

'After I got back home, later that evening, I received a call from Milan and they simply asked me, "Did you sign with Marseille?" I said, "No, I didn't sign." They kept asking me, and I didn't know what to say. They then told me Tapie had already announced he was bringing the "Maradona of the East" to Marseille next year. AC Milan pushed very hard to pay Marseille the compensation to let me free. But Tapie absolutely rejected this possibility.'

With his two fabulous goals against Spain, Stojković showed precisely why Tapie had made that journey to Belgrade, and why he had been the highest-ranked player from eastern Europe in 1989's Ballon D'Or poll (sixth).

'I'd been the best player in Yugoslavia,' he adds, 'the real number ten. What I needed in my career in that moment was the big event, the big competition. It means the World Cup. For my career, it was very important to show the worldwide audience who I was and which kind of player I was.'

He did that with his two goals. The celebration after his slice-of-wonder opening strike at the Stadio Marc'Antonio Bentegodi in Verona is worth recalling too. When he ran back down the pitch in the direction of the Yugoslavia bench, his target was his coach, Ivica Osim. Pushing aside a couple of teammates, he landed in the arms of this big bear of a man in a public gesture of solidarity.

'Osim was criticised very unfairly,' Stojković stresses. Prior to the Spain game, photographs had appeared in newspapers back in Yugoslavia of a bunch of empty bottles left in the restaurant of the team hotel – with the attendant accusation that

Osim was a drunk. 'What made me very angry was when they said that one night he drank eleven bottles or something like that,' Stojković continues. 'It was very bad. Someone who drinks eleven bottles of whisky, normally he dies, you know. It was not true, and I was very angry about this. That's why when I scored against Spain, I ran to him and showed this support.'

FOR STOJKOVIĆ, THE HERO AGAINST SPAIN, THE ULTIMATE TEST awaited in the quarter-finals: Diego Maradona and Argentina. 'This really is a battle of the 10s' is how the *Gazzetta dello Sport* billed the game, and the paper quoted Carlos Bilardo, the Argentina coach, praising the Yugoslavia playmaker: 'He's got everything – acceleration, dribbling, fantasy, personality. And two feet like few players in the world.'

Argentina's journey to Florence from their base at Trigoria, outside Rome, was not straightforward: the air-conditioning on their coach broke, meaning an uncomfortably hot drive of 200km and an arrival 45 minutes behind schedule. Moreover, they arrived with Jorge Burruchaga, Ricardo Giusti, and Oscar Ruggeri all still struggling with injuries. As for Maradona, he would play with the help of another painkilling injection in his ankle.

'It was really, really hot, almost thirty-nine degrees or something like that,' remembers Stojković. 'During the warm-up, I watched him and what he was doing. He was just stretching. He didn't run. Then I said to myself, "Okay, now it's time to show who's better. It is time for me to show my capacity and my talent." That was a really good motivation for me. I played better that game.'

The line-up for that final Yugoslavia World Cup game was as follows: Ivković (Croatian), Spasić (Serbian), Vulić (Croatian), Hadžibegić (Bosnian), Jozić (Bosnian), Brnović (Montenegrin), Sušić (Bosnian), Prosinečki (Croatian), Šabanadžović (Bosnian), Stojković (Serbian), Vujović (Bosnian Croat).

What ensued for this group of players was one last near-miss on Yugoslavia's noteworthy list. They had been World Cup semi-finalists in 1930, twelve years after the founding of the Kingdom of Yugoslavia (with a team shorn of its Croatians, as Zagreb responded angrily to the federation moving its headquarters to Belgrade), and reached the last four again in 1962. They went to Italy with an identical win-loss record in World Cups as Spain. In the European Championship, they were runners-up in 1960 and 1968. They had also lost three Olympic football finals.

A pivotal moment of this latest tale of what-might-have-been came in the 31st minute. It was the moment that Kurt Röthlisberger, the Swiss referee, waved a red card at Refik Šabanadžović, the Yugoslavian given the task of shadowing Maradona. In previous matches, the Red Star Belgrade player had helped stifle Carlos Valderrama and Butragueño. He had already received one yellow card for encroaching at a free-kick, however, when Röthlisberger – who would later receive a lifetime refereeing ban from UEFA for attempted bribery – showed a second for a foul on Argentina's captain.

'Incredible . . . incredible,' says Branislav Ivković. 'I'll never forget this referee from Switzerland. I don't know the name, but I remember the face. It was very difficult as we played for ninety minutes with ten players, but it was one of our best games – dedication, fight, running, jumping, everything. We put everything into the game.'

Yugoslavia had played 120 minutes against Spain four days earlier. Argentina had had two extra days' rest. Yet, Osim's men shrugged off the setback of Šabanadžović's loss. 'He gave us balance in the middle,' Stojković explains. 'We were very surprised to see him sent off so, so easily. It was a really big disadvantage for us, but we played better than Argentina and missed some great chances.'

It was an afternoon when Prosinečki, making his first start of the finals, shone in midfield. Indeed, it seems fitting that Yugoslavia, the Brazilians of Europe, ended that last match with the creative trio of Prosinečki, Stojković, and substitute Dejan Savićević on the field. Savićević might even have won the match in extra time with a stooping header from a Stojković cross, his side's best opening since the unmarked Davor Jozić's early volley had cleared the crossbar.

Argentina had their own moments of danger, with Oscar Ruggeri clipping the goalframe in the second half and Pedro Troglio failing to beat Ivković with a free header in extra time. Right at the death, Jorge Burruchaga did bundle the ball into the net but was ruled to have used his arm.

With the final whistle, Ivica Osim disappeared down the tunnel. He would not follow the shootout from pitchside. 'It was a very stressful time for him,' says Stojković, who would step forward as his country's first taker following José Serrizuela's successful opening kick.

What followed was only the second penalty miss of his career. 'I made a feint, and at the last moment, I saw that [Sergio] Goycochea would go to the left side, and I turned my foot and put the ball at a different angle. I couldn't believe the ball hit the bar. I was a hundred per cent sure I'd score because I saw him dive to the left. Even today, I don't know how it's possible the ball goes too high.'

After Burruchaga and Prosinečki had each converted, Maradona stepped up to take the third Argentina penalty. 'As he came to take his penalty, I shouted, "Diego, I know the side for your penalty",' remembers Branislav Ivković. 'He didn't want to look at me. He kept his head down, only looking down at the ball.'

The pair had history. The previous November, Ivković had foiled the Argentinian in a penalty shootout with his club side, Sporting Lisbon. 'I told him, "I bet you one hundred dollars you don't score the penalty," and he said, "Okay." This was their fifth and last penalty, so if he scored, Napoli would win – but I saved it.'

In an unhappy augury of events in Florence, Maradona's Napoli side still prevailed in the end, though it did not stop the Argentinian entering the away dressing room and giving Ivković his money. Ivković continues, 'I made the same movement as in the Napoli match. I went first to my left side, as he had shot to the left that night in Naples. But I feigned to go left and then went right, and he shot at me.'

Savićević duly made it 2-2 and when Argentina's fourth taker Troglio missed, Yugoslavia held a semi-final ticket in their hands. It soon disappeared. Faruk Hadžibegić stepped forward only for referee Röthlisberger to send him back: Dragoljub Brnović was the fourth man on the official's list, and his weak kick was saved easily by Goycochea. With Gustavo Dezotti then slipping the ball past Ivković, Argentina led 3-2. It fell to Hadžibegić to take the fifth Yugoslavia kick.

'I think it was a mistake by the referee who wrote the numbers down wrong,' he recalls. 'That was my conclusion, but who knows? Perhaps it was destiny that it finished that way. It was someone who made a mistake – either the referee or our staff.'

Hadžibegić had already missed a penalty against Colombia in the group stage but had been persuaded to take one by the squad's elder statesman, Sušić.

Now, Goycochea flew to his left, and he failed again. 'At that time I was with [Gabriel] Calderón who played with me at Betis. He told Goycochea where I'd hit the penalty. I don't think it was so badly taken, but it was an advantage for him as he moved a second earlier.'

It was the end of the road. 'We were all crying,' Ivković remembers. 'I saved two penalties [against Maradona] and lost both games.'

THERE IS A SECOND ENDURING QUESTION WHEN IT COMES TO Yugoslavia's national team in the aftermath of Italia '90. Another big 'what if?' And Darko Pančev is sure of the answer. 'If our generation had had the chance to play in a European Championship or World Cup, we'd have had a big chance,' he tells me.

'We'd have won a trophy. Maybe not in '92, but '94 or '96. One hundred per cent. We had a very strong team. Stojković was a great *fantasista*. He and Prosinečki were so strong in the middle of the pitch. Savićević was the best attacking midfielder. Great passes. When I was twenty-five and played in the finals in Italy, we had [Alen] Bokšić, Šuker, [Predrag] Mijatović on the bench.'

Pančev is speaking to me at his bar in a modest shopping mall in Skopje, the capital of Macedonia. Its name is Café 9, a nod to his old shirt number. Outside, in the burning midday sun, the thermometer nudges forty degrees – the product of a heat wave called Lucifer. Pančev, sipping Turkish coffee, is dressed for the weather in an orange T-shirt and khaki shorts. He is a big man, with big, friendly features.

During Italia '90, the *Gazzetta dello Sport* described him as 'the most cheerful, kind and extrovert player of the conflicted Yugoslavian committee'. Pančev was one of the bright young talents waiting keenly for an opportunity. The Red Star Belgrade forward had been the Yugoslav First League's top scorer with 25 goals – none of them penalties – in the season leading up to the World Cup, but began only two games in Italy, against Spain and the UAE, scoring twice against the latter.

'I wanted to play more; this is normal,' he says. 'In the end, it was okay as I knew our moment would come.' Instead, that moment arrived with Red Star, back on Italian soil, in Bari, on 29 May 1991. It was another penalty shootout involving a Yugoslavian team, this time in the final of the European Cup, and this time with a happy ending.

Pančev had scored a Golden Ball-winning 34 goals that season. All he had to do now was knock a penalty past Marseille goalkeeper Pascal Olmeta, and Yugoslavia would have its first European Cup winners.

'I was very nervous before the penalty,' he reflects. 'Red Star are a big institution. They have five million fans around the world. There were twenty-five thousand supporters in Munich for the semi-final.' That semi-final, in front of 70,000 spectators overall, ended with Red Star inflicting the first defeat by a visiting continental side on Bayern Munich. It featured an outstanding breakaway goal, a six-man move which swept the ball from the Red Star penalty area and into the Bayern six-yard box, where Pančev applied the killer touch.

Back in Bari, he did just that once more, his successful kick completing Red Star's 5-3 shootout success. In the beaten Marseille team was Dragan Stojković, the former Red Star captain. At his leaving party the previous year in Belgrade, he had taken the microphone and said, 'My wish is to see you next season in the European Cup final.' That wish had come true, except Raymond Goethals, the Marseille coach, gave him only eight minutes on the pitch in the final. Stojković then declined the Belgian's request that he take a penalty. After a desperately dull, goalless final, his old club now prevailed.

'It was a change of mentality specifically for that final,' Pančev explains. 'We always played offensively. Yugoslavia never won a medal because of that mentality, as they always wanted to score goals. Italians always played defensively and always won things. Yugoslavia in the European Championship in Belgrade in 1976 were leading two-nil in the semi-finals against the West Germany of [Franz] Beckenbauer and [Gerd] Müller. If that'd been Italy, it would've finished two-nil. But we wanted to score more goals. It was the wrong mentality, and we lost four-two. It was the Brazilian mentality.'

Yugoslavia had their history of near misses, while Partizan and Red Star had each lost a European final before. Bari was different. It had to be. 'This was our moment to win a trophy,' says Pančev. 'We had to be cautious. It wasn't a normal thing for Red Star and it was a very bad game for the spectators. But we'd played Bayern in Munich – they had [Stefan] Effeberg, [Brian] Laudrup, [Olaf] Thon, [Jürgen] Kohler – and beaten them without any problems.'

Federal Yugoslavia was on the brink of collapse, but its footballers – and Red Star's starting XI included three Montenegrins, two Macedonians, and a Croatian – had won the biggest prize in the club game.

In an earlier era, Red Star might have been able to keep that triumphant team together – the regulations did not permit players to depart abroad until the age of 28 – but within twelve months, key players like Prosinečki, Dejan Savičević, Vladimir Jugović, and Sinisa Mihailović had all left for Spain or Italy.

Pančev made his own, ill-fated, move to Internazionale. In Milan, the erstwhile 'Cobra' of the Balkans, the second highest scorer in Yugoslavian top-flight history, scored only three goals and became *il Bidone* – the dustbin.

'I made two big mistakes in my career,' he admits. 'I went to a club that played very defensive and very bad football. It's very important for an attacking player to play in a team that creates chances and plays attacking football. I was a player with a nose for goal. It's normal for that kind of player to depend on the rest of the team to create chances for him.

'My second big mistake – maybe bigger than Inter – was in 1992. [Alex] Ferguson sent [me] a fax to go to Manchester United. I was at Inter. I had a row with the coach [Osvaldo Bagnoli] and didn't play for six months. Ferguson saw I wasn't playing. This was before he signed [Eric] Cantona, and he approached me. I was angry with the coach at Inter, but I decided to stay at Inter to show him I was a good player.'

The laugh he delivers is an acknowledgement of his error. 'I didn't want to go to United. I wanted to prove to Inter I was a good player. United played attacking football and I would've scored a lot of goals there, but when you're young, you make mistakes. When you're young, you have three or four girls you can choose from, and you'll choose the worst one.'

By then, his international aspirations had withered too. In the qualifying competition for Euro '92 in Sweden, Pančev had finished as the ten-goal top scorer, ahead of France's Jean-Pierre Papin and the Netherlands' Marco van

Basten. Yet, there would be no European Championship for him or Yugoslavia.

FOUR DAYS AFTER YUGOSLAVIA'S LAST EUROPEAN CHAMPIONSHIP qualifying fixture in November 1991, the Croatian town of Vukovar fell into Serbian hands after a three-month siege. A massacre of innocent citizens followed. By this point, federal Yugoslavia was already dead, Croatia and Slovenia having declared independence the previous summer. The players from those countries were no longer part of the Yugoslavia team.

When the independence referendum in Bosnia on 29 February and 1 March 1992 brought a wave of shootings and bombings, another player decided to quit: Faruk Hadžibegić, by now national-team captain. He announced his decision after the first Euro '92 warm-up game against the Netherlands later that month.

'Because I'm not someone who's involved in politics, I looked around and consulted everyone I thought I should consult,' he remembers. 'I saw that the war would happen, and I didn't want to accept that. I said, "I can't stand up for a country which makes war on itself." I was captain and I wouldn't take part.'

The siege of Sarajevo began on 5 April, as EC foreign ministers were preparing to announce their recognition of Bosnia and Herzegovina. Croats and Muslims who made up just over 60 per cent of Bosnia's 4.3m population had voted for independence in a poll boycotted by Serbs, who made up 31 per cent and had already voted in their own referendum to stay in Yugoslavia.

Yugoslav air force jets flew low over the capital prompting *The Times'* headline 'Bombers greet Bosnian statehood'. That was on 8 April. The next day, with roadblocks already put in place by hostile militias, petrol supplies ran out.

Hadžibegić, then playing for Sochaux in France, switched his attentions to helping his loved ones back in his stricken home city. 'We started to communicate with people to arrange for everyone in Sarajevo to come over to France,' he recounts. 'I was helped by Serbian and Croatian friends with the transport.'

After finding two private planes to fly to Vienna, he arranged for minibuses to take the party across land to the French border. 'We had twenty-two people living in my house for the duration of the war, so a bit longer than two years.

Five wives, eleven children, parents, grandparents.'

Hadžibegić had carried the Olympic flame when Sarajevo hosted the Winter Games in 1984. He still lives in France and is speaking to me from his home in Paris.

'If you're looking to compare Sarajevo with somewhere, as a cosmopolitan city, you can place it on a level with London, with Paris, with Brussels. Sarajevo is a city which was a model for Europe, in terms of all the cultures living together.'

Even today, the visitor will find in close proximity an Ottoman-era mosque and Serbian Orthodox church both dating from the 16th century, and a synagogue which, at the start of the 20th century, was the third biggest in Europe.

'Religion is different from nationality,' he says. 'To justify the war in the ex-Yugoslavia and these problems between Croatians, Serbs and Bosnians, everyone had the label of Catholic, Orthodox, Muslim, but in each country, there were different religions. In Sarajevo, there were all religions, it was a model for the future – of living together, of tolerance.

'When we speak of nationalism, I think it exists but it exists because today, nationalism is a very good business. It's for economic reasons, for a small number of people. There was a fault in communication and an enormous fault on the part of the international community, because to justify the war, we communicated this idea there was nationalism based on religion – but they're two things that are entirely different.'

Ivica Osim, another resident of Sarajevo, followed his captain's lead when he called a press conference on 23 May 1992 to announce he was standing down as national coach. 'My country doesn't deserve to be at the Euro,' he declared.

Eyes heavy with tears, he added, 'I was born in Sarajevo, and it's the only thing I can do for that town, because you all know what's happening there.' On 31 May, three days after the Yugoslavia squad's arrival in Sweden for Euro '92, they found themselves excluded by UEFA following the United Nations' decision to place the country under sanctions. Denmark, the team who replaced them, ended up holding the trophy.

'I remember in the airport, I was vomiting in the toilet,' Dragan Stojković remembers. 'There was too much stress.'

Stojković is hesitant when asked what Yugoslavia's footballers might have achieved together. 'Nobody knows. This is just opinions. In football, you can't be sure one hundred per cent.'

He played at one more World Cup tournament, alongside Dejan Savićević in a Yugoslavia team made up of Serbia and Montenegro, which reached the last sixteen at France '98.

An even more forthright refusal to speculate comes from Robert Jarni. He played just once for Yugoslavia at Italia '90 but filled a key role as wing-back in the Croatia team which, with the fuel of nationalistic sentiment, reached the quarter-finals of Euro '96 and semi-finals of France '98.

'Honestly, I don't like talking about what might have been if this or that had happened,' says Jarni, who scored his first international goal in Denmark on the evening Yugoslavia beat the eventual European champions 2-0 in a qualifying tie for Euro '92.

'In 1987, there were five or six Croatians in the national team that won the Under-17 World Cup – [Igor] Štimac, Boban, Prosinečki, Šuker, [Dubravko] Pavličić and me,' Jarni says. 'We had six players in the starting line-up. This was a good base after we separated to build a national team.

'During the war, each of us was outside our country, but we were helping people, each doing what we could. Then, we started with the Euro in England, and then the World Cup in France, and all of this pride, all of these emotions came out there. The national team was a huge source of pride. We had this within ourselves, and for me, it was the most important thing – together with our preparations.

'We were together for fifty-five days, and no one argued with anyone in those fifty-five days. Whenever you're working in a team for a week or longer, there's one or two little rows because of the nervous tension, but in 1998, in fifty-five days there was not one argument. There was harmony. We were all fine with one another – a lot of laughs, but on the field, we fought for each other. In '90, there were strong conversations but in '98, nothing at all.'

When Croatia and Yugoslavia met in a decisive Euro 2000 qualifier in October 1999 in Zagreb, where the Maksimir Stadium crowd displayed a giant flag bearing the words 'Vukovar 91' – as a reminder of an appalling atrocity from the Croatian-Serb conflict – Jarni was involved in an ugly incident that brought the sending-off of Serbia's Zoran Mirković.

As Jarni spat some words into the Serbian's ear after he had fallen to ground feigning injury, Mirković grabbed the Croatian's testicles before giving the home crowd the three-fingered Serbian salute on his way off the pitch.

Today coach of Croatia's Under-19s, Jarni may be a patriot, but there is an acknowledgement from him that Europe lost one of its top five leagues with the splintering of Yugoslavia. 'There were four teams who stood out – Dinamo Zagreb, Hajduk Split, Red Star and Partizan,' he explains. 'These were four teams above the rest, but you had other teams you went to play and you could never say, "We're going to win this" – in Sarajevo, for example, against Sarajevo or against Željezničar, or against Velež in Mostar. You had to really sweat to win those games, and where these four teams went, the stadiums were full. But also when other teams played each other, the stadiums were more or less full.

'It's better as it is today, but on the sporting side, we've lost the competitiveness. We train much harder than in other countries, but the problem is the rhythm of the matches. When we go abroad to play European games, after sixty or seventy minutes, we have problems.'

In another sport – basketball – a solution was found in the creation of an Adriatic league. An official from the Football Association of Slovenia told me there had been discussions about a trial league at a junior level, though Dragan Stojković, who was president of the Football Association of Serbia from 2001-05, discounts this idea.

'In the future, I think it's very difficult, almost impossible, because the FAs from each country of the ex-Yugoslavia want to keep their own domestic league, their own football,' he argues. 'It's very difficult from an economical point of view. The first question is who'll guide this competition, who'll be the president, who'll be the general manager, who'll control the financial aspect. It's very, very complicated.'

The current situation is arguably no less complicated. Back in Skopje, Darko Pančev is telling me about his troubles as sports director of Vardar, the Macedonian champions for five of the last six seasons.

'Look, in all parts of the ex-Yugoslavia, football is very weak,' he begins. 'It's really gone downhill. If you've not got a strong championship, it's hard to create good teams. Yugoslavia was the complete opposite. There were lots of great players, lots of great teams, and it was more difficult to play there. Everything has changed now. Here at Vardar, we have a budget of four million euros per year, and it's very difficult to expect Vardar to get into the group stage of the Champions League or Europa League.'

The previous week, Pančev's Vardar side had lost to FC Copenhagen in a Champions League qualifying tie. He adds, 'Copenhagen's budget is thirty or forty million. José Mourinho can say, "Hey, I want this player, here's a hundred million euros." As sporting director, I have to buy players who are worth one hundred or two hundred thousand per year. That's without a transfer fee. I have to pick up players on free transfers.'

The day after our meeting, Skopje will host the UEFA Super Cup between Real Madrid and Manchester United. It has the feel of a Harlem Globetrotters event, the stars on parade. In Macedonia Square in the centre of the city, people queue to have their photo taken with the European Cup trophy in the fan zone. Up on his dais, Alexander the Great – his statue a recent addition to the cityscape along with several gaudy, wedding-cake public buildings – gazes down on the advertising logos of Nissan, Playstation, Heineken, and Pepsi. A slogan on the side of the Pepsi van shouts, 'Football isn't a game, it's a passion'.

WHEN RED STAR, AS THE LAST CONTINENTAL CHAMPIONS FROM eastern Europe, contested the Super Cup against United in 1991, the match was a one-off event at Old Trafford rather than the then customary two-legged contest.

'Red Star were penalised by UEFA,' Pančev argues. 'At that time, for perhaps the first time in football, football was influenced by politics. All the conditions were fine to play in Belgrade; we were penalised for nothing. The year after we won the European Cup, we had to play our home games in Sofia and Budapest.' And they still managed to finish runners-up behind Sampdoria in a group whose winner advanced directly to the European Cup final.

Since then, the farthest any Balkan team has travelled in the continent's premier club competition is the quarter-final stage, as Hajduk Split did in 1995.

Since the turn of the century, three ex-Yugoslavian clubs – Dinamo Zagreb, Maribor and Partizan Belgrade – have participated in the Champions League group stage and between them won just one of 48 matches.

Pančev laments, 'Now everything is centred around this circle [of clubs]. There is Borussia Dortmund, Bayern Munich, Real Madrid, Barcelona, [Manchester] City, United, and perhaps PSG. And that's about it. No other teams exist.

'In my era, Yugoslavia was strong. Russia had strong sides like Spartak Moscow and CSKA. In 1991, when Red Star won the European Cup, Spartak Moscow played the semi-finals too. Since 1991, this hasn't happened – no team from eastern Europe has got close to the semi-finals. Why is this? There's no money, the young players go to the west. This is a big problem. There's no longer a balance between this Europe and that Europe in terms of quality.'

The erstwhile spread of talent was, he adds, 'more interesting for football. Thirty years ago, Real Madrid came to Belgrade to play Red Star, and they lost four-two. This no longer happens. It's more interesting for football, for the public, for journalists, for everybody. Now, perhaps, in all of eastern Europe, you might see one good team. We had Shakhtar [Donetsk] six or seven years ago but not anymore. Then, you might get Dynamo Kyiv or Zenit [St. Petersburg] having a good season. But there's no consistency.'

He is not the only person interviewed for this book to evoke a sense of something lost in the face of football's boom. In this case, though, there is 'Yugo-nostalgia' at force too. 'Older people, over forty, if you did a survey of the population from Macedonia to Slovenia, I would guarantee they'd say they want to live in Yugoslavia,' Pančev insists. 'Not the youngsters, but the older ones.'

Faruk Hadžibegić, whose foiled penalty marked the light going out on Yugoslavia as a World Cup force, as the Brazilians of Europe, is even more forthright about the cost of the conflict that began the next year.

'It was the result of politics and the international community. It's still sad, because what was the result of the war in Yugoslavia?' The question is left hanging.

For the group of men who travelled down with him to Italia '90, the result is easier to define. 'After the war, some declared themselves Croatian, Serb,

Slovenian. I accept that, because Yugoslavia didn't exist any more. Each of us became something else because our country was now Croatia, Serbia, Slovenia, or Bosnia. But it was not a problem between us. War decided the fate of a lot of us. We didn't choose the war. It was international politics that chose it.'

FINALE

Agony and ecstasy

'YOU KNOW, WE DECIDED FROM THE BEGINNING THE FINAL IS IN Rome, the opening in Milan. Semi-final one was Naples, and the other, Turin. The third and fourth play-off in Bari. We tried to cover the entire territory of Italy. Naples was the town of Maradona. We didn't know at the beginning that Argentina would end up in the final. The choice of Naples was very good, the problem was the Italian goalkeeper made a mistake and Caniggia scored.'

Luca Cordero di Montezemolo, general manager of Italia '90

It is football's loneliest walk. And for Aldo Serena, the heavy steps taken from the centre circle of the Stadio San Paolo to the penalty spot felt like its longest walk too.

It is what happens when you have the weight of a nation on your shoulders – and that is precisely what happened to Serena late on the night of 3 July 1990.

He recalls the freeze of fear which swept through him, numbing body and mind after Italy coach Azeglio Vicini asked him to take a penalty kick. The World Cup semi-final between Italy and Argentina had ended with a 1-1 draw, and Vicini needed five takers for the shootout. Serena was number five.

As a centre-forward, the top scorer in Serie A in 1989, he had felt unable to say no. His limbs were now telling him something else, though.

'I remember I was sitting down, and when I stood up, I realised nothing was working as normal – my legs had gone. I tried to do some breathing exercises to control the sense of panic, but nothing. I was struggling to actually feel the ground. The longer it went on, the harder it became. When [Roberto]

Donadoni missed, I had trouble standing up. I couldn't control myself. I was in a state of panic.'

That Donadoni miss meant Argentina led 4-3 and Serena had to score Italy's fifth kick. If not, they faced ejection from their own World Cup by an Argentina led by public enemy number one, Diego Maradona. The Stadio San Paolo was the Argentina captain's home ground. It is a cavernous bowl. Yet Serena, now on his walk to the penalty spot, felt as if there were walls closing in on him.

'When it came to my turn, I could no longer hear the stadium,' he remembers. 'I did some breathing exercises and I told myself to hit the ball in a certain place, but as I wasn't able to feel my legs, I couldn't get the right angle on my shot, and the goalkeeper saved it. The world just collapsed around me. From that moment on, I can't remember a single thing I did that night.

'From the images I've seen after the match, [Roberto] Baggio came straight up to console me, and I'm very grateful to him for that because he was just a boy then, at twenty-three. I really appreciate that gesture. But, I repeat, I've wiped out that evening. I was in a trance, and it's only the images I've seen that have helped me piece together what occurred afterwards.'

Serena is sitting in the lounge of a boutique hotel a short distance from the elegant confection of Milan's Galleria Vittorio Emanuele II shopping arcade. His eyes are bright blue, his hair a sweep of white. Given England's horrible history in big-stage shootouts, it is a source of wry amusement to hear that Serena is something of an Anglophile, a teenaged fan of Pink Floyd who, because of his own prematurely greying hair, developed a soft spot for Peter Reid when watching the Everton midfielder on television at the World Cup in Mexico.

By Italia '90, even more bizarrely, he had cultivated his sideburns in an attempt to copy another former England player. 'I don't have much of a beard, but during the World Cup I had some hair here,' he says, scratching the side of his face, 'because I was a fan of Mick Channon.' It is remarkable, really: a footballer from the land of *la bella figura*, from the same town – Montebelluna – as iconic brands Diadora and Lotto, trying to look like a bloke from Wiltshire. His penalty fate was English enough, and he ended up seeking a place of escape ten thousand miles away. 'I went to Bora Bora in Polynesia,' he says. 'In Italy, they were a bit angry.'

*

FOR ITALY, IT WASN'T MEANT TO END THIS WAY. THE *AZZURRI* HAD a rich World Cup history. They had first won the trophy on home turf in 1934. That was the era of Benito Mussolini's fascist dictatorship, and Brian Glanville, in *The Story of the World Cup*, writes, 'The more sceptical wondered if they would have won anywhere else.'

Win it elsewhere they duly did – in France in 1938, and in Spain in 1982. They reached another final, in Mexico in 1970, when they lost to the most luminous of all Brazil teams.

By 1990, Italy had the best league in the world, home to Europe's grandest set of stadiums and a starry roster of imported talents. Their club sides had just achieved a clean sweep of UEFA's club competitions, Milan having claimed the European Cup (for the second year running), Juventus the UEFA Cup, and Sampdoria the European Cup Winners' Cup.

Serie A was a playground for the world's finest, and it was not just the imports: Italy, according to their 1990 captain, Giuseppe Bergomi, had a squad of players to rival the group who had brought the World Cup trophy home eight years earlier.

'It was a team that was quick, technical, physical – it had everything to do as the '82 team had done,' notes Bergomi of a group who had reached the semi-finals of the European Championship in Germany two years earlier.

Bergomi, who appeared in four World Cups overall, is well placed to make the comparison. He had been an eighteen-year-old in Enzo Bearzot's World Cup-winning team in Spain. The thick, brown slug of a moustache on his lip had already earned him the nickname '*Zio*' – Italian for uncle. It was a moniker given him on his first day of training with the Internazionale first team. By 1990, the moustache had gone, replaced by a different marker of maturity: the captain's armband.

Since '82, Bergomi had seen a gifted crop of players advance to the senior side having excelled together in the Under-21 ranks: goalkeeper Walter Zenga, defenders Riccardo Ferri and Fernando De Napoli, midfielders Roberto Donadoni and Giuseppe Giannini, forwards Gianluca Vialli and Roberto Mancini, and a young substitute called Paolo Maldini had played in the European Under-21 Championship final together in 1986, losing to Spain on penalties.

By the time they began their World Cup campaign against Austria, they had not conceded a goal since a 1-0 friendly loss to Brazil the previous October.

'It was a good team in 1990 because our defence was very strong,' Bergomi reflects. 'It's a real shame not to have won that World Cup because at home, everything was there for us to win it.'

Then, defenders were defenders. Bergomi was one of the best, and he kept illustrious company. There were three *interisti* in the back line – goalkeeper Zenga and fellow centre-back Ferri, along with Bergomi – and two Milan men, in Franco Baresi as libero and left-back Maldini.

The sole member of the unit not from Milan was De Napoli, the right wing-back from newly-crowned champions Napoli. En route to the semi-final, they became the first team to play five matches at a World Cup finals tournament without conceding a goal. By the time of the Naples duel with Argentina, Zenga had recorded ten consecutive clean sheets overall.

Bergomi the player was considered a model of cool, quiet authority (the more cynical Ferri played the bad cop in their pairing), and today, the bespectacled 54-year-old is much the same: thoughtful and meticulous in his responses as we speak at his home in a smart apartment complex a short distance from the San Siro.

He works today for Sky Italia, applying a famously forensic level of detail to his analysis. 'You've come to open some old wounds,' he smiles, before easing back into a leather sofa in his sitting room and shedding light on the workings of that *Azzurri* defence, starting with the charismatic, record-setting goalkeeper Zenga.

'Walter was three times voted best goalkeeper in the world. Character-wise, he could really handle the emotions. He had real speed between his posts and a huge personality which helped him a lot, even in difficult moments.

'Ferri and I had arrived at Inter on the same day and ended up sat together on the bus which took us to our first training session. From there, our careers ran parallel to each other and we had Walter behind.'

There was a familiarity with Baresi too, who, though captain of Milan, was well known to Bergomi through his brother Giuseppe, a regular in Inter's defence. 'Franco was a man of few words but a born leader. He only needed a couple of words to sort us out. He had a great intelligence and could read things before anyone else, so we were all in sync, and then, you had Paolo Maldini. He was extraordinary. The first time I saw him at the European Championship in 1988, I said to him, "Where on earth did you come from?" because he was so good. Perhaps for me, he was the best Italian player of all.'

In 1982 Italy's World Cup-winning defence had operated a man-to-man marking system. The embodiment of this was Claudio Gentile whose approach to man-marking Diego Maradona, legend has it, extended even to rubbing his genitals against the Argentinian to provoke a reaction.

Eight years later, the Italian system had evolved as, with Milan playing a zonal defence under Arrigo Sacchi, national coach Azeglio Vicini sought to blend the two systems.

Bergomi's explanation leads to a reflection on the difference between defending now and then. 'Defenders today should learn man-marking to then play zonally, because when you're in your zone, you have to mark your man. In 1990, Milan were playing zonally, so they had to adapt to the national team's method.

'In 1982, the man-marking was really rigorous and wherever your player went, you followed. In '90, you'd follow the opponent into the zone of Baresi or Ferri and then move back. It was man-marking zonally. I was the right centre-back, Ferri the left centre-back and Baresi the libero. He could interpret the movement of the attacker.

'Now, to be a defender seems much more difficult to me, because all the rules have been turned in favour of attacking football. For us, you'd get a yellow card for your fourth or fifth foul. Now, you do a foul and you're booked immediately. Now, you have to know how to start the move as well as to mark.

'I always give this example. When I was marking Maradona, I'd hit him, I'd put my boot in, I'd foul him, and it was difficult to get booked straight away. Now, by contrast, [Lionel] Messi and [Cristiano] Ronaldo score a sack-load of goals because it's easier for them, because you barely brush against them and you're booked right away, and the second time, you're off. I'd have liked to see

Maradona and other players from our time in today's game, coached with today's methodologies and against these defenders. They'd have surely done even more.'

If that was Italy's defence, upfield they had a man in a sudden state of grace, Totò Schillaci. As Bergomi explains, the Sicilian was following a line of unanticipated Italian scene-stealers: Antonio Cabrini and Paolo Rossi at the 1978 World Cup, himself in 1982, Gianluca Vialli in 1986. Alongside Schillaci, the newly blossomed Roberto Baggio was earning global admiration too, including from American singer Madonna who, in Europe for her 'Blond Ambition' tour, declared herself 'conquered' by the player's 'big green eyes' and posed in an Italy shirt with his number fifteen on the back.

'In 1990, Baggio did some extraordinary things,' says Bergomi. 'Look at the goal against Czechoslovakia – class, talent, unpredictability, personality.

'At the time, there were hierarchies within the squad. In those years, Vialli and Mancini were doing very well as a pair at Sampdoria and had grown up together in the Under-21s. [Andrea] Carnevale had exploded on to the scene with Maradona's Napoli. Then, Roberto Baggio was emerging, and the strength of the coach is to sense the potential of a player and to put him in at the right time. Roberto was a pure talent, a unique footballer.'

Yet, the love for Baggio was not universally felt. His newly inked transfer to Juventus from Fiorentina had outraged followers of the Florence club. Fiorentina had just lost the UEFA Cup final to Juventus. Now, they were losing their favourite player. *Viola* supporters disrupted the squad's pre-finals preparations with protests at Coverciano, the Italian Football Federation base just outside the city, causing the door to slam shut on open training sessions.

Vicini's men found a sense of calm, though, in Marino, the squad's base for the tournament itself. Located close to Castel Gandolfo, the papal summer residence, Marino was fifteen miles from Rome, allowing for swift access to the Stadio Olimpico.

Here, there was a tranquility quite at odds with the storm of excitement breaking across Italy. For Bergomi, the only source of irritation was the smell of cigar smoke that would drift into his room from the balcony next door on which Nicola Berti, a colleague at Inter, had a habit of lighting up. 'The balconies were attached to each other, and Berti would stand outside to smoke a cigar. I'd ask him to stop, but he'd carry on. He'd also have a drink. I saw him not long ago, and he was still smoking his cigars!'

An important source of calm was Vicini, the 57-year-old national coach. Aldo Serena recalls, 'Vicini, at that stage, had done several World Cups as an observer so he knew how important it was, at a mental level, to have some freedom, lightness, laughter, jokes, to help you handle the physical preparation work. He wasn't a club coach. He'd worked his whole career in the federation, so he was a politician who knew the dynamics of the newspapers and how you had to do things.'

If not known as a master tactician, Vicini had the virtue of the human touch, adds Bergomi. 'He knew how to speak to the group, to motivate them in the right way for the challenges we had. He spoke to us in small groups – to the defenders, to the midfielders, to the attackers – and then he'd get us altogether to explain the game and show us some videos of the opposition.'

Motivation was hardly a problem. Prior to the semi-final, Italy's players had played every game in Rome. There was scant need for a team speech, not with the adrenalin-shot sights that greeted them on their way to, and inside, the flag-strewn furnace of the Stadio Olimpico.

'I carry these images in my heart,' says Bergomi. 'We'd set off from Marino between these two banks of people, and it followed us all the way to the stadium. To play in Rome was really beautiful, and it's one of the best memories of my life as a player. The team were swept along by it. When we went out to warm up, there were all these flags and the stadium was already full.'

Serena likens it to an 'ecclesiastical' procession. 'When we went to Rome, the streets were full of flags and people. And when we got to the stadium, it was already filled with tricolour flags, and we'd already won because it gave you so much energy, so much strength.'

The on-field procession had begun against Austria, with Schillaci's spree-sparking header. Next were wins over the United States and Czechoslovakia, the latter confirming the *Azzurri*'s continued presence in the capital.

The next match, against Uruguay, brought Serena's first contribution. He had begun the tournament as fourth-choice centre-forward behind Gianluca Vialli, Andrea Carnevale and Schillaci. Now, he came off the bench and sealed a

2-0 victory. 'I gave the ball to Schillaci for his goal, and then I scored too.'

He returns to the atmosphere in Rome, where another Schillaci goal saw off the Republic of Ireland in the quarter-finals. 'I never thought people could be so involved. I always feel a bit detached from things, and yet in that moment, I saw this great love and warmth – it was something I'd never experienced.

'The closest thing I've seen since was when I was commentated on [Francesco] Totti's farewell game at Roma. It seems absurd to someone who lives in the north, but we're not used to this. Rome, on the other hand, can summon this wave of feeling for sport, which brings together old, young, families and women who wouldn't usually follow football. It was really something special.

'So we got used to a feeling, to a symbiosis with the public. With the stadium and the public there was this give and take of emotions which fed something strong and unique.'

All of this serves to explain the sense of dislocation felt by the Italy squad when they arrived in Naples, a sudden fall in temperature after the ardour of Rome. The reason? Diego Maradona.

The Argentina captain's role as the inspiration for Napoli's Serie A title triumphs of 1987 and 1990 – unprecedented in the club's history – had seared his name on the soul of this football-mad city. His understanding of that Neapolitan soul enabled him to stoke the fires by accusing Italy of racism towards his adopted home. 'In Italy, for three hundred and sixty-four days nobody talks about Naples,' he said immediately after the quarter-final.

The next day, he was an impromptu visitor to Italy's training camp, a 30km drive from Argentina's Trigoria base in his white Mercedes. There, he chatted with his Napoli colleagues Ciro Ferrara, De Napoli, and Carnevale, and even received a massage from the Italy masseur, Salvatore Carmando, who did the same job for the Neapolitan club.

As the semi-final approached, though, Maradona went back to stoking the fire. On the eve of the semi-final, the *Gazzetta dello Sport* ran an article detailing more of the Argentinian's assertions beneath the headline 'Maradona and his people'. He was quoted as saying, 'In the end, the San Paolo will support Italy. The only thing I don't like is that now everyone's asking Napoli to feel Italian. But for the rest of Italy, Naples has always been forgotten, and been slapped in the face.

I know the soul of Neapolitans is Italian, but some people have found this out only now, and that's an awful thing as it's now late.

'Just as it's been awful to discover that in Italy there's so much racism against Neapolitans, racism which deeply affected my national team when we played in the north. The fact Maradona won the *scudetto* with Napoli unleashed a real campaign against Argentina.

'In the whole of Italy, Neapolitans have always been called *terremotati* [earthquake victims], *terroni* [people from the land], but in these moments, they're Italian. Before, they were African, now they're the best people in Italy.'

The Independent likened Maradona to Machiavelli and worse – 'He may have the Hand of God but he has the mouth of Old Nick,' wrote Joe Lovejoy – but his pot-stirring pronouncements had the effect he had been seeking, as Aldo Serena remembers. 'I'm not saying we lost because of this but – we lost the game out on the pitch – but leaving Rome, it was like the spell was broken.

'We got to Naples, and it really was a surprise approaching the stadium on the bus and seeing nothing like that. We had the feeling they were our fans, but they weren't really our fans, because two or three days earlier Maradona had stoked things up with comments that were strong, astute, cunning. Maradona had said simple things, but he'd got into the hearts of the Neapolitans.'

Giuseppe Bergomi offers his own recollection: 'This is a delicate argument because Neapolitans get a bit angry, but I always say the same thing – if we'd remained in Rome, we wouldn't have lost. Maradona was clever in creating that whole atmosphere.

'Napoli's main contenders for the title were Inter and Milan, and in our team, seven of the eleven were from those two clubs – Baresi, Ferri, Maldini, Donadoni, Berti, Serena, Bergomi. During the warm-up on the pitch, there was applause but some whistles. We felt something different. For Naples, Maradona was and still is something incredible. Even now when I go to commentate on games in Naples, they always talk about him.'

Is it any wonder? Before Maradona's arrival in the southern city, Napoli's honours' board featured only two Italian Cups. When he joined the club from Barcelona in 1984, more than 70,000 spectators filled the San Paolo to welcome him. After Napoli's collecting of the 1987 Serie A crown, there were street parties and a graffito on the wall of the city's graveyard saying, 'You don't know what you're missing.'

Francesco Deluca, from Neapolitan newspaper *Il Mattino*, was in the press seats at the San Paolo that evening. Echoing the banner in the stadium which read 'Maradona, Napoli loves you, but Italy is our country,' he insists that only a 'minority' were wishing for a Maradona triumph, and offers some context. 'Anyone who didn't see the Maradona years in Naples can't understand the incredibly strong human bond between Diego and the *Napolitani*. He was a son of the south, of South America, very close to the mentality and passion of the city.'

By 1990, the romance was under strain. In 1989, old photographs of Maradona appeared in *Il Mattino*, the local daily paper: he was partying in a shell-shaped Jacuzzi with members of the Giuliano family – a prominent arm of the Neapolitan mafia, the Camorra, who controlled the city's old quarter. 'I think we can say, after all these years, that Diego knew fully well who these people were,' says Deluca.

Maradona returned late for the 1989/90 season, furious about Napoli denying him a transfer to Marseille. Although Napoli ended the campaign as champions, he had become 'uncontrollable' for the club according to Deluca.

Indeed, within eight months of the World Cup final, in March 1991, it was announced Maradona had tested positive for cocaine following a fixture against Bari. A fifteen-month ban from football would follow.

John Foot, writing in *Calcio*, his history of the Italian game, speculates that, 'It certainly was strange that Maradona was only found positive after the World Cup, as he had been taking cocaine on a regular basis for years.' However, Deluca dismisses the suggestion there was a desire within Italy to punish Maradona: 'There was no wish for a vendetta, even if Maradona and his clan have always thought otherwise.' ✳

FOR ARGENTINA MIDFIELDER JULIO OLARTICOECHEA, VIEWING THE streets of Naples through the windows of Argentina's team bus, there was an early sign of the mood shift that would aggrieve many Italians.

'When we had to play in Naples against Russia, we went the day before the game and saw the city was full of Italian flags,' he notes. 'When we went back there to play Italy, out of respect for Diego, you could see people had taken the flags down from the balconies. It was quite noticeable.'

For Maradona himself, it was the sight of Italy's team sheet which offered the biggest boost, specifically the presence of Roberto Baggio among the substitutes.

Vicini's decision to restore Vialli to the starting XI ahead of Baggio would be a central discussion point during the long post mortem that followed. Vialli had endured an up-and-down season with Sampdoria, stymied by a stress fracture in his foot, and the World Cup had brought further frustration: a penalty against the post against the United States, a problem with his thigh.

'It's real, but nobody seems to believe me,' said Vialli when Italy's medical team could not detect a problem. Yet, he had been Vicini's original first choice to lead the attack, and his name was back on the list of starters.

Aldo Serena says, 'Vicini banked a lot on Vialli and Zenga – they were his two lieutenants in that national team, and he was very close to them.'

Vicini also opted against a recall for Carlo Ancelotti, who had been struggling for fitness with a muscle strain since exiting the opening game against Austria. There would be other talking points to come, including the 73rd-minute removal of Giuseppe Giannini, a proven penalty taker, and the omission of Pietro Vierchowod, a survivor of the Spain '82 finals.

Totò Schillaci's view is that the Sampdoria-based Vierchowod would have been the ideal man to monitor Maradona. 'It was a mistake by the coach,' he says. 'I'd have played Baggio and had Vierchowod man-marking Maradona. But Vicini brought in the old guard – the players he'd had with the Under-21s.'

Instead, Bergomi and Ferri – the two centre-backs – shared the task of marking Maradona and Claudio Caniggia. Bergomi says in Vicini's defence, 'How are you going to change a team that until then had done so well and not conceded a goal?'

Indeed, there had been smiles in the Italy camp when Argentina eliminated Brazil, for they considered the *Albiceleste* the weaker of the two South American powerhouses potentially lurking down the line. Maradona had won none of his five previous encounters with the *Azzurri*. Yet, says Bergomi, Maradona was Maradona. His speed and strength may have been diminished by the kicks and the cortisone and the cocaine, but he remained the wasp in the room; opponents lived with a nagging fear of his capacity to unleash a sudden sting.

'You have to think that when Maradona's on the pitch, you've got a unique player there – absolutely the best I've ever seen play. And you have to think too that the Argentinians are so resourceful. They're sly, cunning, and they're never beaten until the very end. In fact, when you've got Maradona, [Sergio] Batista, Caniggia playing, they were a good team, who were well coached by [Carlos] Bilardo. Then, you've their goalkeeper who made some extraordinary saves.'

In the dressing room beforehand, the Italy team had performed their customary huddle around their captain, Bergomi, placing hands on his back and releasing a shared cry of '*Chi si ritira dalla lotta e' un gran figlio di una mignotta*' – literally, whoever leaves the fight is a son of a slut.

This particular fight had a bright beginning for the hosts. After seventeen minutes, Schillaci had his fifth goal of the competition. He was involved at the start of the sequence, holding on to the ball tenaciously in Argentina territory and then laying it off to Fernando De Napoli, at which point the move sped up: a touch forward from De Napoli, a flick from Vialli, and then Giannini with a flick of his own to lift the ball over a defender's head as he burst into the box. A second Giannini touch, with his head, teed up Vialli who volleyed goalwards. Goycochea parried, but there was Schillaci to gobble up the loose ball. 'I hit it with my shin,' he says.

In the face of that setback, Argentina summoned the best of themselves, showing a coherence not previously seen at this World Cup. *Clarín*'s match report the next day observed that Italy were gradually subdued by the 'fluidity of a team who grew in identity'. Their reward came with Caniggia's equalising goal in the 67th minute.

Julio Olarticoechea, out on the left, collected a Maradona pass five yards from the corner of the penalty box and, with Bergomi standing off, had time to size up, then chip in a near-post cross. As the ball dropped on the line of the six-yard box, Caniggia got his blond head there before defender Riccardo Ferri and flicked it over Zenga, the grey-shirted goalkeeper who had flown out of his goal only to see the ball sail over his head.

Olarticoechea says, 'I saw that Caniggia had made a diagonal run. I paused and waited for him to carry on, and then I floated the ball in. I didn't hit it too hard but clipped it, so it floated over just right. Caniggia's header wasn't easy to flick behind like that.'

'We hadn't made a single mistake until that moment' is Bergomi's rueful recollection. For Zenga, hitherto unbeaten for 517 minutes – still a World Cup record – it was a mistake that left a long shadow.

Bergomi continues, 'Unfortunately, none of us has ever had the courage to say anything. Whenever it's mentioned, he doesn't like to talk about it and changes the subject.

'It's a wound for all of us, Walter included. We all have our own sensibilities, and the feeling of that goal is something he'll carry inside himself, but we carry it too, all of us.

'I've seen it so many times. Olarticoechea has the ball, and I could've been closer to him and not let him cross. When you concede a goal, it's a little bit down to everyone. Perhaps his mistake is the most obvious one, but none of us has ever said anything to Walter.'

With it, some of the belief bled out of Italy. 'The fact of conceding a goal hurt our confidence,' attests Serena. 'It made us fearful and timid. We lost our identity. We were trying to do things but couldn't do them; our timing and attitude weren't right, and neither was our movement. The Argentinians were defending with six players at the back. They shut down the spaces, and it was hard work just getting into their box.

'That's what they played for. In extra time they played not to go forward but to defend, because it was an Argentina squad that was far off their Mexico '86 team. They had a good defence, and Maradona would release Caniggia, and that was it. So it was great for them to get to penalties – that's what they were counting on.'

EXTRA TIME BROUGHT CONTROVERSY WITH A RED CARD AND AN extraordinary time-keeping error. After substitute Baggio had brought a fine save from Goycochea with a free-kick, the Italian forward was then involved in the sending-off of Argentina's Ricardo Giusti following an off-the-ball incident. When Baggio hit the ground and stayed down, referee Michel Vautrot trotted across to Peter Mikkelsen, his Danish colleague running the line, and sought his help in identifying the culprit before calling Giusti across and showing him the red card.

The TV cameras missed the incident. Olarticoechea says, 'He [Giusti] said there was no elbow. He raised his arms.' Giusti's own words to reporters were, 'I wanted to die when he showed me the red card. I turned and opened up my arms, but I didn't manage to touch him.'

Whatever the extent of the contact, the French referee's response was the cue for an explosion of Argentine anger. Bilardo had to push his players away from Mikkelsen as they hurled angry words and jabbed furious fingers at the Dane. Then they swarmed around Vautrot, who, at this stage, was losing control.

When Baggio went down, there had already been five minutes of added time in the first extra period. Ignoring signals from Michal Listkiewicz, one of his assistants, he did not whistle for the change of ends until the stopwatch said 23:21.

'It's inadmissible and incomprehensible,' says Vautrot. 'Fortunately, the refereeing gods were with me in terms of the score not changing during that additional time.

'When I think about it, I still feel a cold sweat running down my back. Did I stop my watch with the number of breaks for players going down and forget to restart it? Did the pressure get to me to the point where I thought we were in a normal half? Why did I ignore the signals of my assistants? There's no answer for that kind of negligence, and it'll go with me to my grave.

'It was far from being the best performance of my career. The fact you had the nervousness of players with a Latin and South American temperament didn't help. And the setting in Naples contributed greatly to that. The Italian players seemed on edge about playing at home without the one hundred per cent support of their supposed public.'

Even with an extra man, there was no way through for Italy, meaning a penalty shootout: a first for the *Azzurri*, whereas Argentina had been through the process, and emerged victorious, only three days earlier against Yugoslavia.

'We played every game to win,' insists Carlos Bilardo. 'I didn't look for penalties.'

Giuseppe Bergomi saw it differently: 'They'd already won a shootout against

Yugoslavia and had a goalkeeper who'd saved penalties.'

Totò Schillaci remembers, 'When we got to the penalties, I wasn't very confident. I didn't want to take one, because by the end of the match, I was exhausted. I was struggling to walk and had a problem with my adductors. I preferred someone in a better condition to take one.'

If Schillaci said no, Serena was one of the five to say yes - albeit reluctantly. 'Vicini came up to me and said, "I'm finding it hard to find people. Aldo, how are you doing?" I said, "If you need me, I'm here, but have another look around." At the age of thirty, I didn't feel right saying no to him. He went round again and found the fourth taker, Donadoni. Then he came back to me and said, "Aldo, I've got four takers, but there's no one else." And so I said to him, "That's alright, I'm going to take one."'

The shootout began with six successful kicks: Baresi, Baggio and De Agostini for Italy, and [José] Serrizuela, [Jorge] Burruchaga and Olarticoechea for Argentina. It was then, at 3-3, that Sergio Goycochea emerged as the hero of the hour. First, he denied Donadoni by flying to his left. Then, after Maradona had sent Zenga the wrong way, he readied himself to foil Serena.

For the Italian, his jelly-legged walk to the penalty spot and failed shot are followed by a blank in the memory bank and a bitter taste in the mouth. 'I still get a feeling, a trace of bitterness, I have to be honest,' he says. 'I have this memory of a unique experience but with a streak of melancholy, of sadness, running through it, for something I feel was unfinished.'

SEEN THROUGH THE EYES OF GOYCOCHEA, THE MAN IN THE Argentina goal, the events in that penalty box down at the Curva B end of the Stadio San Paolo could not hold a more contrasting meaning.

Here was a player who arrived at Italia '90 not having made a single league appearance for his Colombian club Millonarios for over seven months due to the suspension of the championship following the murder of a referee. He was playing only because of first-choice custodian Nery Pumpido's broken leg. And yet, his shootout exploits made him a national hero, those four penalty saves earning him his own personal postcode from the Argentinian post office:

0004 Lima, Buenos Aires.

For Goycochea, the split-second as he dropped to his left and sensed the arrival of Serena's low kick is a moment he would put in a bottle if he could. 'I'd relive in slow motion the moment that the ball's coming towards me, and I know I'm going to save it. It was the most important save of my life.

'It didn't change me, but it changed my relationship with the world. I went to the World Cup as a footballer and came back as a big name. The whole of Argentina knew me. It was so strong what happened at Italia '90 that I still feel the warmth from people today. The most surprising thing is it's kids of twenty-five or thirty who weren't even born then or were just a year or two old. They talk to you about that World Cup as if they've lived it, thanks to technology and all the repeats. It changed my life completely.'

The location for my lunchtime interview with Goycochea leaves no doubt about that. We arrange to meet at his restaurant at the Tortugas Open Mall, a shopping centre some twenty-five miles outside Buenos Aires. The restaurant's name? Italia '90.

The mementos on display inside include a framed Argentina goalkeeper shirt and a set of black-and-white photographs, notably of his penalty saves from Yugoslavia's Faruk Hadžibegić, and Italy's Donadoni and Serena.

These were life-changing feats for Goycochea, opening the door to modelling opportunities and a post-football career in television. Indeed, the first impression as he steps into his restaurant and removes a pair of goggle-style Prada sunglasses is that if Barbie were ever allowed to enter middle age, Goycochea would be the perfect prototype for the accompanying Ken doll given his thick grey quiff and cheekbones as sharp as his reflexes in a World Cup shootout.

Tucking into a juicy slab of sirloin steak – *bife de chorizo* as Argentinians call it – he explains the approach that served him so well. 'You analyse things. I knew Serena wasn't a skilful player but more of a target man. It's different with a player like that, who's left-footed, stepping up than, say, Baggio who's got great technique and vision.

'We practised a lot. We had a method where the player shooting would come and take a penalty against me, and he'd say, "Goyco, it's going to the bottom left". It removed all the pressure over whether the goalkeeper was going here or there, and the taker could concentrate only on the precision of putting the ball there – and ninety per cent of times, it was a goal.

'Bilardo had a thing when it came to penalties that he didn't want anybody to come up and say to me, "Go right, or left, or stay in the middle." He wanted you to analyse the situation alone.'

An exception in the quarter-final shootout against Yugoslavia was the final kick taken by Hadžibegić. 'Before he took it, [Gabriel] Calderón came to me and although Bilardo didn't like it, he said to me, "I played with him in France and normally, he aims for where he put it [to the goalkeeper's left]. Given it's the last penalty and he's got to score to draw level again, the most feasible is that he hits it to his normal side.'

Come the semi-final against Italy, superstition came into play too as Goycochea repeated the exact same steps taken in the lead-up to the Yugoslavia shootout - right down, it turns out, to urinating on the pitch.

An explanation is required. 'It's a question of need. We'd played in thirty-five degrees, and I took on a lot of liquid. At the end of the game, you can't go back into the dressing room, you have to stay on the pitch. I needed to pee, and so I peed on the pitch. Because we won the penalties, then I had to repeat it.'

This begs one very obvious question: how to piss on the pitch during a World Cup semi-final without a single person noticing. The answer, it seems, is 'by pretending you're stretching. It wasn't the most comfortable position, but that's how it was, and there weren't as many cameras as today!'

That night, he had already made a fabulous extra-time save when pawing over a Baggio free-kick. 'That save was harder than the penalties, but the longer the game went on, the more they felt the pressure, as they weren't winning. And because we weren't losing, we were growing, so there was a reverse effect.

'You could tell on their faces before the penalties – they had the possibility of losing something, and we had the chance of winning something. They had the responsibility of winning. We didn't.

'Bilardo said that when you go to the World Cup, you want to play the seven matches. Then, if you end up winning it, all the better. The minimum objective was to play the seven games, so by beating Yugoslavia, we'd achieved that.

'The fact they were whistling our anthem, and the relationship of Diego with

Italy because of his Napoli connection, it all helped us focus. It was, "We're going to show everybody," and we used it in our favour. When they were whistling our anthem, the only thing they were doing was energising us, which is why you had that explosion when we won.'

Maradona's own summing-up of Argentina's progression to the 1990 World Cup final, written in his autobiography, was that, 'We, the motley crew, the injured, the persecuted, had made it to the final.'

The sense of persecution was certainly stronger than ever afterwards, given that the sent-off Giusti and yellow-carded Batista, Caniggia, and Olarticoechea all left the San Paolo pitch having collected suspensions for the final. Bilardo himself would note, 'Italy committed thirty-one fouls and only received one yellow.'

The tears inside the Argentina dressing room were not just of joy. A sleepless night beckoned for the distraught Caniggia. A vivid picture of the state of Maradona, meanwhile, comes from Frits Ahlstrøm, the FIFA media officer at the game.

'After the game, everybody wanted him in the press conference, so I went into the dressing room, and there he was, sitting crying,' he recounts. 'And he said to me, "I can't do it." I saw his legs, and I've never seen anything like that. He was kicked everywhere, he was bleeding, he was blue. He was really in pain, and maybe it was also psychological. Don't forget, he played in Italy, and the way he was treated was with a complete lack of respect for him as a player and human being.'

*

FOR ITALY, THE *NOTTI MAGICHE* WERE OVER. ONE IRONY OF A WORLD Cup recalled with such fondness elsewhere is that in the host country itself, Italia '90 elicits mixed memories. The doleful fate of Vicini's team is a factor. Then there is the question of legacy, with the expenditure on the tournament regarded today as a striking symbol of wasteful public spending.

It is estimated that the overall sum spent on the twelve stadiums for the 1990 World Cup reached 1,250 billion Lira – a total 84 per cent greater than originally envisaged and equal to around £980 million in today's prices. Behind the dazzling scale, the infrastructure was quickly found wanting.

'We did the stadiums badly,' responds Giuseppe Bergomi when asked how the tournament is viewed today. 'They should have been in the vanguard, but they weren't. There were stadiums with running tracks. From the sporting side, Italy didn't win at home, and in those days, the big countries who hosted the World Cup would usually win it. And, if you remember, the stadiums weren't full when they were playing in Bari, for example.'

Bari's San Nicola Stadium, designed by Renzo Piano, one of the architects of Paris's Pompidou Centre, was one of two brand-new venues. The presence of a 58,000-capacity stadium on the heel of Italy owed much to the fact that Vincenzo Matarrese, brother of FIGC president Antonio, was the Bari president. It hosted five matches, including the Italy-England play-off for third place – yet, today with the club absent from Serie A since 2011, it is seldom more than one third full, drawing an average attendance of 16,331 in the 2016/17 season.

The other new stadium, Turin's Stadio delle Alpi, fared even worse. Built in place of the Stadio Comunale, it was an unloved place with a running track surrounding the pitch. In 2008, demolition work began to make way for the new Juventus Stadium, a purpose-built, commercially profitable football arena the club actually owns – something still unique for Serie A.

David Platt, who played for England in their 1990 semi-final at the Delle Alpi, later spent the 1992/93 season as a Juventus player and remembers, 'It was a cold stadium in the sense that whatever atmosphere was in the stadium was lost by the time it arrived on the pitch.'

This sense of a failed legacy would be pivotal in the evaporation of support for a proposed Rome bid for the 2024 Olympic Games – a bid led by Luca Cordero di Montezemolo, who had been general director of the local organising committee for Italia '90.

When asked about mistakes made, he begins with Bari. 'At that time, the team was in Serie A and quite an important team, and soccer is very popular in Bari. The stadium is beautiful, [but] in my opinion, it was too big. Then Bari, after a few years, collapsed. They went into Serie B and then Serie C, and are now in B again.

'But, you know, you have to take a photo of Italy in 1990, and it's different from Italy today. In Turin, they made a mistake to put an athletics track as it's too far from the pitch, but the chairman at that time of the athletics federation said this was a good opportunity to have athletics also. I was against it, but I wasn't responsible. I'm not the mayor of the town.

'We were responsible for the organisation of the event – the referees, the teams, to guarantee the best technology for the press. We weren't responsible for deciding how big you had to do the stadium, [or] in which area of the town you put the stadium. We only said to the towns, "People have to go a stadium with every single seat numbered – every place a seat." This was crucial in the future for safety, because there were lot of stadiums in Italy with standing. Then, they had to cover the press tribune [with a roof] and to put up at least one large screen.

'A lot of towns made, in my opinion, crazy expenses. Why do you have to do the running track in a soccer stadium? Why do you have to build a stadium so big in Bari? Why do you decide in Rome to have a special station for the subway to go to the stadium?'

This last example was one of two stations – Farneto, close to the Stadio Olimpico, and Vigna Clara – whose construction demanded a four-year tunnel-building project and a combined cost of 90 billion Lira (around £40 million). Their days in use did not reach double figures, and by autumn 1990 they were obsolete.

Another white elephant in the capital was Ostiense rail terminal for trains to and from Fiumicino airport. It cost 350 billion Lira (some £160 million) and, owing to its poor location, ceased to operate in 2003 whereupon the squatters moved in. Eventually, in 2012, it reopened as a foodie hub, run by high-end supermarket chain Eataly.

For his part, Giuseppe Bergomi remembers the problems that followed the addition of the San Siro's third tier. This raised capacity to 80,000 ahead of the World Cup but had a damaging effect on the pitch. New turf technology resolved the problem eventually, but Bergomi remembers years of difficulties.

'A disaster for the pitch, unfortunately,' is how the former Internazionale skipper describes it. 'I played for many years on an awful pitch. When you were down on it, you got this smell of mould, of damp. After six or seven games, they'd be having to relay it at a huge cost.

'The third ring was so high. Now, under the new owners, there is a plan to close it, and use only two tiers, and take the capacity to sixty thousand.'

Two evenings before my interview with Bergomi, in May 2017, I sit in the press box at the San Siro, watching Inter close out the season with a 5-2 victory over Udinese. It is a result of little use to a team already out of the running for even Europa League qualification, and the stadium is less than half full, with 36,689 present.

In 1990, AC Milan and Inter were as glamorous as football got. By the time of my visit, the last time either finished in the top three in Serie A was 2012/13, which was also the last time they both played European football in the same season.

It does not help that the San Siro – a futuristic vision to the watching world in 1990 – became a symbol of how *calcio* has been left behind by the colossal commercial engines of club football in England, Spain and Germany.

Commercially, the Milan clubs trail by some distance. Milan fell out of the top twenty in Deloitte's annual Football Money League report published in January 2018. As for Inter, their commercial revenue showed a rise of 137 per cent from £41.1m to £111.8m thanks to the takeover by Chinese electronics retailer Suning. It is the highest figure of any Serie A club but still dwarfed by the £250m-plus that Bayern Munich, Manchester United, Real Madrid and Barcelona bring in. Inter's match-day income, meanwhile, was less than four times what both United and Arsenal earned. Indeed in UEFA's report on 'The European Club Footballing Landscape', also published in January 2018, only Juventus and Napoli of all the Serie A clubs featured in the top thirty clubs for 'average yield per spectator' – and Juventus's €44.50 was less than half the sum earned by Arsenal and Chelsea.

It is not hard for the visitor to the San Siro to find reasons why the Milan clubs lag behind: rows of stalls selling unofficial Inter merchandise stand just beyond the stadium security cordon. Only in 2015 did the two clubs actually set up an on-site San Siro store. The fact they ground-share adds a layer of difficulty, explains one Inter official, as it is necessary to 'Inter-ise' the store one weekend, then 'Milan-ise' it the next. As for hospitality areas, there are five lounges and thirty sky boxes, whereas Arsenal's Emirates Stadium, for instance, has 150 executive boxes and four open-plan suites holding almost 2,000 people.

There are other factors in the decline of Serie A: from the fiercer ambition and superior television deals of other big European leagues to problems which have stripped the sheen from Italy's top flight, including corruption scandals, hooliganism, racism, and falling attendances with the advent of pay-TV.

In the 1990s, Serie A had the 'Seven Sisters' of Juventus, Inter, Milan, Roma, Lazio, Parma, and Fiorentina. Yet, Lazio and Parma suffered with the decline of Cirio and Parmalat, the food companies owned by the respective club presidents. Fiorentina had to start again in the third division after their 2002 bankruptcy.

Bergomi returns, though, to the question of infrastructure. 'Stadiums are a problem for us. When you go to the San Siro, the fans have problems with parking, turnstiles, so many things which don't help. I see the English and Spanish stadiums, and twenty minutes before kick-off, they'll be half-empty, and they fill up and then empty with incredible ease. It's not like that here. And the advent of pay-TV has kept people away from the stadiums. Those Italian families – like Moratti and Berlusconi [at Inter and Milan respectively] – could no longer sustain the costs of their squads, and so we have to accept foreign investors, like the Chinese in our case. It's not quite football poetry, but you accept it because if not, you struggle to keep up.

'Little by little, Italian football lost its power to attract the best players. Football has followed the evolution of the country. Gradually, we've got into difficulties and football, in turn, has got into difficulties. Now, you can see it struggling to bounce back.

'We've only had Juventus recently who've done well on a European level. Other teams have struggled. Italian football needs a strong Milan and Inter, because with their traditions, their shirts have real weight. Roma and Napoli are doing very well. They're playing good football and have invested, but ultimately, they struggle to keep their great players.'

The failure of Italy's national team to reach the 2018 World Cup offered a fresh slap in the face. At the draw for the finals, inside the Kremlin, I watch as Fabio Cannavaro – captain of Italy's 2006 World Cup-winning side – faces a salvo of reporters' questions all amounting to the thing: where did it all go wrong?

'There is not one sole cause,' he said, searching for solutions himself. 'Work ... invest in young players and facilities ... change something in Serie A, Serie B ... reduce some teams ... Something has to be done.'

Cannavaro then remembers his own experience of being at the Stadio San Paolo on 3 July 1990. He was then a sixteen-year-old on Napoli's books and tells me, 'It was a very difficult moment. It was a semi-final, and everyone was confident about winning the World Cup at home. Caniggia's goal was really a shock for us.'

For Giuseppe Bergomi, the failure to do something Cannavaro did sixteen years later – and lift the World Cup trophy – has left an itch, undoubtedly.

Back in his Milan apartment, our interview finished, he leads me upstairs to his office where his 1982 Italy shirt hangs in a frame on the wall. There is no 1990 shirt on display. 'I'm still talking about this with a sense of sadness, with an open wound, because we thought we were going all the way with that squad,' he admits. 'To be knocked out on penalties at home was incredibly bitter. Nobody spoke. They'd walk past and give you a pat on the back, but nobody had the courage to say anything.'

'From Naples, we went directly back to Rome on the bus, but no one slept that night. I remember we had this huge cuddly toy, and we threw it into the swimming pool. We eventually started talking and going over the game, and thinking, "If we'd done this or that . . ." I still ask myself today why our federation moved us and sent us to play the semi-final in Naples.'

Time can only do so much. There are some questions we never stop asking.

Tears in Turin

'NATIONAL TREASURE' READ THE BIG, BOLD LETTERS IN GOLD ON the front of the shiny event programme. And beneath, the name: Paul 'Gazza' Gascoigne.

The setting is a function room in the Birmingham suburb of Edgbaston, filled this Friday evening by 200 or so thirty and fortysomethings. Young women in white squeeze-in dresses and totter-on heels have paraded a series of sporting-auction items. The 1990 England football shirt has been snapped up. The perfunctory meal has been and gone.

During the long wait as £79 meet-and-greet ticket-holders disappear for a snap with the man himself, two Tottenham Hotspur fans on my table reminisce. They were in primary school at the time of Italia '90.

'It was Gazza that made me a Spurs fan,' says one.

'He made me fall in love with football,' responds the other.

The oldest on the table has a different memory. 'It was a coming of age – Italia '90, the rave scene,' he says, remembering illegal parties in aircraft hangars off the M25 and running through cornfields to escape the police. This was the era of acid house and ecstasy, which culminated in the Second Summer of Love in 1989.

Paul Gascoigne's own Summer of Love, his never-ending now, came a year later: youth, mischief, adventure all distilled into his efforts in an England shirt. Its ultimate night was in Turin on Wednesday 4 July, the World Cup semi-final against West Germany. This is why this room is full.

A chorus of 'One Paul Gascoigne' erupts as he strides in, his blue-and-white shirt buttoned halfway down his chest, and takes a seat on a small, central stage alongside Terry Baker, his agent and interrogator for the Q&A that unfolds. The addiction and mental health problems have left a mark on the thinner man we see today, a poignant sight for anybody with a recall of his days as a unique package of puppy fat and puppy power.

Yet, the stories told – reheated as they may be – hold enough of the old wit and devilment to provide a direct line to that time when anything seemed possible.

'I treated it as if I was with you guys,' he says, taking us back in time. 'I played tennis, swimming, I did everything, as well as training. I fitted that in now and again! I roomed with Chris Waddle, and I always remember it was eleven o'clock at night and I can hear someone playing tennis.' Cue a recalled conversation with Waddle:

'"Gazza, you can't – we've got the semi-final tomorrow."

'"I know, but I need to go."

'I went out, and I saw these two guys playing tennis. I went, "I want to play you two. Me against you two."'

'"Where's your partner?"

'I said, "I haven't got one."

'So, I'm playing these guys, and then I heard a voice. Sir Bobby Robson – "Gazza where are you?"'

'I dropped the racket and as I shot off, he says to these fellas, "Do you know who he is? Tomorrow he's got the most important game of his life."'

It is a marvellous tale, and even if the details differ from Robson's account to reporters at the time – 'We discovered he was playing tennis in ninety degrees in the afternoon with an American,' he said during the team's stay in Bologna – pedantry has no place in a greatest-hits package.

And the hits keep coming. He brings the house down with his account of borrowing an ostrich from a zoo and driving it into training at Tottenham Hotspur, where he tells manager Terry Venables, 'Gaffer, I've got this new player for you – he's fast as fuck.'

However, it is the England memories, more than anything, that his audience laps up. 'When I was nineteen, I remember watching England in the World Cup when I was on holiday, and four years later, I'm in one,' he reminisces. 'I just loved pulling on the shirt. After the game you swap your shirts, but I kept hold of mine, I kept hold of every one.'

And he had no fear of the opposition jerseys, no matter who was in them. He recounts his response to Robson when told he would be facing the planet's best footballer in West Germany captain Lothar Matthäus.

'I looked at Sir Bobby Robson and went, "No, I'm sorry but Lothar is – *he's* playing against the best player in the world." I had one of my greatest games. Obviously, I was going to miss the final, and we lost on penalties. Them tears ... I can honestly say that when I finished and I was crying and thanking the fans, I thought that was the end of my football career. I had such a great time with the support I had out there, and ...'

The crack of emotion in his voice demands a pause. 'I just remembered where I grew up and just thought of me on my own and that football. And that was me at the World Cup.'

It was not the end, as he thought, but nor was it the beginning in the way that English football hoped it would be during that dance with greatness.

One Italian newspaper, *Il Giorno,* labelled him as a 'talent superior to Bobby Charlton', his fellow native of the north-east, but within ten months, the spiral of mishaps and self-inflicted injuries had begun with the cruciate ligament rupture sustained in a reckless tackle on Nottingham Forest's Gary Charles in the FA Cup final.

There were still flashes of genius, for Lazio and Rangers and, most memorably, for England against Scotland with a magnificent goal at Euro '96 when he lifted a ball over Colin Hendry and then met it on the other side with a gorgeous volley – but his biggest legacy would be something else. 'Them tears,' as he puts it – the tears that threatened to come with the quivering lip after the booking that ruled him out of the final that never was. The tears that ran and ran at the finish.

It is curious to listen back today and hear ITV commentator Brian Moore's reaction to the sight of a red-eyed Stuart Pearce, one of the two England players to err from the spot. 'He's in tears, Stuart Pearce,' said Moore. 'And I thought he was a really hard man.'

It turned out, though, that tears were alright. Patrick Barclay was at the Stadio delle Alpi on that semi-final night, reporting for the *Independent*. He considers that the impact of Gascoigne's tears cannot be overstated.

'It was the beginning of the process that led to English football being the biggest in the world at club level,' says Barclay. 'Because it was the beginning of football as entertainment with the coincidence of Gazza's tears and a dramatic World Cup. I hope this doesn't sound sexist, but Gazza's tears broadened the audience.'

England, having produced their two most exciting tournament victories since the 1966 World Cup, against Belgium and Cameroon, had now given the record 26.2million audience watching at home another epic contest – and a hero with a vulnerable streak.

'It was one, two, three stunning games – probably among the greatest games England have ever played,' adds Barclay. 'It had a huge effect on English football and it's had a global effect too in that here we are nearly thirty years later, and English football is top of the world because every stadium is full all the time with men and women. You don't see people fighting in the stadiums, and the stars gravitate to it. The TV audiences love it.' Today, England's Premier League is available in an estimated one billion homes around the world.

There was change in the air already back then. 'World Cup adds fuel to a boom,' declared *The Times* on the opening day of the following season, 23 August 1990. The boom in question included rising attendances. The overall Football League aggregate for the four divisions would climb for a fifth consecutive year in 1990/91, for the first time in history. The First Division average crowd of 22,681 in 1990/91, meanwhile, would be the highest for a decade, as the recovery continued following the mid-80s when it had dropped three times below the 20,000 mark for the first time since World War One.

In that same *Times* article, there was news of Arsenal opening 'a massive sports retail store near their stadium', while Gordon Taylor, chief executive of the Professional Footballers' Association, observed, 'A lot of things which were coming together have been crystallised by the World Cup.'

With the fanzines, supporters' groups, and the stadium improvements precipitated by Lord Justice Taylor's 1990 report into the Hillsborough disaster, the gentrification of the game was beginning. In 1991, the Football Association in its 'Blueprint for the Future of Football' underlined this desired direction of travel when it stated that 'the response of most sectors has been to move upmarket so as to follow the affluent middle-class consumer . . . in his or her pursuits or aspirations. We strongly suggest that there is a message in this for football.'

By way of illustration, the play *An Evening with Gary Lineker*, about a group of friends watching the West Germany-England semi-final, reached the West End stage in late 1991 – another measure of the changing mood around a sport described by *The Times* in 1985 as 'a classic British declining industry'.

Comedian Arthur Smith, who co-wrote the play with Chris England, tells me: 'I remember speaking at the Hay-on-Wye book festival and Nick Hornby's book [*Fever Pitch*] had come out and we were there talking about the rebirth of football. It'd gone a bit more middle-class and without realising it, we'd captured a slightly zeitgeisty moment.

'The hooliganism element was a bit dissipated by the trippy ecstasy culture,' he adds. 'People on ecstasy don't want to punch each other. There was a feeling of optimism then, and the end of Thatcherism was maybe part of it too.'

Margaret Thatcher's resignation as prime minister had come in November 1990, eight months after riots in London against her government's unpopular poll tax. It was the end of a divisive eleven-year premiership.

As for Smith's play, it ends with a fantasy sequence in which England do in fact win a semi-final shootout they lost through Pearce and Chris Waddle's unsuccessful attempts. Smith laughs, 'Pearce apparently saw it and leapt up punching the air when we added he'd scored.'

AUTHOR PETE DAVIES HAS HIS OWN RECOLLECTION OF THE POST-Italia '90 climate. 'I remember a good friend of mine that I used to watch Chelsea with, going to the first game of the season in the autumn of 1990,' he tells me. 'He got home that evening and rang me and said, "It's completely different – there are women in the ground."'

Davies's book about the 1990 World Cup, *All Played Out,* features on its cover an image of Paul Gascoigne, teary-eyed and bare-bellied, with his England shirt pulled up to his nose like a giant handkerchief. As the pages inside reveal,

Davies gained a level of access to Bobby Robson and his players that a journalist in 2018 would not even dream about.

Speaking over lunch near his home in West Yorkshire, Davies offers an insight into life with Gascoigne in the England camp that summer. 'That affectionate phrase "As daft as a brush" is the best description there's ever been, and the kindest one,' says Davies, summoning Bobby Robson's oft-repeated quote. 'He was not anywhere near to a grown-up. He had no idea how to behave. I'm not saying he behaved badly. He could be very, very funny. But he had no off-switch.

'The most telling description of it is Waddle having to room with him and knowing he'd been effectively appointed as a babysitter. Gascoigne would be bouncing around the hotel with this infinite sub-fund of energy, and then he'd just stop and sleep for a bit – no routine or rhythm – and then, boing, up again.' Davies is not exaggerating here: Bobby Robson, in his autobiography, *Farewell but Not Goodbye*, cites the night Waddle had to take Gascoigne for an hour-long midnight stroll simply to burn off some of that excess energy.

'I got criticised a lot for stuff I'd put in the book at the time, and you can debate what I did and didn't use,' Davies continues. 'I'm comfortable with it. One of the things I didn't put in was that Gascoigne was drinking around the pool. He had a secret stash of Bailey's that he was putting in his coffee when he was lying by the pool in the afternoon.

'With hindsight, you look back and think, "This guy's going to have a problem." It was like having a child around the place. He'd pile in and contribute some bonkers thing. It might be funny, and then he started to talk to you, and you'd think, "Okay he's initiated a conversation," so you ask him a question and, "No comment," and, boing, he's gone again.'

Terry Butcher has similar tales about Gascoigne, though his recollection of the Bailey's supply is softened by the Labrador-pup lovability that accompanied him back then. 'Gazza always used to get to the hotel first, and he'd get three or four Baileys and put it in his coffee – his cappuccino, or "cappu-t-ino" as he called it. He couldn't say cappuccino.'

He remembers too when the players' wives came to stay and Trevor Steven replaced Waddle on babysitting duties. 'Gazza used to be up all night: "Come on,

Trevor, let's go and play table tennis. Come on, Trevor, let's go and play pool." He was sometimes a pest, but a nice pest.'

There is a line in John Barnes's autobiography where his old England colleague captures the essence of Gascoigne by describing him as a doer rather than a thinker. Barnes writes, "'Oh you two are always going on about football," he said, whenever I went into his room to talk to Chris [Waddle]. He would turn the music up loud or stick his fingers in his ears and chant, "La-la-la, I'm not listening ..." Gazza loved football but he never thought about it. He simply did it.'

In the season leading up to Italia '90, Gascoigne had a few moments where he was clearly not thinking. There was a complaint from the actress inside a Jess the Cat costume when he kicked the furry figure up the backside in a Post Office-sponsored warm-up at Ipswich Town in November 1989.

On New Year's Day 1990, he cracked a bone in his left hand in a clash with Coventry City's Lloyd McGrath. On his return to the Tottenham team at Chelsea five weeks later, he was booked for swinging a punch at John Bumstead.

Owing to ongoing doubts over his reliability – 'He was fat and played only twenty minutes in each half,' as Robson later put it – Gascoigne was not selected for England's friendlies against Italy and Yugoslavia at the end of 1989, joining up with the B team instead.

Indeed, he had made only one start for England, among seven overall appearances, prior to the Wembley friendly against Czechoslovakia on 25 April 1990, which proved his pitch-perfect audition for a World Cup starting role. He provided passes for two Steve Bull goals and a corner for Stuart Pearce to score before adding a late fourth goal of his own.

For one Czech player involved that evening, Michal Bílek, there is a different memory of Gascoigne: 'When we were lining up for the anthems, Gazza was pulling faces! He had three assists in that game, but I couldn't believe what he was doing.'

Everyone has a Gazza story. Bryan Robson's first encounter with his fellow Tynesider came after the then England captain had converted a penalty during Manchester United's 4-2 victory at Gascoigne's Newcastle United in 1986.

'I couldn't believe it, this young kid from the opposition came up to me as I was running back, and he just went, "Aye, that was a great penalty. Well done,"'

Robson tells me.

If Gazza's nickname for Robson was 'Dogshit' – because, as he tells his audience in Birmingham, 'he was everywhere' – the same went for Gascoigne on the night of that Czechoslovakia match.

'The top players rise to the challenge of big games,' Robson recalls. 'I always said to Sir Bobby, "I think it's a nice balance – me sitting in there now and letting Gazza get on with it." I just felt he could do special things on the ball, he could make things happen.

'I said to him, when he came into the team, "You just make sure you're always available, so if I'm working back and getting the ball off the back four or tackling people, I want to get it to you early, so make sure you keep getting into spaces." Gazza was great at that; he was great at getting in little pockets, and he was terrific at running at people or picking a pass.

'Gazza was bordering on being the best player in the world at that time. That's why we got to the semi-finals. You need some very good players, but you need a world-class player to get to the semi-final or win a final in the World Cup. Gazza turned it on unbelievably. He always had real confidence in his own ability. He'd express himself. That's what Gazza did in that 1990 World Cup. He just expressed himself. He wasn't afraid of the competition. He just went out and enjoyed himself.'

The clown prince was now the king of the action. Yet, the court-jesting continued – to the benefit, Robson suggests, of the players in his midst. 'You've got a lot of spare time on your hands, and he was always laughing and joking and enjoying the occasion, and that's sometimes where the England boys fall down a wee bit in competition football over the last sixteen, twenty years. We look as if we're afraid of it, and all the pressure's on you rather than just going there and enjoying it.' The pity for Robson is that by the time England's night in Turin came round, injury meant he was in a BBC studio in London.

ENGLAND'S JOURNEY DEEP INTO THE COMPETITION HAD SURPRISED many people. When the team's families arrived in Turin for the semi-final, their stay began with a lengthy search for accommodation, as Lady Elsie Robson, wife of the manager, recalls.

'The FA hadn't made any provision for hotels or anything because we all thought we were coming back,' she says. 'It was chaotic. We were bouncing around in the back of a bus, and they couldn't find any accommodation. I think Mr Lineker Sr wasn't too happy.'

That inconvenience paled beside difficulties elsewhere. Pete Davies recalls a sense of menace in a city where memories were still fresh of the part played by Liverpool supporters in the 1985 Heysel Stadium disaster.

'It was shit to be a fan in Turin for that game,' Davies says. 'Everything about it – trying to get hold of tickets, trying to find accommodation, trying to feel safe. You didn't know what the police were going to do and what the Italian local boys were going to do, and after the game there was some kicking off between some of ours and some of theirs. I remember getting off the train and thinking, "I don't like the look of this at all."'

For all the nostalgia that this semi-final stirs, the testimonies of those on the ground in Turin suggest a less rosy reality.

'It might be a bit romanticised,' says Steve Beauchampé, one of the organisers of the Football Supporters' Association's fan embassy. 'A lot of it comes from getting to the semi-final and losing the way we did – the whole Gascoigne thing. I wasn't conscious of that. I remember going out to the campsite [for England supporters], and it was under attack from Italian fans because England fans were winding up the Italians. Italy had been knocked out of their own World Cup, and some England fans were driving round sounding their horns.'

The *Daily Telegraph* described the scene at the Parco Ruffini campsite as 'an orgy of wrecking and looting' while the *Guardian* reported that around fifty Juventus supporters had tried to break into the site, prompting gangs of English fans inside to throw bottles, stones, and an iron bar, as the police fired tear gas into both groups.

Despite a police operation involving 7,000 officers, more violence followed on the day of the match. A German was stabbed in the back with a twelve-inch knife after fighting broke out between a crowd of Juventus supporters and English and Germans fans at the main Porta Nuova train station. An England fan was later stabbed in the chest and hands. After the game, back at the station, gangs of stone-throwing Italians, filling the air with shouts about Liverpool and Heysel, left some English victims with blood pouring from head wounds.

Thomas Schneider, a sociologist attending the match with a group of German football hooligans, describes the scene at the station. 'One of my group wanted to go back to Hamburg, and we took him to the train station and dropped him off just as the attack from the Italians started. At first, they were throwing stones. It was absolutely chaotic. They came from the arcades around Turin station. It was some hundreds. The English were really surprised. We were lucky that no stone hit us, but we saw these Turin hooligans with faces full of hate. The thing they were chanting was "Heysel Liverpool". They kept shouting all the time about revenge for Heysel.'

In England, the final whistle prompted eruptions of violence in at least a dozen towns. In Brighton, German students were chased through the streets by a mob of 200 youths, while in Eltham in south-east London, a rampaging gang smashed up German-made cars.

The trouble in Turin was not the first that English supporters had encountered since arriving on the mainland from Sardinia. There were 246 fans deported on a flight chartered by the Italian authorities in Rimini, following brawling outside a bar in the resort, The Rose and Crown. Suspiciously, the number arrested fitted exactly the number of seats on the plane.

Pete Davies suggests that the reporting of incidents involving England supporters had become more balanced by now. 'It stopped being so absolutely blind, two-dimensional – fans bad, hosts good. When people started getting beaten up when they hadn't done anything at all and getting deported for no reason other than they were English, the press started covering that, which in the past, they'd have just ignored.'

Another problem at the semi-final was tickets. While the official attendance at the Stadio delle Alpi would be some five thousand below capacity at 62,628, for England followers, there was a desperate scramble for tickets. Davies, in *All Played Out,* writes that the initial allocation was 'less than 1,000'. Steve Beauchampé, who worked frantically alongside the Football Association to acquire extra batches, relates, 'England had got very few tickets. On the Tuesday evening there were only about three thousand.' (Official ticket prices for the match, incidentally, ranged from between 23,000 and 180,000 Lira – or roughly between £10 and £80.)

As well as empty seats, there was another now anachronistic sight inside the Stadio delle Alpi: the Union Flag of the United Kingdom. Red, white, and blue was then the dominant colour scheme on supporters' flags. It was the flag of choice for the sports pages too. Even Paul Gascoigne, in a memorable TV clip in which Chris Waddle shoves a cake in his face, is wearing a pair of Union Jack swimming trunks.

Within a few years, the flag of England, the Cross of St George, had supplanted it.

Mark Perryman, author of *Ingerland: Travels with a Football Nation,* argues, 'The crucial moment was Euro '96. In '66, the flag was the Union Jack. That was part and parcel of the kind of confusion around our national identity. By Euro '96, there was no way on earth somebody would get the flag wrong – it was St George crosses everywhere. These are the last twelve months of John Major's regime [as prime minister], and it's very clear if New Labour is elected, they'll bring in a devolution referendum [for Scotland and Wales]. In 1990, Thatcherite politics was still reigning.'

The flag was changing and the fan experience too, albeit less quickly than might be imagined. 'Things don't happen overnight,' notes Perryman. The FA did not sell out its allocation for the 1992 European Championship in Sweden and, as Perryman avers, the first trouble-free tournament did not arrive until the 2002 World Cup in Korea/Japan.

*

FOR TERRY BUTCHER, LOOKING BACK ON THE BUILD-UP TO England's semi-final in Turin, the first memory is of a half-finished conversation with his manager, Bobby Robson.

'I was on my sunbed reading my book and he came and sat down on the bed beside me and got his book out. He's asking how the players are, we talked about the families coming out and then he said, "What do you really think about the semi-final?" and I said, "I think we have a great chance." I gave about a five-minute answer and then I said, "Well, what do you think, Gaffer?" and I looked around and he's fast asleep. I went in the pool and dive-bombed next to him and woke him up!

'"Vicky Verky" was one of his sayings – you know, vice versa,' he continues, remembering fondly his old manager's quirks. 'He used to call it Vicky Verky, and all the boys would look at each other snickering. I must say, in 1982, when he first got the job, his team talks were about three hours, and he whittled it down really well, and he was really inspiring and more inspiring than ever in that World Cup. You hung on his every word because there was always a mistake here and there – he got someone's name wrong or timings wrong or teams wrong. But when he really got passionate, it was great, he was like Churchill. Really stirring. It'd put the hairs up on the back of your neck.'

Robson was known to make his players smile with his default response to complaints of cabin fever – 'Hey, them lads who went to war, six years they were away,' as Chris Waddle once told me – so when it came to his team briefing before the semi-final, his players foresaw what was coming.

Gary Lineker explained what followed in the 2015 documentary film *Gascoigne*:

'Bobby Robson wanted a team meeting with all the players, but he was late for the meeting. He was always a bit late, and whilst he was late, I put on this board, "Even money he mentions the war". Then I put the sheet back down, and Bobby comes in, and we're all sitting there, and he goes, "We beat them in the war." It was his first words, and there was this uproar in the whole room.'

It was not just Robson mentioning the war. The back page of *Today* had a mocked-up image of Franz Beckenbauer in a World War One tri-plane and the headline 'England scare snoopy Red Baron' – a negligible reference to Beckenbauer's hopping on to planes to scout future opponents during the World Cup.

There is a loud splutter from Thomas Berthold, the former West Germany full-back, at the discovery that the war remained a topic of the conversation in the England camp.

'Really? Mamma mia!' he laughs. We are sitting in his favourite Italian restaurant in Frankfurt, his home city. So it never came up in the German dressing room at all, then? 'No, never ever. It's too far away for us. My grandfather was in the war but not myself.'

Berthold – for many years a respected TV pundit in Germany and, helpfully, a fluent English speaker – goes on to recall the mood in the opposition camp, beginning with Beckenbauer's dissatisfaction with the quarter-final display against Czechoslovakia, when a rare rage pierced his quiet but absolute assurance.

'Beckenbauer was furious after the match. Maybe it was pressure, but he was out of his mind, crying about how shit we were playing and blah, blah, blah. Klaus [Augenthaler] said, "Calm down now, we're in the semi final." We were winning one-zero with a man extra [after the sending-off of Ľubomír Moravčík], maybe Beckenbauer was expecting more.'

Soon, he was his unruffled self again. 'He asked us if we should leave on the day prior to the match or leave on the match day for Turin,' Berthold explains. '"Match day is fine," we said. We could have lunch there, then take a nap, have coffee, and then go to the stadium. Can you imagine this now? It's impossible.'

By stepping onto the Stadio delle Alpi pitch that night, West Germany established a then-tournament record of 67 matches played on the World Cup stage, surpassing Brazil's 66. It was their third successive semi-final. With a record like that, there was no need to dwell long on England.

Berthold says, 'This was always Beckenbauer's strategy – never talk about our opponents because he said we should play our game and put our strategy on the pitch, because we don't care about the opponents. From the first day, when we met in Italy to prepare the World Cup, I think everybody was convinced we'd make it. There was no doubt about it. Never. Not one second. Total conviction. And I think the manager should transmit this.

'They had great players in this squad, maybe with Gascoigne as the special one who could make the difference. But Beckenbauer said we had to play our match.' The message to his players delivered in typically insouciant fashion in his Bavarian dialect was *'Geht's raus und spielst Fußball.'* In English: go out and play some football.

*

AT THE DUNSTON EXCELSIOR WORKING MEN'S CLUB IN GATESHEAD, there was a rather blunter message left to hang in the air later that evening: 'Smash the German bastards!' It came from John Gascoigne, father of Paul, and was recorded by the reporter whom the *Guardian* had dispatched to Gazza's home patch on the banks of the river Tyne.

The north-east had five of its own involved on semi-final night – alongside Gascoigne, there were Peter Beardsley, Chris Waddle, and substitute Trevor Steven, as well as Bobby Robson.

'There was a real influx of players coming from the north-east in that fifteen, twenty-year period, going on to Alan Shearer,' says Bryan Robson, who would have made it six had he stayed fit. By comparison, since the turn of the century, there have been only three starting appearances by north-east footballers at the World Cup – Michael Carrick against Ecuador in 2006 and Jordan Henderson against Italy and Uruguay in 2014.

It is an arresting statistic, and it reflects the power shift in English football during the Premier League era, away from the old industrial north. 'Power and wealth in English football is increasingly clustered in the south,' wrote the *Guardian*'s Barney Ronay in 2016 when highlighting south London's emergence as a vibrant hotbed for young talents – particularly, in this case, for gifted black or mixed-race youngsters.

His point was underlined by the profile of the England teams who won the Under-17 and Under-20 World Cups in 2017: sixteen of the 27 players to appear in the two finals had progressed through London clubs and came from a black, Asian, and minority ethnic (BAME) background. There was not a single Geordie in either team.

It was all about two Tynesiders in the first 45 minutes in Turin. Inside 45 seconds, from a virtually instant corner, Gascoigne swung a left foot at the ball and tested goalkeeper Bodo Illgner's alertness. Soon, he was dispatching a second shot, again from the edge of the box, that flew into Illgner's midriff.

It was Waddle who shone most vividly in the first period, carrying the ball languidly into dangerous positions, supplying an inviting, outside-of-the-boot cross here, a fifty-yard diagonal ball there, and then pouncing on a loose pass and nearly beating Illgner from 45 yards, the goalkeeper touching the ball on to the crossbar.

'It surprised me a little bit from this distance,' remembers Illgner. 'I was lucky enough to get my fingertips on it. All the other games I didn't work too much, but I had to make some saves against England.'

As it happened, the save was superfluous, the referee having blown for a foul by David Platt on Augenthaler, but the ambition and execution from an Englishman on the world stage, were exemplary. Waddle had arrived at the Stadio delle Alpi minus mullet, having accepted £10,000 from the *Sun* to get those famous straggly strands shorn – a sum he donated to the cancer unit at Newcastle General Hospital. Yet, the Geordie Samson was in no way diminished.

Joining Gascoigne and Waddle in England's three-man midfield was Platt, another instinctively forward-looking player. Graham Taylor, England's next manager, wrote in his World Cup column in *The Times* that there was a 'movement and interchange of position in and from midfield areas that we have not seen for a considerable time in an England team'.

Beforehand Bobby Robson had warned Gascoigne not to stray out of position as he had done against Cameroon, telling him, 'You can't chase the ball'. Gascoigne's response? 'Boss, sit back and enjoy. I know what I have to do.'

Platt credits the manager for keeping the three together, when he could have chosen the more defensive-minded Liverpool midfielder Steve McMahon. 'What Bobby had was the ability to put complete trust in his players. They were a top, top team but you go out on to that pitch, and he puts belief into you as a team and belief as individuals. There's a real trust. It's basically, "You're in the team, now go and play, and I'll back you against Matthäus in midfield." It's a very good trait to have.

'Nobody would have put me, Gascoigne, and Waddle in the same midfield in international football had they looked at the predominant characteristics of the three players. But being in it, what we did have – and Gazza was involved in this as well – was a tactical ability to realise that your predominant characteristics sometimes have to take a back step.

'People would think it was me and Chrissie Waddle that filled in for each other, and one would go forward and one stay back and allow Gascoigne to do what he wanted, but Paul was tactically more astute than people gave him credit for.

'It wasn't a case of watching Matthäus. Sometimes, you have to get forward, you have to help the other two players, but we were never really out of position. If I was forward and Gascoigne was forward, then Chrissie Waddle was sat and vice versa. We dovetailed against our predominant characteristics if you like, and it worked because of that.'

At the other end, with Jürgen Klinsmann subdued by the England defence and Rudi Völler stymied by a calf injury which led to his early substitution, it took West Germany until the last ten minutes of the half to test England goalkeeper Peter Shilton, who smothered an Olaf Thon shot then fisted over Klaus Augenthaler's free-kick.

Terry Butcher reflects, 'We actually played the best football of the tournament in that game. I've seen a replay of the game, and we didn't dominate Germany. It was pretty even-stevens, but I felt at the time, and I still feel, seeing it, that we're going to win it. I still have that belief.'

He was not alone. On the half-time whistle, BBC presenter Des Lynam, back in the studio, turned to the camera and, laconic as ever, declared, 'Well, if you're not having a good time, we want to know why.'

The second half began to a different beat. Shilton made a save after Thon's menacing break into the England box. Then, after 59 minutes, West Germany edged in front. Matthäus had galloped eighty yards down the left touchline to instigate an assault on the England area. With Robson's men unable to escape their half, Thomas Häßler advanced again, Stuart Pearce cut him down outside the box and opportunity knocked for Andreas Brehme from the free-kick.

Thon laid the ball off, Brehme unleashed a shot, and the ball struck the right leg of the onrushing Paul Parker and looped high up into the air before dropping into the net behind Shilton. The goalkeeper had stepped a couple of yards off his line as Brehme shot. Now backpedalling, he got a hand to the ball in vain.

'As soon as he hits it and it gets the deflection, we all knew it was in,' says Butcher. 'Shilts had gone backwards but couldn't react, and it was in the back of the net. Bobby took me off, and then we went to four-four-two. Trevor Steven came on, and we got the equaliser.'

It is ironic that as against Cameroon, it was with the restoration of 4-4-2 that England found a way back. That it was with Lineker's first real sniff of goal was a measure of his clinical touch, as the 1986 Golden Shoe winner struck his tenth goal on the World Cup stage.

Parker played in a hopeful cross from out on the right. Jürgen Kohler misread its flight, and as the ball dropped off his knee, it landed in the path of Lineker. Spinning behind his marker Augenthaler, Lineker steered the ball on with his right knee, then drove it left-footed back beneath the lunging Kohler and into the far corner of Illgner's goal.

'It was a stupid goal,' says Thomas Berthold, one of the three defenders caught in a muddle then, and about to play his part in one of English football's iconic moments as the German floored by the Gascoigne challenge that brought the yellow card, and the tears that followed.

Extra time had begun with two clear openings for Jürgen Klinsmann – a header saved by Shilton, then a volley he sliced wide. Then, in the 99th minute, Gascoigne collected a ball from Peter Beardsley in the centre circle. He shrugged off Stefan Reuter first and then, seeking to evade Matthäus, pushed the ball too far ahead of himself. Cue a lunge at Berthold with the ball long gone and the German hitting the turf like a hooked eel.

'I just wanted my ball back,' Gascoigne said in his autobiography, *Gazza: My Story*. 'I hardly touched him. But he went down in a heap.'

When I point out to Berthold that there were doubts raised about the degree of contact – Ron Atkinson, commentating for ITV, speculated, 'It's a question of whether he actually caught the German player' – he seems genuinely surprised by the suggestion he had exaggerated the impact. 'Do you remember this foul? This was a tough tackle. Watch the video. It can change your mind.'

It is fascinating to revisit these moments in the official FIFA film of tournament. Gascoigne jumps up straight away with both hands raised in apology towards the referee before leaning over Berthold in a show of concern. At this point, he sticks his right forefinger into the defender's mouth. 'He screamed like a baby,' Gascoigne explained later, 'so I tried to put my fingers in his mouth to try and shut him up.'

Berthold chuckles. 'I don't remember this. He did this? Bastard!'

As Brazilian referee José Ramiz Wright raises his yellow card, Gascoigne closes his eyes and grimaces. And then, the never-to-be-forgotten trembling lower lip as Gary Lineker turns to the bench with a concerned look, gestures with a wobbling hand, and says, 'Have a word with him.'

'I don't remember his face, you know,' adds Berthold. 'I was there on the pitch with the physio. For him, it was bad. Now they've changed the rules, it can't happen anymore. To get a yellow card and be out of the final is a stupid rule. He had a great World Cup as well – he was brilliant, dynamic, quick.'

As play moves on around him, Ron Atkinson tells the ITV audience, 'He's in another world.' Yet, several minutes later, Gascoigne shakes a defiant fist to the England supporters crying, 'Come on, Gazza, come on, Gazza.' There is so nearly a goal for them to celebrate with the last kick of the first period of extra time as Chris Waddle latches on to Trevor Steven's header and angles a shot against the inside of the far post. The ball flies back just an inch or two away from the lunging David Platt.

Into the second period of extra time, Augenthaler strikes the same post for West Germany before Gascoigne exhibits remarkable composure as Brehme clatters him from behind, and he rises straight to his feet and shakes the full-back's hand. It shows an uncommon generosity of spirit, and it is hard to picture such a response from a player today.

From Pearce's resulting free-kick, Platt heads a goal which is ruled offside. 'I don't think I was offside when I scored from the free-kick,' he says. 'Nowadays, you'd find out by virtue of the fact there'd be twenty-seven cameras at every single angle.' The replay shows that both Platt and Gascoigne were no worse than level with the last defender. From 25 July 1990, the player level with the second-last opponent was officially no longer offside.

ENGLAND'S FIRST-EVER PENALTY SHOOTOUT WOULD BE THE START of a dispiriting trend. Peter Shilton actually guessed correctly for each of West Germany's first four kicks. Each time, though, the ball flew past him.

In a conversation with Chris Waddle one afternoon at Wembley in 2015, he reflected, 'I always think what a brave decision it would have been to bring Dave Beasant on for the penalty shootout. He was nearly an expert at it. After the tournament, we all thought, "Wouldn't it have been interesting if we'd put Dave Beasant on with thirty seconds to go?"' Two years earlier, Beasant had become the first goalkeeper to save a penalty in an FA Cup final.

For England, Lineker, Beardsley, and Platt all converted, but then up stepped

Stuart Pearce. The left-back, who took penalties for Nottingham Forest, had initially wished to take the third kick, but Robson wanted an experienced man at fourth.

His strike down the middle hit Illgner's shins as the goalkeeper dived to this right. 'I honestly have to say I felt calm and confident going into the penalties,' remembers Illgner, who had been practising spot-kicks along with the rest of the West Germany squad. 'I had the feeling I'd save one or another. Maybe that was youth – when you're twenty-three, you don't get too crazy about things.

'We didn't have any information on the penalty-shooters. I was just observing the striker, the way he was running towards the ball, and where he was placing his foot. Stuart Pearce was unlucky, as if I'd moved a little bit faster towards one side it might have gone in.'

He only needed to make the one save, as Waddle, taker of England's fifth kick, drove his effort high over the crossbar. Waddle took the kick owing to the frame of mind of Gascoigne, the man originally down to take it.

His recollection? 'I was going to put it to the goalie's left, and then when Stuart missed, I just thought, "Hit it." I couldn't strike the ball any better. It's probably not what people want to hear, but it's just one of those things. As soon as I hit it, I thought, "If it goes in, it'll probably be the best penalty anyone's ever seen." But it just kept going, didn't it?'

And it has kept on going. At the time of writing, prior to Russia 2018, England's shootout record is W1 L6. Germany's is W6 L1. The Germans' only defeat was in their first ever shootout, in the 1976 European Championship final.

What is their secret? Berthold, who was down to take their fifth kick against England, says, 'It's about being convinced to make it. It may be in our DNA. We have a huge track record in big competitions when it comes to penalty shootouts. Maybe this history is also in the mind of our opponents: "Shit. Now against the Germans. They always win." It's an advantage.

'When you have a penalty shootout, you need this, you have to be convinced to make it. If you're not convinced, if you have some doubts, you'll never make it. This has mainly been our mentality – there's no fear and no thinking about failure. At the end of the day, you need quality on the pitch and the quality on the pitch is the technical quality and the mental quality.'

This mental strength means that for Berthold, there is something curious about a semi-final defeat holding such a valued place in the collective memory of the English game. 'In Germany, the minimum expectation is to reach the semi-final. If you don't reach the semi-final, it's a disaster. In Germany, the mentality is very important – that you get the mentality to win the tournament. Sometimes, [Germany coach Joachim] Löw maybe was pushing more the mentality than the talented players.'

Of the English mentality, Arthur Smith, whose play *An Evening with Gary Lineker* celebrated a night that ended in tears, remarks, 'I suppose we're famous for always saying sorry when, in fact, someone has trodden on our foot.'

FOR THE WATCHING PELÉ, THE ENGLAND-WEST GERMANY MATCH was the best of Italia '90, a match of 'rhythm, emotion, timing', with only ten fouls committed. It ensured that England would end the tournament with FIFA's Fair Play award.

David Platt recalls, 'There was a big respect that was evident on the pitch. I remember in the penalties: Matthäus had just scored to go two-all, and he came past me and looked me in the eye. It didn't feel like a look of, "Right, now it's your turn, go and miss." To me, it was a look of respect and almost a "Good luck to you" even though he wouldn't have wanted me to score.'

Platt ended up with Matthäus's shirt, while Waddle got a comforting word and a pat on the back from the West Germany captain. Terry Butcher remembers Beckenbauer's stylish response too. 'I'd known Beckenbauer from when he was the manager of the Rest of the World team against the Americas after the World Cup in '86, and I was selected. He came up, and shook my hand, and hugged me.'

If there were tears, the drinks soon began to flow in the England camp. Thomas Berthold even went into the England dressing room, and if midfielder Steve Hodge told him to 'fuck off', to quote Stuart Pearce's autobiography, he recalls a generally 'friendly' response. 'I remember them having some drinks, some cigars,' says Berthold. 'They had a great mentality, this was a team full of characters. In those days, there were really men on the pitch.'

Terry Butcher continues the story: 'The two buses were next to each other, Germany's bus and our bus. We got on our bus having done all the press. We see the Germans on the other side, on their bus – they were only about five or six feet apart. They've got the water and are raising their glasses to us, and we're thumbs up to them. But Gazza finds the beer, so everybody's having a beer. We started singing the songs – "God Save the Queen", "Blaydon Races", "You'll Never Walk Alone". We started having a bit of a party, and the bus was actually rocking, you could feel it move from side to side because we were banging the windows. The Germans must have been looking at us, thinking, "Who's won here? God knows what they'd be like if they won."'

'Then the bus pulled away, and we went back to Juventus's training ground in Asti, and we drank their cellar dry. We just drank everything we could. It was brilliant in as much as it helped you sleep because you were that drunk. But when you woke up the next day, you had the hangover of losing the World Cup semi-final on penalties. Then it really hit home. And it hit home even more when you were on the plane then to Bari [for the third-place play-off] rather than going to Rome.'

Even before the excitement and emotion had sunk in, Michael Calvin, writing in his match report in the *Daily Telegraph*, hinted at the potential power of England's efforts. 'It will take some days for the England players to appreciate the impact of their best performance of an uneven tournament,' he suggested. 'There was much talk – as midnight came and went – of heads being being held high, of national pride being salvaged.'

The pride was palpable on Sunday 8 July, the day of the World Cup final, when 70,000 people greeted the squad as they landed at Luton airport and another 150,000 lined their route around the town. There were fans wearing T-shirts bearing the message, 'Heroes every one. England pride restored. Italy 1990'.

As for Paul Gascoigne, he donned a pair of plastic breasts over his England shell suit as he stood on the squad's open-top bus tour.

Within a few months, Gazzamania had brought the 23-year-old his own Spitting Image doll, an aftershave deal with Brut, and a number two record in the charts: 'Fog On The Tyne (Revisited)' with the Newcastle band Lindisfarne.

Before leaving Italy, Bobby Robson had given the following reflection on the road that lay ahead for Gascoigne.

'He appears to be on the threshold of something that is quite unique in football,' said Robson. 'He is different to everyone else in that he can do so many things ... He's got a terrific future providing he can strike the balance between joviality and seriousness.'

The caveat was telling. There was always one with Gascoigne, and Robson knew this better than anybody. Even in Bari, where Gascoigne was suspended for England's 2-1 defeat in the play-off for third place against Italy, the manager ended up worrying about the whereabouts of his midfielder.

Tony Damascelli, the Italian journalist then acting as media director for the local organising committee, was there that evening and remembers, 'Before the game, Gazza was missing. Bobby said, "Where's Gazza? Where's Gazza? Please, Tony, find him."

'He wasn't in the dressing room, not on the pitch, nowhere to be seen. He was in a private office with Luca Cordero di Montezemolo, just talking about the Italian football market and eating a Toblerone chocolate.'

It was on that evening that Gascoigne, who would end up signing for Lazio the following year, met Gianni Agnelli, owner of Juventus. However, the main recollection of Montezemolo, the man responsible for organising the World Cup, is of a conversation about food with England's star man.

'I met him in the place where they were training before the match. They were very generous with the catering, and I said, "Listen, don't go too far with this pasta." He said, "I love this pasta," as there was this special pasta in Bari called *orecchiette*. He was enthusiastic about Italy – he told me in Sardinia, he'd had a lot of sun, and the sea was fantastic.'

It sounds like a postcard sentiment, but then this was his dream trip. And in Robson, he had the perfect guide. As Gascoigne tells his Friday-night crowd in Birmingham, 'Sir Bobby Robson was like a second father to us; he had someone watching us all the time.'

Probably the most touching exchange between the two, and certainly the most poignant, is the one that appears in subtitles – the work of a lip-reader – to accompany images of manager comforting player on the pitch at the Stadio delle Alpi in the film *One Night in Turin*.

Robson says to Gascoigne, 'You've been absolutely magnificent, haven't you, yeah. You've got your life ahead of you. This is your first.'

It would be Gascoigne's only World Cup. But the connection with his old manager would endure.

'I think the bond was incredible,' says Mark Robson, describing a photograph of his father and Gascoigne on the Tyne Bridge, which hangs on a wall in the family home in Durham. Even on his final public appearance in July 2009, five days before his death, when he attended a charity match at St James's Park featuring players from the 1990 England and West Germany teams, Robson still had one person in particular on his mind.

'That was a few days before Dad died. His eyes were open, but I don't think he could recognise the players. He asked me, "How did Gazza play?" That was the question he asked straight away.'

Wind of change

'NOT UNEXPECTEDLY, THE WORLD CUP IN ITALY SET OFF AN AS YET unequalled echo, which continued to vibrate around the world long after the tournament had ended.'
FIFA general secretary's report to the Executive Committee (December 1990)

The first ball of the 1990 World Cup final was waiting to be kicked, but already the tone had been set. As the band began playing Argentina's national anthem, the screech of thousands of whistling Italians filled the Stadio Olimpico air.

When the TV camera reached the man with the white armband and dark glare at the end of the line of blue shirts, it did not take a lip reader to measure his mood. '*¡Hijos de puta! ¡Hijos de puta!*' he said, each word spat out in turn for the purpose of clarity. *You sons of bitches.* Not just once, but twice. Straight out of the mouth of Diego Maradona. Straight into living rooms around the world.

Edgardo Codesal, the Uruguayan-born, Mexican-affiliated referee of that deciding match between West Germany and Argentina on 8 July 1990, remembers the brief dialogue that came next. 'I said to him, "Diego, calm down. Things are different in a World Cup final, so keep cool and show who you are. Don't get angry."'

Maradona's response? 'No, mate,' as Codesal, speaking from his home in Mexico, recalls it.

Argentina's spikes were out. 'I tried to calm them, but they didn't want to know,' he adds. 'They came out in the wrong frame of mind for the match. The Argentina players started from the first foul in the opening minutes to say they'd been told FIFA didn't want them to win the World Cup, saying that everything was set up against them.'

As it happened, for Argentina's players, the defining moment of a match reasonably regarded as the worst of all World Cup finals did nothing to assuage that suspicion.

It came in the 83rd minute, when West Germany's Lothar Matthäus raced thirty yards from the halfway line and slipped a reverse pass to Rudi Völler down the right side of the Argentina box.

The Argentinian shadowing him, Roberto Sensini, attempted a tackle with his closer foot, his right. It was clumsy, and as Völler made contact with the outstretched leg and tumbled over, Codesal whistled for a penalty. With it, Andreas Brehme would win the World Cup for West Germany.

The ugly reaction of the Argentina players, eight of them surrounding the match official – and even barging into him, in the case of the yellow-carded Pedro Troglio – provided the perfect picture of a disheartening contest in which Codesal ended up dismissing two South American players.

Codesal delivers a rather technical explanation of the biggest decision of his biggest, and last, match as a referee. 'The Argentina player tries to play it with his right foot which, from a biomechanical point of view, is very difficult,' he points out. 'This kind of action you can manage if you use your left. When you use the wrong foot, you aren't going to reach the ball as it's too far and, it's quite probable there'll be contact.

'There's a shot from behind, where you see what I could see, and you can see the Argentina player tries to play it but doesn't touch the ball, and instead touches the opponent. And with his right forearm, he makes contact with the German player's waist, so for me, there was never any doubt.'

Then, the now-dominant argument that any form of contact warrants a fall had yet to gain its grip on the British football consciousness.

'He is a dying swan anyway, Völler,' said Ron Atkinson, co-commentating for ITV with Brian Moore. 'He actually has made contact with Völler,' added Atkinson, 'but Völler knows how to make a meal of it.'

Maradona would later lament that 'They stole that match from us.' The controversy was reignited in 1999, when Jorge Humberto Rojano, an ex-president of the Mexican referees' association, claimed that Javier Arriaga, Codesal's father-in-law and a member of FIFA's Referees' Commission, had told him subsequent to Italia '90 that FIFA had imposed a condition on the final referee that 'Argentina must not win under any circumstances.'

It is intriguing, therefore, to hear more from Codesal. When asked about Rojano's claim, he responds, 'Absolutely not. I was shut away in the hotel. There were no mobile phones then, and the phone in my room was disconnected. I had no information. We were just preparing for the game. It was when I showed the first yellow card after six minutes that various Argentina players said, "We know what's going on." Somebody had put the idea in their head they were going to lose that match.'

What infuriated the Argentinians further was the fact that Codesal had earlier ignored their own penalty claim when Matthäus made contact with substitute Gabriel Calderón inside the West Germany box.

'It's a light step on the toe, which, in that period, as the rules were, was not worth blowing a penalty for,' argues Codesal, noting that he had earlier ignored goalkeeper Sergio Goycochea's collision with Klaus Augenthaler on the edge of the six-yard box. 'If I'd had it in for Argentina, I'd have given a penalty then.'

Afterwards, Pierre Littbarski, the West Germany winger, told reporters that the penalty awarded to Völler 'seemed to be compensation for the foul committed earlier against Augenthaler'. Carlos Menem, Argentina's president, declared simply that Codesal, a doctor in his professional life, 'should stick to medicine'.

It was not just the penalty calls that stirred controversy. Codesal, then 39, became the first referee to send a player off in a World Cup final with his 65th-minute dismissal of Pedro Monzón, an Argentina substitute. The World Cup had waited sixty years for a red card in the final; Codesal waited just another 22 minutes before ordering a second player off in Gustavo Dezotti.

Reliving the first of those decisions, after Monzón caught Klinsmann flush on the shin with a studs-up lunge, Codesal says, 'When I see the way he goes in to hit the player, not to play the ball, clearly for me, it was a red. I have to confess that with my next step, I did think to myself, "There's never been a red card in a final, and this will be the first in World Cup history." I knew Argentina, the whole team, would be against me.'

As with Völler and the penalty, there was scepticism from Ron Atkinson in his ITV commentary position. 'It's a foul,' he said, 'but I'll tell you what, I mean you're giving him 9.5, 9.7, all sorts, when he hits the deck there.'

Klinsmann, for his part, spells out the damage done by the tackle, telling me, 'Monzón's foul was brutal and cut my shin open by four to five inches.'

Codesal flashed the red card again in the 87th minute: the already-cautioned Dezotti had grabbed Jürgen Kohler around the neck and pulled him to the ground after the time-wasting defender refused to hand the ball back.

'The Germany player actually had blood on his neck,' Codesal relates, though the TV images of Kohler show him patting an eye gingerly.

Once again, Ron Atkinson was unimpressed: 'He's one of those six-foot-four hard men, isn't he? About as soft as custard by the look of him.'

The Argentinians, in the meantime, were making their fury known. Dezotti and Pedro Troglio virtually sandwiched the match official as they leant into him, screaming their indignation. José Serrizuela crashed into his back.

Codesal's father, José María, a referee at the 1966 finals in England, had told his son that a World Cup final match official had to retire immediately afterwards - because, as he relates, 'He's been at the top of Everest, and the only thing after that was to go downhill.' In Argentinian eyes, his descent was already done.

'They said it showed they were being robbed, and this was a set-up by FIFA, and I was carrying out orders to make sure they lost,' adds Codesal, who, as he observes, actually had an Argentinian grandfather.

If Codesal looks back today on 'a night of very hard emotions', others look with a sceptical eye on this appointment in the first place, given that his aforementioned father-in-law, Javier Arriaga, was a key figure in FIFA's Referees' Commission in 1990.

Codesal believes it was reward for his efforts in the England-Cameroon quarter-final - 'I had the best game of my life' - but George Courtney, England's representative among the Italia '90 referees, says, 'Eyebrows were raised, yes, but nothing was said publicly. Whether Codesal deserved that on his ability is open to debate, but it didn't look good at the time and didn't sound good.'

Sepp Blatter, then general secretary of FIFA, concurs. 'Yes, yes. I was questioning that,' he tells me. Puffing air from his cheeks, Blatter adds, 'The final wasn't a good final anyway, and the decision of a penalty kick in the last ten minutes ...'

In the aftermath of the final, Maradona was explicit in his accusations of foul play. 'There was a black hand at work,' he said. 'It's a shame I don't have the proof to name names, but a referee can't fail to see the penalty committed on Calderón and then give a penalty for Völler's fall.'

In Maradona's eyes, this was payback for his claims the previous December that the World Cup draw had been fixed to favour Italy. 'Don't talk to me any more about fair play,' he added. 'It's a fairy tale.' *Il Giorno* picked up on his accusations with the front-page headline 'World Cup has stamp of the Mafia'.

When I mention Maradona to Sepp Blatter during an interview with the former FIFA president in Zurich, he replies, 'He's a problematic man, definitely, and I've known him very well.'

I have met Blatter at Der Sonnenberg, a restaurant beside the old home of FIFA, a large villa still housing the governing body's commercial division. We are at an outside table, beneath a canopy of plane trees. The air is sweet, and the view striking as the vineyard below gives way to the rooftops of Zurich and a smooth, blue strip of lake. The FIFA flag curled around its pole indicates the stillness of the warm, late summer day.

It is more than two years since Blatter's departure as FIFA president. Today, after the serial corruption scandals, FIFA.com's 'History of FIFA' section devotes just 53 words to 'The Blatter Years', yet his work as general secretary in the aftermath of the 1990 World Cup should not be ignored.

When asked about his response to Italia '90, Blatter, dressed smartly in a navy cotton jacket and light blue open-necked shirt, takes a scenic route with his answer: 'It was the most exciting World Cup when it came to catering in the stadiums and the reception from the Italians in all the cities. That was just perfect, and it's never been matched so far. The French tried to, but they couldn't, because they were greedy.

'The World Cup [in Italy] was a big theatre, a big event, but the problem was the football itself. One of the most important things was the match control wasn't good – and why? Because at the time, you had referees on the line.

'It was always said it's a team that controls the match, but it was not a team –

and especially in the first matches, they'd even be eager that the one in the middle would commit some mistakes in order that he couldn't go on. Because they had to cut part of the referees after the first part of the competition and were even happy if somebody made mistakes. It's incredible.'

Blatter offers the example of the Italian Luigi Agnolin's conduct as a linesman, describing how 'a referee went to him to ask him something, and he was walking away'. He continues: 'Then, you had the other extreme, and this was [Frenchman Joël] Quiniou in the semi-final in Turin. He kept waving his flag as if to say, "Something's wrong," so the referee [José Ramiz Wright from Brazil] had to go to him and say, "I'm the boss and not you." This was such nonsense to have the best referees and to put them on the line.'

(Edgardo Codesal, incidentally, volunteers another example: Diego Maradona's 1986 'Hand of God' goal, allowed to stand by Tunisian referee Ali Bin Nasser, who later claimed he had waited for a signal from Bogdan Dochev, the Bulgarian running the line. 'There was the notion the assistant could have seen the play but never reacted.')

As FIFA general secretary, Blatter received hundreds of letters from the public following Italia '90, and in his end-of-year report on the World Cup to the Executive Committee, he noted that the criticism of the refereeing had been 'partly justified' and demanded that the 'duties of a linesman must be clearly separated from those of a referee'. There was also a call to consider professional referees.

At every World Cup up to 1990, the match officials selected would perform two roles: refereeing some matches, and running the line at others. It would never happen again. USA '94 featured dedicated referees' assistants for the first time. Since Germany 2006, meanwhile, each referee has worked as a team with assistants from his own country, or, in certain cases, from his confederation.

Along with the standard of refereeing, the other prominent discussion point from Italia '90 was the number of goals scored: 115 in 52 matches which produced the World Cup's lowest scoring rate of 2.21 per game.

Suggested solutions for the former, Blatter wrote at the time, 'varied from increasing the size of the goals to reducing the number of players'.

Franz Beckenbauer, an influential voice, was in favour of exploring the possibilities of both bigger goals and ten-man teams. To take such ideas and develop a plan to uphold football's appeal, Blatter established the Task Force 2000. Its members included Michel Platini, then national coach of France, and Rudi Völler, as well as Graham Kelly, chief executive of the Football Association.

At a meeting, the members gave Italia '90 a mark of 6/10 for the quality of football, though Blatter was more critical, writing, 'The tactical-scientific game has not losing as its main aim, and to this end artistry in football, creativity and technical skills have largely been sacrificed ... FIFA must reintensify its efforts to protect and develop the artistic side of football. "Go for goal" must once again become the main drive in the sport, and here referees can play a key role.'

THE MEETING OF THE IFAB – THE INTERNATIONAL FOOTBALL Association Board, the game's law-makers – which took place in Rome on 28 June 1990 represented a major milestone. There was an amendment to the offside law, in force from 25 July, whereby the attacker was now onside if level with the last defender. Additionally, the IFAB delivered a mandatory instruction that the 'professional foul' denying a goalscoring opportunity must be punished by a red card. This became law the following year.

The change had arrived too late to take full effect at Italia '90: even if the referees had received instructions to this effect beforehand, not everyone put them into practice.

According to Blatter's report to the Executive Commitee, these instructions 'were only assimilated and put into practice by a few – about a third of them [while] another third – sad to say – were unwilling even to consider the new ideas'.

The view of Edgardo Codesal is that some referees felt the instructions arrived too soon before the tournament and 'caused quite a lot of confusion'.

More changes were coming, notably with the 1992 ban on goalkeepers handling back-passes, following a successful trial at the 1991 Under-17 World Cup. In 1995, the concept of passive offside entered the Laws of the Game.

Blatter remembers seeing a succession of back-passes during United Arab Emirates v Colombia first-round match and telling himself, 'Something is wrong in this game.'

He elaborates, 'There was no rhythm. It was a pity to show this match. The United Arab Emirates were playing, and they were the champions of keeping the ball, and they gave it always back to the goalkeeper. If somebody attacked, they gave it back to the goalkeeper. The goalkeeper had it in his hands, gave it to the other side, and then he gave it back, because it was permitted then.

'The back-pass and the foul of the last defender was where we started. You could commit fouls from behind and get a yellow card or perhaps nothing. Really, it would have been wrong if nothing had happened to the game. That's why we decided – and it was my initiative – to have this committee of football for 2000.

'What was difficult to insist to the referees was that the foul by the last defender is a red card, even if it's in the middle of the field. Now, it's obvious.'

As a consequence, where Maradona suffered 53 fouls in seven matches at Italia '90, the equivalent sum for Lionel Messi from the same number at Brazil 2014 was just eighteen. (Arjen Robben, the most-fouled player, was still some way short of Maradona's total with 28.)

Blatter, by his own admission, found himself at odds with the refereeing community at times. He once told journalist Patrick Barclay, 'We should put lead in their flags because if they never raise their flags in a whole game they would make fewer mistakes than they do now.' Yet he certainly knows his history on the subject. He takes me right back to the game's early years at one point in our conversation to explain how a neutral figure would stand at the side of the pitch so that 'when something happens they'll refer to him' and how 'this man became the referee'.

'This is all in books in our library in FIFA,' he adds. 'They're books I read when I started coming to FIFA, and I'm sure that those who are in charge of FIFA, the big bosses up there, haven't looked in these books.'

George Courtney offers his own take on Blatter and the 1990 'watershed', as he describes it. 'I knew Blatter many years, and he loved to court the headlines. He might have been partially right but what he did was put a lot of pressure on referees to stick to the FIFA diktat.

'The problem was, we were told to referee to order to put an end to, I think the term was, violent play. But it was strange to me, because the style of refereeing I'd been used to was that I refereed in a proactive fashion. As with Michel Vautrot, we were of the school that worked with players on the pitch – talking to players, listening to players, sharing a bit of fun – and I think 1990 saw the demise of that style of refereeing. It became much more reactionary, if you like, with the emphasis on yellow cards and red cards.

'FIFA wanted to cut out the late tackle from behind, and that was the beginning of the end of strong tackling. We see so little of good, physically strong tackling now. That has more or less been outlawed, so I think 1990 was a bit of a watershed, but not necessarily for the better in my opinion.'

That said, Courtney does view two changes in a positive light. He recounts that a significant number of Italia '90 referees failed the first fitness test at their initial pre-finals meeting in March that year – 'I remember Blatter raising hell about the poor levels of physical fitness' – and applauds the introduction of dedicated linesmen.

'The performances of the referees who were acting as linesmen wasn't good enough. That was a big change. I ran the line in two games in 1990, and my preparation for that was I ran the line at York, I ran the line at Carlisle, I ran the line at Walsall. For a World Cup, to have that kind of preparation wasn't good enough.'

An example from the penultimate fixture of Italia '90 is still shown today to up-and-coming international referees as an illustration of the bad old days: namely, the header that Italy's Nicola Berti scored against England in the third-place play-off, a goal ruled offside despite the fact four opposition players stood between Berti and goalkeeper Peter Shilton when Roberto Baggio delivered a diagonal cross from deep.

*

THE SUNNY MOOD AT THE END OF ITALIA '90'S THIRD-PLACE MATCH – both teams doing a Mexican wave before the Italy players joined their England counterparts in an arms-pumping 'Let's all have a disco' jig – was certainly not mirrored in the Argentina camp as their players prepared for the final.

Indeed, simmering resentment over their villain-of-the-piece status had already begun to bubble over.

Two days after the semi-final in Naples, Maradona's brother, Raúl – better known as Lalo – decided to take his sibling's red Ferrari for a ride but found himself stopped at the gates of Argentina's Trigoria base by police asking to see his papers. Although Maradona's wife Claudia came and vouched for him, it was not enough. When an incensed Maradona appeared at the scene, trouble erupted. Newspaper reports suggested that both Maradona and his brother-in-law struck police officers after one of them had insulted the Argentina captain. After the ensuing brawl, both a police officer and a security guard needed hospital assistance.

That was not all. Argentina's ambassador to Italy, Carlos Ruckauf, said he had received a call with a hoax bomb alert. Back at Trigoria, two days before the World Cup final, another incendiary incident occurred when the Argentinian flag was ripped down from its pole.

This last insult deepened Maradona's paranoia. 'We were cannon fodder because we'd knocked Italy out of the World Cup,' he claimed. 'They weren't going to forgive us that. We'd buggered up the final the business interests wanted: Italy v Germany! And as if that wasn't enough, we'd knocked Brazil out!'

An alternative theory is that Carlos Bilardo was actually behind a controversy that strengthened his squad's siege mentality. 'They say Bilardo arranged for it to be done,' suggests midfielder Julio Olarticoechea, though naturally, the man himself denies it.

'How was I going to do that?' says the former Argentina coach. 'They've said a lot of things about me in football. But nobody ever produced a photo or a witness. They wanted to insult the players.'

Bilardo is not entirely dismissive of another notion, though – namely, that there were influential forces favouring a West Germany victory. 'That could be true. It was like that with [the rivalry between] South America and Europe. It still happens.'

Others from that Argentina side are more sceptical. 'We're always looking for things like thinking the referee's been bought – it's in our mindset, to mistrust everything,' Sergio Goycochea reasons. 'People make mistakes.'

Olarticoechea goes further still. 'There was that feeling that the referee, with any questionable decisions, always ruled against us. But the reality is we had three key absentees, and Maradona was at half-capacity. I don't like to look for excuses, like blaming FIFA. I don't agree.

'[Maradona] likes that, he likes to take on the world. He has no filter. What he thinks, he says, but sometimes you can't always say what you think. There's a saying, "You're a slave to your words, but master of your silence." This is a country with so much passion, so much madness, but you lose balance when you talk.'

The West Germany camp was a calmer place to be. There was a strong-rooted confidence too. For Thomas Berthold – as with Rudi Völler, his teammate at AS Roma – there was even the advantage of playing the World Cup final at his club's home stadium.

'I remember before the World Cup, I was passing the Piazza Vittorio Emanuele, and the Banca Nazionale del Lavoro is there,' Berthold recounts. 'I was passing by it, and the World Cup trophy was there, just arrived in Rome. I said, "Hey, buddy, in a few weeks, I'll grab you." I remember this day like it was yesterday.

'For Rudi and myself, it was a special World Cup because the venue of the final was Rome, our city where we lived and played. How often does that happen to you as a player in your lifetime?

'In football, you need a tactical set-up; you need skills, but the mental aspect is big. If you're convinced about winning something, it gives you a boost. Most of us were like that.'

Berthold and Völler, together with Andreas Brehme and Lothar Matthäus, were survivors of the countries' 1986 final encounter in Mexico City. 'This was a completely different match,' Berthold continues. 'In '86, Argentina were the favourites and we were the underdogs. In '90, it was a one-way match, because [Claudio] Caniggia was out and he was the best striker, the only weapon they had. Without Caniggia, the rest of the Argentinians were always behind the ball. It was not nice for the viewers. I think Bodo Illgner never caught a ball. Not from the Argentinians.'

Over the ninety minutes, the only save Illgner would make came in first-half stoppage time from a lobbed back-pass by his own teammate, Brehme. 'I was the first one to keep a clean sheet [in a World Cup final],' Illgner recalls. 'I didn't have any work at all, almost.'

On the eve of the game, the Argentina skipper's personal doctor, Rubén Darío

Oliva, had been summoned from his home in Milan to give Maradona an injection in his back. One last numbing of the pain, but it would prove in vain, as midfielder Pierre Littbarski, playing in his second World Cup final, explains.

'We had a four-player plan against Maradona, so every time he had the ball, our strategy was to attack him from four sides. I hear Beckenbauer still saying, "Forget your personal opponent. When Maradona has the ball, we must put four players around him. He can't do anything." That was the only strategy we actually used for Argentina.

'There was one player, [Guido] Buchwald, who played man on man against him. But when he was on our left side and I was standing there, you'd have me and Andreas Brehme, and one central midfielder like Matthäus too. That was the plan.

'I've watched the game again, and you see a few situations where we were able to cut him really out. We said we had to destroy his fun for football, and he got more frustrated and angry.'

It was a match of few pleasures, even for the huge contingent of around 40,000 Germans in the stadium. Brehme's dead balls caused Argentina occasional anxiety. Early in the second half, the unmarked Berthold connected with a Brehme free-kick beyond the far post but could not keep his header down. In the same period, Littbarski, jinking inside from the left, curled a shot a fraction wide.

Carlos Bilardo's last words to his players before they left their dressing room had been, 'Lads, I'm proud of you. We need one more step. Give what you've got left.'

Unfortunately, what they had left was very little. The aforementioned suspensions meant three veterans of the 1986 final – Sergio Batista, Ricardo Giusti, and Olarticoechea – were absent, together with Caniggia.

It was now that Olarticoechea felt the force of this absence. 'Caniggia was crying when he realised he'd miss the final,' he recalls. 'For me, it was the day of the game when my teammates were changing, then I realised what I was missing. You had Caniggia, our striker, and Giusti, who was our motor in the middle, and me – all of us had done really well against Italy.'

For Bilardo, it was the absence of Caniggia that hurt most. 'Germany don't sit and wait. If they can attack you, they will. If you sit back, it's goodnight.

You always need one or two who'll attack. Caniggia was very good up front, and on his own, he'd have made the difference.'

Sepp Blatter has some sympathy for Bilardo. 'It was an ugly game, because the Argentina coach said, "I have no more players." That's also one thing – players could be suspended after the semi-final, and this changed. When going into the semi-final, you nullify the yellow cards. It changed later, but the idea was sowed then.' (Not until after Germany's Michael Ballack missed the 2002 final because of a semi-final yellow card did this change occur – and only in time for South Africa 2010.)

Dezotti, the man deputising for Caniggia, had scored thirteen Serie A goals for relegated Cremonese that season, but he was an isolated figure in the lone striker's role. Instead, he earned the first of his yellow cards after only five minutes for his fiery response to a soft free-kick awarded by Codesal following a challenge on Littbarski.

When Argentina did find a whisper of hope, as José Basualdo won a free-kick on the edge of the box before half-time, Maradona curled his shot over the crossbar.

The goal that put the match out of its misery came with Brehme's penalty six minutes from the end. Lothar Matthäus had scored from the spot against Yugoslavia and Czechoslovakia but now deferred to his Inter teammate. The reason? West Germany's captain was playing in a pair of borrowed boots.

It is something unimaginable today, when Germany players go into major tournaments with four pairs from Adidas, two for hard ground and two for soft. Not in 1990. Matthäus explains: 'We didn't have tons of gear with us and to be honest, I was playing that tournament with one pair of boots. The sole broke in the first half, and at half-time, I had to change into a brand new pair, which someone passed on to me. They were half a size bigger than my real size, so I didn't feel comfortable enough, and I was a hundred per cent sure Andi Brehme would score it.'

The curious thing about Brehme's winning kick was it came from his right foot; his semi-final free-kick against England was a left-foot strike. Now, he tucked a penalty into the bottom-right corner of Goycochea's net with his supposedly lesser foot. 'You couldn't really tell which foot was better,' remembers Illgner.

Brehme's virtuosity was of no comfort to *The Times*, which delivered the following scathing verdict: 'The deplorable World Cup final of 1990 will be remembered not for the way West Germany won it, mechanically and without style, but the manner in which Argentina lost it, disgracefully.'

David Miller, the *Times* writer in question, went on to find fault too in the 'frenzied close-ups' of the celebrating Germans on the giant screens.

This was just one aspect of the big spectacle the organisers signed off with at the Stadio Olimpico. As a forerunner of today's overblown trophy ceremonies, it was perfect: models wearing sweeping robes and tacky headpieces depicting Italian landmarks – including a rather phallic-looking Leaning Tower of Pisa – welcomed the Germany team on to the rostrum to collect their medals and trophy. 'Nessun Dorma' echoed around the stadium, and then 'We Are The Champions'. Cue the dimming of the stadium lights, and a show of fireworks and searchlights and smoke. At this point a graphic declaring West Germany as 'World's champion' [sic] appeared on TV screens worldwide.

Keith Cooper, later FIFA's director of communications, was in the stadium that night and remembers one or two unwelcome surprises. The first, he remembers, came when one of the toga-clad models opened her mouth and issued a distinctly non-Italian 'Nice 'ere, innit?'

The second, when the lights dimmed, was more problematic as Cooper, then working for FIFA's marketing partner ISL, explains: 'It involved turning the entire stadium into darkness at the vital moment of the cup handover. This drove the hundreds of photographers mad, as they had no idea, in those pre-digital days, of how to set their cameras for the historic moment so quality pictures of the German team with their trophy were few and far between. The German FA was obliged to re-stage a photo op with the players in an empty Frankfurt stadium a few days later.'

For Pierre Littbarski, the highlight of the celebrations was a hug – an actual hug – from *Der Kaiser* himself, the imperious Franz Beckenbauer. He grins as he recalls, 'We had this "distance hugging". We didn't want to get his suit wet or come too close to his face. Still, when we meet now, we have a little bit of distance because we have a lot of respect there. He was happy to hug us, but he didn't know how. It was really funny.'

Beckenbauer had just matched the feat of Mário Zagallo in conquering the world as player and coach. His goalkeeper coach, Sepp Maier, had also played in West Germany's victorious 1974 World Cup team, though he was rather less regal in his celebrations.

'I remember that at nine-thirty in the morning, a few of our guys were still in the pool with beers along with Sepp Maier,' says Thomas Berthold, who adds that Maier was showing the effects by the time the team arrived at the airport, bound for home.

'A lady came and asked, "Mr Maier, please be so kind as to tell the players the German ambassador would like to make a speech." And Sepp Maier was drunk, and he said, "German ambassador, who cares? We're the world champions and he is the *bademeister,*" which means the attendant of the public swimming pool. It turns out this lady was the ambassador's wife!'

On the celebrations back in Frankfurt, his home city and site of the DFB headquarters, Berthold adds, 'The highway from the airport was packed, and there were people actually walking beside the bus. It was crazy. When we were in Italy, our families were saying, "You can't imagine what's going on in our country," but we'd not seen German TV. They'd said the whole World Cup was one party, with public viewing, and for us, it was brand new. Maybe this was a change in the mind of German football supporters – celebrating together, with flags, making parties.'

The party concluded at the Römer, Frankfurt's historic city hall. Here, on the balcony, the pink, medieval gabled façade behind them, Beckenbauer and his team stood with their golden prize. Standing in the market square below, on the day of my interview with Berthold, I speak to a woman from the tourist office who was there on that July day in 1990. 'It was a sea of people,' she remembers. 'All you could see were heads.'

✳

FOR WEST GERMANY, IT WAS THE END – AND NOT ONLY OF THEIR Italian adventure. On 19 July, the German Football Association (DFB) made a statement confirming plans to unify the leagues of East and West. Political reunification arrived on 3 October.

Then, eleven weeks later, on 19 December, a football milestone: an all-Germany team faced Switzerland in a friendly match, the first outing of an official Germany XI since 1942. Berti Vogts's squad included five former East Germany players, notably Matthias Sammer and Andreas Thom. The latter scored within 25 seconds of replacing Sammer in a 4-0 win.

Sammer would be a central figure in their Euro '96 success. Michael Ballack, the product of a state-run sports school in the eastern town of Görlitz, drove Germany to the 2002 World Cup final. But not until 2014 did a unified Germany win the trophy again.

On the night of their 1990 World Cup final triumph, Beckenbauer had told reporters, 'With players from the East joining, the German team will be unbeatable. I'm sorry about that for the rest of the world.' It did not turn out that way.

Pierre Littbarski laughs as he remembers Beckenbauer's words. 'He gave that quote which Berti Vogts was not really happy about, because he was taking over the team!'

It was not easy, he adds, for players from the East Germany side to step into a team that had just won the World Cup. 'With players like Ulf Kirsten, Thomas Doll, and Andreas Thom, you know they're fantastic in terms of quality, but you know also that they've grown up in a different environment, in a different training environment.

'I had a good relationship with Falko Götz, and I knew Ulf Kirsten and Andreas Thom, and I knew they were holding back a little bit in the beginning. They were big players in the East Germany team, but they now had to fight in an absolutely new team which was world champion, so this situation was not easy for the players or the coach.'

The late 90s would be a period of relative decline – by German standards – for the national team. Raphael Honigstein's book *Das Reboot* cites several factors, such as the impact of a wave of imports after the 1995 Bosman ruling and the fact that 'the influx of GDR-trained professionals who were supposed to make "Germany unbeatable for years to come" [had] all but dried up along with the state funding.'

In response, the DFB made it compulsory for the clubs in the top two divisions to have academies – the catalyst for the current generation of sparkling talents.

As for those clubs which had led the way in East German football, they faced hard times. In 1991/92, the first season after reunification, Dynamo Dresden and Hansa Rostock stepped into the Bundesliga – and ended the campaign placed fourteenth and eighteenth respectively.

'Football is always a mirror of society, and the first ten years were very, very difficult,' says Jörg Jakob, chief editor of *Kicker* magazine. 'Some guys tried to take over clubs like Dynamo Dresden – one guy from Frankfurt [Ralf-Jürgen Otto, an entrepreneur later imprisoned for criminal offences in connection with his construction firm] almost ruined the club. Dynamo Dresden are a big sleeping giant in Germany with a huge fan base.'

In the 2017/18 season, Dynamo played second-tier fotball. Magdeburg, the only club from the GDR to lift a continental pot – with the 1974 Cup Winners' Cup – were in the third tier. Lokomotive Leipzig – runners-up in the 1987 Cup Winners' Cup – were in the north-east section of the fourth tier. The single eastern club competing in the Bundesliga at the time of writing are RB Leipzig, the Red Bull-fuelled team only in existence since 2009.

Returning to the Germany national team, there is something else Jakob mentions that resonates in a reflection on then and now. It concerns the respective responses to the victorious German World Cup teams of 1990 and 2014. 'In those days, they were footballers; nowadays, they're more young sportsmen playing football,' he argues. 'They have another lifestyle. There's more science and intelligence, and their fitness is better. Those guys [in 1990] were known as footballers with all the good and bad bits. Today they're more the type of young man a mother-in-law would like.'

Curiously, 7,000 miles away across the Atlantic, it is possible to hear a similar perspective from a couple of members of Argentina's 1990 squad.

When the *Albiceleste* flew back to Buenos Aires after their defeat in Rome, their journey from Ezeiza International Airport to the Casa Rosada, the presidential palace, took five hours. There they were met by a crowd of up to 80,000 people. Writing in *Clarín*, Sergio Sinay, the Argentinian essayist and journalist, said, 'Neither in 1978 nor in 1986 did we reach the levels of nervousness, anxiety, emotion, passion, commitment which this team shone the way with, and that 33 million Argentinians shared in.'

Given the nature of their Italia '90 campaign – a feat of endurance that took in two penalty shootouts and tens of thousands of chewed fingernails – Sergio Goycochea suggests it carried an emotional resonance beyond the 2014 Argentina team's run to the final in Brazil against Germany.

'I get people coming up to me, and congratulating me and saying thank you. We weren't world champions, we were runners-up, but it was such a big emotional connection. A lot of people say the best World Cup song was Italia '90, that this was the last great World Cup.

'It has to do with how people feel, how football changed commercially. In 2014, it was the same result against the same opponent. People appreciated it, but they didn't feel it as they felt the runners-up spot in '90.

'The thing is, people identified with us. We started badly. We had injuries. They saw the effort of the players. It didn't matter how we played, as they saw we gave everything. Here in Argentina, you don't [normally] celebrate finishing second.'

Another factor is the game's globalisation. Italia '90 happened in a time before Bosman and super clubs. A time before satellite television and the internet made the football world a small place. A time of local heroes, still.

Of Argentina's 1990 squad, nine of the 22 played at home. By 2014, only three of the 23 were Argentina-based. Seven of their starting XI in the final at the Maracaná had left the country aged 21 or under. An eighth, Lionel Messi, their best player, had never actually played in Argentina.

Goycochea adds, 'They leave the country really young and barely play here, so people have no relationship. We're really used here to people being right on top of you. In Europe, it's done differently so when they come here, players who've been in Europe don't do individual interviews, they give a press conference, whereas the Argentinian journalists are used to something else. I'm not saying it's either good or bad, but they find something they're not used to, and it's a shock.

'I think people have changed too, not just the players. With social media, they have more information, they have a different level of opinion. Also, the lads are formed in a different way. It was more sentimental, with a love of the shirt. It's more commercial now, and this means more of a distance. People will say,

"They've got loads of money." In the past, this insult didn't even exist.'

According to Julio Olarticoechea, these emigrés are accused, unfairly, of having a *'pecho frío'* – literally, a cold chest, that is to say, lacking passion. 'When Argentina lose, they think they don't care, but they're wrong. They lost two finals – to the best Chile in history [in the 2016 Copa América] and against Germany.'

However, he believes one thing has been lost: *picardía*, the cunning and street-smarts, which found its most glaring expression in Diego Maradona's 'Hand of God' goal.

'I talk about it a lot now, that the Argentinian player is losing his cunning. Why? Because there are no *potreros*. This is the waste ground where boys would just play, you'd find them everywhere. We'd play two or three hours a day. After school, you'd play until the sun went down. When you could no longer see, the game would stop. We didn't have mobiles. We didn't have TV, at least not in my town.

'Now I see the children in my town, they all have cell phones; they rollerblade around; they have scooters; and yes, they go to their club and train an hour or two a day, two or three times a week. That's three and a half hours' training a week.

'We had three hours a day. And on the waste ground, you got used to playing with bigger boys, you got kicked, and you had to get used to it. And you'd find bushes, and puddles, and stones, and the ball would jump around; and you'd get a pass, and the ball could fly at you in different directions, and this gave you your technique.'

It is not only in Argentina where you will hear laments like these. The game has left our streets and taken over our screens. Commerce has killed romance.

Planet Football has changed in so many ways since Italia '90. In some ways for the better, in others for the worse. That's the thing about a world in motion, though. It keeps on turning, whether we like it or not.

EPILOGUE

'THE WORLD CUP BETRAYED.' SO PROCLAIMED THE *GAZZETTA DELLO Sport* in an article on 10 July 1990, two days after the final between West Germany and Argentina, in which the Italian sports daily reflected on the good, the bad and the ugly of the 14th World Cup finals.

The irony of Italia '90 nostalgia, be it in England or elsewhere, is that this was the most sterile of all football's global showpieces. It drew the highest attendances since 1970 – with an average of 48,368 – but registered the tournament's lowest-ever goals-per-game ratio of 2.21. As an illustration of the risk-averse approach, there were only two 1990 World Cup matches in which a team came back to win, without recourse to penalties, after conceding the first goal: Costa Rica against Sweden in the group stage and England against Cameroon in the quarter-finals.

Indeed, of the 52 fixtures overall, fifteen of them (28.85 per cent) finished 1-0. Only one World Cup – South Africa 2010 – has produced more 1-0s, though the seventeen recorded there came from 64 matches played (26.56 per cent).

Between them, the champions of Europe and South America – the Netherlands and Brazil – exited the tournament with a shared tally of seven goals from eight matches.

The dearth of goals might be viewed as a fitting conclusion to a previous decade in which only two players, Michel Platini in 1984 and Aldo Serena in 1989, reached the twenty-goal mark in Serie A. And it was not without consequence, focusing minds on the need for a change in approach, which included the proposal of then FIFA president João Havelange to consider a radical switch to four quarters of 25 minutes each.

Amid the searching of souls, FIFA general secretary Sepp Blatter, in his editorial in *FIFA News* in November 1990, wrote, 'The chief motto seemed to be wariness and fear of conceding a goal.'

A month later, in his general secretary's report to the FIFA Executive Committee, Blatter said events in Italy had provoked an unprecedented reaction. In the absence of social-media platforms, football lovers channelled their dissatisfaction in a more traditional way, sending Blatter more than one thousand letters. His own conclusion was, 'As the game has become more and more professionalised – in many countries the top league clubs have developed into business concerns – the emotional side of the sport has been lost. Football has become more of a science, in which tactics are the most important factor and creativity has been suppressed ... The art of football, and also the fun of playing, has been lost.'

Meanwhile, the summary from FIFA's Technical Study Group, laid out in its report on Italia '90, was, 'The history of football is a constant struggle in which attack and defence fight for supremacy. The friction between these poles makes this sport so interesting. At present, the defence is dominant ... The refinement of the attack will be the most pressing task that coaches will have to fulfil in the next four years.'

Andy Roxburgh, Scotland's coach at Italia '90 and latterly technical director of first UEFA and now the Asian Football Confederation, suggests that the sheer infrequency of World Cup tournaments – and worldwide focus they receive – means they are viewed as signposts, even if 'the real direction of the game comes through club football'.

Hence, he says, while AC Milan coach Arrigo Saachi had already introduced an attacking 4-4-2 at Italy's leading club (a trend which led to a majority of four-man defences at USA '94), '1990 did have an impact because it was very high-profile, it had the biggest TV audience ever for a major tournament up to that point, and because it disappointed. The general impression was one of negativity and ugliness.'

It was in the direct wake of Italia '90, in the first half of the new decade, that changes were made to the Laws of the Game to send the pendulum swinging back in the opposite direction.

In 1991, the red card for a professional foul became law – twelve months after the World Cup final referees had received the same instruction.

The following year, as a direct response to events on the pitch at Italia '90, the ban on the goalkeeper handling the ball from a back-pass came into force.

Walter Gagg, then head of FIFA's technical department, remembers well the conversations that followed the World Cup, notably an exchange of ideas with the former Switzerland national coach, Daniel Jeandupeux, then writing columns for the Zurich-based daily, *Tages-Anzeiger*.

Jeandupeux had been collecting the thoughts of coaching colleagues for his newspaper articles, and he approached Gagg and Blatter with one particular suggestion.

'It was a few weeks after the end of the competition, and he gave us this idea: "Why not tell goalkeepers they no longer have the right to handle the ball when it's a back-pass?"' Gagg relates. 'He's a well-known guy, very intelligent, and was national-team coach for two years. We had a conversation, and I think Sepp was also present. This was an absolutely tremendous proposal.'

It was a move designed to speed up the game, and it transformed the job of the goalkeeper. 'The back-pass [ban] has helped the game,' reflects Packie Bonner, the Republic of Ireland's 1990 World Cup goalkeeper. 'It changed dramatically for people like myself and Peter Shilton. At that time, the goalkeepers probably didn't do what they do now tactically. Technically, they weren't as good as they are now, and the goalkeeper is very much a part of the modern game on the offensive side.'

Today, the game is quicker, as fitter players move lighter balls around on carpet-like pitches – though the back-pass ban has hardly stopped time-wasting, with players now breaking the flow of the game by going to ground much more readily than they did in 1990. According to FIFA's statistics, there was actually less pure playing time at South Africa 2010 – an average of 54 minutes per match – than at Italia '90 (56 minutes 15 seconds). As one former international referee pointed out to me, though, playing time back then included when the goalkeeper was holding the ball, or passing it back and forth around his back four and collecting it back from them.

*

THERE WERE OTHER AREAS WHERE ITALIA '90 OFFERED A SIGNPOST for the way ahead. Big Football – in the form of the Champions League and, in England, the Premier League – would officially begin in 1992. The so-called Year Zero for a game where, as a member of England's 1990 World Cup squad confided to me, 'They use the bullshit of television to create drama.'

Football's future as a global TV spectacle was moved a step closer with Italia '90, when the World Cup audience nearly doubled from the 1986 finals, rising to 26.6 billion viewers from the 13.5 billion recorded four years earlier.

A notable factor was that the number of African nations linked to the international signal had jumped from twelve to 25; another was the enormous increase in the number of TV sets in China.

For Australians, meanwhile, it was the first World Cup with comprehensive TV coverage, a point underlined to me by commentator Martin Tyler, who worked at Italia '90 for Australian public network SBS.

'It was bigger for Australia than it'd ever been,' he says. 'FIFA had an arrangement with ABC, which was like the BBC, and also with a terrestrial channel, SBS, who tended to market for the different nationalities in Australia – the Greeks and Croatians. I have letters of gratitude which got passed to me after the tournament, which brought tears to my eyes, from people who'd never thought they'd get to see the whole of the World Cup in a country like Australia.'

With the big audiences, the mega-money would follow. In 1990, FIFA's spoils from TV rights for Italia '90 amounted to $68.7 million. Little over a decade later, TV rights sales for the four-year cycle to 2002 were worth almost $1bn (this after FIFA sold the rights for the 2002 and 2006 events to German media company Kirsch). By 2014, the sum for TV rights for the Brazil World Cup had risen to $2.4 billion.

Club football was looking to TV riches too: two years after Italia '90, UEFA introduced a restructured European Cup and renamed it the Champions League, though even before the World Cup, Silvio Berlusconi, the future Italian prime minister, had been pushing for a makeover of Europe's elite club competition.

In 1988, Berlusconi, then owner of AC Milan and the Canale 5 television channel, had just established Mediaset, the media company which would become Italy's largest commercial broadcaster.

He enlisted the advertising agency Saatchi and Saatchi to create a blueprint for a European Super League, having been disturbed by the sight of Napoli and Real Madrid meeting in the European Cup's first round in 1987 – and the Italian champions falling at the very first hurdle.

'He'd taken over Milan a couple of years previously, and what he saw was that the big, successful clubs produced big, wealthy television audiences,' recalls Alex Fynn, who was assigned to this project by Saatchi and Saatchi. 'He wanted to minimise chance and maximise opportunity and felt if Milan were successful, then he'd get bigger and more revenue-generating audiences through his television station, Canale 5.

'Second, in European terms, he'd be able to have a more cosmopolitan and international audience rather than just a national one. However, what needed to change was what had happened when the champions of Italy drew the champions of Spain and one of these two powerful Latin nations lost their representative in the European Cup. It wasn't, to quote him, modern thinking.

'He used it as a catalyst to force change from UEFA, and as a result of that blueprint UEFA changed the format of the European Cup and created the Champions League. I think this was the impetus.'

Berlusconi had described the European Cup as a 'historical anachronism' in an interview with *World Soccer* magazine, in which he foresaw the football world of today. 'We have to reach an audience beyond the stadium,' he said. 'That means television, the theatre of the global village.

'Football is currently ignoring part of its support. First are the fans in the stadium; but that means only 50,000 or 60,000. Then there are the fans who watch bits and pieces of soccer on the state channels. But the third audience, which we are not reaching, is to be found on pay-TV.'

(That future is now when Liverpool have separate Twitter accounts for 23 different countries and regions; Manchester United have official websites in French, Spanish, Arabic, Chinese, Japanese and Korean; and selfie stick-wielding tourists descend on Anfield, Old Trafford and other famous football venues across Europe.)

If the driving force was Italian, the inspiration for the bells and whistles of the new Champions League, when it did arrive, came directly from Italia '90. The original 'mood board' for the new competition – a series of pictures capturing its supposed essence – came from classical antiquity, along with a shot of Totò Schillaci in the wild-eyed celebration which provided one of that World Cup's enduring images.

The brief was to take football upmarket in the wake of the successful association of opera with football at Italia '90, in the formidable shape of Luciano Pavarotti.

Craig Thompson worked for ISL, the Swiss sports marketing company, on the creation of the Champions League brand, and he recalls: 'The guys that did Italia '90 are the same guys I worked with on putting the Champions League together. We wanted to send a message about the higher image of football and the music was really an important part of that in the Champions League, and there was a parallel there with Italia '90. I was the guy that briefed the composer of the music of the Champions League and that was very much the idea – "We're going to 'class it up.'"

Tony Britten himself, the composer of the Champions League theme, has spoken in the past of the direct line running between Pavarotti, the Three Tenors' concerts, and his reworking of Handel's 'Zadok the Priest'.

For UK football lovers over the age of 35, 'Nessun Dorma' acts as a transporter straight back to summer 1990. Philip Bernie, now head of BBC TV Sport and assistant editor of the corporation's Italia '90 TV coverage, once explained to me how it was chosen to accompany the BBC's opening titles.

'In 1989 I was cutting various montages for the World Cup draw and around that time, I heard Nessun Dorma played on *Desert Island Discs,*' he said. 'The image I thought resonated particularly well was the climactic bit when Pavarotti suddenly goes mad on the final "*Vincerò*", allied to the picture of Marco Tardelli scoring the decisive goal in the 1982 World Cup. He very famously ran away with his arms waving around and his mouth agape – it was a really perfect marriage of vision and audio, and we used that in the montage for the draw, which went down particularly well.

'On the back of that, I advocated that we should use that for the titles at the

World Cup. When you look at it now, it looks quite dated, but the music's still brilliant and that visual bit still works incredibly well. We had the usual discussions with the record company, Decca, who owned Pavarotti's rights, and they came on board and once it was used, it absolutely took off [reaching number two in the UK charts]. The interesting thing was people forget up till then the use of themes around major sporting events was fairly standard so to use something classical and unusual, let alone operatic, was quite a radical departure.'

If it was seen as a bold choice by the BBC, for Luca Cordero di Montezemolo, the man in overall charge of planning Italia '90, as general manager of the local organising committee, it was the obvious one.

Pavarotti was there from beginning to end at Italia '90: from singing at the draw on 9 December 1989, to performing with José Carreras and Plácido Domingo in a 'Three Tenors' concert in the glorious setting of Rome's Baths of Caracalla on the eve of the final.

Montezemolo, an industrialist and one of the most influential men in Italian sport over the past half-century, says, '"Nessun Dorma" is very related with sport. "*Vincerò*" – I will win. So the words are good. Pavarotti was an Italian hero and opera is one of the key core businesses of Italy. Giuseppe Verdi, La Scala ... opera is Italy. I was really very involved with sport and marketing, and so I wanted to give a proper promotion of Italy.'

Explaining the thinking that brought Pavarotti, Carreras and Domingo together, he adds, 'To be honest, this was really my idea, my initiative, and it's very easy. In 1990, the two biggest [Italian] names all over the world were Sophia Loren and Pavarotti. When there was the draw, he was together with Sophia Loren as the two stars of the event. To close the event, Pavarotti alone was not so good because we'd already used him before.

'I was friends with Plácido Domingo and I said, "Listen, if I go to Pavarotti and ask, 'Why don't you consent to [performing with] two others?' he'll become jealous and say, 'Why?' Why don't you go to Pavarotti [and pretend it's] your idea and also Carreras's?"'

'So although I knew Pavarotti well – he's from Modena, and I was with Ferrari as a team manager for many years – I sent Plácido to talk to him. They made an agreement, and that was fantastic. It was a huge night, and, to be honest, something unique.'

A protégé of Fiat supremo Gianni Agnelli, I meet Montezemolo in Rome to hear how Italia '90 foretold the future with respect to both the marketing of the event and the use of technology. We are sitting in his office at the headquarters of the high-speed train company, Nuovo Trasporto Viaggiatori, where he is president. Trains mark a fresh departure for this former president of Ferrari, a handsome septuagenarian with still-sandy hair, an Alain Delon air, and the expensive elegance of a multi-millionaire.

'If you ask me what the main stars of the event are, I'll say, first of all, the technology. This was the first event with mobile phones, with work stations in the stadium for the press, with computers. Every journalist was really impressed as they could see the events on their monitors [in the press box], and could send their articles immediately.'

As well as a mobile phone for each journalist, they had access to fax terminals, photocopiers, and even an electronic mail service. There was also, for the first time, a World Cup database available on monitors in the press centres. For TV viewers, match statistics appeared on screen during broadcasts – such as the mistranslated 'Shots Out' for shots off target.

Naturally, the computers were Olivetti. After all, Montezemolo's canny strategy was to create a second tier of sponsors – official suppliers from the cream of Italian industry – in addition to a first tier comprising Coca-Cola, Anheuser-Busch, Canon, Fujifilm, Gillette, JVC, Philips, Mars, and the local duo of Alfa Romeo and Vini d'Italia.

The suppliers provided their services in exchange for promotional rights.

'Blatter was the general secretary, and he was very open and very curious to see this new approach,' Montezemolo explains. 'I said, "Listen, we're in Italy, you need to have the help of the local industries to organise an event". We had a lot of products – Alitalia for transportation, Fiat for the buses for the teams and referees, and Telecom for telephones. Olivetti at that time was the largest Italian company for computers, so I included these too.

'We were the first to use the technology, the products and the manpower of Italian industry. One of the two largest banks [BNL] gave me not only people to look after the administration of the event, but also we were able to sell tickets in the banks. The banks had offices all over the country, and at that time there was no internet where you could buy tickets. I needed manpower to make the project and to run the project. I had to give them something back – exposure.

'Then I invited a third category. It was "Friends of Italia '90". They could use the logos – but not in the stadiums – and we made a lot of "Friends of Italia '90". It was good to promote the event, to promote some Italian companies, and find money for us without interfering with the big FIFA sponsors.'

One particular feat by Montezemolo was to persuade FIFA to allow Fiat to supplant Opel as the automobile sponsor. General Motors had a contract with ISL – the marketing company closely affiliated with FIFA – whereby Opel would fill this sponsorship slot. However, Montezemolo won the argument with the help of his mentor, Gianni Agnelli.

Sepp Blatter remembers: 'We had a meeting with *l'Avvocato* Agnelli in his home in Turin. It was in the middle of a forest and we flew in his helicopter. I was with [FIFA president João] Havelange and there was [Italian Football Federation president Antonio] Matarrese and Luca Cordero di Montezemolo, along with a representative of ISL.

'I remember he [Agnelli] addressed the president and said, "You want to have this World Cup in Italy and you want to have it with KLM, with Nissan, with whatever. Mr President, you can just forget it. If you want to have this World Cup in Italy, then I'll make sure you have the best promotion by partners and sponsors and they are Fiat, Olivetti, Alitalia. All the Italian industry will be there."

'I remember Havelange was asking me in French, "What about the contracts?" but Agnelli understood. It was, "Do you want Italy or not?" Bang. Finish.'

AUTHOR PETE DAVIES HAS A RATHER DIFFERENT RECOLLECTION OF the Italia '90 sponsors. 'It was the cheese women, the Grana Padano cheese women, who were all not just strikingly attractive but taller than all the other women, so there was a Grana Padano branch of the World Cup who'd successfully gone about employing the tallest, most strikingly attractive women in the whole operation to sell you cheese, for God's sake. It's the fucking World Cup, and they're selling you cheese. I just remember thinking, "What's it turning into?"'

It is nearly thirty years since Davies wrote *All Played Out,* though as the above souvenir suggests, his source of winning lines has not dried up.

For Davies, the commercialisation already evident then has diminished his interest in subsequent World Cups. 'For the game, I feel that it was the last real World Cup. Now I'm a real grumpy old geezer, and of course, that's the tournament I went to, and the tournament where I had one of the best experiences of my life and wrote a book that I loved writing – of course I'm going to love it. But all the signs were there that the corporate takeover was imminent and would be consummated in America, and there was no looking back after that. Then you push up the number of teams taking part, and the thing just became a massive sponsorship bun fight. I'd much rather go and watch Huddersfield Town play than have a press pass for a World Cup today.'

From 2026, the World Cup will have 48 teams – the first rise since 1998 when it expanded to 32. At Italia '90, there were 24. This planned expansion will increase revenue to £5.29bn according to FIFA's own calculations. (Even Sepp Blatter tells me, in a roundabout way, this is a step too far: 'I think the World Cup, as long as it is played with a reasonable number of teams, like thirty-two, as we have in the next World Cup, will be very attractive.')

The transformation of English football in the years since 1990 has been even more striking than the evolution of the World Cup. If this book's aim has been to explore the worldwide legacy of Italia '90, it is inevitable that England will feature prominently given the trajectory from European outcast to home of Planet Football's richest and most popular league, broadcast in 189 of the 193 UN-recognised countries across the world and bringing its clubs in 2016/17 a combined revenue of £2.4 billion.

There is a well-established sequence of events either side of Italia '90 which gave a new momentum to the English game: the 1989 Hillsborough tragedy, which cost the lives of 96 Liverpool supporters before the FA Cup semi-final against Nottingham Forest; the Taylor Report into the tragedy, which precipitated a new wave of safe, all-seated stadiums; and the advent of the Premier League with its unprecedented patronage from satellite television.

The question for Davies is where Italia '90 fits in the chain. He responds, 'The Premier League would have started anyway, but the difference is it made the atmosphere far more favourable. It made it okay to like football. With the widening of the market, of the audience, it just created an atmosphere where it was possible to go forward.

'You look at football in the Eighties – Heysel, Bradford [the 1985 fire which claimed 56 lives at Valley Parade], Hillsborough – it was a wreck. I remember watching Chelsea during the first half of the Eighties when I was living in London. In retrospect, Stamford Bridge was a giant urinal. Italia '90 completely changed the perception of it. People understood that it was the national game and it'd been let down and treated like an unloved orphan.

'Before that, to the ordinary fan who followed a club and loved the game, you'd been lumped into this box of being a pariah. No one thought you could write a book about football because people that watch football couldn't read – that was the idea. And to have a prime minister [in Margaret Thatcher] that seriously suggested that we shouldn't go to the World Cup looks absolutely outlandish now – presidents, premiers, prime ministers of all nations flock to watch their countries playing football.'

Moreover, by the end of the decade, two major satellite broadcasting companies had emerged and were locked in a battle for subscribers: Sky TV and British Satellite Broadcasting (BSB).

'It was happening anyway,' remarks Martin Tyler, then working for BSB. In March 1990, he did his first live BSB commentary at Wembley when England beat Brazil 1-0. 'I did England v Brazil live,' he recalls, 'so it had started. I can remember going on trains up north looking out of the window counting the dishes – and counting the "squarials" [the name given to the company's square aerials] was very hard.

'The technology was there and the appreciation,' he adds. 'A lot of this input came from Australia, where they'd turned sport into more of an entertainment with the cricket particularly – the Kerry Packer stuff and the duck that waddled on at the bottom of the screen if the batsman was out for naught. Some of those guys came to Sky – Sam Chisholm and David Hill – who brought that kind of dynamism into an area where the sports themselves had not really recognised the potential to make some money from it.' November 1990 brought the merger of BSB with Sky to form British Sky Broadcasting.

Academic and author John Williams affirms, 'I think we'd have had the Premier League because satellite television needed something. Satellite television was going down the toilet without a major commodity to sell, and here was the English game transforming itself because of Hillsborough, new stadiums, new marketing campaigns. Italia '90 helped because they heard this operatic singing; they looked at the stadiums; they looked at the players, who didn't look like players here – the Italian players looked like film stars – and it did feel like England were becoming part of something that was about football, rather than "Can we manage these horrible England supporters who are coming here?"'

WEMBLEY STADIUM, LONDON, 10 NOVEMBER 2017. IT IS FRIDAY evening, and the most evocative of all fixtures for English national-team supporters is under way: England v Germany, the first friendly fixture in the run-up to Russia 2018.

As the first paper airplane lands on the turf in the eighteenth minute, I wonder how a visitor from 1990, an England fan brought here, say, on a tour of 2017 by the Ghost of Football Future, would view the spectacle in front of them.

They might well marvel at the majestic scale of the new Wembley and the magnificence of the illuminated arch, yet scratch their head on hearing that Tottenham Hotspur (average attendance in 1989/90: 26,831) are now filling this place every other weekend.

They would surely enjoy the firefly prettiness of all those flickering mobile phones in the second half, but the PA system would feel a bit loud, and the crowd a bit quiet for a meeting of these great rivals. They might feel, in fact, rather like Craig Brewin does when he visits the national stadium. Brewin, who helped run the Football Supporters' Association's fan embassy at Italia '90, finds the modern Wembley experience underwhelming, to say the least.

'It felt like I was in a restaurant in that you could hear this continuous muttering of conversation going on all the way through the game,' he says of a recent visit. 'I was in the lower tier and it didn't feel like a football crowd. There wasn't that coordinated singing or anything or the "oohs" and the "aahs" you get normally at a big game. It was the muttering of conversation. "You want a cup of tea?" "Yeah, I'll get it.'"

Our visitor from 1990 would certainly need a cup of tea after paying £6 for their match programme, and there would be a raised eyebrow on leafing through it and seeing that four of Germany's players were actually with English clubs. In 1990, Italy was the destination for Germany's finest, with five of their World Cup squad based in Serie A.

As becomes clear later in the evening, though, Italy – Europe's most glamorous football nation three decades ago – are about to miss out on qualifying for the latest World Cup after losing a play-off match to Sweden.

But what about England? 'I see a great future in English football' is the headline of an interview with Lothar Matthäus, West Germany's 1990 captain, in the match programme. Yet, as our visitor from the past now discovers, the last 28 years have brought nothing better than another semi-final defeat by Germany at Euro '96.

The view of one of the principal figures behind the founding of the Premier League in 1992, Rick Parry, is that the success of the elite division has come at a cost to the national side.

'I think in three respects,' begins the man who became the league's first chief executive. 'One is in the sheer number of games, and the lack of a winter break, which is a corollary. The second is clearly in the number of foreign players. I think if you have more than fifty per cent foreign players, that goes beyond the natural tipping point.

'The third aspect is the competitive nature now of the Premier League [and] the fact you now genuinely have got six clubs competing for four spots in the Champions League, so every game matters. They can't afford to rest. There's much more competitive pressure in the Premier League than in any other, and all of that has a bearing on fatigue of players.'

On Parry's second point – the number of foreign players – at the first World Cup after the formation of the Premier League, USA '94, there were sixteen Premier League imports involved: nine Norwegians, three Americans, two Swedes, a Russian and a Nigerian (Liverpool-born Efan Ekoku).

The next year brought the Bosman ruling by the European Court of Justice, guaranteeing free movement to players at the end of their contracts and, in the words of Sir Alex Ferguson, 'suddenly, it was a free-for-all.'

At the 2014 World Cup, there were 119 players from English and Welsh clubs involved with their national teams – 97 of them non-English.

In the days after Italia '90, it was not meant to be like this. In 1991 the FA published a *Blueprint for the Future of Football*. It was the response to a Football League document the previous year – *One Game One Team One Voice* – and it included a proposal for a reduced, eighteen-team top division, with the stated ambition of 'establishing the England team at the apex of the pyramid of playing excellence'.

As Parry remembers, the FA had included the chapter on the new league only in response to an approach from the 'Big Five' clubs of the day – Liverpool, Manchester United, Arsenal, Everton, and Tottenham – who had been pushing for a breakaway.

'They held up the printing of the blueprint to allow the chapter to be added in, that's one hundred per cent fact,' Parry explains. When the FA invited the 22 First Division teams to a meeting to unveil the idea of the Premier League, the England-first rhetoric was devalued within minutes.

Parry, seated on the top table with FA chairman Bert Millichip and chief executive Graham Kelly, says, 'Graham unveiled the plans, with the rationale of helping the England team work more closely together, the eighteen-club league, and the two up, two down.

'Ironically, given that the eighteen clubs was for the benefit of the England team, within five or ten minutes of the start of the meeting, Peter Swales, who was the chairman of the International Committee [and also Manchester City], said to Sir Bert, "Is there any scope for compromise on the eighteen clubs?"

'Nobody actually said, "We refuse to go along with it" but that's when Sir Bert memorably said, "It's your league, you will decide". So, the initiative was handed to the clubs within five minutes of the first meeting.

'Maybe that sent a signal to the clubs that if you're going to be able to make a decision on that big issue, then you'll be able to make decision on everything.'

Former Saatchi and Saatchi executive Alex Fynn was involved in drafting the FA's blueprint. Fynn, now a sports, media, and marketing consultant, says, 'In my proposed plan, you could see there was a pyramid – three regional divisions moving up through national divisions higher up. If you only had eighteen clubs in the showcase top division, the England team would naturally rise to the top of the pyramid and would get an attention they've never had before.

'Why didn't any of this happen? Because the FA had no vision, were self-serving, and were more concerned to see off the threat of the Football League. It leaves them further away than they were in 1990, because in 1990, they were very unfortunate not to reach the World Cup final.

'I'd say that so long as we have the present system – and remember that the Premier League is not an English league any more; it's an international league that just happens to be played in England with less than forty per cent of English players – England will never ever win the World Cup or the European Championship.'

Still, predictions about England have backfired before. 'Our World Cup dream looks a bad Irish joke,' moaned the *Daily Mirror* after the national team's dreary opening game against the Republic of Ireland at Italia '90, and just look what happened next.

ACKNOWLEDGEMENTS

I SHOULD START BY THANKING THE MANY PEOPLE I INTERVIEWED for this book who, freely and kindly, gave their time and shared their memories.

My gratitude goes also to those who assisted me on my travels: Martin Etonge in Cameroon; Vicente Casellas and Belén Jiménez in Girona; Dominik Petermann and Michael Schmalholz at the FIFA archives and library in Zurich; Selene Scarsi, Ben Gladwell and Paolo Menicucci in Milan; Ondřej Zlámal in Prague; Ognen Dojcinovski in Skopje; John McAuley in Abu Dhabi; Diego Zandrino in Buenos Aires; David Owens, Dmitri Rogovitskiy and Nathalie Althukova in Moscow.

I owe thanks also to the following people who facilitated some of the 100+ interviews: Liz Luff at the Sir Bobby Robson Foundation; Ioan Lupescu, David Gough and Frank Ludolph at UEFA; Andreas Alf at FIFA; David Wright at Soccerex; Michael Kammarman at US Soccer; Cristian Williams at the Costa Rican Football Federation; Rob Faulkner at Internazionale; Rafa Ramos and Andrés Merello at Espanyol; Darren Griffiths at Everton; Steve Pearce at Ipswich Town; Mark Sullivan at Manchester United; Patrick Bergabo at Sporting Kansas City.

I am similarly grateful to have been able to lean on the contacts of: Graeme Bryce, Neil Custis, Ian Dennis, Graham Hesketh, Alyson Rudd and Sebastien Vaughan at home; and Jörg Jakob, Thomas Renggli, Andrey Vlasov, Magdy Eslam, Lasana Liburd , Ali Khaled and David Barrett abroad; together with the sizeable Balkan contingent of Aleksandar Stojanović, Feđa Krvavac, Elvir Islamović, Slaven Alfirević and Vladimir Stanković.

Valued insights, meanwhile, came from: Bogdan Buga, Mike Cowley, Mark Gleeson, Ian Holyman, Rastislav Hríbik, Michael Keoghan, Andy Lyons, Andy

Mitchell, Pat Nevin, Martin O'Boyle, Jürgen Rank, Zdravko Reic, Tim Rich, James Rogers, Grega Sever, Vara Showman, Pete Smith, Stephen Sullivan, Howard Webb and Paul-Daniel Zaharia.

Elsewhere, David Spratt and Jean-François Rodriguez showed immense generosity in transcribing for me the Cameroon interviews. Adrian Harte offered welcome advice with the Ireland chapters and likewise Lorenzo Amuso and Federico Farcomeni with the Italy sections – along with Ilaria Ianni who also transcribed the Italian interviews. Jim Wirth allowed me to tap into his encyclopaedic musical knowledge, Christophe Roy provided access to FIFA TV's 1990 archive, and Dahlia Kozlowsky helped with archive material from the *New York Times*.

Thanks also to Matt Gatward and Marc Padgett who commissioned Italia '90 interviews from me during their days on the *Independent* and *Independent on Sunday* respectively – parts of which feature in this book – and to another ex-Indy colleague, Ian Herbert, for his moral support.

As for the book itself, Richard Evans helped hugely with his insights when proof-reading the early manuscript, and Patrick Hart and Matt Stone contributed other much-needed pointers.

At deCoubertin Books, James Corbett and Simon Hughes have my deep and lasting gratitude for their trust and good-humoured encouragement – and for answering the odd question or two along the way. I must also thank Jack Gordon-Brown for his brilliant final revision, as well as Megan Pollard, Ceylan Hussein (copy-editing) and Leslie Priestley (typesetting). The look of this book, meanwhile, is down to Thomas Regan, whose artwork means you are very welcome to judge it by its cover. Photography comes from the fabulous Peter Robinson Football Archive.

Last but not least, a word of thanks to my family for their support: to my own Italia '90 crowd of Mum, Dad, Rachel and Patrick – and above all to Mila, who came on board for USA '94 and provided so much wisdom, patience and understanding during the year of living unsociably in which this book came together.

BIBLIOGRAPHY

Barnes, John – *'John Barnes: The Autobiography'* (Headline, 1999)

Bilardo, Carlos and Wernicke, Luciano – *'Doctor y campeón: Autobiografía de Carlos Salvador Bilardo'* (Planeta, 2014)

Bolger, Dermot – *'In High Germany'* (New Island Books, 1999)

Buford, Bill – *'Among the Thugs'* (Secker & Warburg, 1991)

Campomar, Andreas – *'¡Golazo! A History of Latin American Football'* (Quercus, 2014)

Cascarino, Tony with Kimmage, Paul – *'Full Time: The Secret Life of Tony Cascarino'* (Simon & Schuster, 2000)

Conn, David – *'The Fall of the House of FIFA'* (Yellow Jersey Press, 2017)

Corbett, James – *'England Expects'* (deCoubertin, 2010)

Davies, Christopher; Heydari, Keyvan Antonio; Mahoney, Ridge; Polis, John; Robinson, John; Turner, Graham – *'World Cup Italia '90* (Commemorative Soccer Publications, 1990)

Davies, Pete – *'All Played Out'* (Mandarin, 1991)

Doyle, Roddy – *'The Van'* (Minerva, 1992)

Dunphy, Eamon – *'The Rocky Road'* (Penguin Books, 2014)

Foot, John – *'Calcio: A History of Italian Football'* (Harper Perennial, 2007)

Gascoigne, Paul with Davies, Hunter – *'Gazza: My Story'* (Headline, 2005)

Glanville, Brian – *'The Story of the World Cup'* (Faber and Faber, 2001)

Glenny, Misha – *'The Fall of Yugoslavia'* (Penguin, 1996)

Goldblatt, David – *'Futebol Nation: A Footballing History of Brazil'* (Penguin, 2014)

Gough, Richard with Gallacher, Ken – *'Field of Dreams: My Ibrox Years'* (Mainstream, 1993)

Guimarães, Alexandre with Knohr, Erwin Wino – *'La Gran Fiesta'* (Impresión Comercial de la Nación, 1991)

Gullit, Ruud – *'Ruud Gullit: My Autobiography'* (Century, 1998)

Hand, Eoin with Browne, Jared – First Hand: My Life and Irish Football (The Collins Press, 2017)

Hand, Eoin with O'Neill, Peter – *'The Eoin Hand Story'* (Brophy Books, 1986)

Harris, Harry and Van der Kraan, Marcel – *'Ruud Gullit: Portrait of a Genius'* (CollinsWillow, 1996)

Hawkey, Ian – *'Feet of the Chameleon: The Story of African Football'* (Portico Books, 2009)

Honigstein, Raphael – *'Das Reboot: How German Football Reinvented Itself and Conquered the World'* (Yellow Jersey Press, 2016)

Hook, Peter – *'Substance: Inside New Order'* (Simon & Schuster, 2016)

Hunt, Chris – *'World Cup Stories'* (Interact Publishing, 2006)

Kuper, Simon – *'Football Against The Enemy'* (Orion, 1996)

Lynch, Declan – *'Days of Heaven: Italia '90 and the Charlton Years'* (Gill & Macmillan, 2010)

Maradona, Diego Armando with Arcucci, Daniel and Cherquis Bialo, Ernesto – *'El Diego'* (Yellow Jersey Press, 2005)

McCoist, Ally with Brankin, Crawford – *'Ally McCoist: My Story'* (Mainstream, 1992)

McWilliams, David – *'The Pope's Children'* (Gill & Macmillan, 2005)

Mead, Teresa A. – *'A History of Modern Latin America: 1800 to the Present'* (Blackwell Publishing Ltd, 2010)

Milla, Roger with Onana, Charles – *'Une Vie de Lion'* (Éditions Duboiris, 2006)

Montague, James – *'Thirty-One Nil: On the Road with Football's Outsiders'* (Bloomsbury, 2015)

Parreira, Carlos Alberto with Gonzalez, Ricardo – *'Formando Equipes Vencedoras'* (BestSeller, 2006))

Pearce, Stuart with Harris, Bob – *'Psycho: The England Years'* (Headline, 2000)

Pougatch, Mark – *'Three Lions Versus the World'* (Mainstream, 2010)

Riva, Gigi – *'Le dernier penalty'* (Éditions du Seuil, 2016)

Robson, Bobby with Hayward, Paul – *'Farewell But Not Goodbye: My Autobiography'* (Hodder, 2005)

Rowan, Paul – *'The Team that Jack Built'* (Mainstream, 1994)

Schillaci, Totò with Mercurio, Andrea – *'Il Gol è Tutto'* (Edizione Piemme, 2016)

Sheedy, Kevin with Keith, John – *'So Good I Did It Twice'* (Trinity Mirror Sport Media, 2014)

Stott, Richard – *'Dogs and Lampposts'* (Metro Publishing Ltd, 2002)

Tempany, Adrian – *'And the Sun Shines Now: How Hillsborough and the Premier League changed Britain'* (Faber and Faber, 2016)

Toíbín, Colm – *'The Trial of the Generals'* (The Raven Arts Press, 1990)

Valdano, Jorge – *'El Miedo Escénico y Otras Hierbas'* (Aguilar, 2002)

Vialli Gianluca and Marcotti, Gabriele – *'The Italian Job'* (Bantam Books, 2006)

Vidacs, Bea – *'Visions of a Better World: Football in the Cameroonian Social Imagination'* (Lit Verlag, 2010)

Wilson, Jonathan – *'Angels with Dirty Faces: The Footballing History of Argentina'* (Nation Books, 2016)

Wilson, Jonathan – *'Behind the Curtain: Travels in Eastern European Football'* (Orion, 2006)

Winner, David – *'Brilliant Orange: The Neurotic Genius of Dutch Football'* (Bloomsbury 2000)

Winter, Henry – *'Fifty Years of Hurt: The Story of England Football and Why We Never Stop Believing'* (Bantam Press, 2016)

Yallop, David – *'How They Stole the Game'* (Constable, 2011)

NEWSPAPERS

Britain and Ireland
Daily Express
Daily Mail
Daily Mirror
Daily Record
Daily Telegraph
Derby Evening Telegraph
The Guardian
The Independent
Independent On Sunday
Limerick Leader
The Sun
The Scotsman
The Sunday Times
Sunday Independent
The Times
Today

World
Cameroon Tribune
Clarín
Corriere della Sera
Gazzetta dello Sport
Il Giorno
L'Équipe
New York Times
La Repubblica
Sovetsky-Sport
Washington Post

MAGAZINES

World Soccer
Football-Hockey

WEBSITES

Bassavelocita.it
BBC.co.uk
FIFA.com
Ilfattoquotidiano.it
The42.ie
Whoscored.com
Wikipedia.com
Wired868.com
YouTube.com

FILMS

Gascoigne
Italia '90
Lights Of Rome
One Night in Turin
Three Lions (BBC)
The Last Yugoslavia Team

IN MEMORY OF

Benjamin Massing

20 June 1962 – 9 December 2017

www.decoubertin.co.uk